Third Edition

TOTAL GLOBAL STRATEGY

George S. Yip
China Europe International Business School
Shanghai, China

G. Tomas M. Hult
Michigan State University
East Lansing, Michigan, USA

PEARSON

Boston   Columbus   Indianapolis   New York   San Francisco   Upper Saddle River
Amsterdam   Cape Town   Dubai   London   Madrid   Milan   Munich   Paris   Montreal   Toronto
Delhi   Mexico City   Sao Paulo   Sydney   Hong Kong   Seoul   Singapore   Taipei   Tokyo

Editorial Director: Sally Yagan
Senior Acquisitions Editor: Kim Norbuta
Senior Editorial Project Manager: Claudia Fernandes
Director of Marketing: Patrice Lumumba Jones
Senior Marketing Manager: Nikki Ayana Jones
Marketing Assistant: Ian Gold
Senior Managing Editor: Judy Leale
Project Manager: Lynn Savino
Production Project Manager: Debbie Ryan
Art Director: Jayne Conte
Cover Designer: Suzanne Behnke
Cover Art: Fotolia
Full-Service Project Management: Saraswathi Muralidhar, PreMediaGlobal
Composition: PreMediaGlobal
Printer/Binder/Cover: STP Courier
Text Font: 10/12 ITC Garamond

Credits and acknowledgments borrowed from other sources and reproduced, with permission, in this textbook appear on appropriate page within text.

Library of Congress Cataloging-in-Publication Data
Yip, George S.
  Total global strategy / George S. Yip, G. Tomas M. Hult. — 3rd ed.
      p. cm.
  Earlier ed. published as: Total global strategy II : updated for the internet and service era / George S. Yip. © 2003.
  Includes bibliographical references and index.
  ISBN-13: 978-0-13-608983-4 (alk. paper)
  ISBN-10: 0-13-608983-6 (alk. paper)
1. International business enterprises—Management. 2. Strategic planning. 3. International trade. 4. International economic relations. I. Hult, G. Tomas M. II. Yip, George S. Total global strategy II. III. Title.
  HD62.4.Y565 2012
  658'.049—dc23

                                                                                  2011030656

10 9 8 7 6 5 4 3 2 1

ISBN 10: 0-13-608983-6
ISBN 13: 978-0-13-608983-4

To our business partners, clients, and students.

BRIEF CONTENTS

CONTENTS

PREFACE

A lot has changed in the global marketplace since the first edition of *Total Global Strategy* came out in 1992. Even the global changes since the second edition (*Total Global Strategy II*) was published in 2003 have had profound impact on worldwide business. These changes are incorporated into *Total Global Strategy 3e* with a complete rewrite of all chapters, a more integrated view of eBusiness and service issues, and a new slate of innovative and very practical examples in the text and in the case vignettes. A number of other major changes are also incorporated into the new edition (see "New to This Edition"). One significant change is the addition of G. Tomas M. Hult as a coauthor. While the basic tenets of the global strategy framework remain, the collaborative product by the Yip and Hult team has resulted in a uniquely integrated view of today's global strategy issues facing firms while maintaining the framework originally created by Yip which has become such a staple in global strategy research and practice.

NEW TO THIS EDITION

- Each of the 11 chapters has undergone a significant rewrite, revision, and update. This includes incorporating the latest research, practice, and best-in-class benchmarking.
- All practical and research examples in the book and case vignettes are new or significantly updated. In certain cases where a company and/or situation still applies, we kept the story intact but with appropriate revisions and updates. In most cases, however, the examples incorporated into the text and presented in story-telling case vignettes are new to this edition for up-to-date illustrative purposes.
- Issues related to global crises that firms are facing have been incorporated throughout to make the book more valuable in the context of problem-solving scenarios in times of (future) crisis. Since 2003, the world has seen a number of different crises (e.g., economic, natural, human instigated). A firm focused on global strategy needs to be able to handle such crises and move forward in a prosperous way. We have incorporated such issues throughout the text.
- The measurement chapter (Chapter 10) has been rewritten to incorporate measures for all industry drivers, strategy levers, organization factors, and regional focus issues. The earlier versions of the book centered on a smaller subset of these valuable measures. This new version of the book makes the measurement aspects of global (and regional) strategy much more complete.
- All 11 chapters have been revised with the notion of outwardly focused as opposed to inwardly focused global strategy in mind. This means that we view global strategy today more as a mechanism to engage the global marketplace, align the firm with partners and other collaborators in the marketplace, and center attention on global customers (as opposed to a focus on only building the infrastructure of the global firm as a way to be more effective and efficient when an industry is ripe for globalization).

- The notion of global supply chain management (SCM) has been more deeply integrated throughout the book but in particular in the "Locating Global Activities" chapter (Chapter 5). While we do not delve into all intricate aspects of global SCM (e.g., logistics, sourcing, operations), we do incorporate and integrate global supply chain issues throughout. These global SCM issues are becoming critically important for global organizations and, we think, are moving from what was usually viewed as tactical operations to becoming more strategic-focused (i.e., corporate suite) issues in global organizations.

GUIDE TO THE CHAPTERS

Chapter 1 provides the overall global strategy framework within the context of globalization issues that firms face. Each of the building blocks in the global strategy framework is then discussed in detail in the remaining chapters of the book. Chapter 2, one of the longer chapters in the book, describes in detail the operation of industry globalization drivers. A critical aspect of this chapter is to make the reader more knowledgeable about the relative degree of globalization in various industries.

The next five chapters focus on each global strategy lever. Chapter 3 focuses on building global market participation, where a firm should center its attention, and what important aspects of market participation a firm faces in its decision making. Chapter 4 focuses on designing global products and services, preferably from the initial stages of the development process but also as redesigned offerings of the firm. Chapter 5 focuses on locating global activities, that is, where to best leverage knowledge and other resources throughout the value chain of a global firm (including aspects of global SCM). Chapter 6 focuses on creating an appropriate global marketing campaign, what strategic elements are important in global marketing, and the intricate value of global marketing (sometimes at the cost of certain customization). Chapter 7 focuses on the use of global competitive moves—a unique strategic aspect available to global firms that many other types of firms cannot (or should not) engage in worldwide.

Chapter 8 is another long chapter, covering issues related to building the global organization. The infrastructure of the global organization serves both to influence what global strategies the organization can develop and to either enhance or inhibit how the firm implements those strategies. As such, the infrastructure of the global organization is incredibly important for the effective and efficient running of a global strategy. Chapter 9 discusses regional strategy—how firms can develop intermediate strategies that are part of global ones. Chapter 10 provides operational measures for all the industry drivers, strategy levers, organization factors, and regional focus issues discussed earlier. The chapter is particularly helpful for those undertaking a global strategy analysis of the type described in the last chapter of the book. Chapter 11 pulls together the concepts of the book into a systematic, step-by-step approach to conducting a global strategy analysis. This chapter makes the book come full circle, from introducing the concepts in Chapter 1, to detailing each concept throughout various chapters in the book, and to clearly delineating a step-by-step approach to using the global strategy framework in firms.

INSTRUCTOR'S RESOURCE MANUAL

At the Instructor Resource Center, www.pearsonhighered.com/irc, instructors can access the Instructor's Resource Manual available with this text in downloadable format. Registration is simple and gives you immediate access to new titles and new editions.

COURSESMART

CourseSmart eTextbooks were developed for students looking to save on required or recommended textbooks. Students simply select their eText by title or author and purchase immediate access to the content for the duration of the course using any major credit card. With a CourseSmart eText, students can search for specific keywords or page numbers, take notes online, print out reading assignments that incorporate lecture notes, and bookmark important passages for later review. For more information or to purchase a CourseSmart eTextbook, visit www.coursesmart.com.

ACKNOWLEDGMENTS

We wish to first thank Kim Norbuta, our editor at Pearson Prentice Hall, for her persistence and patience in encouraging us to bring out a third edition. Clearly *Total Global Strategy* has been well received in the marketplace, both in 1992 and in 2003, and we are delighted that a new edition has now been produced for practitioners, scholars, teachers, and students of global strategy.

Over the years and editions, many individuals have helped refine the thinking on this topic through various interactions with us. They particularly include Peter Buckley, John Cantwell, Tamer Cavusgil, Diana Day, Susan Douglas, Yves Doz, Johny Johansson, Ahmet Kirca, Gary Knight, Masaaki Kotabe, Andrzej Kozminski, Stefanie Lenway, Arie Lewin, Christopher Lovelock, Shige Makino, David Montgomery, Neil Morgan, Tom Murtha, Matt Myers, Torben Pedersen, Johan Roos, Alan Rugman, Richard Rumelt, Saeed Samiee, Oded Shenkar, Kulwant Singh, José de la Torre, Rajan Varadarajan, and Udo Zander. In addition, Brian Chabowski deserves unique recognition because of his all-around assistance with the third edition of the book.

Finally, we would like to thank our wives—Moira Yip and Laurie Hult—for their incredible support in making the work on this edition possible.

George S. Yip

G. Tomas M. Hult

ABOUT THE AUTHORS

George S. Yip, a native of Asia, and a dual citizen of the United Kingdom and the United States, is professor of management at the China Europe International Business School in Shanghai in China, where he is also codirector of the CEIBS Centre on China Innovation. He divides his time between London, Shanghai, and Maine, USA. He is also Visiting Professor at Imperial College Business School in London, and (former) Emeritus Dean of Rotterdam School of Management, Erasmus University, in the Netherlands. Prior to the RSM deanship he was vice president at Capgemini Consulting. Earlier appointments include professor of strategic and international management and associate dean at London Business School, and positions at Cambridge University, Harvard Business School, and UCLA. Yip has also held visiting positions at Georgetown University, Stanford University, and Templeton College, Oxford. Professor Yip is a Fellow of the Academy of International Business and one of the foremost experts in the world on global strategy.

G. Tomas M. Hult, a native of Sweden, and a dual citizen of Sweden and the United States, is the Eli Broad Professor of Marketing and International Business and director of the Eli Broad International Business Center (IBC) at Michigan State University, USA. He is also the executive director of the Academy of International Business—a professional membership association with more than 3,400 members in some 80 countries. IBC is the developer of the world-leading online source for "international business resources" (per all major search engines) called globalEDGE (globalEDGE.msu.edu). Professor Hult was the 75th most-cited "scientist in economics and business" in the world for 1997–2007, per the ranking provided by Thomson Reuters. He serves as editor-in-chief of the *Journal of the Academy of Marketing Science* and founding editor of *globalEDGE Business Review.* Hult has also held visiting positions at the Copenhagen Business School, University of California at Berkeley, University of Bern, FedEx Center for Supply Chain Management in Memphis, and Leeds University. He was a cofounder of Hult Ketchen International Group. Professor Hult is a Fellow of the Academy of International Business and one of the world's leading experts on research and practice at the intersection of global strategy and global supply chain management.

CHAPTER 1

Understanding Global Strategy

As we entered the third millennium, the debate about firms becoming more global almost ended (or in the language of the wired generation, "game over"). Companies now assumed that they should globalize at least certain aspects of their strategy and organization unless they can find very good reasons not to. Of course, the assumption is that the company engages in the global marketplace. The spread of eBusiness, Internet tools, and Web networks provides compelling reasons. The old saying that any company that mounts a Web site has instant global reach and potential overseas customers really holds true today. And with such global focus come demands for delivery and service. In addition, as more and more evidence shows, companies that globalize achieve better competitive and financial performance.

But globalizing, in the sense of spreading activities around the globe, is not enough. Companies also need to be globally integrated, in the sense of using globally coherent strategies, operating global networks, and maximizing profits on a global basis. However, turning a collection of country-businesses into a worldwide business that has an integrated, global strategy presents one of the stiffest challenges for managers today. Many companies still opt for a smaller selection of countries or a regional approach. Because of its difficulties, being able to develop and implement an effective global strategy is the acid test of a well-managed company. Many forces are driving companies around the world to globalize in the sense of expanding their participation in foreign markets. Companies also need to globalize in another sense, that is, *integrate* their worldwide strategy. This global integration contrasts with the multinational approach in which companies set up country subsidiaries that design, produce, and market products or services tailored to local needs. This multinational model is now in question and may be considered a "multilocal strategy" in contrast to a truly global strategy.[1]

Many managers are asking if they are in a global industry and whether their business should have a global strategy. The better questions to ask are, *How global is the industry* and *How global should the business strategy be?* This is because virtually every industry has aspects that are global or potentially global—some industries have more aspects that are global than others and more intensely so. Similarly, a strategy can be more or less global in its different elements. An industry is global to the extent that there are intercountry connections. A strategy is global to the extent that it is integrated across countries. Global strategy should not be equated with any one element—standardized products or worldwide market coverage or a global manufacturing network. For example, some suggest that a global company needs to have robust sales across many countries, but that focuses on only one of several elements. Global strategy should, instead, be a flexible combination of many elements.

Recent and coming changes make it more likely that, in many industries, a global strategy will be more successful than a multilocal one. Indeed, having a sound global strategy may well be the requirement for survival as the changes accelerate. These changes include the growing similarity among countries in what their citizens want to buy.[2] Other changes are the reduction of tariff and nontariff barriers, technology investments that are becoming too expensive to amortize in one market only, and competitors who are changing the nature of rivalry from country-by-country competition to global competition. Recent events have seen the world converge more and more in customer needs and tastes, the drastic reduction of many government barriers to free trade and investment, an acceleration of globalization enablers in communications, and a surge in globally applicable new technological products and services. All this does not mean that every industry has become entirely global. But today, nearly every industry has a significant global segment in which customers prefer products or services that are much more global than they are local. Around the global segment are still regional, national, or subnational niches. The size of the global segment varies, from very large in, for example, the personal computer industry to relatively small in many parts of the food industry. But the global segment is increasing in size in nearly all cases.

Almost every product or service market in the major world economies has foreign competitors—computers, fast food, medical diagnostic equipment—a nearly endless list that is growing rapidly. Increasing foreign competition is in itself a reason for a business to globalize in order to gain the size and skills to compete more effectively. But an even greater spur to globalization is the advent of new global competitors that manage and compete on an integrated global basis. In the 1980s these global competitors were primarily Japanese. Their central approach to global competition was one of the factors that allowed Japanese companies to conquer so many Western markets.[3] In the 1990s, American and European companies responded to the Japanese challenge by focusing much more on quality. This was exemplified by General Electric's and Motorola's adoption of *six-sigma* quality. In addition, American and, especially, some European companies began to develop new models of globalization that were more flexible than the centralized Japanese one. In the 2000s, Chinese, Indian, and South Korean companies became much more engaged in the global marketplace. These three countries collectively had about 100 of the Forbes 2000 multinational corporations at the end of the decade in 2010.

In addition, the communications and information revolution over the past decade has made it much easier to manage in a globally integrated fashion. Improvements in air travel, computers, satellites, and telecommunications make it much easier to communicate with, and control, far-flung operations. Interestingly, some technology such as the facsimile (fax) machine had to give way for more sophisticated (e.g., intra-networks) and largely less sophisticated (e.g., phone and Web texting) technology implementations.

Carlsberg's Global Strategy

Danish brewery conglomerate Carlsberg Group is the fourth largest brewery group in the world. Unlike its larger competitor, SABMiller, Carlsberg Group has focused on developing core products into global brands. As a result, its brand portfolio is much smaller than SABMiller's, and its sources of non-organic growth are fewer and more significant in their occurrence. For example, in 2008 the Group split up the assets of the British brewery group Scottish and Newcastle with Dutch competitor Heineken. Instead of acquiring more brands for its western European brand portfolio, the company chose to acquire the remainder of the assets of Baltic Beverages Holding in order to take full control of assets that were part of a former joint venture with Scottish and Newcastle. The joint takeover of S&N's provided both companies with access to new noncore target markets: Heineken in Western Europe (especially the United Kingdom) and Carlsberg in Eastern Europe. Acquiring many popular brands in Eastern Europe has allowed Carlsberg Group to move out of its core market and develop growing brands

without sacrificing the growth of its premium market brands. In fact, the establishment of new markets for Carlsberg Group has allowed it to position its core products as premium brands in emerging markets such as Eastern Europe as well as in Asia.

Trade barriers continue to fall. The most important examples include the continuing integration of the North American Free Trade Agreement (among the United States, Canada, and Mexico); the continuing integration of the European Union (also with the addition of new countries); and the formation and (slow) implementation of the World Trade Organization. The rise of the NICs (newly industrializing countries such as Taiwan, South Korea, Singapore, Thailand, Malaysia, Mexico, and Brazil) has also increased the number of viable sites for sophisticated manufacturing operations with low labor costs. In addition, India has increasingly become a power in the industrialized world and the global market economy, joining the so-called BRIC group of Brazil, Russia, India, and China.

Magna International's Diversified Global Strategy

Canada's Magna International is a global OEM (original equipment manufacturer) supplier of automotive components and systems. It attributed its success in the industry to its diversified portfolio of clients and the variety of products and services that it provides. The cases of once-successful specialized suppliers in the automotive industry that fail to diversify are numerous, but Magna's diversified strategy stands in sharp contrast to many competitors that may be global, albeit not always competitive. Many auto manufacturers come to Magna to develop solutions that make new markets for their vehicles, or to extend the life cycle of a niche product that might be good for a brand's image, but is less profitable than more mass-market automobiles. In some

instances, Magna can bring its expertise to a brand by helping implement flexible production systems and global sourcing to produce an automobile for a niche brand that might have a lot of value as a brand but have lackluster expertise in efficient systems for sourcing and assembly. One might consider Magna to be a total car company in its own right; it offers complete vehicle development engineering and assembly services for a number of suppliers, including Chrysler, BMW, and Mercedes-Benz. In 2009, it made the next logical step by taking a controlling stake in German car brand Opel. Magna purchased 20 percent of the company, with an additional 35 percent stake coming from its partner in the buyout, Russia's Sberbank.

These new forms of linking people inside, outside, and across the boundaries of companies created a unique immediacy and completeness of communication that plugged the globe into every executive's desk.

KEYS TO A SUCCESSFUL TOTAL GLOBAL STRATEGY

A total global strategy has three separate components, depicted in Exhibit 1-1:

1. *Developing the core strategy,* which is the basis of sustainable strategic advantage. This is usually, but not necessarily, developed for the home country first. Without a sound core strategy on which to build, a worldwide business need not bother about global strategy.

2. *Internationalizing the core strategy,* through international expansion of activities and adaptation of the core strategy. Companies need to have mastered the basics of international business before they can attempt a global strategy (because the latter often involves breaking the rules of international business).

3. *Globalizing the international strategy,* by integrating the strategy across countries.

Multinational companies know well the first two steps. What they know less well is the third step. In addition, globalization runs counter to the accepted wisdom of tailoring for national markets.[4] *This book focuses on the third step—global integration.*

EXHIBIT 1-1 Components of a Total Global Strategy

1. Develop Core Business Strategy

2. Internationalize Strategy

Country A   Country B   Country C   Country D   Country E   Country F

3. Globalize Strategy

Country A   Country B   Country C   Country D   Country E   Country F

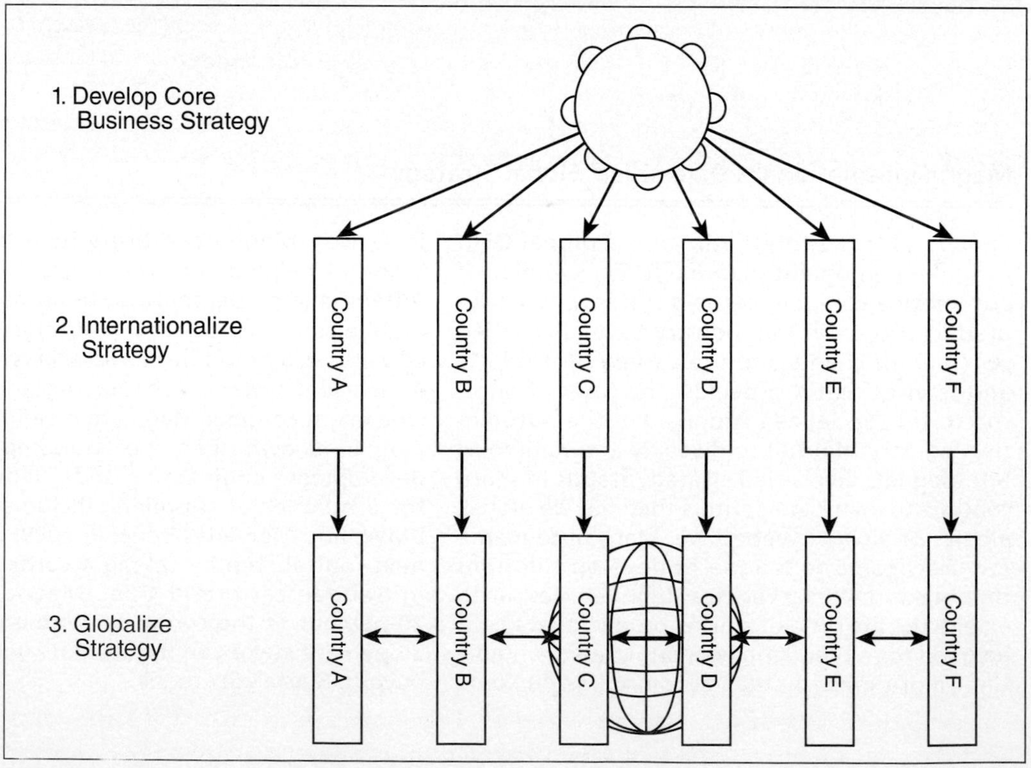

Developing a Core Business Strategy

Each separable business in a company needs its own core strategy.[5] Defining the business in the first place can be a major task. Major parameters of the definition include the types of customers served and the types of products and services offered. The type of product or service can be split into two separate dimensions—the type of need met and the type of technology used to meet that need.[6] For example, one business may be in the total packaging business, while another business may define its business more narrowly as the plastics packaging business.

A core strategy includes several key elements:

- Selection of the type of products or services that the business offers
- The types of customers that the business serves
- The geographic markets served
- Major sources of sustainable competitive advantage
- Functional strategy for each of the most important value-adding activities
- Competitive posture, including the selection of competitors to target
- Investment strategy

Strategy writers have sometimes urged the broadest possible definition of a business and criticize managers who restrictively define their business. But the breadth or narrowness of a business definition is a key element of strategic choice and directly affects sustainable strategic advantage. It is better to devote limited resources to sustaining advantage in a narrowly defined business than to overspread resources so that no advantage is sustained. In recent years the more prominent failures have come from too expansive a business definition. People Express, at one time a highly successful airline in the United States, collapsed when it expanded beyond its East Coast cut-price niche. Saatchi & Saatchi, once the world's largest advertising agency group, had to reverse its expansion into the consulting business. The company had expected, wrongly, to conquer this new business as rapidly as it had conquered its traditional business. Both Matsushita and Sony redefined themselves as entertainment companies and made disastrous acquisitions of movie studios.

Developing an Internationalization Strategy

When a business expands outside its home market, it needs to internationalize its core business strategy. The first and most important step in internationalizing the core business strategy is to select the geographic markets in which to compete. This choice has much more importance for an international business than for a national business. In the early part of its life, a national business does face issues of geographic market selection as it expands within its domestic market. These issues include identifying market attractiveness, potential competition and ways in which to adapt to local conditions, and ways in which to manage the business across a larger geographic area. For some retail or service businesses, geographic market selection continues to be vital because of the importance of site location.

But for most businesses international market selection presents issues that are much more challenging than selection within a domestic market. The sources of this challenge include the role of barriers to trade, such as import tariffs and quotas and foreign ownership rules, as well as differences from the home country in laws, language, tastes, and behavior.[7] Other aspects of an internationalization strategy involve how to adapt products and programs to take account of foreign needs, preferences, culture, language, climate, and so on. *But the end result is typically that the company winds up with strategies and approaches with large differences among countries.* These differences can then weaken the company's worldwide cost position, quality, customer preference, and competitive leverage.

Developing a Globalization Strategy

To overcome the disadvantages created by internationalization, companies need a globalization strategy that integrates and manages for worldwide business leverage and competitive advantage. *What aspects of strategy should be globalized?* Managers can answer this question by systematically analyzing industry conditions or "industry globalization drivers," by understanding the different ways in which a globalization strategy can be used through the use of "global strategy levers," by understanding how the organization's infrastructure factors can affect the implementation of a global strategy, and by evaluating the benefits and costs of globalization.

Exhibit 1-2 presents the framework for diagnosing and developing a globalization strategy. Industry globalization drivers are externally determined by industry conditions or by the economics of the business, while global strategy levers are choices available to the worldwide business.[8] *Industry globalization drivers* (underlying market, cost, and other industry conditions) create the potential for a worldwide business to achieve the *benefits* of global strategy. To achieve these benefits, a worldwide business needs to set its *global strategy levers* (e.g., use of globally standardized products) appropriately relative to the industry drivers, and relative to the *position and resources* of the business and its parent company. The *organization's ability to implement* the formulated global strategy affects how well the benefits can be achieved.

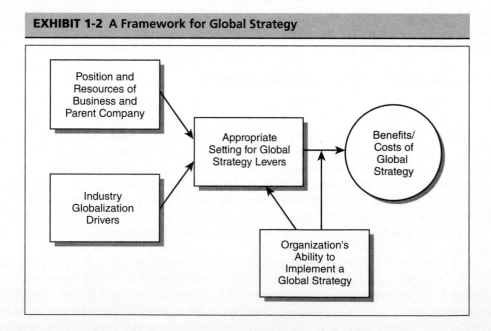

EXHIBIT 1-2 A Framework for Global Strategy

EXHIBIT 1-3 The Globalization Triangle

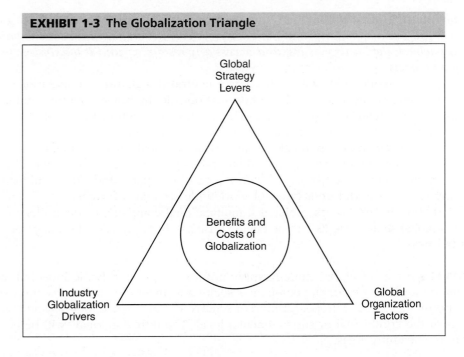

Another way of viewing the relationship among these different forces and factors is in terms of a globalization triangle. As depicted in Exhibit 1-3, industry globalization drivers, global strategy levers, and global organization factors need to work together to achieve potential globalization benefits.

Some Definitions and Distinctions

GLOBAL, GLOBALIZE   The popularity of global strategy has caused overuse of the terms "global" and "globalize." Instead of being used to designate a particular type of international strategy, these terms are being used to replace the term "international." One reason is that "international" has come to represent the now unfashionable distinction between domestic and nondomestic business. Everyone seems to want a global strategy rather than just an international one. As a result of the widespread use of the term "global," we are losing the ability to refer to different types of international strategies. More important, executives will find it easier to delude themselves that they have a global strategy if they are careless as to what they call their worldwide strategy.

A truly global company is one that does business not only in both the eastern and the western hemispheres but also in both the northern and southern ones.[9] In the process, geographic distances and time-zone variations are maximized. With the prominence of many companies in Asia, Latin America, and Eastern Europe, operating in just the "triad" of North America, Western Europe, and Japan is no longer sufficient. Other differences also tend to be sharpened, such as the variety of languages, currencies, cultures, legal and political systems, government policies and regulations, educational backgrounds of managers and employees, levels of national economic development, and climates.

Simply operating globally does not mean that a company possesses a global strategy. *The global company does not have to be everywhere, but it has the capability to go anywhere, deploy any assets, and access any resources, and it maximizes profits on a global basis.*

The term "worldwide" will be used as a neutral designation. "International" will refer to anything connected with doing business outside the home country. "Multilocal" and "global" will refer to types of worldwide strategies. Much of this book will cover what these types of strategies mean. Briefly, a multilocal strategy treats competition in each country or region on a stand-alone basis, while a global strategy takes an integrated approach across countries and regions. "Multilocal" is preferable to "multinational," as the latter term has come to be associated with a type of company. Indeed, a multinational company can pursue different types of worldwide strategies for each of its different worldwide businesses. For example, as a multinational company, General Electric may pursue a global strategy for its turbine engine business, but a multilocal strategy for some other business.

REGIONAL   Issues of global strategy apply not just at the worldwide level but at the regionwide level. For example, companies seeking to meet the challenges and exploit the opportunities of the European Union or ASEAN are, in essence, developing a global strategy at the continental or subcontinental level. The term "regional" will be used to refer to multicountry areas.

COUNTRY   The term "country" can also be problematic. For example, is Benelux one country or three? Legally it comprises three countries, but many companies manage it as one. The same scenario can be said for the Nordic countries—is it one area or more (e.g., Denmark, Finland, Iceland, Norway, and Sweden)? Management is the key. Even more ambiguous is the group of Central American countries lying between Mexico and Colombia. The term "country" will be used to refer to single countries or groups of small, contiguous countries that are managed as one country.

WORLDWIDE BUSINESS   A worldwide business is one that has significant operations on several continents. Furthermore, a worldwide business is defined as one that produces as well as sells in multiple countries (if not continents). Thus a purely export-based business is not a worldwide business in this case. A worldwide business may also not be recognized as such. The company may view it merely as a collection of similar businesses operating in different countries. One topic of this book will be how to recognize a worldwide business. Such a business may use a multilocal or global strategy or some combination in between.

TRANSNATIONAL   Some now argue for "transnational strategy": "In contrast to the global model, the transnational mentality recognizes the importance of flexible and responsive country-level operations—hence the return of *national* into the terminology. And compared to the multinational approach, it provides for linking and coordinating those operations to retain competitive effectiveness and economic efficiency—as indicated by the prefix 'trans.' The resulting need for intensive organizationwide coordination and shared decision making implies that this is a much more sophisticated and subtle approach to MNC management."[10] While we agree with the need to respond to country differences, *where truly* necessary, there is already plenty of advice on how to do that (in most textbooks on international business[11]). What is much harder is to achieve global integration—the focus of global strategy and of this book.

FINANCIAL BENEFITS OF INTERNATIONALIZATION AND GLOBALIZATION

Both internationalization—in terms of globally spreading activities and revenues—and globalization—in terms of globally integrating strategy—can have financial benefits.

Financial Benefits of Internationalization

Many studies have shown that internationalization increases financial returns and reduces risk.[12] Other studies have shown that international spread reduces financial betas for multinational firms, but also that volatile currency markets have vastly increased the impact of exchange risk, so that the net variance in cash flow is higher for multinational firms.[13] This empirical evidence suggests that it is premature to say that multinationals have found a way to eliminate the risk–return relationship. However, it does seem to be the case that firms can simultaneously increase returns to fixed assets and take a portfolio approach to financial risk management by increased internationalization.

While financial risk reduction seems to be less clear-cut today, business risk reduction strategies through international expansion continue to be attractive.[14] If we look at business risk as exposure to unexpected events, international markets offer several advantages. First, extended product life cycles, while perhaps less apparent than in the past,[15] still seem possible in many industries. In some industries, firms that can shift sales of outdated products in industrialized countries to developing countries can gain ongoing returns on their initial investment and may also be able to avoid sudden replacement by new technologies or innovative products. Much evidence also exists to show that strategic maneuvering in concentrated industries is most successful when used by international firms against domestic firms. Finally, political and other environmental risks can be difficult to manage for companies committed to one or a few national markets, while more internationalized firms can shift production, promotion, distribution, and even development among a number of markets to take advantage of (or avoid) local conditions or to increase bargaining power.

Financial Benefits of Globalization

Global integration is still a relatively new phenomenon. So there is relatively little research on its financial benefits. Studies have provided limited evidence, all in favor of, or at least neutral toward, global strategy. One study found no significant difference in profit performance among businesses facing (1) global integration pressures, (2) local responsiveness pressures, and (3) both pressures.[16] A narrower study found that the market share and profit performance of 71 European and Japanese firms serving the U.S. market were negatively related to the extent to which products were adapted for the U.S. market; that is, businesses with globally standardized products performed better.[17] In a study of global industries, companies with a "global, combination" strategy had the best performance on measures of return on assets, and those with an "international, product innovation" strategy had the best performance on return on investment, while the companies with a "domestic, product specialization" strategy had the poorest performance.[18] More broadly, a study of American and Japanese companies found a strong positive relationship between the use of global strategy and superior performance in terms of relative market share and relative profitability.[19]

INDUSTRY GLOBALIZATION DRIVERS

Four groups of "industry globalization drivers"—market, cost, government, and competitive—represent the industry conditions that determine the potential and need for competing with a global strategy.[20] Together these four sets of drivers cover all the critical industry conditions that affect the potential for globalization. While other groupings are possible, these four distinguish among the sources (market or cost, etc.) of the drivers and, therefore, help managers to more easily identify and deal with them. The industry drivers are largely uncontrollable by the worldwide business. As illustrated in Exhibit 1-4 each industry has a level of globalization potential that is determined by these external drivers.

Market globalization drivers depend on customer behavior, the structure of distribution channels, and the nature of marketing in the industry. Cost drivers depend on the economics of the business. Government globalization drivers depend on the rules

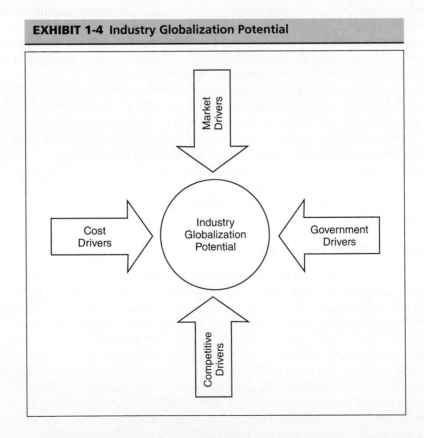

EXHIBIT 1-4 Industry Globalization Potential

Market Drivers

Cost Drivers → Industry Globalization Potential ← Government Drivers

Competitive Drivers

set by national governments. Competitive drivers depend on the actions of competitors. Each group of drivers is different for each industry and can also change over time. Therefore, some industries have more globalization potential than others, and the potential also changes. A common group of changes, increasing the globalization potential of many industries, is spurring the interest of managers in global strategy.

GLOBAL STRATEGY LEVERS

Globalization strategy is multidimensional. Setting strategy for a worldwide business requires choices along a number of strategic dimensions. Some of these dimensions determine whether the strategy lies toward the multilocal end of the continuum or the global end. There are five such dimensions:

- *Market participation* involves the choice of country-markets in which to conduct business and the level of activity, particularly in terms of market share.
- *Products/services* involve the extent to which a worldwide business offers the same or different products in different countries.
- *Location of value-adding activities* involves the choice of where to locate each of the activities that constitute the entire value-added chain—from research to production to after-sales service.[21]
- *Marketing* involves the extent to which a worldwide business uses the same brand names, advertising, and other marketing elements in different countries.
- *Competitive moves* involve the extent to which a worldwide business makes competitive moves in individual countries as part of a global competitive strategy.

For each global strategy lever, a multilocal strategy seeks to maximize worldwide performance by maximizing local competitive advantage, revenues, or profits; while a globalized strategy seeks to maximize worldwide performance through sharing and integration. Intermediate positions are, of course, feasible. A business that has a fully globalized strategy would make maximum use of each of the five global strategy levers and would therefore have complete *global market participation, global products and services, global location of activities, global marketing,* and *global competitive moves.* But, of course, not every business should use such a strategy. An overview of each lever is provided here and then covered in separate chapters in the book.

Market Participation

In a multilocal participation strategy, countries are selected on the basis of their stand-alone potential in terms of revenues and profits. In a global market participation strategy, countries need to be selected in terms of their potential contribution to globalization benefits. This may mean entering a market that is unattractive in its own right but has global strategic significance, such as the home market of a global competitor. Or it may mean concentrating resources on building share in a limited number of key markets rather than more widespread coverage. A pattern of major share in major markets is advocated in the concept of the United States-Europe-Japan triad.[22] In contrast, under a multilocal strategy no particular pattern of participation is required—the pattern accrues from the pursuit of local advantage.

Recent Changes in General Globalization Drivers

Although it is not the purpose of this book to examine general changes in globalization drivers, some of these common changes include the following:

Market Drivers

- Per capita income converging among industrialized nations
- Convergence of lifestyles and tastes
- Increasing travel creating global consumers
- Organizations beginning to behave as global customers
- Growth of global and regional channels
- Increasing establishment of world brands
- Push to develop global advertising
- Spread of global and regional media

Cost Drivers

- Continuing push for economies of scale (but offset by flexible manufacturing)
- Accelerating technological innovation
- Advances in transportation and logistics solutions
- Emergence of NICs with productive capability and low labor costs
- Increasing cost of product development relative to market life

Government Drivers

- Reduction of tariff barriers (e.g., North American Free Trade Agreement)
- Reduction of nontariff barriers (e.g., Japan's gradual opening of its markets)

- Increasing focus on trading blocs (e.g., European Union)
- Strengthening of world trade institutions (e.g., World Trade Organization)
- Decline in role of governments as producers and customers (e.g., denationalization of many industries in Europe and elsewhere)
- Privatization in previously state-dominated economies
- Increasing participation of China, India, and many emerging markets in the global economy

Competitive Drivers

- Continuing increase in level of world trade
- More countries becoming key competitive battlegrounds
- Increased ownership of corporations by foreign acquirers
- Rise of new competitors' intent upon becoming global competitors (e.g., Japanese firms in the 1970s, Korean firms in the 1980s, Taiwanese firms in the 1990s, Chinese firms in the 2000s, and Indian and Russian firms in the 2010s)
- Rise of "born-global" companies
- Growth of global networks making countries interdependent in particular industries (e.g., electronics)
- More companies becoming globally centered rather than nationally centered
- Increased formation of global strategic alliances

Products and Services

In a multilocal product strategy, the products and services offered in each country are tailored to local needs. In a global product strategy, the ideal is a standardized core product that requires a minimum of local adaptation. Cost reduction is usually the most important benefit of product standardization. Others stress the need for a broad product portfolio, with many product varieties in order to share technologies and distribution channels, or stress the need for flexibility.[23] In practice, multinationals have pursued global product standardization to a greater or lesser extent some of the time.[24]

The nature of service delivery makes both standardization and customization equally feasible. Local elements can be easily added to a global formula such as the service provided at Club Med. The well-known chain of resorts has incorporated local

Amazon's Market Participation

For born-global businesses that are largely Internet-based, economies of scope are often demanded by consumers. In marketplaces for consumer products with global reach, goods that command a premium in the marketplace allow for more favorable logistics. While most of the advancements in the global economy take advantage of lower costs of production through scale economies, consumer discretionary income often creates scenarios where atypical niche markets thrive. Sophisticated Web technologies enable rich economies of scope that could not be facilitated to this extent without first connecting businesses to consumers. For example, Amazon .com's Marketplace service allows used booksellers to sell their books globally. Instead of their traditional business model, where a customer's chance of a local store having the used book in stock is slim, consumers can get exactly what they want online. Payment processing is facilitated by Amazon, ensuring customer concerns about making risky transactions with third-party sellers. The company also provides logistical services to sellers, including software to easily load inventory onto Marketplace via bar codes or ISBN numbers. Marketplace has a competitive advantage over other services because Amazon.com was already the industry leader in Web-based new book sales. Integrating used book selling into its site makes it possible for consumers to compare prices between new and used books in one market.

adaptations to its core product. The entertainment available varies from resort to resort, such as Balinese dancing in Indonesia and the game of mah-jongg and more group activities in other Asian resorts. Club Med steers its American customers to English-speaking clubs via strategic segmentation of its brochures and Web sites.[25]

Activity Location

In a multilocal activity strategy, all or most of the value chain is reproduced in every country. In another type of international strategy—exporting—most of the value chain is kept in one country. In a global activity strategy, the value chain is broken up and each activity may be conducted in a different country. The major benefits lie in cost reduction. One type of value-chain strategy is partial concentration and partial duplication. The key feature of a global position on this strategy dimension is the systematic placement of the value chain around the globe.

To provide its global customer support service, Hewlett-Packard maintains a global chain of activity locations—its more than 20 Response Centers around the world are integrated into a global network headed by four major centers: Bracknell (United Kingdom), Atlanta (Georgia) and Mountain View (California) in the United States, and Melbourne (Australia). Each center is staffed during extended daytime hours, seven days a week, by between 12 and 200 engineers. Problems that cannot be resolved in a smaller center may be transferred to one of the major centers. Because of time-zone differentials, at least one of the major centers is always in full operation at any time.

Citibank, one of the world's largest banks, has positioned itself as a "uniquely global consumer bank."[26] The company's objective is to allow its customers to do their banking "any way, any where, any time." To provide this service, it has expanded its Citicard Banking Centers with their automated teller machines to more than 40 countries. These centers are globally linked, allowing 24-hour, seven days a week access. And, of course, noncash transactions can be conducted by phone.

Marketing

In a global marketing strategy, a uniform marketing approach is applied around the world, although not all elements of the marketing mix need be identical.[27] Unilever achieved great success with a fabric softener that used a globally common positioning, an advertising theme, and a symbol (a teddy bear), but a brand name that varied by country. Similarly, a product that serves a common need can be geographically expanded with a uniform marketing program, despite apparent obstacles of differences in marketing environments.

For service businesses,[28] the uncertainty engendered by intangibility requires strong branding to offset it. So the primary task of the brand name or trademark for a service is to offer recognition and reassurance, rather than performing other functions such as positioning or local adaptation. McDonald's, for instance, has to be the same name around the world, so that both locals and travelers know that they will get the genuine McDonald's experience. Travel-related services virtually require the same brand name globally. What use would an American Express card be if the brand were Russian Express in Moscow? One solution is to be both global and local. FedEx combines global and local brand names. In France the company initially used partly localized names: FedEx Priorité, FedEx Rapide, and FedEx Frêt.

Global positioning is also important. McDonald's has a globally consistent positioning and image, but this is not a globally neutral image. It is clearly American, so it stands for "us" in the United States and "them" elsewhere. Similarly, Chili's, a U.S.-based restaurant chain offering Mexican food, has its largest store in Monterrey, Mexico. But customers there go for an "American experience," not a Mexican one. In contrast, Benetton, the Italian fashion clothing concern, is one of the very few global companies that strives for a universalistic, nonnational image.

Competitive Moves

In a multilocal competitive strategy, a multinational company fights its competitors one country at a time in separate contests, even though it may face another multinational in many of the same countries. In a global competitive strategy, competitive moves are

Japanese Global Competitive Moves

Japanese companies seem to make more use of global competitive moves than American or European companies.[29] Bridgestone Company, the Japanese tire manufacturer, has tried to integrate its competitive moves in response to global consolidation by its major competitors: Continental AG's acquisition of Gencorp's General Tire and Rubber Company, General Tire's joint venture with two Japanese tire makers, and Sumitomo's acquisition of an interest in Dunlop Tire. These competitive actions forced Bridgestone to establish a presence in the major American market in order to maintain its position in the world tire market. To this end, Bridgestone formed a joint venture to own and manage Firestone Corporation's worldwide tire business. This joint venture also allowed Bridgestone to gain access to Firestone's European plants. Eventually, Bridgestone made a full acquisition of Firestone. Bridgestone had to be willing to pay the price of its increased global market participation: It had to contend with major losses at Firestone.

Salomon's Retaliation in Skis

Some European and American companies do successfully integrate their competitive strategy, as U.S.-based Salomon did in the ski equipment industry. Tyrolia, an Austrian ski-binding competitor, attacked Salomon's stronghold position in its biggest market, the United States. Rather than fighting Tyrolia only in America, Salomon retaliated in the countries where Tyrolia generated a large share of its sales and profits—Germany and Austria. Taking a global perspective, Salomon viewed the whole world—not just one country—as its competitive battleground.[30]

This last example illustrates that integration of competitive moves is more than just coordination, such as simultaneous or sequenced price moves. Integration requires a concerted effort to compete on a global and not a country-by-country basis. Coordination is part of integration. Other parts include identifying and targeting global, regional, and local competitors. Having a global attack and defense plan for each major competitor is crucial. A major objective may be to limit a potential global competitor to its home country. An American company has devised a strategy to contain a Japanese competitor that has yet to move outside Japan. To prevent this competitor from using joint ventures outside Japan as stepping-stones to globalization, the American company makes preemptive joint venture agreements with the Japanese company's potential partners.

European Hotels Strike Back

Realizing that the competitive terrain is shifting beneath them, European hotel chains are setting out to overhaul their companies along American lines.[31] This has involved tightening management controls, creating a number of brand names instead of one, separating real estate holdings of the company from their management operations, going public, and negotiating strategic alliances with American chains. Although many European hotel companies were profitable in the last decades, they recognize the need to go global in the twenty-first century to continue to be competitive.

With American chains competing in their market, most European hotel companies felt that they did not have much choice but to go global and follow the trail blazed by the American giants. Construction boomed, at both the high end and the low end of the market, and European hotel chains undertook many mergers and acquisitions as they sought allies to strengthen their market positions. Because the European hotel business is a fragmented market and dominated by independents—fully 75 percent of the trade compared with just 25 percent in the United States—it remains vulnerable to penetration by American chains such as Marriott International. The current upheaval, though wrenching, also provides European chains like the Accor group in France an opportunity to become world players. Accor is seizing the opportunity largely by copying the American model. Despite the "Americanization" of the European hotel chains, they insist on not becoming American clones. The regional differences on the Continent are still too great to allow the uniformity of style and service that is possible in the United States.

integrated across countries. The same type of move is made in different countries at the same time or in some systematic sequence, or a competitor is attacked in one country in order to drain its resources for another country, or a competitive attack in one country is countered in a different country. Perhaps the best example is the counterattack in a competitor's home market as a parry to an attack on one's own home market.

BENEFITS OF GLOBAL STRATEGY

Use of the global strategy levers can achieve one or more of four major categories of potential globalization benefits:

- Cost reductions
- Improved quality of products and programs
- Enhanced customer preference
- Increased competitive leverage

Exhibit 1-5 summarizes which lever achieves what benefits. It also summarizes the major drawbacks of global strategy.

Reducing Costs

An integrated global strategy can save worldwide costs in several ways:

- *Economies of scale* can be achieved by pooling production or other activities for two or more countries. For example, production of large volumes of compact disc players can result in economies of scale. Realizing the potential benefit of these economies of scale, Sony Corporation at one time concentrated its compact disc production in Terre Haute, Indiana, and Salzburg, Austria.

- *Lower factor costs* can be obtained by moving manufacturing or other activities to low-cost countries. This has, of course, been the motivation of the earlier surge of offshore manufacturing, particularly by American firms. For example, the Mexican side of the U.S.-Mexico border is now crowded with *maquiladoras*—manufacturing plants set up and run by American companies using Mexican labor.

- *Focused production* means reducing the number of products manufactured, from many local models to a few global ones. Typically, unit costs fall as the number of products made in a factory declines. Such reduction in product variety cuts the costs involved in setup, downtime, extra inventory, and the like.[32]

- *Flexibility* can be exploited by moving production from location to location on a short-term basis to take advantage of the lowest costs at a given time. Dow Chemical takes this approach to minimize the cost of producing chemicals. Dow uses a linear programming model that takes account of cross-country differences in exchange rates, tax rates, transportation, and labor costs. The model comes up with the best mix of production volume by location for each planning period.

- *Enhancing bargaining power,* via a strategy that allows for switching production among multiple manufacturing sites in different countries, greatly increases a company's bargaining power with suppliers, workers, and host governments (*cf.* European Union). This integrated production strategy has greatly enhanced management's bargaining power at the expense of unions.

Improving Quality of Products and Programs

Focus and concentration on a smaller number of products and programs, rather than many products and programs typical in a multilocal strategy, can improve the quality of both products and programs. Global focus is one of the reasons for the Japanese success in automobiles. For example, Toyota weathered the latest economic downturn better than its counterparts. It marketed a far smaller number of models around the world

EXHIBIT 1-5 How Global Strategy Levers Achieve Globalization Benefits

Global Strategy Levers	Benefits				Major Drawbacks
	Cost Reduction	Improved Quality	Enhanced Customer Preference	Competitive Leverage	All Levels Incur Coordination Costs, Plus
Global Market Participation	Increases volume for economies of scale.	Via exposure to demanding customers and innovative competitors.	Via global availability, global serviceability, and global recognition.	Advantages of early entry. Provides more sites for attack and counterattack, hostage for good behavior.	Earlier or greater commitment to a market than warranted on own merits.
Global Products	Reduces duplication of development efforts. Reduces sourcing, production, and inventory costs.	Focuses development and management resources.	Allows consumers to use familiar product while abroad. Allows organizations to use same product across country units.	Basis for low-cost invasion of markets. Offsets disadvantage of low market share.	Less responsive to local needs.
Global Location of Activities	Reduces duplication of activities. Helps exploit economies of scale. Exploits differences in country factor costs. Partial concentration allows flexibility versus currency changes and versus bargaining parties.	Focuses effort. Allows more consistent quality control.		Allows maintenance of cost advantage independent of local conditions. Provides flexibility on where to base competitive advantage.	Distances activities from customer. Increases currency risk. Increases risk of creating competitors. More difficult to manage value chain.
Global Marketing	Reduces design and production costs of marketing programs.	Focuses talent and resources. Leverages scarce, good ideas.	Reinforces marketing messages by exposing customer to the same mix in different countries.		Reduces adaptation to local customer behavior and marketing environment.
Global Competitive Moves				Magnifies resources available to any country. Provides more options and leverage in attack and defense.	Local competitiveness may be sacrificed.

than did General Motors, even allowing for its unit sales being less than that of General Motors. Toyota concentrated on improving its few models while GM fragmented its development funds. The result was that GM was harder hit by the economic downturn in 2008–2010. For example, since the 1990s the Toyota Camry has been the U.S. version of a basic worldwide model and the successor to a long line of development efforts.[33] The Camry has been consistently rated as the best in the class of medium-sized cars. In contrast, General Motors' Pontiac Fiero started out in the early 1980s as one of the most successful small sports cars but was withdrawn after only a few years on the market. Industry observers blamed this on a failure to invest development money to overcome minor problems.

General Motors, in its effort to increase global efficiencies in cost and design, continues to struggle in its proliferation efforts.[34] GM has often relied on Opel, GM's division in Germany, to solve many of GM's globalization problems. However, the high cost of retooling, currency volatility, and local design differences has delayed the process of reducing small car platforms and developing "world cars." Interestingly, world car efforts by U.S. companies have failed in the past. As an example, the Ford Mondeo family sedan sold well in Europe but stalled in the United States due to a perceived small backseat and high price.

In contrast, most Japanese companies have successfully marketed world cars, such as the Toyota Camry and the Honda Accord. Some European companies have also succeeded, albeit with niche offerings—the Volkswagen Beetle at one end of the scale and Mercedes and BMW at the other end. Fiat is now making a serious attempt at a world car with its Palio model, mainly marketed to developing countries.

Enhancing Customer Preference

Global availability, global serviceability, and global recognition can enhance customer preference through reinforcement. Soft drink and fast-food companies are, of course, leading exponents of this strategy. Many suppliers of financial services, such as credit cards, have to provide global presence because of the travel-related nature of their service. Manufacturers of industrial products can also exploit this benefit. A supplier that can provide a multinational customer with a standard product around the world gains from the worldwide familiarity within the customer organization. Computer manufacturers have long pursued this strategy.

Increasing Competitive Leverage

A global strategy provides more points to attack and counterattack against competitors. In an effort to prevent the Japanese from becoming a competitive nuisance in disposable syringes, Becton Dickinson, a major American medical products company, decided to enter three markets in Japan's "backyard." Becton entered the Hong Kong, Singapore, and Philippines markets to prevent further Japanese penetration.[35]

DRAWBACKS OF GLOBAL STRATEGY

Globalization can incur significant management costs through increased coordination, reporting requirements, and even added staff. Globalization can also reduce management effectiveness in individual countries if overcentralization hurts local motivation and morale. In addition, each global strategy lever incurs particular drawbacks.

Whirlpool's Global Expansion in Appliances

The American appliance company, Whirlpool, is going global aggressively, and paying the price, too. Although Whirlpool's revenues have doubled since the inception of its aggressive globalization efforts, the company now faces major problems as a result of these efforts.[36] The business requires that Whirlpool offer a host of customized products that meet regional preferences and understand the logistics of local manufacturing. Whirlpool's inability to standardize these products, and the poor quality associated with Asian operations in comparison to Japanese operations, caused a reduction in profits to the company. In addition, the company saw its high start-up costs in Asia reduce profit potential.

Whirlpool had not counted on the difficulty in marketing appliances—largely homogeneous in the United States—to the fragmented cultures of Europe.[37] Because of lifestyle differences that range widely from country to country, appliance makers must target products to specific markets. For instance, clothes washers sold in northern countries like Denmark must spin-dry clothes much better than in southern Italy, where consumers often line-dry clothes in the warmer weather. Whirlpool was also caught with higher material costs, which cut into its profit margins. And the Whirlpool name, not well known in Europe, took a while to catch on with the locals. Distributors were more familiar with brands such as Electrolux, the Swedish appliance maker and Whirlpool's largest European rival. Despite the difficulties, Whirlpool remains committed to its globalization strategy.

A global strategy approach to market participation can incur the drawbacks of an earlier or greater commitment to a market than warranted on its own merits. Many American companies, such as Motorola, struggled from the 1980s onward with long-term efforts to penetrate Japanese markets, mostly in order to enhance their global competitive position rather than to make money in Japan for its own sake. Similarly, many foreign companies have struggled since the 1990s in their efforts to build positions in China, attracted by the promise of future reward.

Product standardization can result in a product that fully satisfies customers nowhere. The product may have been developed with the most universal features to be globally acceptable but provides limited value to many customers because of its lack of customization and/or inflexible features.

Concentrating activities distances those activities from customers and can reduce responsiveness and flexibility. It also increases currency risk by incurring costs and revenues in different countries. Modern communications can offset some of the disadvantages of geographic concentration. For example, Perth, on the coast of Western Australia, is perhaps the most isolated major city in the world, with more than 2,000 miles of desert between it and other major Australian cities. But Accor Asia Pacific, the Asian arm of France's Accor, one of the world's largest hotel companies, chose Perth as the home of its global reservation center for 2,400 Accor hotels worldwide. Accor chose Perth because it is the home of Telstra, the Australian-based telecommunications corporation; it is in close geographic proximity to Asia; it offers a time-zone advantage; it is cost-effective; and it has ready access to a multilingual labor force.[38]

Uniform marketing can reduce adaptation to local customer behavior and the marketing environment. For example, the head office of British Airways (BA) mandated that every country use the "Manhattan Landing" television commercial developed by its advertising agency, Saatchi & Saatchi. While the commercial won many awards, it was criticized for using a visual (of New York City) that was not widely recognized in many countries. From the mid-1990s the firm set about transforming itself from a British airline with a global reach to an airline of the world that just happens to be based in Britain.[39] As part of a 1997 campaign, the planes took on a completely different look—with new logos and paintwork. BA commissioned dozens of designs from regional artists— African murals, Japanese calligraphy, and Scottish tartan plaids. Then the airline transposed these multicultural images onto ticket jackets, cabin crew scarves, business cards, and the tails of planes. Unfortunately for BA, many of its British customers objected to this transformation. Most notably, the former British prime minister, Margaret Thatcher, when confronted with a model of the new design covered the offending tail with her handkerchief. Other critics called the airline's new designs "global graffiti," and Virgin Atlantic countered by adding the British flag to its planes. By 1999, in the face of criticism and poor profits, BA began to replace the artists' designs on the tail with a new, less traditional version of the British flag. And, as of February 2007, BA's advertising agency is Bartle Bogle Hegarty, and BA is a tier one partner of the 2012 Olympics and Paralympics.

Integrating competitive moves can mean sacrificing revenues, profits, or competitive position in individual countries. This is particularly true when the subsidiary in one country is asked to attack a global competitor in order to send a signal or to divert that competitor's resources from another country.

FINDING THE BALANCE

The most successful worldwide strategies find a balance between overglobalizing and underglobalizing. The ideal strategy matches the level of strategy globalization to the globalization potential of the industry. A business in an industry with low globalization potential should have a strategy that is not very global. A business in an industry with high globalization potential should have a generally global strategy. A business suffers *global strategic disadvantage* by using a strategy that is less globalized than the potential offered by its industry. The business fails to exploit potential global benefits such as cost savings via product standardization. In contrast, a business suffers *national strategic disadvantage* by being too globalized relative to the potential offered by its industry. The business does not tailor its products and programs as much as it should. While there is no systematic evidence, comments by executives generally suggest that far more businesses suffer from not enough globalization than from too much, or at least that their focus of attention is on increasing their level of globalization.

Managers should avoid viewing industries as global or not global, but rather as being more global or not in particular dimensions. For example, an industry may have high globalization potential for globally standardized products but low globalization potential for centralized manufacturing. The paint industry satisfies fairly similar needs around the world, particularly in interior applications where intercountry differences in weather and surfaces are less. So global paint products are perfectly possible. But the low value of paint relative to its bulk and weight renders it uneconomic for long-distance shipment. So globally centralized manufacturing is not possible for most paints.

Managers should also avoid viewing strategies as global or not global. They should focus on the extent to which different dimensions of strategy are globalized. For example, M&M Mars, the confectionery manufacturer, standardizes most of its products while maintaining different marketing approaches and even, in some cases, different brand names.

MORE THAN ONE STRATEGY IS VIABLE

Although they are powerful, industry globalization drivers do not dictate one formula for success. More than one type of international strategy can be viable in a given industry.

Industry Variation across Drivers

First, no industry scores high on every one of the many globalization drivers. A particular competitor may be in a strong position to exploit a driver that scores low on globalization. The dominance of national government customers offsets the globalization potential from other industry drivers, because government customers typically prefer to do business with their own nationals. In such an industry a competitor with a global strategy can use its other advantages, such as low cost from centralization of global production, to offset this drawback. At the same time, another multinational competitor with good government contacts can pursue a multilocal strategy and succeed without globalization advantages; and single-country local competitors can succeed on the basis of their very particular local assets. The hotel industry provides examples of both successful global and successful local competitors.

Global Effects Are Incremental

A second factor affects why globalization drivers are not deterministic. The appropriate use of global strategy levers provides *additional* competitive advantage that is *incremental* to other sources of competitive advantage. These other sources may allow individual competitors to thrive with international strategies that are mismatched with industry globalization drivers. For example, superior technology provides a major source of competitive advantage in most industries, but it can be quite independent of globalization drivers. A competitor with sufficiently superior technology can use that to offset disadvantages in globalization. At the same time, effective global strategies can leverage worldwide a technology or other advantage.

Position and Resources of Business and Parent Company

The third reason why drivers are not deterministic has to do with resources (the top left box in Exhibit 1-2). A worldwide business may face industry drivers that strongly favor a global strategy. But global strategies are typically expensive to implement initially even though there should be great cost savings and revenue gains later. High initial investments may be needed to expand within or into major markets, to develop standardized products, to relocate value activities, to create global brands, to create new organization units or coordination processes, and to implement other aspects of a global strategy.

The strategic position of the business is also relevant. Even though a global strategy may improve the business's long-term strategic position, its immediate position may be so weak that resources should be devoted to short-term, country-by-country improvements. The automobile industry has very strong globalization drivers. But American automobile manufacturers had, in avoiding bankruptcy in 2008–2011, to deglobalize by selling off a lot of their international automotive businesses. Financial survival was more important at that point. Lastly, there may be greater returns in investing in nonglobal sources of competitive advantage, such as superior technology, than in global ones, such as centralized manufacturing.

Limitations in Organization

Finally, organization factors such as structure, management processes, people, and culture affect how well a desired global strategy can be developed and implemented. Differences in organization among companies in the same industry will, therefore, constrain the extent to which the companies can, or should, pursue the same global strategy.

CHALLENGES OF IMPLEMENTATION

Implementing strategy is always difficult. Implementing global strategy is particularly challenging because of the multiple countries and nationalities involved. Furthermore, in many cases a key part of the global strategy is not so much the content of the strategy (e.g., a standardized global product) but the decision to operate with a globally integrated management process (e.g., a global product development process). Implementation can be so disruptive and difficult that there may not be enough benefit in pursuing a highly global strategy. In particular, strategy globalization often requires changes that involve one or more countries having to give up long-established strategies, products, and the like. A European consumer packaged goods business had, under a multilocal strategy, developed different versions of the same basic product. One major country marketed a product made of *opaque* plastic parts and another major country marketed the same product made of *translucent* plastic parts. There seemed to

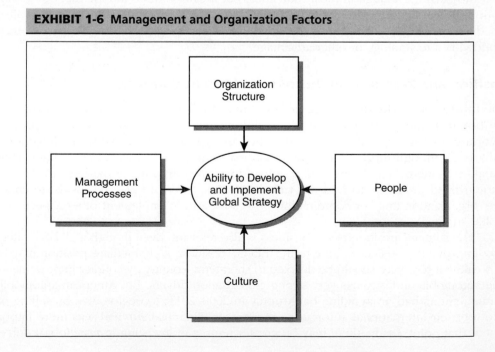

EXHIBIT 1-6 Management and Organization Factors

be no real reason why consumers might prefer opaque over translucent or vice versa. But the managers of each country felt committed to their version and were loathe to risk the potential marketplace disruption involved in change. It was implementation issues like this one that posed roadblocks for this business's attempt to rationalize its worldwide product lines.

Four key organization and management factors determine a business's ability to develop and implement a global strategy. Exhibit 1-6 summarizes these factors.[40]

- *Organization structure* comprises the reporting relationships in a business—the "boxes and lines."
- *Management processes* comprise the activities such as planning and budgeting, as well as information systems, that make the business run.
- *People* comprise the human resources of the worldwide business and include both managers and all other employees.
- *Culture* comprises the values and rules that guide behavior in a corporation.

Chapter 8 will elaborate on the application of these organization and management factors in discussing building the global organization.

Discussion and Research Questions

1. What trends are there in general globalization drivers? Provide company examples.

2. What forces currently work against globalization?

3. Select a company and describe its total global strategy in terms of its core business strategy, its internationalization strategy, and its globalization strategy. How successful has this company been in each aspect of its total global strategy?

4. What are the most globally successful companies from your country (region)? Why?

Notes

1. Hout et al. (1982) coined the term "multidomestic" to apply to industries rather than strategies. See Thomas Hout, Michael E. Porter, and Eileen Rudden, "How Global Companies Win Out," *Harvard Business Review,* September–October 1982, pp. 98–108. The term "multilocal" seems better when applied to strategies, in that domestic implies a company competing in its home market, while a great deal of local competition occurs between companies, none of which are in their home markets.

2. See Theodore Levitt, "The Globalization of Markets," *Harvard Business Review,* May–June 1983, pp. 92–102, and Kenichi Ohmae, *Triad Power: The Coming Shape of Global Competition* (New York: The Free Press, 1985).

3. See Philip Kotler, Liam Fahey, and S. Jatusripitak, *The New Competition* (Upper Saddle River, NJ: Prentice Hall, 1985). For works on Japanese management, see James C. Abegglen and George Stalk, Jr., *Kaisha: The Japanese Corporation* (New York: Basic Books, 1985); William G. Ouchi, *Theory Z: How American Business Can Meet the Japanese Challenge* (Reading, MA: Addison-Wesley, 1981); and Richard Tanner Pascale and Anthony G. Athos, *The Art of Japanese Management: Applications for American Executives* (New York: Simon & Schuster, 1981).

4. This accepted wisdom is laid out in one of the rejoinders provoked by Levitt's article; see Susan P. Douglas and Yoram Wind, "The Myth of Globalization," *Columbia Journal of World Business,* Vol. 22, No. 4, Winter 1987, pp. 19–29.

5. There are many sources of guidance on core business strategy. See, for example, Kenneth R. Andrews, *The Concept of Corporate Strategy* (New York: Dow-Jones Irwin, 1971); Michael E. Porter, *Competitive Strategy: Techniques for*

Analyzing Industries and Competitors (New York: The Free Press, 1980); ———, *Competitive Advantage* (New York: The Free Press, 1985); Kenichi Ohmae, *The Mind of the Strategist* (New York: McGraw-Hill, 1982); Robert M. Grant, *Contemporary Strategy Analysis* (Oxford, England: Blackwell Publishers, 1998); and Constantinos C. Markides, *All the Right Moves* (Boston, MA: Harvard Business School Press, 1999).

6. See Derek F. Abell, *Defining the Business: The Starting Point of Strategic Planning* (Upper Saddle River, NJ: Prentice Hall, 1980), for an extensive framework for business definition.

7. For a complete framework on how to select and enter foreign markets, see Franklin R. Root, *Entry Strategies for International Markets* (San Francisco: Jossey-Bass, 1994). For a general review of how to conduct international business, see, for example, Michael R. Czinkota, Ilkka A. Ronkainen, and Michael Moffett, *International Business* (New York: Harcourt, 2000), and Paul W. Beamish, Allen J. Morrison, Philip M. Rosenzweig, and Andrew C. Inkpen, *International Management: Text and Cases,* 4th ed. (New York: Irwin McGraw-Hill, 2000).

8. This framework was first presented in George S. Yip, "Global Strategy . . . In a World of Nations?" *Sloan Management Review,* Vol. 31, No. 1, Fall 1989, pp. 29–41.

9. Christopher H. Lovelock and George S. Yip, "Developing Global Strategies for Service Businesses," *California Management Review,* Vol. 37, No. 3, Winter 1996, pp. 64–86.

10. Christopher A. Bartlett and Sumantra Ghoshal, *Text, Cases, and Readings in Cross-Border Management,* 3rd ed. (Boston, MA: McGraw-Hill, 2000), p. 13.

11. See, for example, Paul W. Beamish, Allen J. Morrison, Philip Rosenzweig, and Andrew C. Inkpen, *International Management: Text and Cases,* 4th ed. (New York: Irwin McGraw-Hill, 2000).

12. See, for example, Will Mitchell, J. Myles Shaver, and Bernard Yeung, "Getting There in a Global Industry: Impacts on Performance of Changing International Presence," *Strategic Management Journal,* Vol. 13, No. 6, 1992, pp. 419–32, and Peter Mason and Karl Moore, "The Impact of Globalisation on Company Performance" (Templeton College, Oxford: The Oxford Executive Research Briefings, 1998).

13. David M. Reeb, Chuck C. Y. Kwok, and H. Young Baek, "Systematic Risk of the Multinational Corporation," *Journal of International Business Studies,* Vol. 29, No. 2, 1998, pp. 263–80.

14. This section on risk reduction comes from Stephen B. Tallman and George S. Yip, "Strategy and the Multinational Enterprise," in Thomas Brewer and Alan M. Rugman, Eds., *The Oxford Handbook of International Business* (Oxford, England: Oxford University Press, 2001), Chapter 12.

15. Raymond Vernon, "The Product Cycle Hypothesis in a New International Environment," *Oxford Bulletin of Economics and Statistics,* Vol. 41, No. 4, 1979, pp. 255–67.

16. Kendall Roth and Allen J. Morrison, "An Empirical Analysis of the Integration-Responsiveness Framework in Global Industries," *Journal of International Business Studies,* Vol. 21, No. 4, Fourth Quarter, 1990, pp. 541–64.

17. Masaaki Kotaabe and Glenn S. Omura, "Sourcing Strategies of European and Japanese Multinationals: A Comparison," *Journal of International Business Studies,* Vol. 20, No. 1, Spring, 1989, pp. 113–30.

18. Allen J. Morrison, *Strategies in Global Industries: How U.S. Businesses Compete* (Westport, CT: Quorum Books, 1990).

19. Johny K. Johansson and George S. Yip, "Exploiting Globalization Potential: U.S. and Japanese Strategies," *Strategic Management Journal,* Vol. 15, No. 8, October 1994, pp. 579–601.

20. The concept of industry conditions affecting the potential for global strategy was first developed by Michael E. Porter in "Changing Patterns of International Competition," *California Management Review,* Vol. 28, No. 2, Winter 1986, pp. 9–40, and in "Competition in Global Industries: A Conceptual Framework," *Competition in Global Industries,* Porter, Ed. (Boston, MA: Harvard Business School Press, 1986). The concept of industry globalization drivers was first presented in George S. Yip, Pierre M. Loewe, and Michael Y. Yoshino, "How to Take Your Company to the Global Market," *Columbia Journal of World Business,* Winter 1988, pp. 37–48, and more fully developed in George S. Yip, "Global Strategy . . . In a World of Nations?" *Sloan Management Review,* Vol. 31, No. 1, Fall 1989, pp. 29–41.

21. For a full description of the value-chain concept, see Michael E. Porter, *Competitive Advantage* (New York: The Free Press, 1985).

22. Kenichi Ohmae, *Triad Power: The Coming Shape of Global Competition* (New York: The Free Press, 1985).

23. Gary Hamel and C. K. Prahalad, "Do You Really Have a Global Strategy?" *Harvard Business Review,* July–August 1985, pp. 139–48; Bruce Kogut, "Designing Global Strategies: Profiting from Operational Flexibility," *Sloan Management Review,* Vol. 27, Fall 1985, pp. 27–38.

24. Peter G. P. Walters, "International Marketing Policy: A Discussion of the Standardization Construct and Its Relevance for Corporate Policy," *Journal of International Business Studies,* Summer 1986, pp. 55–69.

25. Lovelock and Yip, "Developing Global Strategies for Service Businesses."

26. Pei-yuan Chia, "Citibanking the World," *Bank Management,* July/August 1995.

27. The possibilities and merits of uniform marketing have been discussed by Robert D. Buzzell, "Can You Standardize Multinational Marketing?" *Harvard Business Review,* November–December 1968, pp. 102–13, and by John A. Quelch and Edward J. Hoff, "Customizing Global Marketing," *Harvard Business Review,* May–June 1986, pp. 59–68.

28. These examples come from Lovelock and Yip, "Developing Global Strategies for Service Businesses."

29. See Philip Kotler, Liam Fahey, and S. Jatusripitak, *The New Competition* (Upper Saddle River, NJ: Prentice Hall, 1985), p. 174.

30. I thank Pierre M. Loewe of The MAC Group for this example.

31. Based on "Room Service à la Américain, Old World Charm Bumps into New World Economics," *New York Times,* October 3, 1997, pp. C1 and C4.

32. Two very experienced consultants who worked for The Boston Consulting Group have estimated the potential cost savings in focused production. They found that if the number of products produced is halved, total factory labor costs should fall 30 percent, and total costs including materials should fall 17 percent, while breakeven should be reduced to 60 percent of capacity. See James C. Abegglen and George Stalk, Jr., *Kaisha* (New York: Basic Books, 1985), p. 87.

33. The Toyota Camry was first introduced into Japan in 1980. An export version was created in 1985. Another long-lived Japanese automobile model is the Honda Accord, first introduced into Japan in 1976. See Kiyonori Sakakibara and Yaichi Aoshima, "Company Growth and the 'Wholeness' of Product Strategy," Working Paper No. 8904, Graduate School of Commerce, Hitotsubashi University, April 1989.

34. "Can Opel Deliver the 'World Cars' GM Needs?" *Business Week,* December 4, 1995, p. 52.

35. Reported in Marquise R. Cvar, "Case Studies in Global Competition: Patterns of Success and Failure," in Michael E. Porter, "Competition in Global Industries: A Conceptual Framework," *Competition in Global Industries,* Porter, Ed. (Boston, MA: Harvard Business School Press, 1986).

36. Based on "Did Whirlpool Spin Too Far Too Fast?" *Business Week,* June 24, 1996, pp. 135–36.

37. Based on Carl Quintanilla, "Whirlpool Seen Retrenching After Its Effort to 'Go Global,'" *The Wall Street Journal,* December 12, 1997.

38. Based on "Accor, World's Largest Hotel Group, Chooses Australia for Its Reservation Center," *IAC (SM) Newsletter Database (TM),* March 20, 1996.

39. Based on "Flying High, Going Global," *Fortune,* July 7, 1997, pp. 195 97.

40. This particular concept of management and organization factors affecting global strategy was first presented in George S. Yip, Pierre M. Loewe, and Michael Y. Yoshino, "How to Take Your Company to the Global Market," *Columbia Journal of World Business,* Winter 1988, pp. 37–48. Other authors such as Christopher Bartlett, Yves Doz, Sumantra Ghoshal, and C. K. Prahalad have done a great deal of work on the role of management and organization in global strategy. See Christopher A. Bartlett and Sumantra Ghoshal, *Managing Across Borders: The Transnational Solution* (Boston, MA: Harvard Business School Press, 1989), and C. K. Prahalad, and Yves L. Doz, *The Multinational Mission: Balancing Local Demands and Global Vision* (New York: The Free Press, 1987).

CHAPTER 2

Diagnosing Industry Globalization Potential

Industry globalization drivers are the underlying conditions in each industry that create the potential for using global strategy. Here we will examine each driver in more depth and, in addition, discuss how drivers affect the industry competitive forces of the threat of entry and rivalry among competitors. We will also examine possible differences in globalization drivers for service businesses,[1] and how the Internet affects globalization drivers.[2] *To achieve the benefits of globalization, the managers of a worldwide business need to recognize when industry conditions provide the opportunity to use global strategy levers.* These industry conditions are the industry globalization drivers and can be grouped into four categories—market, cost, governmental, and competitive. Each key industry globalization driver affects the potential use of global strategy levers (global market participation, global products and services, global location of activities, global marketing, and global competitive moves). The drivers are as follows:

Market Globalization Drivers

- Common customer needs and tastes
- Global customers and channels
- Transferable marketing
- Lead countries

Cost Globalization Drivers

- Global scale economies
- Steep experience curve effect
- Sourcing efficiencies
- Favorable logistics
- Differences in country costs (including exchange rates)
- High product development
- Fast-changing technology

Government Globalization Drivers

- Favorable trade policies
- Compatible technical standards
- Common marketing regulations
- Government-owned competitors and customers
- Host government concerns

Competitive Globalization Drivers

- High exports and imports
- Competitors from different continents
- Interdependence of countries
- Competitors globalized
- Transferable competitive advantage

Industry globalization drivers relate to, but are different from, the industry competitive forces identified by Michael E. Porter—threat of entry, rivalry among existing firms, pressure from substitute products or services, bargaining power of suppliers, and bargaining power of buyers.[3] In most cases, but not always, increases in industry globalization will increase the strength of competitive forces. Particularly for the threat of new entrants and rivalry among existing firms, increased industry globalization heightens competition by increasing its geographic scope. The specific effects on these two competitive forces vary in interesting ways depending on the specific industry globalization driver, and so will be addressed later for each of the drivers. Increased industry globalization also increases the pressure from substitutes by increasing the geographic scope of where these substitutes might come from. This effect is fairly straightforward and consistent, and so need not be discussed for individual industry globalization drivers. Lastly, the effects of industry globalization on the power of suppliers and the power of buyers can be positive in some cases and negative in others. In particular, the globalization of customers themselves (the "global customers" driver) increases their bargaining power relative to industry competitors, while the globalization of competitors reduces the bargaining power of customers. The same effects apply for the bargaining power of suppliers.

Globalization can also change the fundamental strategy required for managing competitive forces. In *Competitive Strategy,* published in 1980, Porter, in effect, recommends that companies seek to compete in markets with weak competitors and weak customers.[4] In *The Competitive Advantage of Nations,* published in 1990, Porter argues instead for participating in national markets with the strongest rivals and most demanding customers, in order to build international competitiveness.[5] The difference between his two positions is explainable by the difference between a closed, domestic industry and an open, globalized industry. In a closed, domestic industry, a company accustomed to weak competitors and undemanding customers has little to fear: There is no source of new competitors who might grow strong in more demanding competitive arenas. In an open, globalized industry, such newly strong competitors abound. *That is why it is important to understand how industry globalization drivers affect the threat of entry and rivalry among existing competitors.*

GLOBALIZATION DRIVERS FOR SERVICE BUSINESSES

How do the distinctive characteristics of service businesses affect globalization and the use of global strategy?[6] This is a crucial question for managers in numerous industries. Not only are services continuing to grow rapidly in domestic economies, but international trade in services is increasing too. The United States, like some other developed countries, has a trade surplus in services that helps offset the deficit in merchandise trade. In contrast, Japan has been much less successful in internationalizing its service businesses.[7] So it is essential to national competitiveness that governments, as well as companies, achieve a better understanding of how to develop effective global strategies for different types of service businesses.

Service businesses have eight primary characteristics that distinguish them from manufacturing businesses.[8] These characteristics begin with the nature of the output—a performance rather than an object—and also include customer involvement in production, people as part of the service experience, greater likelihood of quality control problems, harder for customers to evaluate, lack of inventories for services, greater importance of the time factor, and availability of electronic channels of distribution. Although these characteristics provide a useful starting point for thinking about the distinctive aspects of service management, not every service is equally affected by all of them.

It is also useful to distinguish among three broad types of service businesses: people-processing services, possession-processing services, and information-based services:

PEOPLE-PROCESSING SERVICES   involve tangible actions to customers in person. These services require that customers themselves become part of the production process, which tends to be simultaneous with consumption. In such businesses as passenger transportation, health care, food service, and lodging services, the customer needs to enter the "service factory" (although we know it by such names as an airliner and air terminal, a hospital, a restaurant, or a hotel) and remain there during service delivery. Either customers must travel to the factory or service providers and equipment must come to the customer. In both instances, the firm needs to maintain a local geographic presence, stationing the necessary personnel, buildings, equipment, vehicles, and supplies within reach of target customers. If the customers are themselves mobile—as in the case of business travelers and tourists—then they may patronize a company's offerings in many different locations and make comparisons between them.

POSSESSION-PROCESSING SERVICES   involve tangible actions to physical objects to improve their value to customers. Examples include freight transport, warehousing, equipment installation and maintenance, car repair, laundry, and disposal. The object needs to be involved in the production process, but the customer does not, since consumption of the output tends to follow production. Again, the service factory may be fixed or mobile. A local geographic presence is required when the supplier needs to provide service to physical objects in a specific location on a repeated basis. In the case of smaller, transportable items, the vendor can provide remote service centers for servicing—although transportation costs, customs duties, and government regulations may constrain shipment across large distances or national frontiers. Modern technology now allows a few service processes to be administered from a distance, using electronic diagnostics to pinpoint the problem.

INFORMATION-BASED SERVICES are, perhaps, the most interesting category from the standpoint of global strategy development, because they depend on collecting, manipulating, interpreting, and transmitting data to create value. Examples include accounting, banking, consulting, education, insurance, legal services, and news. Customer involvement in production of such services is often minimal. The advent of modern global telecommunications, linking intelligent machines to powerful databases, makes it possible to use electronic channels to deliver information-based services from a single "hub" to almost any location. Local presence requirements may be limited to a terminal—ranging from a telephone or fax machine to a computer or more specialized equipment like an automated teller machine—connected to a reliable telecommunications infrastructure. If the latter is inadequate, then use of mobile or satellite communications may solve the problem in some instances.

Service production and delivery systems can be divided into "back office" and "front office," the latter being the portion of the service factory encountered by customers.[9] People-processing services necessarily involve a high degree of contact with service personnel and facilities; possession-processing and information-based services, by contrast, have the potential to be much lower contact in nature. Retail banking, for instance, can take place either through traditional branch banks or through channels such as mail, telephone, and the Internet.

In this chapter and later ones, I will examine how globalization drivers and the use of global strategy might apply to various types of services, and what differences might exist relative to manufacturing businesses.

MARKET GLOBALIZATION DRIVERS

Market globalization drivers—common customer needs and tastes, global customers, global channels, transferable marketing, and lead countries—depend on the nature of customer behavior and the structure of channels of distribution. These drivers affect the use of all five global strategy levers. As illustrated in Exhibit 2-1, different industries have different levels of market globalization drivers. *These comparative rankings are approximate only and will also change over time.*

Common Customer Needs and Tastes

Common customer needs and tastes represent the extent to which customers in different countries want the same things in the product or service category that defines an industry. Many factors affect whether customer needs and tastes are similar in different countries. These factors include whether differences in economic development, climate, physical environment infrastructure, and culture affect needs in the particular product or service category, as well as whether the countries are at the same stage of the product life cycle.[10] Common customer needs particularly affect the opportunity to use the global strategy levers of global market participation, global products and services, and global competitive moves. Common needs make it easier to participate in major markets because a few product varieties can serve many markets. Thus, fewer different product offerings need to be developed and supported. Japanese companies have been particularly successful at exploiting common needs when they first entered world automotive

EXHIBIT 2-1 Strength of Market Globalization Drivers for Selected Industries

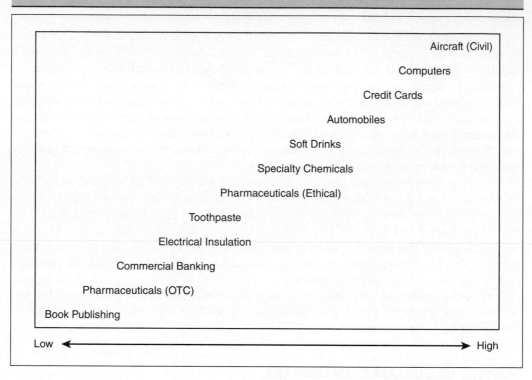

markets. Toyota, Nissan, and Honda chose to focus on fundamental needs common to all countries—such as reliability and economy—rather than to focus on peripheral differences—such as styling. The underlying commonality of needs meant that their highly standardized global products were quite acceptable in most countries. Common needs also allow the sequenced invasion of markets with highly standardized products—again, a successful approach of many Japanese companies.

Common customer needs and tastes make entrants more dangerous by reducing the number of products or services that they need to develop for different countries. Success in one country with a global product can be used as a springboard for entering other countries. Thus, it is not surprising that Japanese entrants were most successful in the 1980s and 1990s in markets with fairly common customer needs—electronic and automotive products. These successes continued into the 2000s for Japanese electronic manufacturers, but were tempered by competitors from South Korea as well as the 2008 economic downturn. As a result, some former competitors merged in the electronic products sector.[11] Meanwhile, Japanese automotive manufacturers became even more competitive and challenged automobile producers in the United States for global supremacy in innovation as well as market share.[12]

In addition, the Japanese turned in the 1990s to financial services. The common need of corporations around the world for sources of financing from debt or equity encouraged the Japanese big four brokers—Yamaichi, Nomura, Daiwa, and Nikko—to try their luck in the U.S. and European financial markets. The Japanese entered the

Nestlé's Localized Innovation Strategy

Nestlé conducts research and development (R&D) on a global scale with 28 R&D facilities worldwide. The goal of the company's R&D network is to develop new products and assist in the evolution of the company to not only make value-added food products but also provide innovative products with superior health benefits. One example of this strategic initiative resided in the 2010 opening of an R&D location in Santiago, Chile, to focus specifically on biscuits and cereal-related products.[18] Another example is in Nestlé's plans to open an additional global R&D facility in India in 2012 to focus specifically on nutrition-based products marketed to lower income consumer groups.[19]

Much of Nestlé's current R&D efforts are concerned with creating global products that are easily adaptable to different locations. As a result, based on its product and positioning strategy, Nestlé is often considered a local company in the many countries it has operations.[20] In fact, the company leverages its superior logistics advantages of short supply chains and manufactures in about 500 factories across 100 countries. By taking a decidedly local approach to its logistics as well as its innovation, Nestlé can maintain its strategy as long as it responds to marketplace needs better than competitors.

Nestlé does not, however, simply rely on its R&D network to develop innovative products for the company. The company's unique approach to R&D, "Open Innovation," brings knowledge from strategic partnerships developed worldwide by Nestlé.[21] This approach allows information from outside the organization to become a part of the new product development process at the company such that Nestlé has become, for example, the largest producer of food conforming to the Muslim dietary restrictions of halal.[22] Creating innovations that successfully allow its products to be adaptable to local preferences and produced in a vertically integrated fashion is an ambitious long-term goal. However, it is increasingly a necessity to develop global competitive advantages through product differentiation. And, in Nestlé's case, its Open Innovation initiative is one such way to accomplish widespread local acceptance.

New York market by selling the "financial equivalent of Toyotas" (simple, high-quality products)—Treasury bills, mortgage-backed securities, corporate bonds, and commercial paper. At the same time, they established a presence in European financial markets.[13] But the Japanese found much less success in financial services.[14] In essence they lacked the specialized institutional and country knowledge needed in this highly regulated and relationship-based industry. Similarly, if the companies appearing in *Fortune*'s Global 500 list for 2010 is any indication, the Japanese have failed to make headway in industries with significant variations in customer needs and tastes, particularly consumer packaged goods.[15] Here, the companies with a head start in deciphering local variations, such as Danone, Nestlé, and Unilever,[16] have maintained their dominance.[17] As indicated in the Nestlé example, the ability to identify differences across local market conditions is integral to marketplace performance.

Common needs and tastes across countries also make it more difficult for competitors to differentiate themselves from one another. Rivalry, therefore, becomes more severe. (It might be argued that globalization creates larger global segments that should have more room for competitors and, therefore, less rivalry. In practice, however, the lure of the large global market seems to raise the ambitions of competitors.) Consumer tastes in magazines are sufficiently common in Europe so that publishers can now sell pan-European offerings. Cultural differences do not seem great enough to prevent some magazines from crossing borders; consequently, publishing firms are making an effort

How DuPont Avoids the Race to the Bottom

Based in Wilmington, Delaware, E. I. du Pont de Nemours & Company (DuPont) has been very effective at turning product-based brands into a strategic advantage. While it is usually abnormal for consumer durable manufacturers to mention the brand of materials constituting a particular product, many manufacturers have boasted that their products are equipped with DuPont brand materials such as Teflon, Nylon, Kevlar, and Tyvek. For some time, the company has been successful at adding value in its product portfolio by developing a brand identity in an industry that is extremely price-sensitive. DuPont's strategy of value-added branding has made the company a preferred materials supplier for use in consumer durable manufacturing. During 2005–2007, DuPont was able to raise the average selling price of its products from 3 to 5 percent.[24]

When DuPont sells a material, it is not considered a commodity. Instead, the company sells a product that commands a premium in the market and reduces the propensity for customers to respond to global price fluctuations.[25] For instance, in the case of Teflon pans, manufacturers are able to command a premium price in the market by citing the superior durability of a Teflon-equipped product otherwise unattainable if a generic substitute material were purchased.

DuPont products command a premium price through differentiation using multiple strategies. First, based on considerable innovation and research,[26] patented innovations shut out competitors and give DuPont exclusive rights to production of many materials. Second, the company's products are customized to meet the demand of different market segments. Some manufacturers demand greater performance, while others demand greater customer service.

Still, DuPont cannot ignore the price-sensitive demands of a global market. As such, the company can mitigate the risk of a "race to the bottom" through aggressive product differentiation, materials innovation, and market segmentation. In fact, DuPont is continuing in this tradition by introducing a new biofiber, Sorona,[27] and other advances in industrial biotechnology.[28] Therefore, there is little doubt that DuPont should be well-positioned in the marketplace to deliver unique and competitive products in sectors typically focused on the importance of price as the key point of distinction.

to sell those magazines to all of Europe with only slight changes in content. The result is significant heightening of rivalry. In the mid-1980s, *Bella* was successfully launched as a European women's magazine, first in Western Germany, then in Britain and Spain. Since then, *Elle* magazine has become a global women's fashion journal, publishing over 42 editions in more than 60 countries.[23]

How common customer needs are across countries clearly varies greatly by industry and depends on factors such as the importance of national culture and tastes, income elasticity, and physical conditions that might affect the use of the product. For consumer businesses, the book publishing and magazine industries fall at the low end of the spectrum in commonality of needs, because of differences in both content and language, although both of these factors are changing rapidly. At the other end of the spectrum, travel-related industries, like airlines and traveler's checks, have needs that are inherently common across countries. Among consumer packaged goods, most food products tend to lie at the low end while household and personal care products are nearer the middle of the spectrum. For industrial businesses, commodities, such as many chemicals and other raw materials, tend toward very high commonality of needs. This is noticeable in DuPont's ability to remain competitive over a prolonged period of time.

In contrast, more complex industrial products, such as computer equipment and process controls, range from moderate to highly common needs. Customer needs may, however, be more common than most executives think. *Managers, particularly those with single-country responsibilities, tend to focus on the differences between countries, because it is the differences that require effort in adaptation. But executives can find more commonality if they look for it.* This may also explain the varying strategies of companies. Some companies have looked for commonality and acted accordingly. Canon, for example, did this in developing a global photocopier that sacrificed the ability to copy certain sizes of Japanese paper in order to capture a larger share of the worldwide market. Based on the company's corporate philosophy of *kyosei* (or, global harmony in life and work),[29] Canon is now a dominant player in the global photo-copier market.[30]

COMMON CUSTOMER NEEDS AND TASTES IN SERVICE BUSINESSES   Service businesses usually involve the customer in production. But this effect reduces the degree to which many services can be standardized and still meets the needs of a broad cross section of customers around the world. In general, the less the involvement, whether physical or psychological, the better the opportunity for a global approach. So we are more likely to see global standardization in fast food and airlines, where customer involvement is tightly controlled, than in medical care or education, where customer involvement is both stronger and more prolonged. Note that these observations apply to the broad "middle market" rather than to the relatively small market segment composed of affluent, highly educated, cosmopolitan customers.

Service staff form part of the service experience. This also limits the potential commonality of customer needs and tastes. Differences can arise even within the same industry. In banking the service provided by human tellers is far less standardized and standardizable than that provided by automated teller machines. Accounting services depend heavily on people. The higher status of accountants in Britain than in the United States means that British accountants provide more general business advice than do their American counterparts. And U.S.-style psychotherapy is unlikely to yield a global "McShrink" franchise.

EFFECT OF TECHNOLOGY ON COMMON CUSTOMER NEEDS AND TASTES   The Internet has increased global commonality in customer needs and tastes. When customers in an industry have needs and tastes that are mostly common across countries, companies can make more use of global strategies, especially in offering globally standardized products and services. The Internet has further exposed customers to global offerings and other lifestyles. Individuals can now gain global exposure and attain global learning effects with ease. So they are more likely to migrate to the highest or most popular global standard.

The Internet has had at least two effects. First, it has reinforced the appeal of those brands that are already globally recognized. Potential customers can get more information about these product offerings and have their desires further reinforced. At the same time, global technological communication creates more opportunities and churns in the next tier of contender brands. Relatively unknown brands will be able to rapidly build up word-of-mouth and global presence via the Internet. Superior Web site design can make up for currently low recognition. Both Schwab and Dell Computer massively shifted their marketing and ordering systems. The dramatic effects on their businesses are well recorded. Less obvious is that this shift helped propel both companies from the "possible" category of suppliers to the "must consider" category. Even if someone does not end up choosing Schwab or Dell, most potential customers now have to consider these two companies in their respective industries.

Another example is Barnes & Noble's response to Amazon's unique value proposition in published materials. Identifying the imminent technological threat which Amazon posed in the 1990s, Barnes & Noble strengthened its online presence to remain competitive. After weathering Amazon's marketplace challenge, it became obvious that a status quo emerged based on an intense distribution rivalry.[31]

Global Customers and Channels

Global customers buy on a centralized or coordinated basis for decentralized use, or at the least they select vendors centrally. As such, "global customers" can be distinguished from "international customers," "foreign customers," and "local customers," as shown in Exhibit 2-2. Global customers, compared with other types, have both more internationalized purchasing (in the sense of buying outside domestic markets) and

EXHIBIT 2-2 Types of Customers

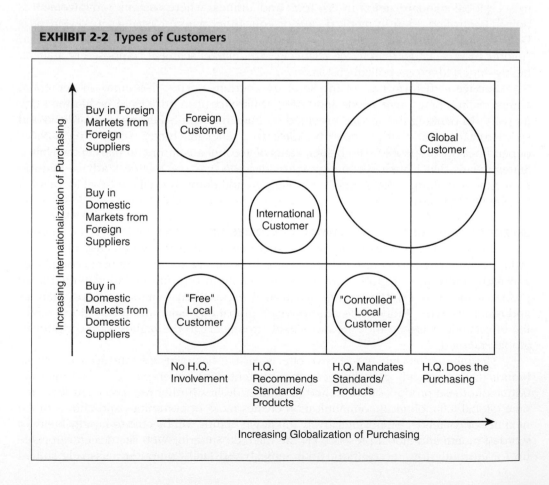

more globalized purchasing (in the sense of global control by headquarters). A recent study found that multinational companies are rapidly increasing the globalization of their purchasing and are in turn demanding more in the way of global customer management from their vendors.[32]

There are two types of global customers—national and multinational. A *national* global customer searches the world for suppliers but uses the purchased product or service in one country. National defense agencies are a good example. A *multinational* global customer also searches the world for suppliers and uses the purchased product or service in many countries. Examples are the World Health Organization for medical products and some automotive companies. The existence of global customers affects the opportunity or need for global market participation, global products and services, global activity location, and global marketing. Even if they do not purchase centrally, having global customers drives a business toward developing globally standardized products. Similarly, global customers can compare prices charged by the same supplier in different countries and tend to be unhappy with unexplainable discrepancies. Global customers usually occur in industrial categories, although in some consumer categories—such as cameras, watches, and luxury handbags—a significant portion of sales is accounted for by those buying while outside their home country.

The definition of a global customer or channel can be extended to "influencers" such as physicians who prescribe drugs, architects who specify building materials, and engineers and other technical experts who specify or recommend equipment and the like. Japanese trading companies, such as Mitsubishi and Mitsui, also act very much like global channels, although they typically make most of their "purchases" in one country—Japan.

To serve its global customers, the business needs to be present in all the customers' major markets. The U.S. advertising agency that used to have the Coca-Cola account (one of the largest in the world) was unable to serve Coca-Cola when it expanded to Brazil. So McCann-Erickson, another American but more global agency, took the account in Brazil. Then McCann used the Brazilian relationship to win the entire Coca-Cola account worldwide.[33] Chiat Day, famous for having created the world's greatest commercial ("Apple Macintosh 1984"), lost the Reebok (athletic shoes) account partly because it did not have an international network. In consequence, Chiat Day sold itself to a global agency, TBWA.

In 1994, IBM replaced over 40 different advertising agencies that were serving it around the world and consolidated the company's entire $500 million account at one top 10 global agency, Ogilvy & Mather Worldwide. By 2009, IBM's marketing budget had expanded to $1.25 billion with a critical global digital marketing component.[34] Seeking to distance itself from its stodgy roots, IBM made a concerted effort to utilize social media in nontraditional ways to differentiate its consulting services with a centralized message.[35]

Offering standardized products can also be a necessity for serving global customers. Increasingly, such global customers are requiring their suppliers to play the role of global coordination. General Electric (GE) has told many of its suppliers that it expects them to be responsible for ensuring that GE businesses get uniform products around the world. Some activities—such as development engineering, selling, and after-sales service—may need to be concentrated, or at least globally coordinated, in order to effectively serve global customers. Lastly, uniform marketing programs may be needed. Global pricing policies may be particularly important. Suppliers that implement global account management programs have to beware of global customers using the unified account management to extract lower global prices.

The latter provides an example of how the existence of global customers also requires the content of the marketing mix to be uniform. It is also important to recognize potential global customers. These are multinational customers who currently do not buy or coordinate centrally but may start to do so. A global supplier can gain a first mover or preemptive advantage by being the first to treat a potential global customer as an actual global customer.

Analogous to global customers, there may be channels of distribution that buy on a global or at least a regional basis. Global channels or middlemen are also important in exploiting differences in prices by performing the arbitrage function of transshipment. Their presence makes it more necessary for a business to rationalize its worldwide pricing. Global channels are rare, but regionwide ones are increasing in number, particularly in European distribution and retailing. By 1998, the largest retailers each operated in several countries: the United States' Wal-Mart with $137 billion in revenues in 9 countries, France's Carrefour/Promodès with $56 billion in 26, Germany's Metro with $49 billion in 23, France's Intermarché with $37 billion in 7, the Netherlands' Ahold with $35 billion in 17, and Japan's 7-Eleven with $35 billion in 18.[36] Through 2008, this international trend continued, with some dominant retailers like Wal-Mart expanding to 15 countries with $406 billion in revenues, Carrefour to 36 with $130 billion, Metro to 32 with $100 billion. Others maintained position like Intermarché's position in 8 countries with $45 billion or Ahold's 9 with $38 billion. As shown in the importance of Tesco in 13 countries with $96 billion in revenues, new players challenged the largest international retailers as well.[37]

The existence of global (or regionwide) channels requires, like the existence of global customers, globally coordinated marketing and uniform marketing mix content. Global customer and channel issues also apply to regional (e.g., Asian or European) customers. Indeed, regional customers are probably growing at a faster rate than global customers, particularly in Europe. As such, the importance of regional strategy will be detailed in Chapter 9.

The existence of global customers or channels cuts both ways for the threat of entry. On the one hand, it is much more difficult to displace an incumbent who is serving a customer in many countries. On the other hand, the essence of a global customer—centralized buying for multinational use—also makes a global account vulnerable to rapid total capture. A competitor may be able to capture a global account by selling to the head office only. Global or regional channels of distribution can also be exploited for rapid entry. Owing to the different regulatory, currency, and tax environments across Europe, many insurance companies have found the need to form alliances with foreign banks in order to enter new markets. By forming these alliances, insurers can take advantage of the banks' distribution networks (branches). For example, Germany's Allianz originally sold life insurance policies through the branches of Spain's Banco Popular under a joint venture. The relationship between the two companies became so advantageous that Allianz has considered merging with Banco Popular.[38]

The presence of global customers or channels increases rivalry among existing competitors. Global customers or channels become prizes to be fought over, and the fight is global in scope. As marketers aim to expand their brands to more countries, advertising agencies have been reorganizing in order to meet the demands of their global customers. In a preemptive move with its double-page advertisement in the *Wall Street Journal* and the *Financial Times* in 1984, Saatchi & Saatchi was the first agency to publicize its global capabilities. This move annoyed many rivals with more extensive global experience and customers. Some of these rivals then moved to enhance their own credentials. Both BBDO Worldwide and Lintas: Worldwide created European boards of directors; Ogilvy & Mather removed three subregional posts and appointed a European creative director and a new European chairman; DDB Needham Worldwide relocated its international headquarters to Paris from New York. By 2009, the largest advertising agencies were configured into 15 consolidated networks to respond to worldwide competitive pressures.[39] Each network was headed by one of five global advertising companies: Tokyo-based Dentsu, London-based WPP, New York-based Interpublic Group, Paris-based Publicis Groupe, or New York-based Omnicom Group. In effect, each agency had developed internal mechanisms to respond to many possible strategic moves by competitors on a global scale.

The reinsurance industry provides a more classic type of global customer. In the search for reinsurance, insurance companies, many of them multinational, scour the globe for the lowest premiums and best contracts. The high information content and relatively standardized nature of the product make it easy for reinsurance buyers to behave as global customers.[40]

GLOBAL CUSTOMERS AND CHANNELS IN SERVICE BUSINESSES   As large corporate customers become global, they often seek to standardize and simplify the array of services they consume. For instance, firms may seek to minimize the number of auditors they use around the world, using "Big Four" accounting and professional services firms (Deloitte Touche Tohmatsu, Ernst & Young, KPMG, and PricewaterhouseCoopers) that can apply a consistent worldwide approach (within the context of national rules within each country of operation). Corporate banking, insurance, business logistics, and management consulting are further examples. Individuals act as global customers when they purchase goods and services on their travels. The service characteristics of "a performance rather than an object" and "greater importance of the time factor" create special opportunities for travel-related services, a very large and growing segment that starts with transportation but extends to credit, communication, and emergency support.

Global customers for possession-processing services prefer common procedures and standards. For example, airlines absolutely depend on their aircraft being maintained in the same way everywhere and, increasingly, so do customers of factory and machinery maintenance services. Global customers for people-processing services may care particularly about ubiquity, especially when traveling. The New Zealander who breaks her leg in Pamplona needs medical treatment on the spot. Global customers for information-based services may have a more diffuse set of needs, but these certainly include comprehensiveness, accuracy, and accessibility. The American executive who has lost his traveler's checks in Shanghai needs reimbursement there, now, not back home in Indiana, later.

EFFECT OF TECHNOLOGY ON GLOBAL CUSTOMERS AND CHANNELS   Multinational companies increasingly act as global customers by globally coordinating or centralizing their purchases. But there are many obstacles, both external (finding and coordinating with vendors around the world) and internal (agreeing and coordinating requirements across international subsidiaries). The Internet has made it easier to become a global customer. Customers can search for suppliers from anywhere in the world. Or they can go even further and place requests for proposals and bids on their own Web sites and wait for vendors to respond.

The Internet has accelerated the growth of regional and global channels of distribution, allowing traditional firms to more easily complete their networks. And, of course, firms like Amazon jump straight into existence as global channels, although the real Amazon distribution system was Amazon + Ingram (the United States' largest book wholesaler, based in Seattle, since displaced by Amazon's own warehouse operations) + United Parcel Service in the United States and various other package deliverers elsewhere.

Lastly, the rise of Internet intermediaries (pure online firms with no physical assets), such as Autobytel and China's Alibaba.com, creates a new dimension to longtime vendor–distributor relationships. In the automobile sector, carmakers have traditionally focused on mostly subnational, and occasionally national, area agreements. The Internet bypasses these relationships to seek out the best deals on a national basis (as Autobytel does in the United States). The immediate effect is that carmakers much adapt their pricing as a certain level of price convergence has been introduced in the marketplace.

Transferable Marketing

The nature of the buying decision may be such that marketing elements, like brand names and advertising, require little local adaptation; that is, brand names and advertising are readily transferable. Transferable marketing makes it easier to expand participation in markets: The business need not develop a new marketing approach. A worldwide business can also adapt its brand names and advertising campaigns to make them more transferable or, even better, design global ones to start with. Exxon chose its new name after an intensive worldwide search for a unique and easily pronounced name to replace Esso and a mixture of other brand names. The Exxon example also highlights the importance of trademark availability. Other companies owning the rights to the names desired hamper many companies in their efforts at consolidating around one global trademark or name. By definition, transferability enables the use of uniform marketing strategies. Offsetting risks include the blandness of uniformly acceptable brand names or advertising, and the vulnerability of relying on a single brand franchise.

The accepted wisdom in international marketing has long been that marketing approaches need to be tailored for each country. For example, advertising should be developed locally and designed to appeal to the local audience. But companies are finding ways to succeed with uniform or only slightly modified marketing.[41] Such transferable marketing greatly lengthens the reach and punch of global competitors.[42]

Marketing elements that are transferable across countries can both raise and reduce entry barriers. On the one hand, incumbent competitors can leverage global marketing to build high barriers in almost every market. Coca-Cola has created not just national but global barriers to entry with its global brand franchise. This franchise has been built in part through global advertising and packaging. On the other hand, potential entrants can use transferable marketing as a "gateway to entry."[43] Entrants can apply the advertising, packaging designs, and so on, that they have developed elsewhere. Transferable brand names and reputation need the additional factor of spillover media, foreign travel by potential customers, or other vehicles of communication before they can be used to reduce international entry barriers.

Transferable marketing adds a dimension to rivalry among existing competitors. Not only must rivals try to develop the best marketing programs in each country, but they must also compete in their ability to transfer successful programs from country to country. Companies without a transfer mechanism can find themselves out-marketed one country at a time by a rival that globally leverages a successful approach. In the toothpaste market, Colgate-Palmolive achieved global share leadership partly through its successful application of a global approach to branding, packaging, and advertising. In contrast, rivals like Unilever and Beecham lagged with different approaches in different countries.

TRANSFERABLE MARKETING FOR SERVICE BUSINESSES Some kinds of marketing may make more use of local people for service than for manufacturing businesses, and thus be less globally transferable. For example, television commercials may feature service staff. For locally provided services, these would have to be depictions of local staff. So the executions would need to be different for each country, although the copy strategy and script may well be the same. In some cases, where the concept of the service has strong national traditions, even the strategy and script may have to differ. Interestingly, the need for adaptation depends on the extent to which the service proposition is itself globalized. A hotel chain that stresses its global uniformity, such as Holiday Inns, would use a more globally common advertising strategy. The target audience would also make a difference. Advertising to international travelers would be more common, while advertising a hotel's restaurants to local customers would be more local.

EFFECT OF TECHNOLOGY ON TRANSFERABLE MARKETING The Internet has two effects on the transferability of global marketing—enabling and demanding. In terms of *enabling* global marketing, Internet-based marketing has inherent global reach. In fact, the impact of social media on marketing is a technological example of the way companies can communicate with an increasingly technologically savvy marketplace.[44] Further, users share a common style of interaction—they have been conditioned to interact with electronic communications in certain ways—browsing, blogging, and impatient. Third, many users, by self-selection, have a working knowledge of English, itself the dominant language of the Internet, even though nearly three-quarters of the 2 billion Internet users speak languages other than English.[45]

In terms of *demanding* global marketing, the Internet mandates that vendors use globally standard brand names. A simple example suffices to illustrate this new commandment. In a different era, the original launch of Amazon.com would probably have meant the Amazon in Brazil only, but Mississippi.com in the United States, Thames.com in the United Kingdom, Rhine.com in Germany, and Yangtze.com in China. However, the founder of Amazon chose the *world's* largest river as his company's global brand name. Similarly, other elements of the marketing mix, particularly price, need to be more uniform than before.

Lead Countries

Innovation in products or processes may be concentrated in one or a few countries because of the presence of innovative competitors or demanding customers or both. In that case it becomes critical for global competitors to participate in these "lead countries" in order to be exposed to the sources of innovation. Customers may view market position in a lead country as a surrogate for overall quality. Companies frequently promote a product in one country as, for example, "the leading brand in the U.S.A."[46] Lead countries can be easily identified as those in which the most important product or process innovations occur.

In many industries, there are lead countries in which major global competitors are based and where the bulk of innovations occur. For example, Japan has been a lead country for consumer electronics, Germany for industrial control equipment, and the United States for technology and services. In such industries it is critical for all competitors with global ambitions to participate in the lead countries. In many industries the key lead countries are the United States, Japan, and major European countries like Germany or the United Kingdom. Other countries, of course, do take the lead in particular industries, such as Denmark for insulin and Italy for ceramic tiles.[47] Most American and European companies had until the 1990s a very small presence in Japan and worried that they were missing out on innovations in that country. In the 1990s American companies started to make the major commitments needed to set up R&D operations in Japan so as to be able to tap into the growing stream of Japanese innovations. By 2008, MNCs also sought to develop operations in South Korea to benefit from the heightened innovative environment in both Asian countries.[48]

The existence of lead countries can increase the threat of entry. Potential entrants can readily identify the key innovations, even if they choose to enter other countries first. Furthermore, the lead countries become prized targets for entry. As Japan increasingly becomes in many industries an innovator rather than an imitator, American and European companies are increasingly recognizing the criticality of Japan as a lead country. There is a gap to date as measured by the far higher ratio of patents filed internationally versus domestically by Japanese and South Korean companies relative to American companies.[49] In addition to the role both Japan and South Korea play in worldwide innovation, both China and India will likely become key lead countries in Asian technological development for the foreseeable future.

Rivalry is fiercer in lead countries as competitors recognize the strategic as well as financial importance of success there. In particular, companies need to recognize the value of investing to build a strong position in lead markets, particularly if those markets are the home of major global rivals.

LEAD COUNTRIES IN SERVICE BUSINESSES   Lead country effects apply equally for service businesses. Interestingly, the United States is far more dominant as a lead country for global service businesses than it is for manufacturing ones. In many categories of service businesses, the United States sets global trends and standards: in chain restaurants, hotels, entertainment theme parks, health care, delivery services, car rental, and so on. This may be because global service businesses depend less on technology or skilled labor and more on having a strong business concept that is systematically applied globally.

EXHIBIT 2-3 Strength of Cost Globalization Drivers for Selected Industries

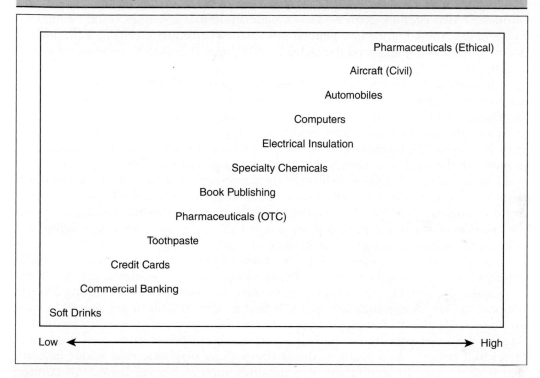

Pharmaceuticals (Ethical)

Aircraft (Civil)

Automobiles

Computers

Electrical Insulation

Specialty Chemicals

Book Publishing

Pharmaceuticals (OTC)

Toothpaste

Credit Cards

Commercial Banking

Soft Drinks

Low ⟵——————————————————⟶ High

COST GLOBALIZATION DRIVERS

Cost globalization drivers—global scale economies, steep experience effects, favorable logistics, differences in country costs, high product development costs, and fast-changing technology—depend on the economics of the business. These drivers particularly affect the use of the global activity location lever, as well as the global market participation and global product levers. Exhibit 2-3 ranks on cost globalization drivers, the same industries ranked on market globalization drivers in Exhibit 2-1. Notice some of the differences: Pharmaceuticals (ethical) rise to the top of the cost rankings, while soft drinks fall to the bottom.

Global Economies of Scale and Scope

Global scale economies or scope economies apply when single-country markets are not large enough to allow competitors to achieve optimum scale. Scale at a given location of an activity can then be increased through participation in multiple markets, combined with product standardization and/or concentration of selected value activities. But corresponding risks of increasing scale at one location include rigidity and vulnerability to disruption. There has been a shift in the economics of the electronics industry. As the cost of electronic components has decreased, the cost advantage has gone to companies that can produce them at the lowest cost. Size has become a major asset. Among others, Thomson, the French electronics maker, realized the need to have a worldwide presence in an industry characterized by economies of scale. Accordingly, Thomson instituted a major global expansion that included the acquisition of GE's RCA consumer electronics business.[50] However, by 2007, Audiovox understood that synergies could be attained by owning distinct brands in a general portfolio of consumer electronics products.[51] As such, Audiovox purchased the rights to RCA from Thomson to leverage size with adaptive capabilities.

In many cases it seems to be *economies of scope* (the gains from spreading activities across multiple product lines or businesses) rather than economies of scale (the gains from increasing the volume of an activity) that push businesses to internationalize or to globalize. In consumer household products, such as detergent and toothpaste, economies of scale at the manufacturing level can typically be achieved by national plants in most but the smallest countries. In soft drinks, large cities in China can support several bottling plants. Yet these industries are dominated by a handful of multinational firms—Unilever, Procter & Gamble, Colgate-Palmolive, Coca-Cola, and PepsiCo. It seems that the economies of scope involved in consumer research, product development, and the creation of marketing programs are a major source of the competitive advantage enjoyed by multinational companies in these industries.

Global scale economies reduce the threat of entry, particularly from potential entrants that are national companies. Where global scale economies apply, it will not be possible for an entrant to achieve competitive economic scale by entering a single national market. A non-multinational will find it very difficult to get started in such an industry. In the disposable syringe industry, the minimum economic size in production has been estimated to be 60 percent of the combined markets in the United States and Japan.[52] As a result, national competitors play little role in this industry that is dominated by multinational companies such as Becton Dickinson (United States) and Terumo (Japan). Still, such experience in the disposable syringe industry allows for expansion into related industries such as cardiovascular systems.[53] Conversely, where economies are not at a global scale, an entrant can start in a smaller country-market and gradually build the experience that will allow it to export to larger markets. That is why the U.S. market has become so vulnerable to imported personal computers and other products that can be effectively manufactured in low volumes.

Global scale economies also broaden the scope of competitive rivalry. With national scale economies, competitors have to worry about national market share in order to stay at the economically efficient scale. In the presence of global scale economies, competitors have to worry about their global share. Loss of share in any country will impact the cost position of any sister country with which activities are shared.

GLOBAL SCALE ECONOMIES IN SERVICE BUSINESSES   Certain service characteristics—lack of inventories, customer involvement in production, and people as part of the service experience—all work against being able to concentrate production to achieve scale. As Yum! Brands has found in its worldwide expansion, service companies typically have to find global scale economies by standardizing production processes rather than through physical concentration, and in concentrating the upstream, rather than the downstream, stages of the value chain.

The effect of cost globalization drivers, like global scale economies, varies sharply according to the level of fixed costs required to enter an industry (although equipment

The Multi-brand Strategy of Yum!

Yum! Brands is the world's largest quick service franchisor and the parent brand to well-known restaurant franchises including Taco Bell, Pizza Hut, KFC, Long John Silvers, A&W Restaurants, and Wingstreet. Known as Tricon for a time prior to re-branding efforts in 2002, Yum! Brands was spun off from PepsiCo in 1997 and has been successful in its international activities.

With unmistakable American designs and services, Yum! Brands has been able to globalize without significant marketing strategy adaptation by country. In fact, in locations outside the United States, Yum! has become the world's largest retail developer by opening approximately four new restaurants every day in 2007.[54] In 2008, KFC and Pizza Hut were listed on *BusinessWeek*'s Top 100 Global Brands ranking.[55] Also, Pizza Hut has been ranked as the most trusted food service brand in India for several years.[56] Though Pizza Hut has vied with McDonald's for the top position of the quick service category on a yearly basis, Yum! Brands has three of its restaurant chains in the top 10 of this category.[57]

In fact, the company has over 30,000 stores worldwide.[58] As such, Yum! Brands has shown few signs of slowing its worldwide retail expansion. Recent strategic moves have included aggressive tactics with existing KFC operations in France,[59] China,[60] and India.[61] Also, benefiting from its success with KFC and Pizza Hut in south Asia, Yum! has plans for introducing its Taco Bell franchise in India.[62] As such, combining significant market power with customer satisfaction makes Yum! Brands formidable, should competitors seek to develop global marketing potential.

leasing schemes, or awarding franchises to local investors, provide a way to minimize such entry barriers). So cost globalization drivers may be less favorable for services that are primarily people-based and face lesser scale economies and flatter experience curves. One common solution for the would-be global company is to substitute equipment for labor in order to achieve lower costs and better performance than local companies using traditional business systems, as has been done by McDonald's.

EFFECT OF TECHNOLOGY ON GLOBAL SCALE ECONOMIES   The Internet drives down global economies of scale and scope. The technological transformation of businesses generally reduces minimum efficient scales. First, many physical activities can be replaced by virtual and social media activities. Therefore, many scale and investment barriers to global spread are bypassed. For example, many already globalized companies are running down their international distribution systems, while newly internationalizing companies need to spend much less on international distribution. Second, value chains and business systems are being broken up or "deconstructed."[63] Inevitably, this means a consolidation of players and market share takes place at the deconstructed stages and therefore a larger scale. On the one hand, this means that there is less pressure on the new entities to globalize. But on the other hand, these new entities have clearly focused business models and competitive advantages that are easily transferable and leverageable internationally.

This reduction in economies of scale and transaction costs will particularly help aggressive and well-managed smaller firms from emerging markets. For example, small firms in developing and emerging economies will be able to combine to achieve global reach, reducing the customer proximity advantage of firms in developed economies.

Zara's Fast Fashion Success

Spanish clothing retailer Zara has reaped tremendous benefit from a lean and well-orchestrated value chain. Instead of outsourcing the majority of manufacturing to disparate low-cost countries such as competitor H&M,[65] Zara keeps most of its value chain in-house. Approximately 40 percent of Zara's products are manufactured in company-owned facilities, half of which are located in Spain.[66] As such, the close proximity of designers to the procurement and production process increases the possibility that logistical and cost considerations can be part of the design and development process.

Zara has been an industry leader in affordable fashionable clothing or "fast fashion"—a market where consumers demand the latest designs in extremely short product life cycles. Annually the company produces more than 10,000 new products, which is between three and five times more than its competitors.[67] In fact, a Zara clothing item can go from concept to customer in a matter of weeks.[68] Efficient economies of scope allow the company to take risks with new designs and obtain information about what is selling and what is not, adjusting production quickly to respond to demand. With this in mind, Zara launched its online retail strategy with considerable success, thereby leaving its competitors to evaluate the landscape.[69]

Keeping a vertically integrated value chain has been critical to its competitive strategy, but this could also prove to be a barrier to true global expansion. Low government barriers to trade allow Zara to flourish in Europe, but cost advantages diminish worldwide. For example, in the United States, products in Zara's stores can cost considerably more than they would in Spain.[70] In order to satisfy emerging markets for its products, the company will have to revise much of its integrated strategy to scale production.

Steep Experience Curve

Even if scale and scope economies are exhausted, expanded market participation, product standardization, and activity concentration can accelerate the accumulation of learning and experience effects (learning effects apply to direct manufacturing while experience effects apply to the entire production process). The steeper the learning and experience slopes, the greater the potential benefit. *Managers should beware, though, of the usual danger in pursuing experience curve strategies—overaggressive pricing that destroys not just the competition but the market also.* A steep experience curve has similar effects as global scale economies on the threat of entry and rivalry among competitors.

Global Sourcing Efficiencies

The market for supplies may allow centralized purchasing to achieve savings in the cost of production inputs. In the past, companies strove to attain efficiencies in global sourcing by trading with locations well known as low-cost sourcing providers. However, based on increased market instability, some corporate decisions have increased the importance of sourcing from nearby locations to reduce risk in the supply chain when possible. Along with other concerns related to product quality, one example related to European companies looking again at eastern European countries to attain cost efficiencies.[64] Thus, as is evident in the Zara example, companies in certain industries will continue to weigh the risks of low-cost countries with available capacity in closer locations—be they in-house or through external partnerships.

GLOBAL SOURCING EFFICIENCIES IN SERVICE BUSINESSES   Many service businesses produce at the location of the customer and, hence, have multiple national sites. In many cases, satisfactory supplies can be sourced locally. But in many other cases, the need to maintain global standards will require global sourcing at higher cost. When McDonald's first went into Russia, the company imported some ingredients (potato chips) and set up special supply arrangements for others (beef). The company invested $45 million to guarantee its ability to deliver consistent quality amid the adverse conditions McDonald's encountered.[71] Similarly, professional service firms often face the need to fly in qualified staff from overseas for a time until sufficient investment can be made to create a self-sustaining sourcing system in strategically integral markets.

EFFECT OF TECHNOLOGY ON GLOBAL SOURCING EFFICIENCIES   The Internet enhances global sourcing efficiencies. Prior to the advent of the Internet, globally centralized purchasing required complex, paper- and phone-based coordination of geographically dispersed subsidiaries and suppliers. Today, subsidiary requirements can be managed efficiently and can be coordinated through technology-based networks. For example, General Motors, Ford, and Chrysler created the Automotive Exchange Network (ANX) to support automated interactions with their parts suppliers. ANX defines a set of technology and service-quality standards for exchanging critical transaction and planning documents over the Internet.[72] The concept has served as an example of effective and efficient global sourcing to many industrial sectors. In fact, European and Japanese companies have developed similar systems. In electronics, Panasonic (formerly known as Matsushita) built an integrated network linking its factories and suppliers to be more competitive.

Favorable Logistics

A favorable ratio of sales value to transportation cost enhances the ability to concentrate production. Other logistical factors include nonperishability, the absence of time urgency, and little need for location close to customer facilities. Low transportation costs allow concentration of production. Even the shape of the product can make a crucial difference. Cardboard tubes, such as those used as cores for textiles, are not economically shippable because the tubes are mostly air. In contrast, cardboard cones are transportable because they can be stacked, allowing many more units in the same space. In general, higher priced/higher quality products within any category face more favorable logistics. So French *vin de table* stays home while good Burgundies travel everywhere.

Favorable logistics increase the threat of entry. The low costs make it much easier for foreign entrants to enter markets, by exporting. Favorable logistics also increase rivalry among existing competitors by expanding the geographic scope of competition. Rivals can readily shift products from country to country, such that competition is between global production capabilities.

FAVORABLE LOGISTICS IN SERVICE BUSINESSES   Low transportation costs allow concentration of production for physical goods. For services, "customer involvement in production" raises the logistical stakes in globalization. In most people-processing services, the need for convenience prevents concentration. But in some possession-processing services, customers are willing to transport their possessions to another location for better service. Thus, many airlines bring their aircraft to Singapore. Some people-processing services have achieved similar success in having customers come to them. London hospitals maintain a flourishing business among wealthy Middle Eastern patients, as do Miami hospitals for patients from Latin America.

Companies have to balance the trade-offs between logistics and appeal. Disney favored logistics over appeal in selecting northern France rather than southern Spain for the location of Euro Disney. More people can get more easily to the Euro Disney site outside Paris, but once there they often face cold weather and colder service. Service businesses can also create their own favorable logistics. Club Med organizes charter flights from urban centers to its off-the-beaten-path locations. Some airlines provide limousine ground transport to and from their first-class flights.

Lastly, logistics is seldom a barrier to globalization for information-based services. Using electronic channels to deliver such services allows providers to concentrate production in locations that have specific expertise and to offer cost savings or other meaningful advantages. For instance, banks in the Cayman Islands are not conveniently located from a purely geographic standpoint, but money can be shipped there electronically to take advantage of the tax benefits conferred by offshore status.

EFFECT OF TECHNOLOGY ON FAVORABLE LOGISTICS   The Internet speeds up global logistics and facilitates the operation of global production and supply networks. Boeing has created the Boeing Partners Network to connect with its 40,000 trading partners around the world. For example, separate regulatory agencies in the United States, Canada, Japan, Russia, and Europe have used the Boeing intranet to collaborate on its space station project. In addition, new Boeing projects such as the 787 Dreamliner benefit from such logistics efficiency to provide performance advances to the industry.

Differences in Country Costs

Differences in country costs can provide a strong spur to globalization. Factor costs generally vary across countries, and more so for particular industries. The availability of particular skills also varies. Concentration of activities in low-cost or high-skill countries can increase productivity and reduce costs. But managers need to anticipate the danger of training future offshore competitors.[73]

Large variations in costs among the countries that produce or might produce a particular product increase the threat of entry from foreign sources. Japan—and then the "four tigers" of South Korea, Taiwan, Hong Kong, and Singapore—has very successfully leveraged low factor costs in entering many international industries. Similar success has been made by China and India. Other Asian countries such as Thailand and Vietnam are also making entries in high labor cost industries. Eastern European countries have made strides thus far by exploiting low-cost but high-skill labor. However, regardless of the location of manufacturing activities, having a low cost of goods sold, relative to the selling price, is often an industry's best protection from cheap imports as it represents continued investment in manufacturing capabilities difficult to attain immediately in a low-cost sourcing country.

Differences in country costs increase rivalry among existing competitors by creating differential sources of competitive advantage. Rivalry heightened between Japanese and European consumer electronics manufacturers when the Japanese discovered that it was cheaper to produce Europe-bound products in the United States than at home. Ricoh assembled photocopiers containing 90 percent Japanese parts in California and reexported them to Europe. Furthermore, Sony produced audio-visual products in Alabama and Florida to subsequently ship them to Europe for sale. Similarly, the United Kingdom became the preferred European manufacturing site for many Japanese companies. As a result the UK government became embroiled in a dispute with other European Union (EU) governments on the extent of local content needed to qualify as "Made in Europe." In fact, reflecting manufacturing and competitive dynamics, serious concerns emerged in the EU concerning the future of "Made in Europe" market offerings.[74]

Exchange rates, and changes in them, provide a major source of the variation in costs between countries. But the effect of exchange rates works in one direction for the cost of local inputs, such as labor and some raw materials, and usually in the opposite direction for imported inputs and foreign services. So it is usually only labor-intensive industries, or those in which local materials and supplies are both important and plentiful, where exchange rates can have a major impact on relative country costs.

DIFFERENCES IN COUNTRY COSTS IN SERVICE BUSINESSES   Service businesses vary in their ability to exploit differences in country costs. People-processing businesses can do so the least as they usually need local operations wherever their customers are. Possession-processing businesses have more opportunities. Centralized processing facilities may have such low costs that they can afford to bring the possessions to the facility. For example, airplanes are now often serviced at specific hubs operated by third parties rather than the airlines owning the planes. Information-based services have the most opportunity as, in many cases, they can be based nearly anywhere worldwide.

EFFECT OF TECHNOLOGY ON DIFFERENCES IN COUNTRY COSTS   The Internet does not change relative country costs and skills, but it enables many activities to be shifted to lower cost countries. First, the Internet can be used as a means of efficient communication and coordination to make possible the "offshoring" of activities that would otherwise be too complex to manage. For example, taking advantage of time-zone differences as well as lower costs, some consulting firms have shifted document production to India as well as other locations. While U.S.- and Europe-based consultants sleep, their documents and presentations are being produced for them. Second, the deconstruction of activities creates specialized Web-based functions such as customer service (particularly for information-rich services) that can easily be shifted to lower cost locales. The information database can remain in the home or another key country while being accessed by the Internet from lower cost and perhaps less secure countries.

High Product Development Costs

High product development costs relative to the size of national markets act as a driver to globalization. Philips, the Dutch multinational, estimated that technology developments in public telecommunications increased the cost of product development by enormous multiples. In the 1950s development costs for conventional electromechanical switching systems were about $10 million, and they had an expected life cycle of about 25 years. By the beginning of 1970 when the analog system was introduced, development costs had jumped to $200 million, while the life cycle fell from 12 to 15 years. In the 1980s, when the first digital systems were developed, costs had risen to $1 billion for a life expectancy of 8 to 12 years. Philips calculated that digital development expenses of $1 billion required roughly 8 percent share of the world market just to recover costs. The largest single market in Europe—Germany—could in total deliver less than that share.[75]

By 2000, developing a new pharmaceutical or agro-chemical product could cost $200 million or more, developing a new automobile platform could cost at least $1 billion, and developing the next generation of super-jumbo jets was projected to cost over $10 billion (for the Airbus A380). The A380 program was so large that Airbus needed alliances in Russia, China, and Japan, and substantial U.S. content. A decade later, development costs for Boeing's 787 were estimated at $2.5 billion.[76] Similar to the complexity of the A380 program, Boeing developed alliances outside its home market with partners from Australia, England, France, Italy, Japan, South Korea, and Sweden.

Developing a few global or regional products rather than many national products can reduce high product development costs. But the process for designing global products must not be so cumbersome as to slow the entire process. The automobile industry is characterized by long product development periods and high product development costs. One reason for the high costs is duplication of effort across countries. In the 1990s, companies such as Ford consolidated design efforts, with different regions specializing in particular activities. This approach to automotive design paid off during the financial crisis of 2008–2009 as Ford declined governmental intervention to prevent bankruptcy whereas the company's primary American competitors required such assistance.[77] As such, high product development costs have had a similar effect as global scale economies increase the threat of entry and rivalry among competitors.

EFFECT OF TECHNOLOGY ON PRODUCT DEVELOPMENT COSTS   The Internet reduces product development costs to varying degrees. Some aspects of the product, particularly supplementary ones such as service, can be shifted out of the physical product and into a service setting such as the Internet. This allows the development of a simpler, global core product with lower development (and production) costs. In some cases, the customer can do the final customization online. As a very common practice, both Nike and Dell allow customers to design and order their own customized products. Another cost reduction arises when companies manage globally dispersed product development teams technologically, thereby also enhancing effectiveness.

Fast-Changing Technology

Fast-changing technology, in products or processes, usually accompanies high product development costs, and in itself already increases industry globalization potential:

- The cost of embodying the technology changes typically drives companies to amortize that cost across as many markets as possible.

- Companies that pioneer a particular technology usually feel pressured to rapidly globalize that technology in order to exploit it before imitators do so. So both the cost and preemption reasons just cited spur companies to increase their global market participation.
- A company can better exploit and protect its new technologies by using globally integrated competitive moves that include a clear prioritization of when and where to use the technology against competitors.

FAST-CHANGING TECHNOLOGY IN SERVICE BUSINESSES   For information-based services, the growing availability of broadband telecommunication channels, capable of moving vast amounts of data at great speed, is playing a major role in opening up new markets. But there may be no need to duplicate all informational elements in each new location. Significant economies may be gained by centralizing "information hubs" on a global basis, as FedEx does in Memphis. For all three types of services, the use of information technology may allow companies to benefit from favorable labor costs or exchange rates by consolidating operations of supplementary services (such as reservations) or back-office functions (such as accounting) in just one or a few countries. While a globalization driver in its own right, information technology also interacts with all of the other drivers.

GOVERNMENT GLOBALIZATION DRIVERS

Government globalization drivers—favorable trade policies, compatible technical standards, common marketing regulations, government-owned competitors and customers, and host government concerns—depend on the rules set by national governments and affect use of all global strategy levers. Exhibit 2-4 ranks on government globalization drivers, the same industries ranked on market and cost globalization drivers in Exhibits 2-1 and 2-3. Again, notice some of the differences: Toothpaste rises to the top while electrical insulation falls near the bottom of the rankings.

Favorable Trade Policies

Host governments affect globalization potential in a number of major ways: import tariffs and quotas, nontariff barriers, export subsidies, local content requirements, currency and capital flow restrictions, ownership restrictions, and requirements on technology transfer.[78] Governments' exercise of these trade barriers makes it difficult for companies to use the global levers of global market participation, global products and services, global activity location, and global marketing and affects the need to use the lever of global competitive moves. Government policies greatly restrict global market participation in the media industries.

In many countries, foreign control of the media is restricted or prohibited. Some countries also impose other special restrictions. In Canada magazines must be printed in the country or else be charged a higher postal rate—in effect a local content requirement that restricts a company's choice on activity location.[79] The newsprint industry also has faced unfavorable trade conditions, probably because of its political salience as part of the natural resource sector but also the result of the decentralizing effect of the Internet as an information source.[80]

EXHIBIT 2-4 Strength of Government Globalization Drivers for Selected Industries

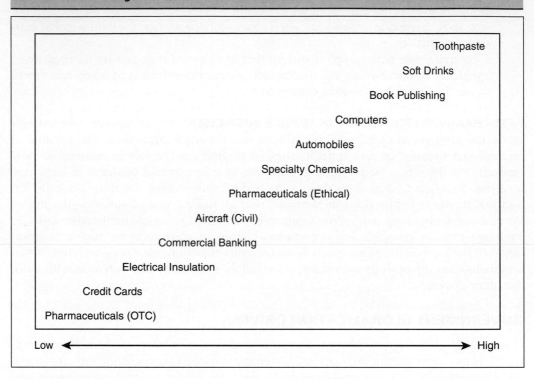

In the 1970s many national governments responded to the oil crisis and consequent business bankruptcies by intervening with subsidies, tax laws, cartels, and delays in scheduled tariff reductions and quota increases.[81] During the global recession of 2001, many national governments were struggling to find ways to support failing flagship companies, especially airlines. This again became a source of political concern in the financial crisis of 2008–2009 as national governments intervened in the automotive, financial, and other sectors to reduce bankruptcies on an unprecedented scale.[82]

National trade policies particularly constrain the extent to which companies can concentrate manufacturing activities. Aggressive U.S. government actions and threats on tariffs, quotas, and protectionist measures helped convince Japanese automobile manufacturers and other manufacturers to give up their concentration of manufacturing in Japan. Reluctantly, Japanese companies opened plants in the United States. Honda even made a public relations virtue out of necessity. It gave great publicity to the first shipment of an American-made Honda car to Japan.

The easing of government restrictions can set off a rush for expanded market participation. European Community regulations for banking and financial services were among those harmonized in 1992. The EC (now EU) decision to permit free flow of capital among its member countries in 1992 led to a jockeying for position among European financial institutions. Until then, the Deutsche Bank had only 15 offices outside Germany, but it has since established a major presence in French markets. Deutsche Bank also moved into the Italian market by acquiring Bank of America's 100 branches there. After the expansion of the EU into eastern European countries, Deutsche Bank continued to develop its pan-European presence by acquiring United Financial Group in 2005 to strengthen its position in the Russian market.

Favorable trade policies increase rivalry among existing international competitors by making it easier for them to compete in each other's markets. The opening up of European financial markets, created by the Europe 1992 changes, has made rivals of national European banks. Until the changes, banks such as Germany's Deutsche Bank, Britain's Barclays Bank, and France's Banque Nationale de Paris (BNP) competed only in fringe activities. Recognized by each other as major rivals for some time, the financial sector has increased its standing considerably, with sales now rivaling other dominant economic sectors.[83]

TRADE POLICIES IN SERVICE BUSINESSES   For services, customer involvement in production may mitigate many government barriers to global strategy. Government drivers are often favorable for people-processing and possession-processing services that require a significant local presence, since they create local employment opportunities. On the other hand, governments often impose regulations to protect home carriers in the case of mobile services, such as passenger and freight transportation. For instance, restricting foreign airlines' landing rights or ability to pick up passengers at an intermediate stop ("third freedom" rights) provides a way to protect home-based airlines on international routes.

Nations may perceive both an economic and a cultural threat in unrestricted imports of information-based services through electronic channels. Government regulations range from controls on international banking to bans on private ownership of satellite dishes (as in countries such as China, Singapore, and Saudi Arabia). Some nations are now trying to manage citizen access to the Internet. However, as events in the Middle East have indicated, such controls on access to electronic media can have a limited impact.[84]

For people-processing services, government barriers to global strategy include country differences in social policies (e.g., health) affecting labor costs, the role of women in frontline jobs, and the hours or days on which work can be performed. For possession-processing services, tax laws, environmental regulations, and technical standards may decrease/increase costs and encourage/discourage certain types of activities. For information-based services, special policies on education, censorship, public ownership of communications, and infrastructure quality may apply; technical standards may vary; and government policies may distort pricing.

Most global efforts at reducing trade barriers focused for many years on the movement of goods. But now bodies such as the World Trade Organization (WTO) and the EU are also freeing up services. The French insurer AXA's 1996 acquisition of rival UAP provides a good example of how governmental policies are helping to spur changes in the global insurance industry. The unification of Europe through the EU as well as its expansion into Eastern Europe propelled AXA to consolidate with another massive French insurance company to become the largest insurance company in the world. As a result of the unification, many tariffs and artificial price supports that protected the insurance industry in Europe were destructed. French insurance companies like AXA, therefore, were faced with increased competition from non-French insurance companies. In order to remain competitive in the global insurance industry, AXA chose to acquire its rival UAP.[85]

EFFECT OF TECHNOLOGY ON TRADE POLICIES   The Internet weakens many government barriers to globalization, often sidestepping trade policies. Technological advances reduce trade barriers in several ways, particularly in bypassing import duties and taxes. Most governments find it impossible to monitor or tax services delivered over the Internet, unless the government is actively engaged in monitoring and censoring traffic, as do a few authoritarian regimes. For products and services ordered over the Internet but delivered physically across borders, governments should, in theory, be able to catch these at the frontier. But in practice, most governments miss a significant portion of the increasing numbers of relatively low-value items.

Compatible Technical Standards

Differences in technical standards among countries affect the extent to which products can be standardized. Government restrictions in terms of technical standards can make or break efforts at product standardization. Often, standards are set with protectionism in mind.

MOTOROLA'S STRUGGLE WITH JAPANESE STANDARDS   Motorola, a leading American electronics manufacturer, found that many of its products were excluded from the Japanese market on the grounds that these products operated at a higher frequency than permitted in Japan. Motorola spent many years, with some notable successes, to get Japan to change its standards. For a time, Motorola exited the Japanese cell phone market. However, the company returned after changes were made both in Motorola's corporate structure and in the Japanese market.[86]

Over-the-counter pharmaceuticals, being sold directly to the public, face strict standards that vary from country to country. Maximum allowed dosage is perhaps the greatest source of incompatibility. In contrast, while still strict, governments are more liberal with prescription pharmaceuticals, so that standards are typically more compatible. At the other end of the scale, the airline industry has to have highly compatible technical standards in order to function at all. For example, all international airports have similar runway lengths to accommodate the largest passenger jets; and the universal language used around the world in cockpits and control towers is English.

Telecommunications have been regarded by governments as contributing to national security. So they have tended to rely on domestic suppliers. Consequently, the world faces a hodgepodge of standards in telecommunications. In Europe, Spain has a three-second busy tone while Denmark has a two-second one. German telephones operate on 60 volts while other European countries use 8 volts, and so on.[87]

OPENING OF TELECOM MARKETS   The protection of national telecom markets is falling fast. In 1997, WTO brokered an agreement among 69 countries to open their telecom markets to competition, most by 1998.[88] In scope alone, the agreement was the most ambitious yet as it opened the three big telecom markets—America, the EU, and Japan—to allow international and domestic competition by 1998. A total of 15 other countries would join them, and another 16 would open their markets over the next seven years (1997–2004). Most of the WTO signatories agreed, not because they abruptly saw the virtues of competition but in grudging recognition of the fact that developments in technology and business were making change inevitable.

Compatible technical standards can make it easier for new entrants to achieve the needed scale. With one product they can enter many markets at once. Lack of major differences in country technical standards greatly helped Japan's Canon enter the photocopier market in the early 1970s. Canon was able to design a single global product that needed only minor modifications for individual countries. In fact, compatible technical standards also increase rivalry among existing competitors by making it easier for them to invade each other's market. This is noticed with Canon as the company became a dominant competitor in the global photocopier market.

EFFECT OF TECHNOLOGY ON TECHNICAL STANDARDS The Internet spurred global technical standards. The move to put standards on government Web sites and to allow public access is gradually increasing the transparency of the standard-setting process and should encourage the spread of global standards. For example, Japan lobbied other G8 nations for unified global rules on electronic financial trading.

Common Marketing Regulations

The marketing environment of individual countries affects the extent to which uniform global marketing approaches can be used. Certain types of media may not be allowed or may have restrictions on their use. The United States is far more liberal than Europe in the kinds of advertising claims that can be made on television. The British television authorities even veto the depiction of socially undesirable behavior, such as scenes of children pestering their parents to buy a product. And, of course, the use of sex is different. At one extreme, France is far more liberal than the United States about sex in advertising. There can also be limitations on various promotional devices, such as lotteries. In the United States promotional competitions cannot require skill or special knowledge!

Common marketing regulations increase rivalry among existing international competitors by making it easier for them to invade each other's markets. British Airways (BA) has used a uniform global advertising campaign to help increase its market share in many countries around the world.

EFFECT OF TECHNOLOGY ON MARKETING REGULATIONS The Internet confronts diverse marketing regulations. Governments lag in their efforts to regulate marketing on the Internet. Differences in rules on Internet marketing can themselves pose a barrier to globalization. For example, the EU is applying increasingly strict rules to prevent marketing e-mail from originating outside the EU. Many marketers are thus finding that, just like traditional producers, non-traditional companies need to set up operations inside the EU. Germany forbids all unsolicited marketing contact of consumers, including via e-mail. France forbids e-Bay and similar online auction services from allowing French users to access Web sites outside France itself.

The Internet also depends on national legal systems. Both overly weak and overly strong national legal systems deter international business. The critical issue revolves around the protection of free speech. Jurisdictions vary in the protection extended to Web site content, particularly regarding deceit, pornography, and defamation. Some countries such as the United Kingdom have consumer protection groups which monitor and act on Internet marketing communications deemed illegal, dishonesty, or untrue.[89] However, with pornography the problem lies with the huge variations in interpretation. What may be quite innocent in a liberal nation may be deemed criminal elsewhere. With defamation, some jurisdictions allow portal and feed operators the defense that they do not know what is mounted by third-party content providers. Others do not. In response many service operators are shifting operations to host countries with more liberal rules.

Government-Owned Competitors

The presence of government-owned competitors can increase the globalization potential of an industry. Such competitors frequently enjoy subsidies as well as protected home markets and are often a major source of foreign exchange earnings. This combination both allows and spurs them to aggressively pursue foreign markets. In response other competitors need to have a global plan for fending off government-owned competitors.

The existence of government-owned competitors increases the threat of entry. Similarly, government-owned competitors increase rivalry because of their differing motivations from private competitors. According to a disgruntled American competitor, Spanish and Italian government-owned manufacturers of aluminum products typically act to depress prices in the European market.

Government-Owned Customers

In contrast to government-owned competitors, the presence of government-owned customers provides a barrier to globalization. Such customers usually favor national suppliers. The privatization of most European telecommunications companies spurred greater global competition in the equipment-supplying industry.

Host Government Concerns

Lastly, in addition to the specific government drivers just discussed, firms pursuing a global strategy need to be aware of the concerns of host governments:

- Global businesses will quickly respond to shifts in the relative factor cost competitiveness of various manufacturing locations by relocating to different countries.
- Global integration gives multinational companies more opportunity to bias the financial results of subsidiaries to decrease total tax liability.
- Value-chain specialization within global businesses will keep key competencies outside their countries.
- The weakening of national decision centers under global strategy makes it more difficult for governments to deal with multinational companies.[90]

In addition, governments and companies usually have a desire for local reliance in major or strategic industries, for example, the textile industry in a number of Asian countries.

So governments will seldom allow such major industries to depend for key inputs on supply from foreign countries, particularly distant ones.

COMPETITIVE GLOBALIZATION DRIVERS

Competitive globalization drivers—high exports and imports, competitors from different continents, interdependence of countries, and globalized competitors—raise the globalization potential of their industry and spur the need for a response on the global strategy levers. Exhibit 2-5 ranks on competitive globalization drivers, the same industries ranked on market, cost, and government drivers in Exhibits 2-1, 2-3, and 2-4. For example, civil aircraft and computers rank high in competitive drivers while book publishing ranks low in most developed economies.

High Exports and Imports

The most basic competitive driver is the level of exports and imports of both final and intermediate products and services. The more trade there is between countries, the more competitors in different countries interact with each other. A global strategy is, therefore, more necessary. Furthermore, high levels of trade change the nature of competitive forces as discussed earlier on the threat of entry.

EXHIBIT 2-5 Strength of Competitive Globalization Drivers for Selected Industries

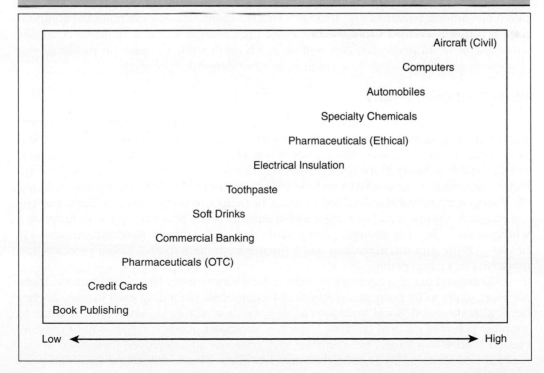

Competitors from Different Continents and Countries

Another obvious driver of industry globalization potential is the extent to which major competitors come from different continents or countries. Because their differing backgrounds spur different objectives and approaches, global competition among rivals from different continents tends to be more severe.

Interdependent Countries

A competitor may create competitive interdependence among countries by pursuing a global strategy. This effect arises from the sharing of activities. For example, a business may use a plant in Mexico to serve both the U.S. and Japanese markets. So market share gains in Japan will affect volume in the Mexican plant, which in turn will affect costs and ultimately the business's market share in the United States. Thus, with interdependent countries, a competitor's market share in one country contributes to its overall cost position and, therefore, its share position in another country. Such interdependence helps a company to subsidize attacks on competitors in different countries. But it also requires the company to jointly manage its competitive position in each country, rather than leave that task just to local management. Other competitors then need to respond via increased global market participation, global marketing, or globally integrated competitive strategy to avoid a downward spiral of sequentially weakened positions in individual countries.

Interdependence among countries makes entry more difficult. An incumbent competitor can be expected to retaliate more fiercely in order to protect its interdependent position. Protecting the share of a subsidiary becomes doubly important when that also means preserving the cost position of subsidiaries in other countries. Interdependence among countries also increases rivalry among existing international competitors. It requires competitors to worry about their market share in multiple countries simultaneously. In particular, they will be much more willing to give up profits in one country in order to protect their position in other dependent countries.

Globalized Competitors

Competitors are globalized to the extent that they use the global strategy levers of global market participation, global products and services, global location of activities, global marketing, and global competitive moves. When a business's competitors use global strategy to exploit industry globalization potential, the business needs to match or preempt these competitors. These moves include expansion into or within major markets, being the first to introduce a standardized product, or being the first to use a uniform marketing program. Competitors pursuing a global strategy place pressure on the industry as a whole to globalize. For example, competitors that push globally standardized products or use globally uniform marketing will influence customers to find global products and marketing more acceptable.

Globalized existing competitors reduce the threat of entry from new entrants: There are more likely to be powerful multinational incumbents defending each market. Incumbents with integrated global strategies can draw on their worldwide assets and resources to suppress potential national entrants. Major U.S. consumer goods companies have typically viewed Europe as a single, broad market and, consequently, deployed their assets across national boundaries. This globalized posture has made it more difficult for their European competitors to enter and compete in markets other than their home country. In contrast, until spurred by Europe 1992, European companies tended to focus their efforts in a single, national market. A 1988 study of 45 major European food companies found that half had a presence in only one or two countries.[91] Two decades later, the food industry in Europe was still fragmented as over half of the companies were small or medium-sized.[92]

Globalized existing competitors also increase industry rivalry by increasing the geographic scope of competition. Competition between globally integrated competitors becomes battles between global systems, not just single-country one-on-one combat. In one household, product category competitors began to pay more attention to each other once one company clearly became global and started to make major inroads into the other competitors' markets.

CITIGROUP'S MOVES IN ASIA   In the 1990s, Citicorp sought to strengthen its presence in Asia, a region where stiff competition already existed.[93] Chase Manhattan and J. P. Morgan, two other U.S.-based banks at the time, and HSBC, a Hong Kong-based bank that already operated in 71 countries in the mid-1990s, were formidable Citigroup rivals in Asia.[94] Despite this stiff competition, Citigroup continued to generate impressive profits. Citigroup was able to build a successful franchise in Asia because Asians perceived the bank to be a sophisticated place to work and a harbor for serious money. Because of such an impressive image among Asians, Citigroup has been able to woo wealthy customers who demanded exceptional service. However, given its aggressive marketing of some products, Citigroup suffered some losses in large markets such as India.[95] Still, Citigroup's reputation remained reasonably intact and—as a result—the opportunity to expand into new Asian markets such as Indonesia, Malaysia, Thailand, and Vietnam should continue for some time to come.[96]

Transferable Competitive Advantage

Perhaps the ultimate globalization driver is the global transferability of competitive advantage. Some competitive advantages, such as technology-based ones, are easily transferable with little adaptation. In consequence, global companies engaged in global competition populate such industries. Other advantages are much more locally rooted, especially advantages based on local knowledge or local relationships. Industries based on those advantages tend to be multilocal. The legal industry perhaps typifies the type of industry based on local knowledge (of laws) and local relationships (with mostly national or local clients). In consequence, there are few genuinely global law firms, although there are a number operating as global alliances.

GUIDELINES FOR DIAGNOSING INDUSTRY GLOBALIZATION POTENTIAL

Getting a good understanding of industry globalization potential is the starting point for developing an effective total global strategy.[97] In diagnosing this potential, managers should find the following guidelines useful:

- Do not assume that industries are either global or not global. Instead, nearly every industry has globalization potential in some aspects and not others.

- Different industry globalization drivers can operate in different directions, some favoring globalization and others making it difficult and inadvisable.
- Businesses can respond selectively to industry globalization drivers, by globalizing only those elements of strategy affected by favorable drivers.
- The level of globalization potential changes over time.
- Industry globalization drivers can work at a regional or continental scale as well as at a global scale.
- Industry competitors can themselves affect some globalization drivers. The competitors that stimulate these changes typically reap the major benefits.

Discussion and Research Questions

1. Select an industry and analyze its globalization drivers as they were five years ago, today, and what they are likely to be in five years' time.
2. Which aspects of this industry are most in favor of the use of global strategy? Which aspects are least in favor of its use?
3. What other drivers of globalization are not included in this chapter but should be?
4. How do industry globalization drivers affect companies' choice of global strategies?
5. What is different about globalization drivers for service industries?

Notes

1. Comments on service businesses are adapted from Christopher H. Lovelock and George S. Yip, "Developing Global Strategies for Service Businesses," *California Management Review,* Vol. 37, No. 3, Winter 1996, pp. 64–86. Additional examples were developed with the assistance of Christine Blanchet and Dominique Litmaath, both MBA students at the Anderson School at UCLA.
2. Comments in this chapter and elsewhere on the effects of the Internet are based on George S. Yip, "Global Strategy in the Internet Era," *Business Strategy Review,* Vol. 11, No. 2, Winter 2000, pp. 1–14.
3. Based on Michael E. Porter, *Competitive Strategy: Techniques for Analyzing Industries and Competitors* (New York: The Free Press, 1980).
4. Ibid.
5. Michael E. Porter, *The Competitive Advantage of Nations* (New York: The Free Press, 1990).
6. Comments in this chapter and elsewhere about service businesses are drawn primarily from Christopher H. Lovelock and George S. Yip, "Developing Global Strategies for Service Businesses," *California Management Review,* Vol. 37, No. 3, Winter 1996, pp. 64–86.

7. Johny K. Johansson, "Japanese Service Industries and Their Overseas Potential," *The Service Industries Journal,* Vol. 10, No. 1, January 1990, pp. 85–109.
8. Christopher H. Lovelock, *Services Marketing,* 2nd ed. (Upper Saddle River, NJ: Prentice Hall, 1991); Christopher H. Lovelock, *Product Plus: How Product + Service = Competitive Advantage* (New York: McGraw-Hill, 1994).
9. Richard B. Chase, "Where Does the Customer Fit in a Service Operation?" *Harvard Business Review,* November–December 1978, pp. 137–42.
10. See also Pradeep A. Rau and John F. Preble, "Standardization of Marketing Strategy by Multinationals," *International Marketing Review,* Autumn 1987, pp. 18–28.
11. "Fujitsu to Takeover Toshiba's Mobile Unit," *Wall Street Journal,* June 17, 2010, http://online.wsj.com/article/SB10001424052748704198004575311623251254624.html.
12. "The 50 Most Innovative Companies," *Bloomberg Businessweek,* April 15, 2010, http://www.businessweek.com/interactive_reports/innovative_companies_2010.html.

13. William Glasgall, "Japan on Wall Street," *Business Week,* September 7, 1987, pp. 82–90.

14. "Japanese Securities Firms Lose Bond Deals," *New York Times,* December 22, 1997, http://www.nytimes.com/1997/12/22/business/japanese-securities-firms-lose-bond-deals.html.

15. See *Fortune*'s Global 500 list for 2010, http://money.cnn.com/magazines/fortune/global500/2010/full_list/.

16. Lorraine Heller, "Danone Beats Unilever and Nestle in Food Categroy Dominance," *Dairy Reporter,* May 14, 2010, http://www.dairyreporter.com/Markets/Danone-beats-Unilever-and-Nestle-in-food-category-dominance.

17. For a further analysis of Japanese global strategy, see George S. Yip, "Global Strategy as a Factor in Japanese Success,"*The International Executive,* Vol. 38, No. 1, pp. 145–67, special issue on Japan, January/February 1996, and Yoko Ishikura and George S. Yip, "Chapter 2. Japan—Still Bubbling," in George S. Yip, *Asian Advantage: Key Strategies for Winning in the Asia-Pacific Region (Updated Edition—After the Crisis)* (Cambridge, MA: Perseus Publishing, 2000).

18. Nestlé Press Release, January 5, 2010, http://www.nestle.com.

19. Nestlé Press Release, September 22, 2010, http://www.nestle.com.

20. Bob De Wit and Ron Meyer, *Strategy: Process, Content, Context: An International Perspective,* 4th ed. (Hampshire, United Kingdom: Cengage Learning, 2010).

21. Michael Fitzgerald, "Open Innovation at Nestle," *BNET,* April 30, 2009, http://www.bnet.com/blog/business-books/open-innovation-at-nestle/689.

22. Beth Kowitt, "Nestlé: Tailoring Products to Local Niches," *Fortune,* June 2, 2010, http://money.cnn.com/2010/07/02/news/companies/nestle_refreshes_brand.fortune/.

23. Find information about *Elle* magazine at http://www.hfmus.com/hfmus/media_kits/fashion_beauty_design/elle/about_us.

24. From DuPont's 2007 Annual Report.

25. V. Kasturi Rangan, Rowland T. Moriarty, and Gordon S. Swartz, "Segmenting Customers in Mature Industrial Markets," *Journal of Marketing,* Vol. 56, No. 4, October 1992, pp. 72–82.

26. "Chemical Reaction," *Wall Street Journal,* March 7, 2011, http://online.wsj.com/article/SB10001424052748703580004576180183375640192.html.

27. "Better Living Through Chemurgy," *The Economist,* June 26, 2008, http://www.economist.com/node/11632861.

28. "Chemistry Goes Green," *The Economist,* July 1, 2010, http://www.economist.com/node/16492601.

29. Canon's Corporate Philosophy of Kyosei, http://www.canon.com/about/philosophy/.

30. "Canon U.S.A. Earns #1 Ranking in 2010 Total Copier Market Share," *CNBC,* March 17, 2011, http://www.cnbc.com/id/42129412.

31. Jason Boog, "Barnes & Noble Writes Open Letter to Amazon Affiliates," *Galleycat,* February 14, 2011, http://www.mediabistro.com/galleycat/barnes-noble-writes-open-letter-to-amazon-affiliates_b23292.

32. David B. Montgomery and George S. Yip, "The Challenge of Global Customer Management," *Marketing Management,* October–December 2000.

33. David J. Collis, "Saatchi and Saatchi Company, PLC," Case No. 1-387-170 (Boston, MA: Harvard Business School, revised 4/88).

34. Rupal Parekh, "Euro Replaces Digitas as IBM's Global Digital Agency," *Advertising Age,* November 9, 2009, http://adage.com/article/agency-news/euro-replaces-digitas-ibm-s-global-digital-agency/140401/.

35. Hoag Levins, "IBM's Zany Viral Video Chief," *Advertising Age,* September 21, 2009, http://adage.com/article/video/ibm-s-zany-viral-video-chief/139154/.

36. Data from McKinsey & Company study, "Managing International Retailers," London, 1999.

37. Data from Deloitte study, "Emerging from the Downturn: Global Powers of Retailing 2010," London, 2009.

38. "Spain's Popular Mulls Allianz Unit Sale—Website," *Reuters,* February 17, 2011, http://www.reuters.com/article/2011/02/17/popular-allianz-idUSLDE71G0DC20110217.

39. "*AdvertisingAge* Agency Report 2010," New York, April 26, 2010.

40. Takayuki Amano, Sheila Colgan, and Mika Palosuo, "Reinsurance Industry," unpublished study (Washington, DC: Georgetown Business School, 1989).

41. See John A. Quelch and Edward J. Hoff, "Customizing Global Marketing," *Harvard Business Review,* May–June 1986, pp. 59–68, and Dean M. Peebles, "Don't Write Off Global Advertising:

A Commentary," *International Marketing Review,* Vol. 6, No. 1, 1989, pp. 73–78.

42. Gatignon and Abeele suggest that one test for the transferability of marketing is the extent to which sales response elasticities to marketing expenditures are the same across countries. Thus, if the response of sales to advertising expenditure is similar in two countries, that is a starting point for assuming that the content of the advertising may be transferable. See Hubert Gatignon and Piet Vanden Abeele, "Can You Standardize Marketing Programs Internationally? Cross-Country Determinants of Marketing Mix Effectiveness," Marketing Science Institute Mini-Conference on Global Marketing, Cambridge, MA, May 1990.

43. See George S. Yip, "Gateways to Entry," *Harvard Business Review,* September–October 1982, pp. 85–92.

44. Al Ries, "Social Media Will Usher in Golden Age of Global Branding—If Marketers Get Message Right," *Advertising Age,* January 10, 2011, http://adage.com/article/al-ries/social-media-usher-golden-age-global-branding/148062/.

45. Based on information from Internet World Statistics, which estimates that about 1.5 billion of the nearly 2 billion people who use the Internet speak languages other than English. (*Internet World Stats,* June 30, 2010, http://www.internetworldstats.com/stats7.htm.)

46. See Thomas Hout, Michael E. Porter, and Eileen Rudden, "How Global Companies Win Out," *Harvard Business Review,* September–October 1982, pp. 98–108, and Michael E. Porter, *The Competitive Advantage of Nations* (New York: The Free Press, 1990).

47. See Porter, *The Competitive Advantage of Nations,* who searched 10 countries, including smaller ones like Denmark and Switzerland, for industries in which these 10 countries led.

48. Jim Andrew and Andrew Taylor, "The Geography of Innovation: BCG's List of the World's Most Innovative Countries," *Perspectives,* Boston Consulting Group, December 17, 2010.

49. Brian Bergstein, "World of Ideas," *Technology Review,* March/April 2011.

50. See also Janice McCormick and Nan Stone, "From National Champion to Global Competitor: An Interview with Thomson's Alain Gomez," *Harvard Business Review,* May–June 1990, pp. 127–35.

51. "Audiovox Acquires Thomson CE Business, Including RCA Brand," *Consumer Electronics Daily News,* October 16, 2007, http://www.cedailynews.com/2007/10/audiovox-acquir.html.

52. Marquise R. Cvar, "Case Studies in Global Competition: Patterns of Success and Failure," in Michael E. Porter, Ed., *Competition in Global Industries* (Boston, MA: Harvard Business School Press, 1986), pp. 483–516.

53. Kanoko Matsuyama and Hideki Sagiike, "Terumo's TRI Catheter Sales to Rise 67% in the U.S.," *Bloomberg,* May 26, 2010, http://www.businessweek.com/news/2010-05-26/terumo-s-tri-catheter-sales-to-rise-67-in-the-u-s-update1-.html.

54. See Yum! Brands Web site, http://www.yum.com.

55. "Best Global Brands 2008," *BusinessWeek,* http://www.businessweek.com/interactive_reports/global_brand_2008.html.

56. "India's 100 Most Trusted Brands," *The Economic Times,* August 31, 2010, http://economictimes.indiatimes.com/articleshow/6468721.cms.

57. See Yum! Brands Web site, http://www.yum.com.

58. Cathy A. Enz, "Multibranding Strategy: The Case of Yum! Brands," *Cornell Hotel & Restaurant Administration Quarterly,* February 2005 (access via *Entrepreneur*: http://www.entrepreneur.com/tradejournals/article/128253023.html).

59. Paul Ziobro, "KFC Seeks Secret Recipe for France," *Wall Street Journal,* May 5, 2010, http://online.wsj.com/article/SB10001424052748703866704575223892236926372.html.

60. "Colonel Sanders' Secret Ingredient: China," *Forbes,* December 9, 2010, http://blogs.forbes.com/investor/2010/12/09/colonel-sanders-secret-ingredient-china/.

61. Julie Jargon and Arlene Chang, "Yum Brands Bets on India's Young for Growth," *Wall Street Journal,* December 16, 2009, http://online.wsj.com/article/SB100014240527487045410045746001140586300226.html.

62. Ibid.

63. See Philip Evans and Thomas S. Würster, *Blown to Bits: How the New Economics of Information Transforms Strategy* (Boston, MA: Harvard Business School Press, 1999).

64. Jesús de Juan, Victor Du, David Lee, Sachin Nandgaonkar, and Kevin Waddell, "Global Sourcing in the Postdownturn Era," *Boston Consulting Group,* September 2010.

65. "Global Stretch," *The Economist,* March 10, 2011, http://www.economist.com/node/18333093.

66. Kristin Thoney-Barletta and Lisa Hartman, "Zara Fast Forward Workshop," *Journal of Textile and Apparel, Technology and Management,* Winter 2006, Vol. 5, No. 1, http://www.tx.ncsu.edu/jtatm/volume5issue1/Zara_fashion.htm.

67. Kasra Ferdows, Michael A. Lewis, and Jose A. D. Machuca, "Zara's Secret for Fast Fashion," *HBS Working Knowledge,* February 21, 2005, http://hbswk.hbs.edu/archive/4652.html.

68. Sten Stovall and Christopher Bjork, "Inditex Fashion Formula Hard to Beat," *The Source,* March 17, 2010, http://blogs.wsj.com/source/2010/03/17/inditex-fashion-formula-hard-to-beat/.

69. Christopher Bjork, "Zara Tries a Fast One on the Net," *The Source,* September 22, 2010, http://blogs.wsj.com/source/2010/09/22/zara-tries-a-fast-one-on-the-net/.

70. Tushar Mital, "Zara," Know the Co, January 16, 2009, http://knowtheco.com/index.php?news=20.

71. Janet Adamy, "As Burgers Boom in Russia, McDonald's Touts Discipline," *Wall Street Journal,* October 16, 2007, http://online.wsj.com/article/SB119248482397359814.html.

72. J. E. Frook, "Automotive Extranet Lights Fire Globally," *Internet Week,* special volume, April 20, 1998, p. 1.

73. See Constantinos C. Markides and Norman Berg, "Manufacturing Offshore Is Bad Business," *Harvard Business Review,* September–October 1988, pp. 113–20.

74. James Kanter, "Can 'Made in Europe' Survive?" *New York Times,* April 16, 2005, http://www.nytimes.com/2005/04/15/business/worldbusiness/15iht-wbmade.html.

75. Estimates provided by Gerrit Jeelof, vice-chairman, Board of Management, Philips N.V. See Gerrit Jeelof, "Global Strategies of Philips," *European Management Journal,* Vol. 7, No. 1, 1989, pp. 84–91.

76. Steve Wilhelm, "Boeing Puts Some Certainty on 787 Development Costs," *Puget Sound Business Journal,* August 28, 2009, http://www.bizjournals.com/seattle/stories/2009/08/24/daily55.html.

77. Matthew Dolan, "Ford Targets Rivals as Loss Eases," *Wall Street Journal,* April 25, 2009, http://online.wsj.com/article/SB124056802228652509.html.

78. See also Yves Doz, *Government Control and Multinational Management* (New York: Praeger, 1979), and ———, "Government Policies and Global Industries," in Michael E. Porter, Ed., *Competition in Global Industries* (Boston, MA: Harvard Business School Press, 1986), pp. 225–66. In addition, Spence cites three public sector activities that can protect domestic competitors: blocking access to the domestic market, providing subsidies, and creating spillovers in research and development. See A. Michael Spence, "Industrial Organization and Competitive Advantage in Multinational Industries,"*American Economic Review,* Vol. 74, No. 2, May 1984, pp. 356–60.

79. Jane Ashton, William Kummel, Elizabeth Powell, and Mary Colman St. John, "The Magazine Publishing Industry: A Global Strategy Analysis," unpublished report (Washington, DC: Georgetown Business School, 1989).

80. Russell Adams, "Online Ads Pull Ahead of Newspapers," *Wall Street Journal,* December 20, 2010, http://online.wsj.com/article/SB124056802228652509.html.

81. Susan B. Berg, Richard B. Bruno, Michael J. Derr, R. Scott Handel, and Stephen B. Straske, "The Newsprint Industry: An Analysis of Globalization Potential," unpublished report (Washington, DC: Georgetown University, 1989).

82. Matthew Karnitschnig, Deborah Solomon, Liam Pleven, and Jon E. Hilsenrath, "U.S. to Take Over AIG in $85 Billion Bailout; Central Banks Inject Cash as Credit Dries Up," *Wall Street Journal,* September 16, 2008, http://online.wsj.com/article/SB122156561931242905.html.

83. *Fortune*'s 2010 Global 500 Ranking, http://money.cnn.com/magazines/fortune/global500/2010/.

84. "Signalling Dissent," *The Economist,* March 17, 2011, http://www.economist.com/node/18386151.

85. Based on Joseph B. Treaster, "A Huge Insurance Merger: AXA and UAP in France," *The New York Times,* November 13, 1996, p. C2.

86. Michiyo Nakatmoto, "Changes in Japan's Phone Market Boost Opportunities," *Financial Times,* January 3, 2006, http://www.ft.com/cms/s/0/982f5a38-7bfd-11da-ab8e-0000779e2340.html#axzz1H5ECmgvF.

87. Stephen Bowen, senior vice president, Northern Telecom Limited (Canada).

88. Based on "Not Quite Magic," *The Economist,* February 22, 1997, pp. 67–73.

89. "New Online Remit Enhances Consumer Protection," Advertising Standards Authority, March 1, 2011, http://www.asa.org.uk/Media-Centre/2011/

New-online-remit-enhances-consumer-protection
.aspx.

90. These four concerns are raised by Yves L. Doz, "Government Policies and Global Industries," in Michael E. Porter, Ed., *Competition in Global Industries* (Boston: Harvard Business School Press, 1986). See also Yves L. Doz, *Government Control and Multinational Strategic Management* (New York: Praeger, 1979), and Dennis J. Encarnation and Louis T. Wells, Jr., "Competitive Strategies in Global Industries: A View from Host Governments," in Porter, *Competition in Global Industries.*

91. Study conducted by The MAC Group for *The Cost of Non-Europe,* Basic Findings, Vol. 12, Part B, Commission of the European Community, Brussels, 1988.

92. "Competitiveness of the European Food Industry: An Economic and Legal Perspective," *European Commission,* November 2006.

93. "The Top 500 World Banks," *Thomson Bank Directory,* June–November 1995.

94. Carol J. Loomis, "Citicorp: John Reed's Second Act," *Fortune,* Vol. 133, No. 8, April 29, 1996, pp. 88–98.

95. Tony Munroe and Saeed Azhar, "Retreat from Asia Unlikely for Embattled Citigroup," *New York Times,* October 20, 2008, http://www.nytimes.com/2008/11/20/business/worldbusiness/20iht-citi.1.17992621.html.

96. Kevin Brown, "Citigroup Focuses on SE Asia Growth," *Financial Times,* September 22, 2010, http://www.ft.com/cms/s/0/ad5e982e-c65d-11df-9cda-00144feab49a.html#axzz1H5ECmgvF.

97. For an example of an analysis of the globalization potential of an industry, see George S. Yip and George A. Coundouriotis, "Diagnosing Industry Globalization Potential: The World Chocolate Confectionery Industry," *Planning Review,* January/February 1991, pp. 4–14.

CHAPTER 3

Building Global Market Participation

This chapter presents a new, global-strategy-oriented way of viewing market partici-pation. Instead of selecting country-markets on the basis of stand-alone attractiveness, managers need to consider how participation in a particular country will contribute to globalization benefits and the global competitive position of the business.

Participating in markets outside the home country acts as a lever for both interna-tionalization (the geographic expansion of activities) and globalization (the global inte-gration of strategy). But in the internationalization mode managers select countries based on stand-alone attractiveness. In contrast, when used as a global strategy lever, market participation involves selecting countries on the basis of their potential contribution to globalization benefits and to the global competitive position of the business. The same considerations also apply to determining the level at which to participate—primarily the target market share—and the nature of participation—building a plant, setting up a joint venture, and so on. Managers may, of course, often make market selection deci-sions from a mixture of motives, and many multinational companies have grown that way.[1] The key is to recognize that there is a difference in the two motivations and in their potential consequences.

BASIS FOR GLOBAL EXPANSION

Chapter 2 discussed how industry globalization drivers decide the potential for compa-nies in an industry to use global strategies. But the company itself and its characteristics also affect its potential for globalization. How does a company decide whether it even has a basis for global expansion? It is critical to have one or more of the following:

- A business model that is internationally transferable
- A strong basis of competitive advantage that can be leveraged internationally
- An economy where the company's industry is more developed than those in most other economies

Transferable Business Model

Companies seeking to globalize need a globally transferable business model. Let's first distinguish between a *business model* and a *strategy*. A business model can be viewed as the way in which a company transforms inputs to add value for particular customer groups and includes the way in which it is managed. For example, McDonald's has a very clear business model: It takes relatively low-quality food ingredients, unskilled labor, retail locations, and buildings and—through a very rigorous, standardized process—transforms them into a particular kind of food service experience for mass-market customers. A strategy can be better viewed as the way in which a company changes its business model. And global strategy can be thought of as the way in which a company adapts and globally expands its domestic business model to achieve a global business model.

At its simplest, the most globalizable business models are those that seek to impose the company's logic on the marketplace. The model requires customers to change their behavior rather than the company changing to meet customers' existing behavior. This sounds like the opposite of the marketing concept. But reflection will show that many of the most successful new products and services have changed customer behavior—Xerox copiers, Polaroid cameras, Sony Walkmans, Boeing 747, Apple Macintosh, and McDonald's, as well as Internet services such as Amazon and Google. This kind of model finds international success easy because it minimizes the need to adapt to local conditions and customers. By focusing on the importance of enhancing interpersonal communication in a digital age, the example of Nokia illustrates this very well.

In contrast, business models that depend on adaptation and customization find globalization much more difficult. Three examples from clothes retailing illustrate this point. Italy's Benetton has been successful in global expansion, while Britain's Marks and Spencer has undergone considerable transition. In 2001, the Benetton Group operated in 120 countries, while Marks and Spencer was in the process of closing most of its overseas ventures. Benetton's business model has been to provide fashion clothing that has no distinct national characteristics and to promote it on the basis that wearers become part of Benetton's global community, "The United Colors of Benetton." In such a business model, finding and maintaining the right fashion edge is the difficult part, but globalizing it is easy. Benetton does little local adaptation, even though it allows local stores autonomy in what they order from the company's fixed global ranges. As such, Benetton has maintained its corporate position worldwide without widespread international venture reductions. Based on a similar approach, Spain's Zara clothing stores focus on a globally standardized range that imitates expensive designer labels. By 2001 Zara had expanded to 33 countries, and its parent company, Inditex, went public in the same year, achieving a market capitalization of $10 billion. After a decade, Inditex's market value reached nearly $50 billion to indicate the compelling value provided by Inditex in general and Zara in particular.[5]

By comparison, Marks and Spencer's business model has been to meet the distinct clothing (and grocery) needs of the middle market of Britain. While quality and service are also essential parts of this model, it is adaptation to the special needs of British customers that is the central part of the model. Inherently such a model is far more difficult to export. The company tried and failed to adapt this model to meet the special needs of French customers in France and other European countries. Its purchase of Brooks Brothers, an American company with a similar business model of local adaptation (albeit for a more upscale clientele), created no value as Marks and Spencer could add

Nokia Utilizes a Transferable Business Concept

With the emergence of cellular phones, Nokia was able to create a business model transferrable across Europe and worldwide. By facilitating communication between people with its product offering, Nokia has established itself as a global leader in the telecommunications industry. Even though the company must continue to alter its perspective to remain at the forefront of this dynamic portion of the global economy, Nokia has a long history on which to base its business model.[2]

In 1981, Nokia was able to capitalize on the need for communication by introducing new mobile phone technologies and creating the first ever international cellular network to reach customers in Nordic countries. The network's creation helped Nokia create a boom in the use of mobile phones. By the 1990s, Nokia expanded beyond Europe and into North America, South America, and Asia. Through revolutionizing the use of mobile phones, Nokia was able to expand into new markets and maintain a standardized product across countries and continents. Instead, customers in most parts of the world started changing their own behaviors to accommodate the introduction of mobile phones. In fact, by 1998, Nokia had become the world leader in mobile phones.

A fundamental shift in the marketplace, however, has forced Nokia to reevaluate its core strategy. Even though its customer retention is vastly more competitive than many others in the market, the company must contend with new forms of competitors—mainly computer manufacturers and software developers.[3] Still, as the company is valued at nearly $30 billion, Nokia continues its standing as an integrated telecommunications company.[4] Thus, the company will undoubtedly continue to build on its past experience of facilitating communication.

nothing. As such, this British-focused business model was in serious trouble in 2001. However, after a decade which saw a series of divestitures as well as an emphasis on corporate ethics, the company was able to rebound and maintain competitiveness.[6]

In contrast to Marks and Spencer, the U.S.'s Wal-Mart chain of discount stores continues to be hugely successful in its domestic market. But like Marks and Spencer, Wal-Mart has found great difficulty in international expansion. For example, it took the company a number of years to learn to adapt to the Argentine market. Why the difficulty? The problem lies in the broad scope of both Wal-Mart's and Marks and Spencer's product ranges, inherent in being general merchandise stores. Niche retailers such as Benetton, Zara, and IKEA need to make only minimal adaptations: Foreign customers either like their focused offerings or they do not. Mass retailers need to adapt to *many* aspects of the lives of their foreign customers, a far harder task.

Leverageable Competitive Advantage

Firms usually need an initial competitive advantage that they can leverage into international markets. Recent research shows that for newly internationalizing firms, the initial competitive advantage is the single greatest determinant of international success, outweighing the process used in internationalization.[7]

While there are many different bases of competitive advantage, companies may find it useful to think about six categories of advantage: customer market, products and services, business system or value chain, assets and resources, partners, and scale and scope. Exhibit 3-1 depicts these categories around a hexagon, illustrating the idea that a company can start from any corner of the hexagon but needs eventually to add strength at every point.[8]

EXHIBIT 3-1 The Hexagon of Competitive Advantage

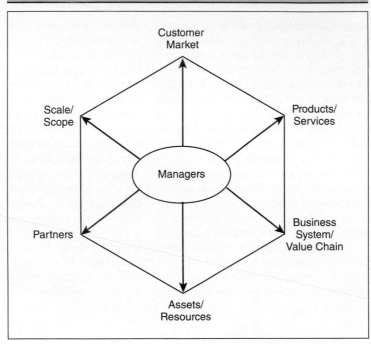

Source: George S. Yip, "Bases of Competitive Advantage," in Stuart Crainer and Des Dearlove, Eds., *Financial Times Handbook of Management,* 2nd ed. (London: Financial Times/Prentice Hall, 2001), pp. 253–263.

CUSTOMER MARKET ADVANTAGE   Being the first company to enter or create a new market, or the first to serve a group of customers, constitutes one of the most common early bases of competitive advantage. Initially, such a company has no competitors at all, which is the ultimate competitive advantage. When Xerox created the market for plain paper photocopiers, it totally dominated this new market, protected by its patents and unique products. Market dominance is a better way of viewing Xerox's competitive advantage at this stage rather than, say, product superiority. There simply were not any competitive products. Many new dot-coms also have this as their first basis of advantage (which also makes clear that once competition comes in, dot-coms need other bases of advantage).

It is also important to note that some successful companies never achieve an advantage in terms of market or customer dominance other than through other bases such as product superiority, which then yield preference by customers in market segments. A quintessential example is Singapore Airlines, which, starting from one of the smallest countries in the world (Singapore even today has a population of fewer than 3 million), has become one of the world's leading airlines and consistently one of the most profitable and most highly rated among business travelers. Lastly, owning a customer market can be a major basis of advantage even if the customers do not like the company. It has been estimated that in Britain the average bank account lasts longer than the average marriage. Do customers love their banks? No. But they stay with them through inertia.

In contrast, some companies have such a good relationship with their customer base that the latter will buy almost anything from them—in the case of Britain's Virgin group, everything from air and train travel to music to investments.

PRODUCT AND SERVICE ADVANTAGE   Having a superior product or service is, of course, a very common basis of competitive advantage. Such superiority can range from minor items to very major ones. Toyota's innovation of a coffee cup holder in its automobile models represents perhaps one of the smallest yet most successful product-based advantages. This product feature, costing less than .01 percent of the total value of the car, gained Toyota many sales in the United States during the brief period before its competitors imitated this product innovation. At the other extreme, product superiority can be so great as to constitute a new category that in turn yields the additional basis of advantage of market dominance. Product superiority can also be built up slowly over time. Both Singapore Airlines and Toyota, starting from initial positions of product inferiority, continually improved their products until they achieved superiority in many aspects of their offerings. Only continuing product superiority has kept Apple Computer alive in its fight against the Microsoft standard, outnumbered more than 10 to 1 in installed base. At the same time, companies may be successful with inferior products, most famously in the case of Microsoft's DOS operating system.

We also have to be careful to understand the underlying reality of an apparent product-based source of competitive advantage. Often, this advantage springs from other bases in the hexagon. For example, the best-selling book *The Discipline of Market Leaders*[9] cites product superiority as a primary reason for Hertz's success in the automobile rental market, such as in its faster, more efficient express service (Gold Service in the United States). But why can Hertz offer a service superior to that of its competitors? Is it because Avis and National do not know how Hertz does it? No. There are no secrets in the car rental business. Nor is it because Avis and National do not have the desire to imitate Hertz. The real barrier to imitation lies in the sixth base of competitive advantage—scale. By virtue of being larger than its competitors, Hertz has more buses circling airports, larger facilities, better computer systems, more cars, and more staff. It is these scale-based advantages that yield the advantage of product superiority and not the other way around. So Hertz is not number one because it offers superior service. It is able to offer superior service because it is number one.[10]

BUSINESS SYSTEM/VALUE-CHAIN ADVANTAGE   The value-adding chain, also known as the business system, comprises all the activities that a business conducts. A typical sequence begins with research and development, runs through production, and finishes with selling, marketing, distribution, and after-sales service. The value chain can provide advantage to a company, first, if the company is superior in one or more elements of the value chain. Many companies have built up superiority in particular elements over long periods of time: 3M's superior research and development capability, Procter & Gamble's (P&G) marketing skills, Dell Computer's distribution system, Sony's innovative designs, Toyota's superiority in production operations, and companies such as American Express in customer service.

An alternative or additional source of value-chain superiority is to coordinate the chain better than competitors.[11] The just-in-time movement can be interpreted as an effort at better coordination of the value chain. The enthusiasm for business process

Technology Increases Value-Chain Superiority

Many businesses find that globalizing the scope of their manufacturing can drive down cost and increase advantage in the marketplace. Often times, responding with cost globalization drivers is only one part of an effective global strategy. In fact, it can sometimes prove difficult to establish information networks that connect together physical networks. Still, these technologically-based components can prove critical to global companies in an increasingly competitive market.

The rise of common technical standards and all-in-one business software allow businesses to convert disparate physical networks into an integrated information network. For instance, emerging developments in Internet-based "cloud computing" software services have transformed the expensive and capital-intensive risks associated with enterprise software. In fact, cloud-based office suites such as Google's Apps for Business allow distant global business hubs to be linked together in a highly secured electronic environment.[12] Lenovo group was able to reduce end-to-end expenses in its supply chain by 17 percent during the 2007–2008 fiscal year.[13] Thus, relocating software solutions to the "cloud" can provide a new level of consolidation in the value chain by reducing organizational expenses yet maintaining the integrity of the data used. Therefore, with the consolidation of information and reduction of operational expenses with this emergent technology-based approach, a company's entire value system stands to gain a global competitive advantage.

reengineering also qualifies as a way of obtaining competitive advantage through reconfiguration of the value chain. Southwest Airlines became the most profitable airline in the United States, partly through redesigning its value chain in order to speed up turnaround. This required the coordination of several elements of the business system: the passengers, the check-in process, the boarding process (boarding not by row numbers but by position in the row—window seats first, then center seats, then aisle seats), and in terms of operations and turnaround service of inbound and outbound flights. A number of Hong Kong hotel chains, such as The Peninsula and the Mandarin Oriental, are renowned for their impeccable service, the best in the world. But this service is merely the tip experienced by guests of an entire business system dedicated to supporting the point of customer interface. As shown in the technology-based examples of Google and Lenovo, one way of viewing the efforts at achieving value-chain superiority is that they all have the same end objectives of delivering products and services better, faster, or cheaper.

ASSETS/RESOURCES ADVANTAGE   Assets—tangible ones, which can range from factories to patents, and intangible ones, such as brand names and reputation—provide another powerful basis for competitive advantage. Perhaps the most interesting aspect of asset-based competitive advantage is that these assets have often been generated in much earlier periods. One of Coca-Cola's primary bases of competitive advantage is the fact that it has the best known brand name in the world (a fact confirmed in numerous surveys). Yet the power of this brand name has been built up over a period of 100 years through continual investment in advertising and other forms of promotion, as well as association with Coca-Cola's high-quality products. (But brands are a particularly tricky form of asset. For example, some analysts value Microsoft's brands at over $60 billion.[14] But people do not buy Microsoft products because of the brand. Without the patents and installed base, Microsoft's brands are worth almost nothing.) Another key basis of

Coca-Cola's advantage is its asset of both its physical distribution system—comprising many company-owned bottling plants and trucks, warehouse, and other distribution facilities—and its less tangible network of franchised bottlers. This asset has also taken decades to build up. So a very high proportion of Coca-Cola's current competitive advantage is based on assets built up by previous generations of managers.

Sometimes an asset-based advantage can come from a complementary asset rather than one that is directly in the value chain of the company. Not least among Singapore Airlines' competitive advantages is the fact that its base, Singapore's Changi airport, is one of the world's finest. This airport is not directly owned by Singapore Airlines but by the government of Singapore, which is also the primary shareholder of Singapore Airlines. Most noteworthy is the fact that while Singapore is one of the world's smallest countries, with a physical area of only 250 square miles, its airport is among the most spacious in the world. The Singaporean government has chosen to make this investment.

For many natural resource companies, assets are often the sole basis of competitive advantage. This is the case for many state-owned energy companies, whose primary competitive advantage is the fact that they have assets in the ground—oil and gas reserves—that can be extracted at lower cost than those of rival countries. Generally, companies operating in the natural resource sector typically owe their competitive advantage to ownership or access to low-cost and/or high-quality sources of raw materials. Like any other basis of competitive advantage, assets and resources can be under-utilized, perhaps more so. The dramatic improvement of Disney's fortunes from the late 1980s to the late 1990s, under Michael Eisner's stewardship, lay primarily in his ability to make much better use of Disney's underexploited assets of film properties, brand names, and characters. Under Eisner's successor Robert Iger, the company has continued this trend of innovative conceptual development. In fact, Disney has expanded its scope to include education in emerging markets to further utilize its brands in a different setting.[15]

PARTNER ADVANTAGE   Having the right partners can also provide a very powerful basis of competitive advantage. Microsoft's true initial basis of competitive advantage was its partnership with IBM. Rover was in serious difficulties until it acquired Honda as a new joint venture partner in the 1980s. Honda was able to help Rover so much that the British company became a valuable property and was able to sell itself to BMW in 1994, much to Honda's chagrin (but perhaps subsequent relief seeing that BMW turned out to be not such a successful partner). Many companies have gone on to surpass their partners. Microsoft's fortunes have certainly prospered much more than those of IBM. Numerous Asian manufacturers have begun as original equipment suppliers to American and European partners, only to overtake them later. The emphasis on strategic alliances illustrates the criticality of having the right partners. Indeed, Caterpillar, the U.S. heavy equipment manufacturer, identifies its ability to create and manage partnerships as one of its critical sources of competitive advantage.

SCALE AND SCOPE ADVANTAGE   Companies can also gain advantage from economies of scale or of scope, economies of scale being the reduction in unit cost with increased production volume, while economies of scope come from sharing costs across multiple products or lines of business. Market share usually drives these economies. Depending on the industry, economies of scale may flatten out at relatively small market shares.

Caterpillar Develops Competitive Advantage with Partners

Supported by its logistics, remanufacturing, and financial services divisions, Caterpillar is able to develop a powerful basis for competitive advantage with partners worldwide.[16] In fact, the company developed partnerships with both Ford Motor Company and SAP to build a management application for its service parts.[17] Both partners were chosen for their unique knowledge of supply chain management, but SAP became a partner based on its understanding of logistics software implementation.[18] The result of this collaboration was a fully integrated order management system which allowed for materials and warehouse capabilities management. Necessary for operations all over the world, the system reduces logistics complications, streamlines order requirements, and responds more quickly to customer needs to make Caterpillar more efficient and effective.

Another example is Caterpillar's partnership with Mitsubishi Heavy Industries. Their collaborative efforts combined to make one of the top producers of construction and mining equipment in Japan. By targeting Asia, Caterpillar's long-standing relationship with Mitsubishi provides an ideal position to capitalize on rapid expansion and development in emerging markets such as China.[19] In fact, the trend toward increased standing in the Asia-Pacific market is evident in Caterpillar's increased sales.[20] Therefore, the partnership strategy Caterpillar has recently forged appears to have lasting momentum. By continuing with this trend, the company should be able to further develop competitive advantage by identifying new customers and findings partners so Caterpillar can deliver value to the marketplace.

Such industries are fragmented ones in which no competitor can dominate the industry or gain a large share, such as many retailing sectors, apparel manufacturing, and the like. Economies of scale and scope, or even just sheer size, can yield many advantages, some of which may not be obvious to the companies themselves or their competitors. This chapter has already referenced the example of Hertz's express service. Other companies recognize that size is perhaps their main advantage. In early 2000, Barclays Bank began an advertising campaign in Britain to stress how "big" the company is, linking bigness to customer benefits such as being able to provide free Internet banking. By inference, Barclays was admitting that it could offer few other advantages. After the onset of the 2007 global financial crisis, the firm was able to relate its size with substance to weather fashionable market trends. Though not a complete break from its traditional message of being "big," the shift indicates Barclays's ability to change its positioning to some degree.

ADDING TO BASES OF ADVANTAGE   While it is important to be superior in some basis of advantage, the real power comes not from being good in one base but from putting together multiple bases of advantage. The truly successful companies are the ones that manage to build on their initial base of advantage, increasing the advantage in that base, while continually adding other bases of advantage.

USING COMPETITIVE ADVANTAGES TO GLOBALIZE   Clearly, the more transferable advantages a company has, and the more dominant these advantages, the easier it is to globalize. Companies with highly dominant positions, such as Microsoft, can globalize very quickly indeed.[21]

EXHIBIT 3-2 The Pyramid of International Competitive Advantage

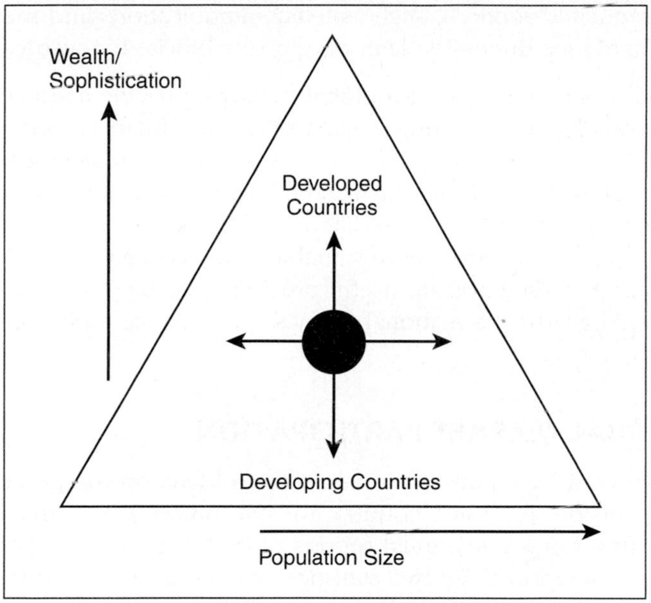

Source: Stephen B. Tallman and George S. Yip, Chapter 12, "Strategy and the Multinational Enterprise," in Thomas Brewer and Alan M. Rugman, Eds., *The Oxford Handbook of International Business* (Oxford, England: Oxford University Press, 2001).

Being from a More Developed Economy

In the case of global expansion, having an advantage need only be relative to each specific country entered. Hence, a firm with weak competitive advantages at home may still have a competitive advantage in foreign markets. This would be particularly the case for firms moving from more developed economies to less developed ones. This effect is illustrated by the "pyramid of international competitive advantage" in Exhibit 3-2. In this pyramid, firms selling "down" to less developed economies (which usually but not always have less demanding markets) find it relatively easy to have a competitive advantage in the entered market. Firms selling "sideways" to economies of similar development need to work a bit to create an advantage, perhaps through local adaptation. Lastly, firms selling "up" to more developed economies have to work really hard to establish a competitive advantage, perhaps through lower prices or by focusing on a market niche.[22]

GLOBAL MARKET PARTICIPATION FOR SERVICE BUSINESSES

Global market participation can often be easier for service businesses:

- Being less visible, they usually provoke fewer trade and investment barriers (an interesting exception being that, despite the North American Free Trade Agreement, Canada prevents U.S. management consultants from entering the market in a substantive way).

- Often having lower minimum efficient scale, service businesses can set up incrementally, incurring less risk, commitment, and competitive retaliation.
- But many regulated services, such as telecommunications and media, find foreign entry very hard (see discussion later on globally blocked industries).

Services that operate as part of a global network provide a special case in global market participation. For network firms—such as airlines, financial services, and logistics companies—highly specific geographic locations may be seen as essential. No financial service firm with global ambitions, for instance, can afford not to have a presence in New York, London, and Tokyo. Travel-related services benefit from wider global market participation: The service becomes more valuable to a customer. Thus, American Express traveler's checks and credit cards are useful precisely because they are widely accepted in most countries. Similarly, international airlines can enhance their appeal as they fly to more destinations.

TYPES OF GLOBAL MARKET PARTICIPATION

The traditional view of being international tends to focus on the percentage of a business's revenues outside the home country and the number of countries in which the business participates. Corporate annual reports of both American and European companies almost invariably report these two statistics. But these two measures are of little use when we take a global strategy view of market participation. Knowing that a concern has 50 percent of its revenues outside the home market is meaningless without knowing the percentage of the worldwide market that is outside the home country. Similarly, being present in 10 countries that include the United States, Japan, and Germany is far more important, in most industries, than being present in 30 countries that exclude these three but include many small, less advanced countries.

To have a global level of market participation requires significant global market share, a reasonable balance between the business's geographic spread and the market's spread, and presence in globally strategic country-markets. Allianz Versicherungs AG, Europe's largest insurance group and headquartered in Germany, has a global strategy of gaining leading market positions in the United States, Europe, and Asia. Allianz built up a strong position in Europe primarily through acquisitions and pursued a similar acquisition strategy in the United States with its 1990 bid for Fireman's Fund, one of the largest insurance companies in the country. This continued with the purchase of PIMCO in 2000.[23] However, success in the United States has been mixed to date.[24] Still, alliances and relationships developed in Asia have been particularly successful for Allianz in India, Indonesia, and Malaysia.[25] As such, the company appears able to sustain its global participation in the near future.

Global Market Share

Achieving high market share in single-country markets has long been a key objective for most managers. The benefits include being able to exploit economies of scale, possessing greater bargaining power with suppliers and distribution channels, and enjoying more ready acceptance by customers. Some researchers have questioned these benefits.[26] But these benefits of high share seem even greater in highly global industries. As in the example of Inbev and Anheuser-Busch, the advantages of high market share can be

Inbev and Anheuser-busch

When Inbev acquired Anheuser-Busch in late 2008, considerable potential was created to enter new markets and increase brand strength for both companies. Anheuser-Busch already had a strong market position in the United States and Canada. Also, it had a presence in China and a stake in Grupo Modelo, manufacturer of the Corona brand beer. On the other hand, Inbev had greater access to the European market, where Anheuser-Busch had previously not been as successful. In fact, Inbev's CEO, Carlos Brito, indicated that the merger of the two companies would make a diversified player in the industry to create a balance between high-growth developing markets and more stable mature markets.

As such, the acquisition allowed the major brands of each company an opportunity to expand into growing markets, competing with local brands and other global brands as well. When discussing the merger, Tom Pirko, president of Bevmark LLC, said, "In a global market, you're going to gain your profits not by sitting tight in the United States in a flat and declining market. You're going to make your money in China and Russia and India and Brazil."[27] Pirko made his point by saying the company needed to market itself in emerging markets to grow and be successful. Since the merger, Anheuser-Busch Inbev has capitalized on its market position and found considerable success in large developing countries.[28] With plans to introduce more of the company's flagship brands in unsaturated markets such as Brazil and Russia, it appears that Anheuser-Busch Inbev has developed a strategy to leverage its many assets and maintain growth.

leveraged across many countries and not just one. If done right, the advantages can be used again and again. A business that takes a global approach to manufacturing—by concentrating production in one or a few countries—in an industry where economies of scale are large can exploit the resultant low-cost advantage in country after country. That strategy worked for Japanese companies in industry after industry. Low-share competitors may be able to resist in individual countries by developing specialized strategies, but that approach is unlikely to be available in the majority of countries.

Global Balance

High global market share is important but not sufficient for global market participation. A global business also needs to have its geographic distribution of revenues in reasonable balance with that of the worldwide market. That is, the business should usually not have most of its revenues concentrated in just a few countries, and its market share in each country should not be too different from its global market share. Global balance is important as a counterpoint to large market share, because the business usually needs to have significant presence in many countries in order to fully benefit from a global strategy. On a country-by-country basis, in some industries it may be better to have a large, significant share in some countries and a small share in others than to have a moderate share level everywhere.[29] But this effect may well be offset by the damaging effect of uneven market share on the ability to operate a global strategy.

An imbalanced level of market participation weakens the use of each of the other four global strategy levers. A business with revenues concentrated in a few businesses will find it difficult to develop global products that have wide appeal. Inevitably, the desires of the few dominant countries will take precedence. While this may be fine in the short term, such a situation makes it more difficult to expand geographically in the future. For the same reasons, and with the same consequences, such a business will find it difficult to develop global marketing programs. A concentrated business may also find it difficult to develop a globalized network of value-adding activities. Ideas for where to locate activities may be biased toward the needs of the dominant countries. In addition, there is usually a strong reluctance to move away from the status quo. Perhaps, most important, *a business with imbalanced market participation will find it difficult to make effective integrated competitive moves*. Because of its weakness in many markets, such a business will have fewer opportunities and leverage points for making preemptive and counterparry moves against competitors. Being aware of global balance can change the perception of competitive threats. A competitor with a large share but limited presence can be less of a threat than a competitor with a smaller share but broader market presence.

Most American companies have a significant imbalance with too great a proportion of revenues in the United States. In effect, it appears that a more balanced participation in the global marketplace is required for American companies to remain competitive.[30] Furthermore, in most industries the U.S. market is growing more slowly than the rest of the world, so that the imbalance has the possibility of growing worse.

Presence in Globally Strategic Markets

Lastly, a large global market share and global balance need to be combined with presence in key or globally strategic country-markets. Perhaps the most important difference between market participation for the sake of internationalization and that for the sake of globalization is the role of *globally strategic countries*. Such countries are important beyond their stand-alone attractiveness. There are several ways in which a country can be globally strategic as a market:

- Large source of revenues or profits
- Home market of global customers
- Home market of global competitors
- Significant market of global competitors
- Major source of industry innovation

LARGE SOURCE OF REVENUES OR PROFITS   The size of a market is, of course, a major factor in country stand-alone attractiveness. Size is also important for global strategic reasons. The larger the market, the more it can contribute to a competitor's global scale economies. Success in a large market can, therefore, drive down worldwide costs for a competitor that shares costs across countries. Success in a large market can also provide funds to subsidize the business in other markets. Active subsidization across countries is a key feature of a global strategy. For these reasons it is critical to succeed in large markets and to deny success in such markets to global rivals. American and European companies suffer a common disadvantage in that Japan, the third major market after Western Europe and the United States, is so much more difficult for foreign competitors than are these other two markets.

In most industries, Japanese competitors enjoy at home a well-protected major source of revenues and profits.[31] Conversely, the size of the U.S. market is rapidly turning from an advantage to a liability for American companies. When they had little global competition, American businesses could use their home scale advantage to muscle their way into overseas markets. But new, tough, and newly tough foreign competitors are irresistibly drawn to the U.S. market—still the largest single-country market in the world.

Markets that are large relative to their region can also be strategically important, particularly where it is impractical to ship between continents. For this reason, Brazil is commonly regarded in many industries as strategically important. This is despite the difficulties of doing business there. Brazil has had some of the highest trade barriers in the world, so that in most industries multinational companies have to set up local production rather than being able to import.

HOME MARKET OF GLOBAL CUSTOMERS   Global competitors need a strong presence in the home market of global (and other major) customers. Relationships can be maintained best at the customer's home. The customer's foreign subsidiaries will also look askance at a supplier that does not have a major share of its home country business. Major customers are also the key source of ideas for innovation. So it is important to have a research and development presence in these customers' home markets. Having demanding customers can also be a key to global success.[32]

HOME MARKET OF GLOBAL COMPETITORS   For many global competitors their home market represents a major source of revenues or profits, although the home market need not be the country in which the parent company has its head office.[33] A business needs a strong presence in these enemy home markets in order both to limit funds flow to its competitors and to act as a hostage for good behavior. One executive characterizes this motivation as an "in your face" strategy. Equally important, the business can learn firsthand how the competitor operates and more closely monitor developments. Being in the home market of major competitors greatly reduces the chance of being surprised. Kodak has now greatly strengthened its position in Japan, but at a far higher cost than if it had committed to Japan much earlier.

The air-conditioning industry provides an example of the dangers of ignoring the Japanese market. Major U.S. producers, who long dominated the world market, made much less of an effort in Japan, now the world's largest market for air conditioning (in revenues). Japanese manufacturers successfully applied a technology invented in the United States—the ductless split (which provides a smaller and quieter central air-conditioning system than conventional methods)—and now seek international markets.[34] A stronger presence in Japan might have alerted American producers to the growing attraction of this technology rather than having to make up lost time now. Recognizing this failing, the U.S.'s Carrier Corporation, the original inventor of air conditioning, formed an alliance in 1999 with Toshiba, a Japanese leader in this and related products. The synergy related to the joint venture has focused both companies' efforts to develop a more environmental-friendly product line for the United States market.[35]

SIGNIFICANT MARKET OF GLOBAL COMPETITORS   Participating in significant markets of global competitors brings benefits similar to those realized from participating in competitors' home markets. Sixt, a dominant car rental company in Germany, has sought to expand into its rivals' major markets. But it faces formidable competitors—such as Hertz, Avis, and Europcar—that will protect their home markets and possibly retaliate in the German market.

MAJOR SOURCE OF INDUSTRY INNOVATION   As discussed in Chapter 2, most industries have a few markets that act as "lead countries" in the sense of being the primary source of innovations. Very often, lead countries are also the home markets of global customers and global competitors. But identifying lead countries further helps the process of making correct decisions on market participation.

GLOBALLY UNIMPORTANT COUNTRIES

Just as less important markets need not be entered as part of a global strategy, the same markets, if already entered or entered for reasons of stand-alone attractiveness, can be left out of the global integration effort. So these countries need not be included when applying the other four global strategy levers of global products and services, global location of activities, global marketing, and global competitive moves, or they can be left to last in the globalization effort. In addition to the factors affecting global strategic importance, other factors should be considered in deciding whether a country should be integrated into the global strategy. These other factors include market size; competitive position; extent of ownership and control of the subsidiary; quality of the subsidiary's management; and the benefits, costs, and risks of change.[36]

BENEFITS OF GLOBAL MARKET PARTICIPATION

A global approach to market participation provides global benefits in each of the categories: cost reduction, improved quality, enhanced customer preference, and competitive leverage.

Cost Reduction

Expanding market participation helps reduce costs by increasing volume for economies of scale. That benefit applies whether the expansion takes place for internationalization or for globalization reasons. But a global strategy approach to selecting the markets into which to expand, and in which to participate, can help make choices that have a more direct effect on the ability to achieve global scale economies.

Improved Quality

Presence in lead countries, and exposure to their demanding customers and innovative competitors, can help a business improve the quality of its products. But a company reaps such benefits only if it is willing to learn from these countries. In general, Japanese companies have been much better at applying such lessons than American and European companies.

Enhanced Customer Preference

As in the case of McCann-Erickson serving the Coca-Cola account, global market participation can enhance customer preference through global availability, global service-ability, and global recognition. The greater the percentage of purchases accounted for by global customers (whether organizations or consumers), the more benefits arise from global market participation. With the rise of global account management programs to serve global customers (discussed in Chapter 6), suppliers are finding it more necessary to participate in markets that are important to their global accounts. The supplier may not find a particular country profitable on a stand-alone basis but needs to be there to support the total global account.

Competitive Leverage

A global strategy approach to market participation can increase competitive leverage in the various ways already described. In summary, these gains include the advantages of earlier entry into key markets, providing more sites for attack and counterattack, and creating hostages for good behavior. If choices need to be made among countries for participation, an important consideration is the choice among countries where global competitors are present and where they are not.

A global presence also helps guard against complacency and gives the ability to retaliate against competitors in their home markets, as mentioned in Chapter 1. For example, the strength of the Kellogg Company in global markets for ready-to-eat cereals has been a major reason why large foreign competitors such as Nestlé have a limited presence in the U.S. cereal market.[37] Indeed, Kellogg's archrival, General Mills, has had to resort to establishing a partnership (Cereal Partners Worldwide) in Europe with Nestlé, which will manufacture and market General Mills' products.[38]

DRAWBACKS OF GLOBAL MARKET PARTICIPATION

A global approach to market participation also has the clear drawback of an earlier or greater commitment to a market than warranted on its own merits. In addition, the more the business is managed on a globally integrated basis across many geographic markets, the more coordination costs will be incurred. The cost of coordinating across countries depends in part on the differences and barriers between the countries. Using Profit Impact of Market Strategy (PIMS) data, it was found that continental-scale businesses in Europe performed financially worse than national-scale businesses in 1972–1987, that is, before the 1992 creation of the single European market would reduce barriers. This study also found that, in the United States by contrast, where barriers and differences between regions are much less than in Europe, continental-scale businesses performed better than regional-scale businesses. Other drawbacks arise from the crossing of national frontiers and the loss of customer focus.[39] Still, with the emergence of the European Union and the Euro zone, the costs related to coordination across national boundaries have been reduced considerably throughout Europe.

Coordination Costs

Expansion in geographic scope across national boundaries is particularly likely to increase coordination costs. The simple need to set up separate legal entities much of the time provides one major source of additional complexity. Furthermore, the legal entity usually requires some management structure to be responsible for it. Thus, a multicountry business will typically require more layers of management than a national business covering the same geographic size of territory. Other sources of increased coordination cost include international differences in technical standards, language, culture, and operating practices.[40]

Crossing National Frontiers

A business that operates across national frontiers incurs trade barrier costs, transportation costs, and inventory costs. Tariff and nontariff trade barriers hurt performance by reducing sales and increasing costs. Transportation is slower and more costly because of border checks. Also, the combination of trade barriers and transportation difficulties may require a multicountry business to maintain more inventory relative to sales than a single-country business.

Losing Customer Focus

Multicountry businesses are also less likely to be able to customize for buyer needs than single-country businesses. A multicountry business may have to offer many more product versions or else provide lesser customer satisfaction than single-country competitors. Offering more products incurs more cost, while providing less customer satisfaction hurts sales.

GLOBALLY BLOCKED INDUSTRIES

In some industries, government barriers prevent direct participation in foreign markets. In particular, regulated industries allow only limited internationalization, such as in sensitive industries like defense, where home governments discourage the overseas relocation of critical activities; or in industries where the minimum efficient scale of operations, particularly production, is so great that concentration is best. Typical companies and industries are British Aerospace and Northrop Grumman in their defense-related businesses, British Telecom and other national telecom service operators, most airline companies, most utility operators, most law firms, and many media companies.

For internationally blocked industries, there are three main paths for global expansion. First, they can make acquisitions of foreign participants in the same industry, if allowed. But there are severe restrictions in many industries on foreign ownership—including airlines, defense, and media. Rupert Murdoch had to become a U.S. citizen in order to be able to buy U.S. radio and television companies. Second, they can form international strategic alliances. As indicated in the recent merger with Iberia Airlines, British Airways continues to build international alliances that can operate as seamlessly as will be allowed by national regulators.[41] Its global One World alliance (co-led with American Airlines), the Star Alliance (spearheaded by the U.S. United Airlines), and the pan-European Miles & More alliance[42] all seek to achieve in alliance mode what their members are not allowed to do as national air carriers. Third, companies in blocked industries can hire out their expertise to foreign partners or customers, or globalize in unrestricted activities. For example, Singapore Airlines has many training and support contracts with other carriers and also operates globally some specialized airline-related businesses, such as catering. By developing a competitive advantage based on in-flight service in its own company-wide operations, Singapore Airlines has been able to leverage its distinct capabilities in particular areas of the industry. After its ground and cabin services subsidiary SATS was divested, the spinoff company expanded its operations to strengthen its position in Asia through the acquisition of airline caterer TFK from Japan Airlines.[43]

THE SPECIAL CASE OF JOINT VENTURES

International joint ventures represent a special case in market participation.[44] They provide a rapid way of expanding the geographic scope of a business. Managers need to beware, however, of thinking that setting up a joint venture in a country means that market is covered and can be counted as part of a business's global presence. Whether joint ventures represent genuine market participation depends on how the venture is set up and on how the partners behave. Strategic success in global joint ventures may depend more on how partners behave than on how the venture is set up.[45] Let's look at one situation. An American multinational company, "AMSUPP," had very strong market positions in an industrial supplies business in all major countries except Japan. There they had set up a joint venture with the leading Japanese company in the industry, "NIPPONSUPP." The venture gave AMSUPP a 45 percent ownership in return for technology transfer as well as capital investment. In discussing global coverage and global market share, the AMSUPP managers included Japan in their calculations. With Japan, AMSUPP's global market participation looked very complete. Japan's inclusion was particularly important because, using the criteria discussed earlier in this chapter, the AMSUPP managers identified Japan as the most globally strategic country, even more than the United States. Unfortunately, the way in which the venture was set up and the way in which the AMSUPP managers operated really negated the possibility of genuine participation by AMSUPP.

First, AMSUPP owned a share only of the manufacturing subsidiary of NIPPONSUPP and not a share of the parent company, which was responsible for marketing and sales. AMSUPP, therefore, had no legal right of access to NIPPONSUPP's markets and customers. Second, while NIPPONSUPP had sent marketing representatives to the United States to learn from AMSUPP about the American market, AMSUPP had not done the same in Japan. Many American companies have found that in joint ventures with Japanese companies, the latter have gained far more access to their American partners' knowledge than have the former to their Japanese partners' knowledge. In effect, AMSUPP did not participate in the Japanese market in any strategic sense: They had merely a financial investment and not a very profitable one either. When the AMSUPP managers understood their problem and tried to change it, they found that they were in the proverbial position of riding a tiger: They could not get off for risk of being eaten. In this case, if AMSUPP ended the joint venture, they would lose all their business in Japan. Worse, they had created the tiger themselves by setting up NIPPONSUPP with the best technology. This, combined with NIPPONSUPP's manufacturing skills, resulted in NIPPONSUPP's products being of higher quality than those manufactured by AMSUPP. AMSUPP now had to maintain the relationship in order to prevent NIPPONSUPP from becoming a fearsome global competitor. So, joint ventures and alliances help much more in strengthening the core strategy and the internationalization strategy than the globalization strategy.

DIFFERING STRATEGIC ROLES FOR EACH COUNTRY

A global strategy approach to market participation also means that different countries should have different roles within the total business. The collection of country-businesses should be viewed as a strategic portfolio rather than as a passive one. The Boston Consulting Group (BCG) popularized the use of cross-subsidization of businesses

EXHIBIT 3-3 Business-Growth/Competitive-Strength Matrix[1,2,3]

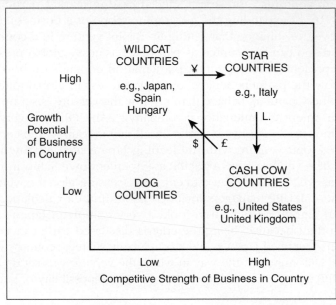

[1]Adapted from the Boston Consulting Group's growth share matrix.
[2]Arrows indicate desired direction of cash flow.
[3]Countries are for illustration only.

within a corporate portfolio. The same approach can be applied to countries in global strategy. Typically, the home country needs to subsidize markets that are newer to the business. That contrasts with what has been a common mindset in companies dominated by the home business. Such companies often treat international markets opportunistically as ways to balance capacity utilization.

Business-Growth/Competitive-Strength Matrix

A comprehensive way of allocating country roles is to use an adaptation of the BCG matrix.[46] In Exhibit 3-3, the horizontal axis uses competitive strength (which includes market share) instead of BCG's relative market share (and is reversed in direction from the BCG matrix), and the vertical axis uses growth potential of the business instead of BCG's industry growth rate. In this business-growth/competitive-strength matrix, "cash cow" countries provide funds for investment in "wildcat" countries that may become future "star" countries. For a typical U.S.-based business, the cash cow countries might include the United States and the United Kingdom; the star countries might include Italy; and the wildcat countries might include Japan, Spain, and Hungary.

Global Strategic Importance/Competitive-Strength Matrix

Another important way of allocating roles to countries is to take a competitive approach based on the global strategic importance of each country. The country strategic importance/competitive-strength matrix in Exhibit 3-4 keeps the same horizontal dimension as Exhibit 3-3 but uses as the vertical axis the global strategic importance of each country.

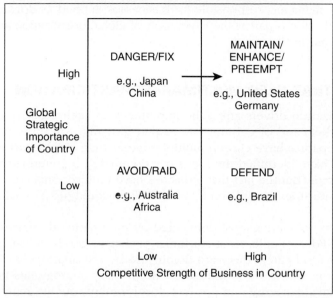

EXHIBIT 3-4 Country Strategic Importance/ Competitive-Strength Matrix[1]

[1]Countries are for illustration only.

Countries in each cell of the matrix have a different competitive prescription. *Maintaining* and *enhancing* the business's position in countries that are of high global strategic importance, and where the business is strong (upper right cell), must be viewed as a very high priority. It may also be important to *preempt* possible competitive threats. For a typical U.S.-based business, countries in this cell might include the United States and Germany. The top left cell, where countries have high global strategic importance but the business has a weak competitive position, presents a *danger* area that managers need to *fix*. For many, perhaps most American (and European) businesses today, Japan and China loom large in this cell. As the arrow indicates, the business should seek to move itself in Japan or China to the upper right cell. The lower right cell represents countries with low global strategic importance but where the business has high competitive strength. The business should *defend* its position in these countries, but not at exorbitant cost. For a typical American business, many Latin American countries might today be in this cell. Lastly, the lower left cell indicates countries that have low global strategic importance and where the business has low competitive strength. These countries should probably be treated opportunistically. Managers should *avoid* them or *raid* them for short-term profits. For many American businesses, countries like Australia might fall in this cell.[47]

Implementation Issues

In using both matrices shown, attention should be paid to likely changes over time as country-markets evolve. Users may also want to use refinements such as placing businesses in positions that straddle two cells or designating likely or planned directions of movement. Another very important consideration is the organizational and political aspects of designating portfolio roles to countries. The corporate portfolio approach came to some grief in the 1980s because of both conceptual flaws and the demotivating effects it had on managers responsible for businesses dubbed as dogs or cash cows.[48] The issue of motivation is part of the larger topic of global organization and management that will be covered in Chapter 8.

INDUSTRIES THAT NEED MULTIMARKET PARTICIPATION

Industry globalization drivers affect the importance in each industry of participating in multiple markets and of defining the market globally. Are there particular industries where companies have chosen multiple- rather than single-market participation? Various studies have identified the industries dominated by multinational rather than national companies. But the fact that industries have multinational companies does not mean that the industries are inherently global. They could just as easily be inherently multilocal.

Some of the industries most dominated by multinational companies have been very multilocal. For example, most consumer packaged goods industries—detergents, toiletries, many food categories—are dominated by multinationals—Unilever, P&G, Nestlé, and so on. But in these industries the primary strategy has been to transfer the multinational's expertise—in product development, quality manufacturing, and marketing—but then to manage each country on a more or less stand-alone basis. But, as cited elsewhere in this book, even in these industries companies have taken a more global approach.

GUIDELINES FOR BUILDING GLOBAL MARKET PARTICIPATION

Participating in the right countries and at the right level provides the foundation on which a successful total global strategy needs to be built. The following guidelines summarize the global, rather than multilocal, approach to building market participation:

- Managers need to select countries for entry and investment on the basis of global strategic importance as well as of stand-alone attractiveness.
- The most strategic countries can often be the most expensive ones in which to build up a significant market presence.
- Managers should particularly worry about the home countries of major global competitors or *potential* global competitors.
- Managers need to evaluate multiple, sometimes conflicting, criteria in identifying globally strategic markets. So selecting the markets in which to participate is somewhat more complicated than using a simple rule of thumb like "be in the 'triad' markets of the United States, Europe, and Japan."
- Different countries can play different strategic roles as part of the total global strategy.
- Alliances and joint ventures can provide a quicker and easier way to build global market participation, but also weaken the potential for a fully integrated global strategy.

Discussion and Research Questions

1. What are the most important countries in which a global business should participate today, and why? What will this list of countries look like in 5 years' time? What will it look like in 10 years' time?
2. How should a company select countries for market participation?
3. Compare and contrast the "multilocal" and "global" approaches to market participation.
4. What priorities should be assigned by a multinational technology company to North America, Latin America, Western Europe, Eastern Europe, the Middle East, Japan, East Asia, and other regions? How would your answer differ for other types of companies? How would your answer differ based on the home country of the company in question?
5. What is different about global market participation for service businesses?

Notes

1. The literature on foreign direct investment (FDI) provides extensive treatment of companies' motivations for internationalization. See, for example, Peter J. Buckley and Mark Casson, *The Future of the Multinational Enterprise* (New York: Holmes and Meier Publishers, 1976), Alan M. Rugman, *International Diversification and the Multinational Enterprise* (Lexington, MA: Lexington Books, D. C. Heath, 1979); Peter J. Buckley, *The Theory of the Multinational Enterprise* (Uppsala, Sweden: Acta Universitatis Upsaliensis, *Studia Oeconomiae Negotiorum* 26, Uppsala, Sweden, 1987); and John H. Dunning, "The Eclectic Paradigm of International Production: A Restatement and Some Possible Extensions," *Journal of International Business Studies,* Spring 1988.
2. Nokia company Web site, "Story of Nokia," http://www.nokia.com/A4303001.
3. Lars Klemming and Diana ben-Aaron, "Nokia's Business Model Changes as New Rivals Emerge," *Bloomberg,* April 23, 2009, http://www.bloomberg.com/apps/news?pid=newsarchive&sid=aBx4tHh5mCBw.
4. Interbrand's Best Global Brands 2010, http://www.interbrand.com/en/best-global-brands/best-global-brands-2008/best-global-brands-2010.aspx.
5. "Inditext Founder Amancio Ortega Names Isla Chairman," El País, January 10, 2011, http://www.elpais.com/articulo/english/Inditex/founder/Amancio/Ortega/names/current/CEO/Pablo/Isla/chairman/elpepueng/20110110elpeng_2/Ten.
6. "M&S Set to Launch Fairtrade Range," *BBC News,* January 30, 2006, http://news.bbc.co.uk/2/hi/business/4660410.stm.
7. George S. Yip, Javier B. Gomez, and Joseph Monti, "Role of the Internationalization Process in the Performance of Newly Internationalizing Firms," *Journal of International Marketing,* Vol. 8, No. 3, 2000, pp. 10–35.
8. This section is based on George S. Yip, "Bases of Competitive Advantage," in Stuart Crainer and Des Dearlove, Eds., *Financial Times Handbook of Management,* 2nd ed. (London: Financial Times/Prentice Hall, 2001), pp. 253–63.
9. Michael Treacy and Frederick Wiersema, *The Discipline of Market Leaders* (Reading, MA: Addison-Wesley, 1995).
10. Hertz is now only the second largest car rental company in the United States, behind Enterprise rent-a-car, but it is still the largest for business and vacation rentals, as Enterprise focuses on accident replacement rentals.
11. See Michael E. Porter, *Competitive Advantage* (New York: The Free Press, 1985), and Michael E. Porter, "What Is Strategy?" *Harvard Business Review,* November–December 1996.
12. Michal Lev-Ram, "Google Enterprise Chief: Data Is Safer on Our Cloud Than Your PC," *Fortune,* March 10, 2011, http://tech.fortune.cnn.com/2011/03/10/google-enterprise-chief-data-is-safer-on-our-cloud-than-your-pc/.
13. See Lenovo 2007/2008 Annual Report, http://www.pc.ibm.com/ww/lenovo/2008annualpopup.html.
14. Interbrand's Best Global Brands 2010, http://www.interbrand.com/en/best-global-brands/best-global-brands-2008/best-global-brands-2010.aspx.

15. James T Areddy and Peter Sanders, "Chinese Learn English the Disney Way," *Wall Street Journal,* April 20, 2009, http://online.wsj.com/article/SB124017964526732863.html.

16. "Cat Sinks Its Claws Into Services," *Businessweek,* December 5, 2005, http://www.businessweek.com/magazine/content/05_49/b3962096.htm.

17. Information from Cat Logistics Web site. "SAP-Cat Logistics Success Story," http://logistics.cat.com/cda/components/fullArticle?m=115228&x=7&id=394024.

18. Marc L. Songini, "Ford, Caterpillar Team with SAP on Supply Chain Project," *Computerworld,* August 5, 2002.

19. Miriam Marcus, "Caterpillar Tilts Toward China," *Forbes,* March 26, 2008, http://www.forbes.com/2008/03/26/caterpillar-mitsubishi-china-markets-equity-cx_mlm_0326markets19.html.

20. Information from Caterpillar Annual Report 2007.

21. For a discussion of how newer companies are globalizing quickly, see Harry Korine, "Fresenius AG: High Speed Globalization,"*Business Strategy Review,* Vol. 11, No. 2, Summer 2000, pp. 47–57.

22. See also Stephen B. Tallman and George S. Yip, Chapter 12, "Strategy and the Multinational Enterprise," in Thomas Brewer and Alan M. Rugman, Eds., *Oxford Handbook of International Business* (Oxford, England: Oxford University Press, 2001).

23. "PIMCO: A 'Quantum Leap' for Allianz," *Businessweek,* January 24, 2000.

24. Nick Elliott, "Bribery Looms as High Priority for New Compliance Officers," *Wall Street Journal,* December 23, 2010, http://blogs.wsj.com/privateequity/2010/12/23/bribery-looms-as-high-priority-for-new-compliance-officers/.

25. Gregory J. Millman, "Insurance in Asia: Interview with Allianz's Heinz Dollberg," *The Source,* March 3, 2010, insurance-in-asia-interview-with-allianzs-heinz-dollberg.

26. There is significant controversy in the academic literature about the direction of causation between market share and profitability, and some even question whether there is a positive association. The key literature on this topic includes Robert D. Buzzell, Bradley T. Gale, and R. G. M. Sultan, "Market Share—A Key to Profitability," *Harvard Business Review,* January–February 1975, pp. 97–106; Richard P. Rumelt and Robin Wensley, "In Search of the Market Share Effect," *Proceedings, Academy of Management Annual Meeting,* pp. 2–6, 1981; Robert Jacobson and David A. Aaker, "Is Market Share All That It's Cracked Up to Be?" *Journal of Marketing,* Vol. 49, No. 4, Fall 1985, pp. 11–22; John E. Prescott, A. K. Kohli, and N. Venkatraman, "The Market Share—Profitability Relationship: An Empirical Assessment of Major Assertions and Contradictions," *Strategic Management Journal,* Vol. 7, 1986, pp. 377–94; Robert D. Buzzell and Bradley T. Gale, *The PIMS Principles: Linking Strategy to Performance* (New York: Free Press, 1987); and Robert Jacobson, "Distinguishing Among Competing Theories of the Market Share Effect,"*Journal of Marketing,* Vol. 52, No. 4, October 1988, pp. 68–80.

27. Sarah Theodore, "Beer Has Big Changes on Tap," Beverage Industry Magazine, September 15, 2008, http://www.bevindustry.com/Articles/Cover_Story/BNP_GUID_9-5-2006_A_10000000000000427113.

28. John W. Miller, "Emerging Markets Give a Boost to Anheuser," *Wall Street Journal,* November 3, 2010, http://online.wsj.com/article/SB10001424052748704462704575591573400416184.html.

29. See, for example, Porter's ideas about the disadvantages of being "stuck in the middle": Michael E. Porter, *Competitive Strategy: Techniques for Analyzing Industries and Competitors* (New York: The Free Press, 1980).

30. Abbey Klaassen, "Fareed Zakaria Sees Role for Mad Ave in U.S.'s Growth, If Country Can Fix Its Issues," *AdvertisingAge,* March 8, 2011, http://adage.com/article/special-report-4as-conference/fareed-zakaria-sees-role-madison-avenue-u-s-s-growth/149286/.

31. Yoffie and Milner argue that, contrary to classical trade theory, preserving access to large markets can justify government intervention in trade, when competitors practice protectionism in industries characterized by large economies of scale, steep learning curves, or sizable R&D requirements. See David B. Yoffie and Helen V. Milner, "An Alternative to Free Trade or Protectionism: Why Corporations Seek Strategic Trade Policy," *California Management Review,* Summer 1989, pp. 111–31.

32. See Michael E. Porter, *The Competitive Advantage of Nations* (New York: The Free Press, 1990).

33. Ibid.

34. Todd Vogel and Chris Perry, "How Japan Is Beating the Others Cold," *Business Week,* September 3, 1990, p. 79.

35. Marcel Michelson, "Interview: Toshiba Carrier to Sell Japanese Aircons in U.S.," *Reuters,* February 9, 2010, http://in.reuters.com/article/2010/02/09/idINIndia-46019420100209.

36. See also Pradeep A. Rau and John F. Preble, "Standardization of Marketing Strategy by Multinationals," *International Marketing Review,* Autumn 1987, pp. 18–28.

37. Kasra Ferdows et al., *The Internationalization of U.S. Manufacturing: Causes and Consequences* (Washington, DC: National Academy Press, 1990), p. 13.

38. This partnership was announced in 1991.

39. See George S. Yip, "A Performance Comparison of Continental and National Businesses in Europe," *International Marketing Review,* Vol. 8, No. 2, 1991, pp. 31–39.

40. Hofstede's classic study has highlighted the major differences in culture within one multinational corporation. See Geert Hofstede, *Culture's Consequences: International Differences in Work Related Values* (Beverly Hills, CA: Sage Publications, 1984).

41. See "British Airways Trades for Last Time Ahead of Iberia Merger," *The Guardian,* January 20, 2011, http://www.guardian.co.uk/business/2011/jan/20/british-airways-trades-last-time-merger.

42. Though affiliated with the Star Alliance, Miles & More's two flagship members are Lufthansa and Austrian Airlines Group.

43. "SATS to Buy Stake in TFC," *The Straits Times,* November 29, 2010, http://www.straitstimes.com/BreakingNews/Money/Story/STIStory_608584.html.

44. Joint ventures are a very large topic in their own right. See, among others, Larry G. Franko, *Joint Venture Survival in Multinational Corporations* (New York: Praeger, 1971); Kathryn R. Harrigan, *Strategies for Joint Ventures* (Lexington, MA: Lexington Books, 1985); ———, *Managing for Joint Venture Success* (Lexington, MA: Lexington Books, 1986); and Joseph L. Badaracco, *The Knowledge Link* (Boston, MA: Harvard Business School Press, 1991). See also Michael E. Porter and Mark Fuller, "Coalitions and Global Strategy" and Pankaj Ghemawat, Michael E. Porter, and Richard E. Rawlinson, "Patterns of International Coalition Activity" in Michael E. Porter, Ed., *Competition in Global Industries* (Boston, MA: Harvard Business School Press, 1986). See also Michael Y. Yoshino and U. Srinivasa Rangan, *Strategic Alliances: An Entrepreneurial Approach to Globalization* (Boston, MA: Harvard Business School Press, 1995); Paul Beamish and Peter Killing, Eds., *Cooperative Strategies* (Lanham, MD: Lexington Books 1997).

45. See Gary Hamel, Yves L. Doz, and C. K. Prahalad, "Collaborate with Your Competitors and Win," *Harvard Business Review,* January–February 1989, pp. 133–39.

46. See also Jean-Claude Larréché, "The International Product-Market Portfolio," in Jean-Claude Larréché and Edward E. Strong, Eds., *Readings in Marketing Strategy* (Palo Alto, CA: The Scientific Press, 1980).

47. A key challenge for governments in such countries is to increase the global strategic importance of their markets.

48. See Philippe Haspeslagh, "Portfolio Planning: Uses and Limits," *Harvard Business Review,* January–February 1982, pp. 58–73, and Richard G. Hamermesh, *Making Strategy Work: How Senior Managers Produce Results* (New York: John Wiley & Sons, 1986).

CHAPTER 4

Designing Global Products and Services

Developing and maintaining global products and services constitutes the second global strategy lever. Globally standardized products or "global products" are, perhaps, the one feature most commonly identified with global strategy. However, *the idea of a fully standardized global product that is identical all over the world is a near myth that has caused great confusion.* Such products are not very realistic and extremely hard to attain, like an "edible Walkman"—the dream of some multinational food companies.[1] Instead, standardization occurs along a continuum, from very customized products (e.g., specialty foods) to very standardized products (e.g., certain Sony products). Instead of standardizing the complete product, a better approach is to reap the benefits of global products (or services) by standardizing the core product or large parts of it while customizing peripheral or other parts (Exhibit 4-1). For example, many of Sony's consumer electronic products are primarily standardized except for the parts that meet national electrical standards.

Recent developments in the passenger automobile industry provide an excellent example of the wide range of global standardization, both between companies and between model lines within a company. At one end, both Mercedes and Honda, for example, sell products that are highly standardized globally. At the other end, General Motors (GM) historically has had little in common between its North American and European product offerings, although that is now changing with the rapid restructuring and developments within GM. Furthermore, all of the automotive manufacturers are striving to increase their level of standardization. Ford does this in part by assigning responsibility to different parts of the company in developing major portions of a new car for world markets. Most major automobile manufacturers have also cut the number of suppliers used for the parts in a car to about a third of what it used to be previously (i.e., comparing the 2000s with the 2010s). Mazda, in Japan, of which Ford owns a small share of 3.0 percent, has the responsibility for small cars, Ford in Europe for medium-sized cars, and Ford in North America for larger cars. Ford's link to Mazda is unique. While Ford's ownership in Mazda has been reduced significantly, from roughly a third of the company to just a

EXHIBIT 4-1 The Ideal Global Product

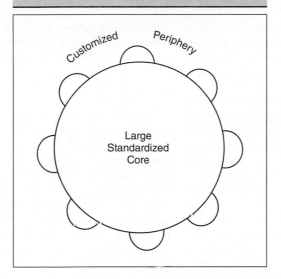

few percentage points, both companies have agreed to continue their strategic partnership which spans 30 years with a focus on joint ventures, joint projects, and exchange of technology information.

In passenger automobiles product standardization comes primarily in the "platform" (underbody, or chassis, of a car and suspensions with the axles) and to a lesser extent the engine. Developing the platform can account for 30 percent of the total development cost of a new vehicle. As such, automobile companies hardly ever design different platforms for different countries but may use different bodies on standardized platforms.

Honda's Adjustable-Width Platform

To solve the car platform problem, Honda developed in the late 1990s and early 2000s the world's first adjustable-width automobile platform.[2] The platform, developed over a three-year period by Honda's engineers, allowed three distinct Accords that cost 20 percent less to bring to market than the single Accord developed in 1994. Honda's strategy in developing this global platform differed from the larger automakers that budget much higher research and development expenditures. Honda executives challenged its engineers to come up with different designs for each region while working on a very small budget. A single frame was the only solution, and engineers developed a way to vary the platform's width by using adjustable brackets. The brackets allowed Honda to cheaply and easily push the car's wheels together or apart. The innovations have allowed Honda to inexpensively and without difficulty customize and design products for each region around the world. In Europe, the Accord has a short, narrow body geared to handle tiny streets; in the United States, the body was stretched to allow for a roomier interior that caters to the family midsized market. This flexibility might give the Honda Accord the distinction of being the first truly global car, defined as the single car that can satisfy the masses worldwide.

Toyota's Flexible Manufacturing

Faster new product development methods coupled with flexible manufacturing have also allowed manufacturers to develop and produce many more models than before, making it more possible to customize for local markets while enjoying global scale economies. So, for example, Toyota, which used to field fewer passenger car models than its American rivals, by 1990 offered more models than Ford (59 versus 49). But Toyota developed and made these 59 models from just 22 basic designs. So the company still benefits from focus on a relatively small number of core products. The smaller number of core products became a true benefit for Toyota in the late 2000s when most automobile manufacturers saw a downturn in their operations and sales, mainly as a function of the downturn in the economic climate in the world. Improvement in design and development methods, particularly in the use of overlapping rather than consecutive stages of development, allowed Toyota and other Japanese manufacturers to drastically shorten the time from drawing board to market.[3] At the same time, the scale (i.e., volume of production) needed by Toyota to meet market demand caught up with the company in the late 2000s, when production quality and oversight affected its automobile outputs and sales. At the same time, flexible manufacturing, including the use of just-in-time inventory management, has allowed Toyota to relatively efficiently produce the large number of models put out by the development process. In summary, Toyota now seems to be able to benefit from both the global benefits of product and production focus and the local benefits of product proliferation, but it still needs to focus on quality controls with the much larger volume now produced than previously.

Volkswagen's Overcustomization

Volkswagen's experience as the first foreign manufacturer to locate in the United States provided a poignant story of the risks of not standardizing enough, that is, customizing *too much* for local tastes. Volkswagen had set a target of increasing its U.S. market share from 2 to 5 percent by targeting the 60 percent of buyers who normally considered domestic models only. So Volkswagen adapted its products to American tastes by softening the suspension and the seats, placing carpeting instead of map pockets on the insides of the doors, and color coordinating the interiors to liven up the standard gray Volkswagen interiors. The result was disastrous. Subsequent market research showed that instead of attracting domestic-loyalists, the changes merely drove away import-loyalists! Volkswagen has taken this lesson very much to heart and today insists on retaining the special German and Volkswagen characteristics whenever localization to suit different market conditions is undertaken.

For example, the Ford Fusion appears to be a somewhat different car from the Mazda 6 sedan, but both use the same platform. Interestingly, if you park a Ford Fusion next to a Mazda 6, very little would indicate that these automobiles are related. The Ford is even slightly larger than the Mazda 6.

Businesses can standardize the worldwide *mix* of products as well as the *content* of a product. A globally standardized product mix means that the business sells the same range or list of models around the world. In contrast, global content standardization involves the extent to which individual product items or models are the same around the world. For example, candy companies like M&M Mars try to sell pretty much the same range of products around the world, even though the products themselves vary in content to allow for differences in tastes.

Fiat's Third-World Global Car

Fiat used its Brazilian market as a base for designing a global car, the Palio, for poorer countries.[4] From its design to its manufacturing, the Palio was different from Fiat's European cars. Utilizing an experienced staff who understood the necessary adaptations to meet the demands of Brazilian roads and tastes, Fiat produced a car tailored to local tastes. For example, the Palio was bigger and stronger than its European counterpart.

These features attracted consumers by handling better on the rough interior roads in Brazil and by serving as the sole family car for many Brazilian buyers. Now Fiat is seeking to extend the Palio to other third-world markets, such as India and China. The Palio is produced in Argentina, Brazil, China, India, South Africa, and Turkey. In addition, the Palio is also built under licence in North Korea, named the Pyonghwa Hwiparam.

It can be helpful to map mix standardization against content standardization for the business and its competitors. Exhibit 4-2 illustrates a situation in an American chemical additives business. The business had long pursued a product line strategy of customizing to meet differing customers' needs. The result was a very broad product line, most of which was offered in every country. Furthermore, there was little standardization within each product line, so that the business maintained an inventory of many thousands

EXHIBIT 4-2 Options in Global Product Line Strategy

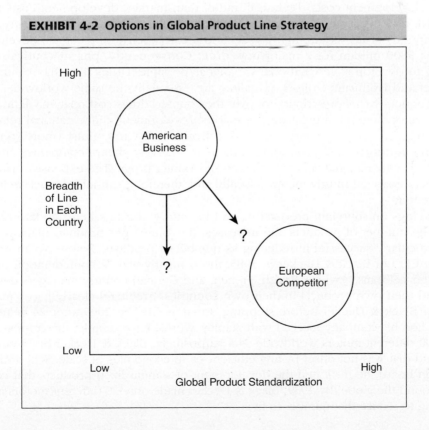

of individual items. In contrast, its leading competitor, a European firm that was just as profitable, sold a much narrower product line that was also much more standardized across countries. Presenting the information in the manner of Exhibit 4-2 helped raise two questions. First, did the competitor's approach suggest that customer needs were as different as this business's executives assumed? Second, did this business's product line strategy incur unnecessary costs?

BENEFITS OF GLOBAL PRODUCTS AND SERVICES

We have identified four categories of benefits from globalization: cost reduction, improved quality, enhanced customer preference, and competitive leverage. Each of these benefits applies to global product or service standardization.

Cost Reduction

Reducing costs is probably the most common motivation in standardizing products. These cost savings include development, sourcing, production, and inventory costs. Thus, as described in Chapter 2, high product development costs act as a globalization driver of product standardization. The higher the development cost relative to expected revenues, the more need there is to develop a few global or regional products rather than many national products. It is important to distinguish between technical and market development costs. Technical, rather than market, development costs act as a driver for product standardization. For example, in the pharmaceutical industry, ethical (prescription) drugs require many years and great expense in technical development, perhaps $800 million for a major new drug. Consequently, pharmaceutical companies try to develop as few national variants as possible: Drugs like GlaxoSmithKline's Tagamet and Hoffmann-La Roche's Valium are essentially the same worldwide. In contrast, proprietary (nonprescription or over-the-counter) drugs cost relatively little in technical development but a great deal in market development. Since national regulations for nonprescription drugs vary a great deal from country to country (more so than for prescription drugs), and developing variants is relatively cheap, companies are happy to market many national versions of over-the-counter drugs. The expensive market development costs are mostly incurred locally and, therefore, cannot be much reduced by globalization.

Savings on sourcing, production, and inventory accrue when standardization reduces the number of products and increases the volume per product. Black & Decker was particularly successful in reducing its number of products. Before Nolan Archibald became CEO of Black & Decker in 1985, the company was "a confederation of nearly sovereign fiefdoms,"[5] where British, French, and German country managers developed and sold their own products in their own countries. Archibald clearly had a major impact on Black & Decker before stepping down as CEO in 2009 after 24 years at the helm when his company merged with Stanley Works. For example, the company made over 100 different motors worldwide. Not surprisingly, Black & Decker had tremendous overhead that was not offset by any efficiencies or economies of scale. When Archibald came on board, he instituted the development of standardized products that could be sold around the globe. By 1989, Black & Decker made only 20 different motors and was planning to reduce that number to five.

Tata nano

Although many major automobile manufacturers operate on a global scale, their customer base is generally limited to relatively affluent customers in developing nations. It is clear now that the auto industry has a large potential for growth in emerging markets, but successfully accommodating the demands of these markets requires a transformation in the way auto firms understand what consumers want, as well as a transformation the way the companies build and sell cars. For many manufacturers, designing models for emerging markets seems to be somewhat of an afterthought. Often, an outdated Western automotive design is produced, simply with fewer amenities. Thus far, one of the most innovative automobile designed for emerging markets has been the Tata Nano—also called the "People's Car from Tata Motors." The Nano costs about $2,200, nearly half the cost of the next cheapest automobile in India. Hitting this low price point has been possible through careful design and modular manufacturing. Despite being low in price, Tata has employed high-quality suppliers such as Bosch, Mahle, and Saint-Gobain to help its design components. Additionally, the Nano's modular construction allows the vehicle to be exported and assembled in facilities with very low start-up costs. This business model may seem strange, but many early western automobiles at the turn of the century were also sold partially assembled. Tata's innovation is the use of careful, frugal product design combined with modern manufacturing technology.

Product standardization also multiplies the gains from concentrating production to exploit economies of scale. As will be discussed in Chapter 5, activity concentration can reduce costs even without product standardization, but with it the potential savings become far greater.

Improved Quality

Less obvious than cost reduction, but potentially as important, product standardization can also improve the quality of the products themselves. Reducing the worldwide number of products, through standardization, allows financial and management resources to be focused on the smaller number of products. Braun—the German manufacturer of shavers, coffee makers, and other consumer durable goods, and now a subsidiary of Proctor & Gamble—maintains a very high reputation partly by restricting the number of products it offers. This parsimony applies across countries as well as across the product line. Braun does little tailoring for national tastes but single mindedly maintains its distinctive, global design style.

Enhanced Customer Preference

Although product standardization can reduce customer preference by failing to tailor for national needs, in many situations standardization can actually increase preference. For consumer products and services that are bought while abroad as well as in the consumer's home country, the availability of the same product or service can frequently be a plus that reinforces preference. Frequently consumed products like soft drinks, fast food, cigarettes, and candy lend themselves most to this effect. Not surprisingly, Coca-Cola, McDonald's, Philip Morris, and Nestlé derive much of their revenues from globally standardized products. In contrast, products that are seldom purchased while abroad, like detergent or floor wax, do not gain preference from global standardization.

Similarly, travel-related consumer services, from credit cards and traveler's checks to airlines and automobile rental, all need to be as standardized as possible. Some companies like American Express do an excellent job, while others are surprisingly lax. Automobile rental companies such as Hertz and Avis have largely failed over the years to standardize the way in which they classify their types of vehicles and do not even provide a guide to comparing American and European classifications. Because few American travelers are familiar with individual European automobile models, they sometimes wind up renting cars in Europe that are too small for their families and luggage. Europeans have the opposite problem. They can find themselves trying to drive an "intermediate" automobile in North America that is larger than most passenger cars on European roads.

Global standardization also enhances consumer preference when being global is an essential part of the category's or brand's appeal. Thus, part of Benetton's appeal to teenagers is the implication that wearing its (globally standardized) clothes somehow contributes to world unity; part of Louis Vuitton's appeal is that wealthy and discerning buyers around the world have the same taste in luggage and accessories. Furthermore, when users of Benetton or Louis Vuitton products travel, the items bring global recognition of the travelers' affinity, taste, or wealth. So LVMH, the parent company of Louis Vuitton and other luxury brands, adapts its product ranges very little around the world: Its luggage, watches, and champagnes are globally the same. Even its DFS duty-free chain retained the same approach and merchandise mix as it expanded from Asia to the United States.

Industrial or commercial products and services sold to multinational customers can also gain increased preference from standardization. The more the customers themselves have a global strategy, the more need they have to purchase globally standardized products and services. Some executives worry that standardizing products will make it easier for competitors to steal business with imitative products. But this risk can be greatly reduced by continuing to differentiate *among* multinational customers while standardizing *within* a given multinational customer.

Competitive Leverage

Globally standardized products can increase competitive leverage by providing low-cost products that can be the basis for invading markets. When they first entered international markets, most Japanese companies lacked the resources to develop and support different products for different countries. Turning this weakness into a strength, they focused on a small number of globally standardized products that initially via low cost, then via superior quality, allowed them to conquer market after market. In contrast, companies from developed nations that are market share followers tend to defend against larger competitors by offering locally customized products. The Japanese experience suggests that smaller competitors may have greater need for standardized products.

DRAWBACKS OF GLOBAL PRODUCTS AND SERVICES

The most important drawback of global product standardization is that some aspects of national needs may have to be sacrificed. As a result, customer preference in some countries may be less than for a product customized for the local market. Stories abound of companies that have made mistakes by not customizing for local needs, such as American appliances that are too large for Japanese kitchens or Japanese calculator pads too small for American fingers. The key is to find a balance between the benefits and drawbacks of standardization. Furthermore, the benefits can be increased and the drawbacks reduced by designing global products from scratch. These global products (or services) should seek to satisfy the most important common needs of the most important markets.

Canon's product strategy when it first entered the photocopier business in the early 1970s provides one of the most powerful examples of sacrificing the ability to meet local needs. Canon chose to design from scratch a global product. In doing so, Canon realized that it could not keep the feature of being able to copy all sizes of Japanese paper if the product cost was to meet its target. Canon willingly gave up the ability to meet all the needs in its *domestic* market in order to maximize its prospects in the *global* market.[6] Few companies would find it easy to make such a decision.

GLOBAL STANDARDIZATION IN SERVICE BUSINESSES

One of the greatest dilemmas in global strategy for manufacturing businesses is the need to balance global standardization with local customization. Designing, then manufacturing, a global product with a degree of local customization requires major trade-offs. In contrast, the nature of service delivery—at the point of consumption in many cases—makes both standardization and customization equally feasible. Local elements (e.g., mariachi bands in Mexico) can be easily added to a global formula (Club Med vacations); using local nationals as service providers may overcome the foreignness of a standardized service (e.g., use of local cabin crews by international airlines). The practice of augmenting a core service with many supplementary elements makes it relatively easy to provide a globally standardized core service augmented (and differentiated) by nationally customized supplementary service elements. This tends to be easier than for manufacturing businesses.

So services can be particularly easy to both globalize and localize. In perhaps the most extreme example, McDonald's opened restaurants in India that, in deference to Hindu reverence for cows, do not serve hamburgers at all. Were McDonald's a goods-based business, that could be equivalent to selling a car without an engine. But as a service-based business, the other core and supplementary elements can make up for the lack of beef. McDonald's also adds items, such as Veggie Burgers, to menus to meet local tastes. In Britain, McDonald's includes both tea and coffee in its menus, while in France and Germany, it also serves beer. Interestingly, these local variations are in the food itself, the product element, rather than in the service elements. In services, McDonald's allows little variation in its core formula of restaurant design, service approach, and key menu items. In opening its Moscow restaurants, McDonald's made great efforts to maintain its standard formula, right down to the smiles of the servers.

Hewlett-Packard is a global leader in computer-based customer support services. It maintains a globally standardized set of services that range from site design to systems integration and remote diagnostics. This global standardization includes seamless service at any hour of the day or night from anywhere in the world.

Professional service firms vary in their ability to provide a globally standardized service. Some firms, such as those in the accounting industry, face significant international differences in technical standards, making uniformity more difficult. But it is also a matter of strategy. Andersen Consulting (now Accenture) chose to lead in offering globally standardized services. Its competitors had to play catch-up. Similarly, advertising agencies face international differences in culture and consumer behavior, but some have chosen to overcome these differences.

Given that people are part of the production system, some service businesses have to work quite hard at global standardization. To implement its ambition of becoming the world's premier global consumer bank, Citibank is investing heavily in technology to ensure that the 65,000 Citibank personnel worldwide, many speaking different languages, deliver the same experience. The global standard also applies to the "model" branch, by 1997 in place in over half of its 1,100 plus branches around the world. While fast-food chains commonly standardize formats, banks have typically been given the latitude to choose their own layout at the local level. Citibank, however, intends to give customers the same retail services and experiences everywhere.

WHEN TO USE GLOBAL PRODUCTS AND SERVICES

As with the other global strategy levers, the condition of industry globalization affects the use of global products and services.

Market Globalization Drivers for Global products

Among market globalization drivers, the extent of *common customer needs* and of the importance of *global customers* provides the main stimulus to using globally standardized products and services.

COMMON CUSTOMER NEEDS   The extent to which customers in different countries have the same needs and tastes in a given product or service category provides the primary determinant of how much to standardize. In the pharmaceutical industry, fundamental customer needs are highly common as disease and ailments strike all of humanity and in mostly similar ways. Many afflictions are universal: from the common cold to heart disease. There are some geographic differences, with tropical diseases being the largest group of location-specific afflictions. Similarly, national diets and lifestyle affect the relative incidence of different diseases, such as the well-known high incidence of heart disease in developed countries arising from high-fat diets and the high incidence of hypertension in Asian countries arising from high-salt diets. But, like other differences in national habits, these dietary differences and their related health consequences are declining. Ice cream is becoming increasingly popular in Japan, while Oriental food is increasingly on the menu of American fast food. So overall, needs are highly common. But even if the *incidence* of a particular disease varies, its treatment is usually the same. So multinational drug companies are able to market nearly identical products around the world, and successes in one country can rapidly become global successes.

At the same time, national practices differ somewhat in how ailments are treated. Some countries are more eager users of surgery, some rely more on medicines prescribed by doctors, and others depend on over-the-counter remedies suggested by pharmacists. In particular, the preferred form of the medicine varies greatly. For example, in Britain many people prefer to take aspirin in powder form dissolved in water instead of the tablet or capsule form popular in the United States. People in some countries like to take medicine via suppositories. Preference for folk remedies over manufactured medicines also varies. The return-to-nature trend has created the new category of "phaetopharmaceuticals," which are made from natural, nonchemical ingredients. These new medicines have captured a very large share of the market in Germany. Even diagnosis can be affected by national culture: Americans tend to focus on head pains, while Japanese tend to focus on stomach pains. National difference in treatment tends to be much greater for over-the-counter drugs, which consumers select for themselves, than for prescription drugs, which are chosen by doctors.

Computer products also have high levels of global standardization. While local business practices and government regulation may affect the content, format, and frequency of, for example, accounting reports, the need for hardware is not fundamentally affected by these variations. So in the computer industry, companies usually find it easier to globally standardize hardware than software. But various cultural factors affect both hardware and software: Computing is particularly affected by language differences. For example, Japanese *kanji* characters require two bytes to store, in contrast to one byte for Western alphabetical characters. One computer company accommodated these differences by designing a global product from the start, with broad capabilities. Also, in Japan, dedicated word processors (capable of handling Japanese characters) are far more common than in Western Europe and the United States, where dedicated word processing machines have dwindled as a product segment. The need to translate software and documentation for the various European and Asian markets also poses a barrier to the easy dissemination of application software. In health care software systems, the key distinction between countries in the commonality of software needs turns on whether medicine is socialized.

In textbook publishing, the potential for global products is limited by the desire of teachers to use books that reflect the national perspective on history, sociology, psychology, and other subjects. Other than primary sources and some scholarly books, college textbooks in the social sciences and humanities remain largely domestic in origin. Textbooks at the precollege level are even more restricted to national markets. One significant exception to the lack of global textbooks is English as a second language (ESL) instruction, where standardized texts abound. Even so, the world market has long been divided between instruction in American English and British English, with textbook sales following the relative influence of the two countries. For example, American English is taught in Japan, but British English is taught in Malaysia. In some countries, such as Brazil, there is competition between the two forms of English.

GLOBAL CUSTOMERS   Global customers often demand global products and services. So the incidence of global customers has a major effect on the need and potential for product standardization. In the computer industry, customers who globally coordinate their purchases are becoming an increasingly important driver. As customers become more sophisticated computer system buyers, and as they become globalized themselves, they are also becoming more willing to look beyond a single vendor. Their purchasing criteria have changed from focusing on the security provided by a single vendor to maximizing system performance at minimal cost. Further, as companies adopt "open systems" architectures, they frequently do so with the realization that their corporate information systems need to be coordinated on a global scale. But as yet, only perhaps 10 to 15 percent of buyers act as global customers. A larger number of buyers (perhaps 20 to 25 percent) look regionally.[7] But because of their investment in proprietary systems, many buyers are reluctant to consider new suppliers. Even multinational firms may choose to replicate their headquarters' computer system in their foreign affiliates instead of adopting a newer global hardware standard because the costs of transferring software, writing new programs, and training staff on new systems can be prohibitive.

A Stanford–UCLA study of 165 multinational companies found that while the average revenues from all international customers were 46 percent, those from multinational customers were 26 percent, and those from globally coordinated multinational customers were only 13 percent.[8] So although revenues from all international customers were 46 percent (fairly typical of a Fortune 500 type of firm population), only 13 percent of revenues were from truly global customers. While 13 percent may seem low, these revenues usually come from the most prestigious and most sophisticated customers. Few multinational suppliers can afford to underserve such customers. Furthermore, this percentage will increase, as other evidence shows. Suppliers' use of all aspects of global account management was at the moderate level, somewhat below the levels of customer demand. But suppliers expected to greatly increase their use of all aspects, with scores in the five-figure range.

In the process control industry, many multinational customers now demand globally standardized products. For example, Royal Dutch Shell, a major customer, might order 16 identical units for its different plants around the world because it wants each plant to be a mirror image of the others.

Most consumer packaged goods industries have few global customers, but the chocolate industry provides an interesting exception. The chocolate industry has global customers in one special sense. Many consumers buy chocolate as a gift to others (or for themselves) while traveling abroad. The ease of customizing chocolate to incorporate local specialties also encourages purchases by travelers (chocolate with macadamia nuts in Hawaii or with kiwi fruit in New Zealand). Such purchases abroad expose consumers to different types of chocolate around the world, helping to establish global standards in perceived quality and perhaps taste also. So companies can benefit by maintaining similar brand images, packaging, and quality standards for their chocolates around the world. The impact of global customers is even greater for more frequently purchased consumer packaged goods items like soft drinks and cigarettes.

Cost Globalization Drivers for Global Products

Among cost globalization drivers, *global scale economies, high product development costs,* and *fast-changing technology* have the most effect on the need for global products and services.

GLOBAL SCALE ECONOMIES   Global-level scale economies in the production process encourage businesses to centralize production. Typically, the technological imperatives that yield global scale production economies also yield important production economies in product rationalization. Thus the gains from centralized production can usually be multiplied when combined with a focused, global product line. Both Black & Decker in small appliances and Becton Dickinson in disposable syringes have greatly benefited from using global product ranges with limited items.

HIGH PRODUCT DEVELOPMENT COSTS/FAST-CHANGING TECHNOLOGY   High product development costs provide a major motivation for using globally standardized products and services. This motivation is particularly important in industries with rapidly changing technology, such as electronics, or risky development efforts, such as pharmaceuticals. As technology becomes more important in more and more industries, companies in even the food industry are finding that it no longer pays to develop national products. In the coffee industry, for example, the cost of developing new forms of soluble coffee is so great now that companies work on developing new forms (e.g., freeze dried) for global markets only, even though they may adapt blends (e.g., types of coffee beans used) for individual markets.

Government Globalization Drivers for Global Products

Among government globalization drivers, *favorable trade policies* and *compatible technical standards* have the greatest effect on the potential for global products and services.

FAVORABLE TRADE POLICIES   Trade barriers, particularly nontariff ones such as quotas and local content rules, can greatly restrict a company's ability to produce and market a globally standardized product line. In products where the source of raw materials is critical, or the production process is difficult to reproduce in some countries, trade restrictions can prevent the use of global products.

COMPATIBLE TECHNICAL STANDARDS   Differences in technical standards and related rules directly affect the extent to which products can be globally standardized. Fortunately, differing national standards are converging in many industries toward common global standards. The increasing convergence of standards in telecommunications is making it easier to design global products in that industry. For example, instead of designing products for just the North American market, as it used to do, Nortel Networks Corporation, the Canadian telecommunications company, now designs global products for all of its markets, making only minor software modifications.

Competitive Globalization Drivers for Global Products

Lastly, having *globalized competitors* who themselves use globally standardized products or services provide a powerful spur to developing global products of one's own. It is Japanese companies who have tended to lead in this strategy, forcing their rivals to play catch-up in designing global products, for example, American and European manufacturers in both automobiles and consumer electronics.

DEVELOPING GLOBAL PRODUCTS AND SERVICES

There are two primary ways to develop global products and services. The first, and preferred, method is to develop products and services with the global market in mind, as Canon did for its first photocopier. This approach has the obvious advantage of taking into consideration the needs of major markets right at the start, rather than having

Global Standardization in Financial Services

Despite regulatory barriers, many companies in financial service industries manage a surprisingly high degree of global standardization. Although differences in financial products exist, many are becoming increasingly standardized.[9] Barclays, a leading British bank, aims to ensure through its global customer information system that its multinational corporate customers have access to a uniform range of products at a uniform level of service in a familiar Barclays environment. Because credit cards have become standardized, Citicorp introduced its bank cards into Europe with little modification. American Express is, perhaps, the master of offering a standardized global product in financial services. French banks have introduced standard leasing arrangements with particular success in Spain and Portugal. Letters of credit have been standardized to the extent that they are almost exclusively written in English to facilitate international transactions and to ensure consistency of contract language. Some products, however, are difficult to standardize because of long-standing differences in national practices. In the United States, the 30-year mortgage is standard, while in Europe the 10-year mortgage is more common. Despite these differences, many financial product modifications are not too costly, so that national differences can often be accommodated. The potential for further global standardization seems high as regulatory changes continue to further standardize banking practices and foster greater international competition.

to retrofit a product developed for one national market. *Managers should start by identifying globally strategic markets and then understanding the needs of those markets. Perhaps, most important, managers should search for commonalities rather than for differences.* Such an approach should allow managers to design the largest possible standardized core, while allowing for necessary customization at the same time.[10]

The second, less desirable but more common, approach is to adapt existing products or services. In adapting from an existing mix of national products, managers need to start by understanding the causes of the national variants. Have these variants arisen from a deliberate response to real differences in needs and tastes? Or are they accidents of independent development? Very often the answer is much more accident than deliberation. Many businesses wind up with product lines that are much less standardized than they could be, simply by not having a global perspective, so that countries make decisions independently of each other.

A European manufacturer of semidurable consumer products found itself with half the countries in the world selling products in one set of colors and the other half in another set. These were not major color differences, but differences, for example, in the shade of blue. This situation arose because most of the world was supplied out of two manufacturing plants, one in the United Kingdom and one in Germany, and the two general managers in these two countries made decisions independently. When first asked to explain the difference, the executives in this business tried to justify their decisions on the basis of differences in consumer preference. But when pushed, the executives admitted that the differences did not arise from perceived consumer differences but from the independent decision-making process. In contrast, the business's major competitor had great success with a highly standardized product line, confirming that customer preferences were not that different.

GUIDELINES FOR DESIGNING GLOBAL PRODUCTS AND SERVICES

Successfully designing global products and services requires managers to make tough trade-offs between global and local demands. Several guidelines apply, including the following:

- Globally standardized products and services can bring the benefits of not just cost savings, but also of improved quality and customer preference.
- The best global products are usually those that are designed as such from the start rather than being adapted from national products later.
- Designers of global products and services should try to maximize the size of the common global core while also providing for local tailoring around the core.
- In investigating customer needs around the world, managers should look for similarities as well as for differences.

Discussion and Research Questions

1. What is the difference between a local product and a global product?
2. Identify a global product or service. Describe what is standardized about it and what is localized.
3. Which of the following products and services are more globally standardized and why?
   Apple iPad
   American Express Gold Card
   Disney theme parks
   Mercedes automobiles
   Nestlé coffee
4. How should a company go about developing a global product?
5. Select one product or service and discuss which aspects of it are global and which local, and why.
6. Which service elements are more easy to standardize globally?
7. How does the Internet affect product standardization and localization?

Notes

1. This term was coined by David Stout, head of Economics, Unilever PLC.
2. Based on "Can Honda Build a World Car?" *Business Week,* September 8, 1997, pp. 100–8.
3. See George Stalk, Jr., and Thomas M. Hout, *Competing Against Time* (New York: Free Press, 1990).
4. Based on "A Car Is Born," *The Economist,* September 13, 1997, pp. 68–9.
5. John Huey and Sandra L. Kirsch, "The New Power in Black & Decker," *Fortune,* January 2, 1989, accessed March 14, 2011, http://Money.Cnn.Com/Magazines/Fortune/Fortune_Archive/1989/01/02/71444/Index.Htm.
6. See also Michael E. Porter, "Changing Patterns of International Competition," *California Management Review,* Vol. 28, No. 2, Winter 1986, pp. 33–4.
7. These estimates of global customers and global channels were made by senior executives in a major computer manufacturing firm.
8. David B. Montgomery and George S. Yip, "The Challenge of Global Customer Management," *Marketing Management,* Vol. 9, No. 4, Winter 2000, pp. 22–9.
9. This paragraph is based on Julie Carson, Sanjay Dube, Shyh-jaw Chien, Eric Crabtree, and Mitsuhisa Ashida, "Worldwide Commercial Banking in the Late 1980s," unpublished report (Washington, DC: Georgetown Business School, 1989).
10. See also Ilkka A. Ronkainen, "Product-Development Processes in the Multinational Firm," *International Marketing Review,* Winter 1983, pp. 57–65. For a comprehensive description on how to develop multinational product policy, see, for example, William H. Davidson, *Global Strategic Management* (New York: John Wiley & Sons, 1982).

CHAPTER 5

Locating Global Activities

The global location of activities represents the third global strategy lever. Where to locate a business's activities and how to coordinate them constitute critical choices in global strategy.[1] Every functional or value-adding activity, from research to manufacturing to customer service, is a candidate for globalization. Traditionally, multinational companies have faced two choices in activity location. On the one hand, they can duplicate an activity in multiple foreign locations. The classic multinational strategy has been to reproduce activities in many countries, particularly the production function by setting up factories and other manufacturing assets. On the other hand, multinational companies can keep activities concentrated in the home country. Exhibit 5-1 summarizes some key choices in terms of location and coordination.

The classic *export-based strategy* has been to locate as much of the value chain as possible back home, while locating overseas only downstream activities—such as selling, distribution, and service—that have to be performed close to the end customer. This was the typical strategy of Japanese and South Korean companies in the 1970s and 1980s, before they began to move production overseas. Not much coordination is needed as there are few assets overseas and little international variation in product offerings.

As discussed in earlier chapters, there is also a *multilocal strategy* in which activities are geographically dispersed and only loosely coordinated. Dispersed activities combined with high coordination can be viewed as *controlled foreign direct investment* (FDI). This is a form of global strategy and is often a transition phase from multilocal strategy. For example, many older European multinational companies found themselves in the 1980s and 1990s with activities that were too dispersed for the new conditions of a globalizing world. An initial response was to increase coordination as a precursor to reducing the number of locations for activities.

A *pure global strategy* also concentrates activities, but in contrast to an export-based strategy, these activities are not all concentrated in the home country but in one or a few best different countries for each different activity. For example, such a strategy might locate research in the United Kingdom, development in Germany, raw material

EXHIBIT 5-1 Choices for Locating and Coordinating Activities

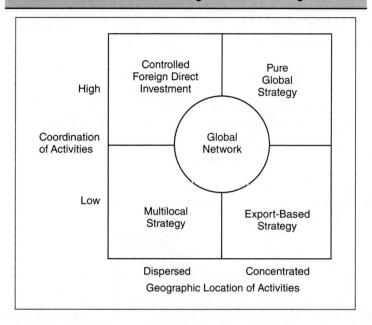

processing in Mexico, subassembly in the United States, final assembly in Ireland, and so on. Exhibit 5-2 shows an extreme case of a global value chain in which every activity occurs in one different country only. In reality most companies would, and should, provide for some duplication of most activities. Such duplication provides security against supply disruptions and provides some flexibility in the system. Another way of viewing the global approach to activity location is the following. Global activity location means deploying one integrated, but globally dispersed, value chain or network that serves the entire worldwide business, rather than separate country value chains or one home-based value chain.

Increasingly, multinational companies are trying to head toward the center position in Exhibit 5-2, that of the *global network*.[2] Here there is more dispersion and perhaps less coordination than in a pure global strategy. No part of the organization, whether headquarters or subsidiary, is self-sufficient. Instead, all work together in a network. The global network is made possible as technical developments in the transfer of data and falling transportation costs make it less and less necessary to co-locate functions.[3] It is now common to integrate operations on a global basis and put parts of the value chain in different parts of the world. Denso, a Japanese producer of air conditioners and other automobile parts, operates an Asia-Pacific network in which powertrain controls as well as thermal and electric systems are made in Thailand; air conditioning components, spark plugs, and relays in Malaysia; refrigeration units for automobiles and buses in the Philippines; and automotive and specialty industrial products in Australia.[4]

Most leading American, European, and Japanese companies (e.g., Toyota and Sony) are now converging on the global network model for specific product lines, albeit from different starting points—many Japanese companies from pure global strategy, many

EXHIBIT 5-2 The Extreme Global Value Chain

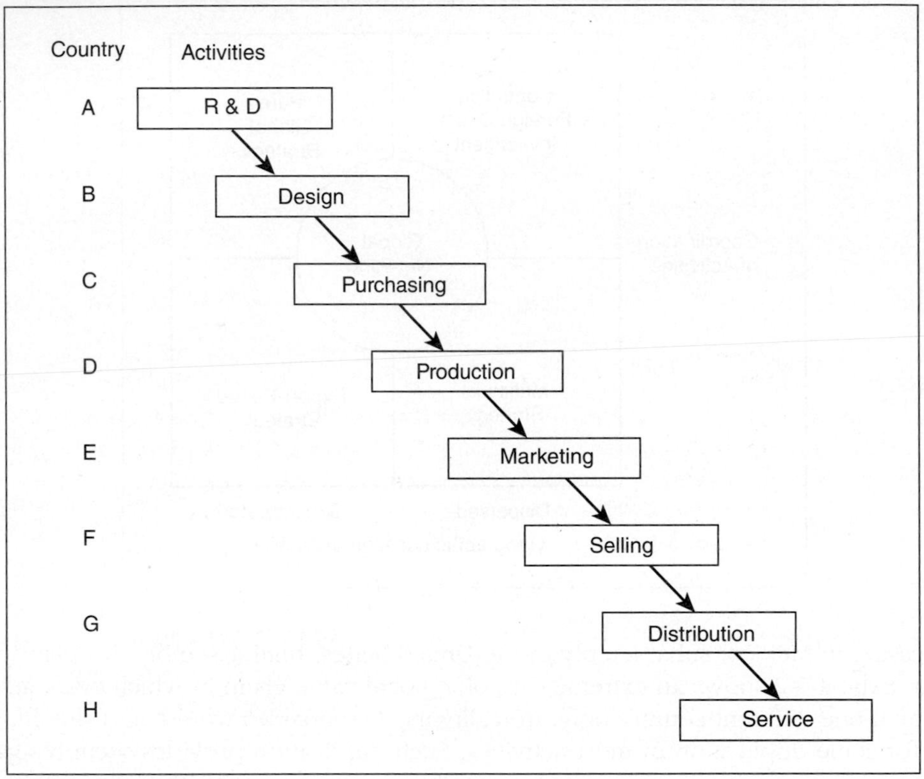

Country   Activities

A   R & D

B   Design

C   Purchasing

D   Production

E   Marketing

F   Selling

G   Distribution

H   Service

older European companies (e.g., Philips and Unilever) from multilocal strategy, and many American companies (e.g., Coca-Cola and General Electric) from controlled FDI. The Internet has made the global network the dominant model of multinational companies for the foreseeable future. This model seeks to reduce duplication of activities. Near instant communication offers companies maximizing this mainstay of the global economy the potential to complete the process of de-duplication.

Perhaps the most important consideration in a global strategy approach to activity location is to take a "zero-based" view and to ask what would be the optimal pattern and location of each activity if the company could start from scratch. Hardly any company is likely to be able to conclude that its current pattern of location is optimal. Because globalization conditions have changed and continue to do so, and because of a lack of global thinking in the past, many, perhaps most, companies find themselves saddled with activity networks unsuited to the globalization potential of the industries in which they operate. Companies in Europe in the 1980s provided the most extreme example. With the coming single European market at that time, many companies there found themselves with factories 50 kilometers apart on either side of a frontier that would no longer exist. The 1990s saw major restructuring and concentration of production and other activities in Europe, and this process continued in the 2000s. Clearly, changing the location of activities, particularly of major fixed assets like factories, is expensive and, in many cases, not justified. But global managers need to operate with an understanding of where their activities ought to be located even if they cannot easily move them there. Such knowledge is essential in planning investments to upgrade or expand existing facilities and to create new ones.

ROLE OF NATIONAL FACTORS

Many factors affect the choice of location for activities. Global managers need to distinguish between traditional country considerations and global strategic importance, among other considerations.

Traditional Country Considerations

Traditional international economic theory has stressed the importance of "comparative advantage" in addressing where multinational companies should locate their activities.[5] In particular, they should locate in countries where the costs of raw materials, labor, and other production inputs ("factor costs") are lowest for a given level of productivity. But production cost is only one consideration. Furthermore, production costs themselves are subject to broader influences such as tax benefits and other forms of aid that may be provided by national and other country authorities. Japanese automobile manufacturers seemed particularly astute in garnering the maximum governmental benefits from their production location decisions. In placing their American production plants in the 1980s, not only did they extract many concessions from states eager for their patronage, but Honda, Nissan, and Toyota each located in a different state (Ohio, Tennessee, Kentucky, respectively), perhaps to maximize their political lobbying effectiveness by each having two senators to represent their concerns. Interestingly, in the 1990s, two German car firms located new factories in yet two other states: BMW in South Carolina and Mercedes in Alabama. By 2008, Honda had expanded its network of assembly plants to Indiana and Alabama, while Toyota located facilities in Indiana and Nissan had operations in Mississippi.

Other considerations include broader issues of productivity and quality, convenience for shipping to other countries, reliability of the workforce, the cost of capital, the economic infrastructure, and the extent of political risk. Some developing countries with low costs and high productivity may seem ideal, but they may need to be avoided because of their high level of political risk. While the risk of outright expropriation has declined, the risk of government interference as well as political and economic disruptions continues. For example, many Western companies manufacturing in China and other countries have suffered from sudden clampdowns on foreign exchange that they needed to purchase raw materials, equipment, and supplies. Multinational companies also need to worry about the social and ethical standards of suppliers from developing countries, especially if they are not themselves controlling the factories. In the 1990s, Nike, Wal-Mart, and many others were hit by protests and negative publicity about the practices of their third-world suppliers.[6] In fact, publicity problems persisted with suppliers to both Nike[7] and Wal-Mart[8] for decades. However, as indicated in the Levi Strauss example, some companies go to considerable and unexpected lengths to ensure that supplier conditions are consistent with a company's stated policies.

Another type of issue concerns the so-called country-of-origin effect, in which customers give preference to goods produced in certain countries or that they believe to

Levi Strauss and its Terms of Engagement

Levi Strauss has strict guidelines to follow in its evaluation of current and potential locations for global sourcing and operating. The guidelines include two parts: country assessment guidelines and business partner terms of engagement, or TOE.[9] Established in 1991, the TOE's goal is to protect worker rights and act as a fundamental part of the company's sourcing strategy and its relationships with contractors worldwide.

In fact, the country assessment guidelines examine health and safety conditions, the human rights environment in country as well as its legal system and political, economic, and social environment. By using these measures as a basis for assessment, Levi Strauss aims to ensure that every country with corporate operations meets the expectations the company has come to set for itself, its workers, and its consumers. By using a tool called an Eco Index,[10] each possible country is compared for the company's required support to protect company trademarks, investments, and other commercial interests as well.

As such, the TOE are used to find business partners who operate by workplace standards that are consistent with Levi Strauss's overall corporate mission. To support this company-wide approach to sourcing, the company only engages in partnerships with contractors who do not hire child labor, who do not use prison or forced labor of any kind, and who do not use corporal or any other forms of mental or physical coercion. They also examine whether working hours, wages and benefits, organizing possibilities, and skill-based hiring are within acceptance levels. The result is that Levi Strauss is more sensitive to the interests of its consumers,[11] thus making it competitive and appealing in the apparel industry.

come from those countries.[12] The country-of-origin effect in the U.S. automobile market partly explains why the Toyota Corolla, a nearly identical car to General Motors' Geo Prizm, and produced on the same assembly line in the United States during the 1990s, commanded a 10 percent or so price premium in the market. (Chapter 6, on global marketing, will also address this effect.) All of these considerations in the location of activities, including from where to source production inputs, should be familiar to multinational companies in developing their internationalization strategy. So in keeping with the focus of this book on globalization rather than internationalization, the author assumes a basic understanding of these issues and addresses them only in terms of how they affect globalization strategy.[13]

Globally Strategic Countries for Activity Location

Just as countries can be globally strategic from the viewpoint of market participation, they can be globally strategic in terms of activity location, for some of the same, but also some different, reasons. Two activities, research and development (R&D) and production, particularly need to be located in globally strategic countries.

FOR R&D LOCATION   For R&D, globally strategic countries have the following characteristics:

- Major source of industry innovation
- Presence of highly skilled and/or low-cost R&D workers
- Highly demanding customers

As in the case of market participation, the R&D activity benefits from location in countries that are major sources of industry innovation. R&D workers in those countries can gain direct access to the many sources of the innovations being created—via face-to-face contacts with university researchers, participation in conferences, quicker access to publications, competition in the job market, and so on. Monitoring from a distance cannot achieve the full benefits possible through physical location. For example, many scientific journals in Japan are published only in Japanese and circulate little outside the country. While the countries making the major innovations in an industry also tend to have the most skilled R&D workers, other countries can also be important sources of highly skilled or low-cost staff. Several Asian countries have demonstrated this capability.

Lastly, locating R&D in countries with highly demanding customers helps the R&D staff there to better understand the nature of their needs. In fact, China and India are two emerging markets which fit this profile well. Though China has a clear advantage with basic R&D opportunities, India is more specialized in the skills available to multinational corporations. In specific, operations in China typically focus on electronics while R&D in India emphasizes pharmaceuticals.[14] Still, continued investment by each country in skilled labor is planned to encourage the location of R&D facilities by multinational corporations in each country. The result for entering companies is not only skilled R&D labor but also insight into the needs of customers that might not otherwise be possible.

FOR MANUFACTURING LOCATION For manufacturing, globally strategic countries are those that offer an attractive investment climate as well as factors and conditions on which to build comparative and strategic advantage. Companies choosing to make investments in manufacturing facilities, as opposed to sourcing from outside suppliers, need to consider a long list of factors affecting the investment climate. This list includes the level of political stability, government policies toward foreign investment, trade policies, tax policies, legal factors, the macroeconomic environment, and policies on international payments. These considerations are the usual ones that have to be dealt with when a company internationalizes through FDI.[15] The additional factors that produce comparative and strategic advantage—and, therefore, render a country globally strategic for manufacturing—include the following:

- Favorable factor conditions
- Close location to major markets
- Favorable country-of-origin effect
- Manufacturing presence of global competitors

Favorable factor conditions—such as low-cost raw materials or labor, or highly skilled or productive labor—form the traditional basis for comparative advantage of one country relative to others.[16] Similarly, location close to major markets can be viewed as a type of factor advantage that lowers transportation cost or speeds up response time, thus providing both comparative and strategic advantage.[17] Countries that lead in innovation, that produce high-quality products, or that have highly demanding customers often enjoy a positive country-of-origin effect, though typically only within specific product categories. Lastly, as indicated in the example of the automotive industry in Mexico, the manufacturing presence of other global competitors can create a positive spiral of rivalry and imitation that continually upgrades the level of manufacturing capability for all competitors in the country.[18] So a global strategy for activity location can also be viewed as a means to get access to resources on which to build both comparative and strategic advantage.

Transportation Costs in the Automotive Industry

When the costs of transportation rise, it is essential for multinational and global companies to reconsider the implementation of company strategies with regard to the location of manufacturing facilities. For a considerable amount of time, China has been identified as an ideal location for companies to conduct manufacturing due to the large available work force, stable education system, and low labor costs. However, when transportation costs increase, many automobile manufacturers look to countries located close to their targeted markets.

Many automobile manufacturers have targeted Mexico as a country to locate manufacturing operations because of its opportune access to the North American—particularly the United States—market.[19] Though Mexico does not have the advanced educational systems that India and China have,[20] the country can be seen as a potential growth opportunity for both the Mexican government and the automobile industry based on the premise that investment in education can ensure quality manufacturing and products for years to come.

As evidence of the automotive industry's commitment to Mexican manufacturing, Ford, General Motors, Nissan, and Volkswagen have substantially increased operations in Mexico based on superior access to the U.S. market as well as lower labor costs.[21] With operations so close to a large target market, transportation costs are decreased and assembly plants are able to conduct just-in-time sourcing more effectively.[22] This, in turn, allows companies to be more responsive to marketplace demand and—as a result—make them more competitive.

ROLE OF EXCHANGE RATES

Currency exchange rates have a direct effect on relative country costs and, therefore, on the competitive positions of companies. In the construction equipment business Caterpillar Tractor depended heavily on U.S.-based production, while its Japanese rival, Komatsu, manufactured mainly in Japan. In 1979 Caterpillar was the low-cost producer, but by 1985 most of its product lines were priced over 40 percent above Komatsu's. One reason was that the U.S. dollar had increased by 50 percent over the yen and most key European currencies. This price difference greatly helped Komatsu to penetrate many of Caterpillar's traditional markets.[23] In response and as an operating hedge against currency fluctuations, the company moved much of its manufacturing overseas during the 1990s. By 1998, approximately half of Caterpillar's plants were overseas. One decade later, a weaker dollar helped the company's profits[24] and facilitated acquisitions in the United States to keep Caterpillar competitive in emerging markets.[25]

Companies that shift to lower cost countries for offshore production are taking a bet, in part, that these low costs will not be eroded by currency changes. The European introduction of the Euro in 1999 and its nearly immediate drastic fall in value (by about 25 percent against the U.S. dollar as of mid-2001), and Britain's retention of its pound sterling, caused great problems for exporters who had located in Britain while it was relatively low cost compared to Continental Europe. In 2001, foreign investors, such as Japanese and German automobile companies, were threatening to move production out unless Britain rapidly joined the single European currency. However, by 2002, the Euro recovered and peaked against the U.S. dollar in 2008. The Euro's recovery against the

British pound was more gradual. Still, Japanese and German automobile manufacturers have facilities in the United Kingdom.

Perhaps most important, *companies need to recognize the strategic as well as financial risk posed by currency changes*. Traditional definitions of currency exposure concentrate mainly on foreign currency flows that relate to the company's own operations. This internal focus ignores the fact that an unfavorable currency movement may not just be unfavorable; it could be favorable to the competition. But exchange rate changes can also favor a company in the short term and hurt it in the long term. In the late 1980s depreciation of the U.S. dollar relative to the Japanese yen improved the competitive position of American companies relative to their Japanese rivals. But the higher value of the yen also allowed Japanese companies to make many bargain acquisitions across borders that would enhance their long-run competitive capabilities. So exchange rate changes can act as catalysts in the international restructuring of companies and industries.[26]

But forecasting long-term exchange rates is generally acknowledged to be very difficult. About the only consensus is that the currencies of countries with high or fast-growing productivity tend to appreciate relative to currencies in countries with low or slow-growing productivity rates. Even so, differences in productivity did not account for the down-up-down, doubling, and halving path of the U.S. dollar against the Japanese yen, Deutsche mark, and other major currencies in the 1970s and 1980s. Nor were many experts able to predict this path. Currency volatility continued in the 1990s, spurred in part by financial crises in Latin America, Russia, and Asia. Though the introduction of the Euro in 2002 added some stability to international currencies, global instability compelled Europe, Japan, the United Kingdom, and the United States to intervene and protect currency markets.[27]

One view is that companies should locate production in countries with low productivity, with the expectation that the currency will stay weak. Furthermore, these companies can increase their advantage by increasing their productivity in the country faster than the country's overall rate of productivity growth. Another view takes into account "parity purchasing power" exchange rates that adjust for differences between countries in the prices of similar goods and services. So a country with a high relative nominal (official) exchange rate but high relative prices also has a lower parity purchasing power exchange rate. Some studies provide evidence that nominal exchange rates tend to move toward their parity purchasing power exchange over time.[28] Thus the latter rate can be used to forecast the movement of the official exchange rate.

Perhaps the best that can be said is that companies looking for exchange rates that will stay weak should locate operations in countries with weak economies. Even then, it is only the nominal exchange rate that might weaken, and real exchange rates might still go up with wage and other factor price increases. Offsetting that exchange rate benefit is, of course, all the other disadvantages in terms of infrastructure and productivity inherent in weak economies.

On the other hand, if a company wishes to locate in strong, or at least, developed economies, it should probably not make its choice among such countries on the basis of expected currency movements. Any likely differences in nominal exchange rates are likely to be offset by movements toward the parity purchasing power exchange rate. To maintain its comparative advantage over foreign competitors, a producer also needs to increase its productivity, *relative* to that of the country in which the production activity is located, *faster* than its competitor does in its country. Otherwise, the firm will find its productivity gains more than offset by increases in the currency exchange rate where it is located. So it is dangerous to invest in locating activities in a country with one strong sector, unless the activity is in that sector. For example, because of the effect of oil exports on strengthening Norway's exchange rate, other industries there have had great difficulty in being competitive internationally.[29]

So given the difficulty of forecasting exchange rates, global managers can choose among alternative ways of handling the uncertainty. They can speculate, hedge, or be flexible.[30] *Speculation* involves committing to one or a small number of countries as production sites. This approach, of course, runs the risk of betting the wrong way. *Hedging* means spreading out production and other activities so that losses from exchange rate rises in one country can be offset by gains from exchange rate declines in other countries. But diversifying the manufacturing base around the world may be insufficient. Managers also need to consider what competitors are doing. So a global strategy needs to consider strategic foreign exchange exposure as well as operating exposure, and strategic flexibility as well as operating flexibility. A strategy of *being flexible* means investing in excess capacity in several locations and then shifting production with exchange rate shifts. This last option provides the best chance of reducing strategic risk as well as reducing operating risk. In particular, a really cautious strategic approach to being flexible would be to manufacture in some of the same locations as major global competitors. That way, the competitor would stand less chance of gaining an advantage from movements in exchange rates.

STRATEGIC ADVANTAGE VERSUS COMPARATIVE ADVANTAGE

The previous discussion of exchange rates highlights the difference between strategic advantage and comparative advantage. In global competition, companies need to exploit both. *Strategic* advantage springs from the core business strategy, as discussed in Chapter 1. This advantage can be spread and applied around the world without depending on country-based sources of *comparative* advantage such as low labor costs or superior technological infrastructure. Apple Computer's strategic advantage came primarily from its pioneering position in the personal computer (PC) business, its unique user-friendly designs, and the strong name recognition and loyalty that it quickly built. But as both domestic and international competitors encroached on Apple's turf, the company had to add comparative advantage also by shifting some of its production activities offshore in order to reduce costs. So, today, Apple's remaining competitive advantage depends on a combination of strategic and comparative advantage.

FedEx developed a core business strategy for the document and package delivery market that gave it significant strategic advantage in its home country, the United States. The company then sought to expand its business globally. A key issue was whether its core strategy could provide the same extent of strategic advantage abroad. But it came up against entrenched competitors: DHL in Europe and, to a lesser extent, Australia's TNT in Asia-Pacific. FedEx's home-based strategic advantages were insufficient to overcome the local first mover advantages of these foreign rivals. And as a service business based in many countries, FedEx could not exploit comparative advantage either. So FedEx has been significantly less successful outside its home market. In contrast, Japanese automobile manufacturers, such as Toyota, in the 1980s successfully added quality-based and design-based strategic advantages to the cost-based comparative advantage with which they entered international markets in the 1960s. In fact, by locating manufacturing facilities worldwide, Toyota was able to leverage its quality and design advantages to solidify its position in Europe, Latin America, and North America. *The best global strategies combine strategic and comparative advantage to yield global competitive advantage.*[31]

Exhibit 5-3 illustrates some possible combinations of strategic and comparative advantage. Companies with only strategic advantage have a *core-formula strategy* (upper left cell), as Caterpillar, the construction equipment manufacturer, had in the 1970s and FedEx in the 1980s and 1990s. Similarly, Club Med's all-in vacation resorts continue to benefit from the company's highly successful core formula, although this has gradually changed as the company's client base has aged. Companies with only comparative advantage tend to have to compete on the basis of low cost as many Japanese companies did in the 1960s, many South Korean companies did in the 1980s, and many Chinese companies (such as Haier in air conditioners) in the 1990s and 2000s, in a *cost-based export strategy* (lower right cell). Some South Korean concerns like Samsung's microwave oven business were able to move beyond low-cost-based comparative advantage to add quality-based strategic advantage. Others, like Leading Edge in microcomputers, succeeded for a while on the basis of comparative advantage but lost their position

EXHIBIT 5-3 Combinations of Strategic and Comparative Bases of Advantage

		No	Yes
Strategic Advantage	Yes	CORE-FORMULA STRATEGY Caterpillar in 1970s FedEx in 1980s and 1990s Club Med in 1950s to 2000s	GLOBALLY LEVERAGED STRATEGY Sony in 1980s to 2000s Toyota in 1980s to 2000s Nokia in 1990s to 2000s Samsung in 1990s
	No	UNTENABLE STRATEGY British Leyland in 1970s Chrysler in 1980s Marks & Spencer in 1990s	COST-BASED EXPORT STRATEGY Toyota in 1960s Samsung in 1980s Leading Edge in 1980s Hyundai in 1990s Haier (China) in 2000s
		Comparative Advantage	

when they could not develop high enough quality to achieve strategic advantage. Still other South Korean concerns, such as Hyundai's passenger automobile business, were at the cusp of transition in the 1990s. However, faced with competitors such as Toyota and Honda, Hyundai has found it difficult to complete this transition. Still, companies with both sources of advantage have a *globally leveraged strategy* (upper right cell), as Sony has had for a long time and that Toyota achieved in the 1980s. Companies with neither source of advantage have an *untenable strategy* (lower left cell) and will fail to hold their position, as happened to British Leyland and Harley-Davidson in the 1970s, Chrysler in the 1980s, and Marks and Spencer in the 1990s.

The sources of strategic and comparative advantage also change over time. They change for external reasons, such as differing productivity growth rates among nations and the advent of new technologies, and for competitor-driven reasons, such as one competitor committing to exploit an emerging technology, as Seiko did to the quartz technology for watches in the 1970s. Similarly, Japanese competitors' commitment in the 1980s to multipurpose, rather than specialized single-purpose, automated industrial equipment dramatically enhanced their strategic advantage relative to American competitors. In the 1990s, investment in flexible manufacturing provided one of the most important sources of strategic advantage. In the 2000s, the Internet's emergence as a form of communication provided some of the greatest sources of competitive advantage for companies, which can in turn be leveraged globally. Both Dell Computer and Schwab (in investment brokerage) transformed their existing business models using the Internet, while newcomers, such as Britain's easyGroup (owner of easyJet, easyCar, easyHotel, etc.), use the Internet as the starting points and bases of their business models.

BENEFITS OF GLOBAL LOCATION OF ACTIVITIES

A global strategy for activity location can achieve each of the major globalization benefits of cost reduction, improved quality, enhanced customer preference, and increased competitive leverage.

Cost Reduction

Multinational companies, whether using multilocal or global strategies, need to minimize the tariffs, taxes, and transportation costs they pay. In addition, compared with a multilocal approach, a global approach to activity location can reduce costs in further ways. It can *reduce duplication of activities* by eliminating and consolidating identical activities from many country locations into one or two globally centralized locations. In 1973, Unilever had 13 factories for soap production in Europe. As part of its globalization and Europeanization drive, Unilever had reduced these to three factories and one finishing plant by 1989. This allows the company to focus on customer-focused environmental initiatives otherwise not possible.[32] Similarly, N. V. Philips closed 80 factories in the 1970s to consolidate and to reduce duplication. In the 1980s Philips changed the role of the remaining factories from local production operations to "international production centers" that provided large-volume production for world markets.[33] Lastly, although a global approach to activity location means fewer locations than under a multilocal strategy, it may involve more locations and duplication than under a pure export approach.

A global approach to activity location can help exploit *economies of scale* by pooling production or other value-adding activities. For each activity, there can be an overall effect for the industry as a whole. The global benefits of manufacturing concentration are generally greater in the commercial aircraft business than in the apparel business—because the minimum efficient production scale requires a much higher share of the global market in aircraft than it does in apparel. But the specific effect for individual firms depends on the actual production technology used by the firm and by the market position of the firm. So firms that use a lower scale technology face fewer potential benefits from global concentration unless they change their technology approach also. Similarly, firms with a large share of large national markets will, other things being equal, gain less from global concentration than firms with small market shares, because these larger firms may already be able to achieve the minimum efficient scale. Smaller firms usually face a tough choice. They can try to overcome their size disadvantage by concentrating more than their larger competitors, but they run the risk of being swamped if these competitors adopt the same strategy. Or the smaller firms can stay with multiple, low-scale, national activities that depend on differentiation, quality, service, and other non-cost-based sources of strategic advantage. In industries where price is the primary customer concern, such strategies restrict the user to a small portion of the market. Furthermore, even in industries where product features and quality are also important, a cost advantage can be converted into not just lower prices but greater investment in improving product features and quality.

In the commodity chip market, economies of scale and learning/experience effects result in lower cost for high-volume plants. These drivers resulted in huge factories in Japan belonging to companies such as NEC, Fujitsu, and Hitachi. The output of these factories was much more than any one market could absorb, both allowing and requiring the Japanese companies to make large-volume sales in the United States. In the United States, on the other hand, companies such as Texas Instruments and Micron Technology (of Boise, Idaho) had smaller plants and higher costs, putting them at a cost disadvantage. The consolidation of production by the Japanese chip makers and the global strategy that they have followed were two of the factors responsible for their greater competitiveness in the global commodity chip market. This greater competitiveness is illustrated by the growth of their world market share in all memory products from 25 percent in 1980 to 64 percent in 1986 (before declining in the face of new South Korean competition).[34] In the 1990s, U.S. chipmakers recaptured the lead, with 45 percent global market share by 1996, in large part due to Intel's dominance of the PC market and subsequent economies of scale, as well as technological leadership. Though the status of U.S. companies in chipmaking and supercomputing was maintained for a decade, a resurgence of Japanese competition as well as Chinese companies slowly became apparent by 2010.[35]

The global concentration of activities can exploit *economies of scope* (which apply to the gains from spreading activities across multiple product lines or businesses) as well as economies of scale. The same types of issues apply, with the complicating need to coordinate across different product lines and businesses. These complications include the possibility that one link in the value-added chain should be global for one business but local for another business and will be further addressed later in this chapter.

Exploiting flexibility can be another way in which a global approach to activity location can reduce costs and applies primarily to production and sourcing activities.

Partial concentration allows flexibility in regard to changes in exchange rates and in bargaining with suppliers, labor unions, and host governments. The requirement for achieving this benefit lies not so much in the existence of multiple locations, which a multilocal strategy would have, and even more so, but in the capability to switch activities between locations. Such a capability has to exist in the configuration of physical assets, in the product policy, and in the management structure, policies, and processes of a company. First, flexibility in production requires investment in excess capacity that can produce to meet the needs of multiple countries. But such investment may be too costly in some industries and companies. Second, such production flexibility is greatly enhanced by the use of global products—products with a high degree of cross-country standardization. (The specific strategy of "flexible manufacturing" will be discussed shortly.) Third, the management system must allow production to be switched between countries without penalizing the individual managers and units giving up that production. Often, these management issues pose the greatest barrier to global flexibility. Chapter 8 will devote itself to the role of management and organization in global strategy. Putting these three requirements together—excess capacity, global products, and a global management system—can create a global network that allows a business to profit from the uncertainty of the world market.[36]

Improved Quality

A global approach to activity location can improve product and program quality by focusing on a smaller number of products and programs than under a multilocal strategy. This quality-enhancing focus can occur in a number of elements in the value-added chain, particularly for R&D and production activities. Concentration of the R&D function allows a company to devote greater resources to the projects undertaken. At the same time, a concentrated R&D function can also be the center of a global network that taps into selected skills and knowledge in particular countries.

Concentration of the production function allows investment in better facilities and equipment than can be afforded under a multilocal strategy. These superior assets can then produce higher quality as well as lower cost products. *Studies increasingly show that low cost and high quality are not alternative, but complementary, strategies.*[37] In highly globalized industries, having both low cost and high quality is particularly important because buyers have more choice in where they buy and have access to the best products or services offered in the world. In addition, competitors will be able to pursue low-cost strategies through global centralization and standardization. Concentration of the production function should also allow more consistent quality control.

Lastly, taking the zero-based approach inherent in a global approach to activity location may open up unlikely and fascinating possibilities. McKinsey & Company centralized all production of PowerPoint presentations in one of its offices in India and takes advantage of time-zone differences as well as lower cost and higher accuracy. The British Post Office routes to India photo images of envelopes that cannot be read by machines. There, individual readers retype the addresses and route them back electronically.

Enhanced Customer Preference

Globalized activity location has only an indirect effect on customer preference, via possible improvements in product design and quality. Other global strategy levers—global market participation, global products, and global marketing—have more direct effects. On the other hand, globalized activity locations that are too far from customers can cause problems. Obviously, activities that are time- or service-sensitive or that require a great deal of customer interaction need to be located close to customers. But the Internet and other forms of communication are making it easier to achieve both global activity concentration and effective customer interaction.

Increased Competitive Leverage

A global strategy for activity location can increase competitive leverage by bringing the resources of the worldwide network to bear on the competitive situation in individual countries. Under a multilocal strategy in which products are supplied by local manufacturing facilities, each subsidiary's competitive position—as based on its cost and quality position—depends on that subsidiary's own market share and revenues. So a subsidiary that loses market share under competitive attack also loses the operating scale needed to maintain the very cost and quality advantages needed to defend its market position. This was the losing position in which Philips, with its highly independent subsidiaries relying on local production, found itself in country after country, facing the Japanese electronics onslaught in the 1970s and early 1980s. In contrast, under a global strategy, each subsidiary's cost and quality position depends much more on the global market position of the worldwide business. So loss of local market share has little effect on cost and quality. In other words, *a global strategy for activity location can greatly reduce the dependence of each subsidiary's competitive position on local conditions.*

Recently, Philips has sought to unify its operations such that conditions in each country will have a minimal impact on the company's strategy. Though numerous restructuring attempts during the 1990s had little effect, Philips instead decided to focus on design simplicity and customer benefit beginning in 2004.[38] This gave rise to the company's involvement in product development for medical industry wireless technology[39] as well as three-dimensional printing.[40] As a result, Philips is developing offerings which respond to more general, overarching needs which are not as dependent on specific local conditions.

Such independence from local conditions also applies under an export strategy for activity location. But, as discussed in relation to exchange rates, a global approach with a network of locations provides more flexibility relative to exchange rate and other changes. So, again, a global approach can provide more leverage against competitors.

DRAWBACKS OF GLOBAL LOCATION OF ACTIVITIES

A global strategy for activity location also has drawbacks. Exhibit 1-5 in Chapter 1 summarizes the major potential problems in such a strategy. These possible drawbacks include lessened responsiveness to customers, increased currency risk, increased risk of creating competitors, and difficulties in managing the value-added chain.

Lessened Responsiveness to Customers

In comparison with a multilocal strategy in which most activities are located in the same countries as customer markets, a global strategy of partial concentration of activities distances many of these activities from customers. The same applies even more so, of course, to an export-based strategy of total concentration. Obvious drawbacks include increased inventory costs, transportation expenses, and tariffs. These additional costs need to be less than the cost savings discussed earlier.

Increased Currency Risk

Performing value-adding activities in countries where the company obtains little revenue means incurring costs in currencies different from that of revenues. As discussed earlier, this currency risk needs to be managed in a number of possible ways. Such management can verge on speculation, and companies need to beware of playing the foreign exchange markets for the sake of trading gains alone.

Increased Risk of Creating Competitors

One approach to building a global manufacturing network is to use "offshore manufacturing" in which the home country-market is supplied from production facilities located elsewhere. This strategy is, of course, a special case of the more general one of global activity location. But offshore manufacturing has received the most attention and criticism, particularly in regard to the danger of "hollowing out" the corporation as more and more parts of the value-added chain are moved offshore.[41] Offshore manufacturing is particularly risky when the suppliers are collaborators rather than fully owned subsidiaries. Numerous offshore suppliers have learned the business of their customers sufficiently well to develop into full-fledged competitors.[42] Even the use of fully owned subsidiaries runs the risk of creating new competitors if local managers spin off on their own.

Difficulties in Managing Value-Added Chain

A global network of activities, in which interdependent elements of the value-added chain are spread across different countries, is inherently difficult to manage. In contrast, the centralized network of an export-based strategy or the mostly independent value-added chains of a multilocal strategy pose much less of a management task. If managed badly, a global network can be both less efficient and more costly. However, as shown in the Lenovo example, successful implementation of a global network can have considerable benefits as well.

GLOBAL ACTIVITY LOCATION FOR SERVICE BUSINESSES

It is difficult to speak broadly about product-service differences in activity location. But it is somewhat easier when we focus on the next level of distinction: among people-processing, possession-processing, and information-based services (as elaborated in Chapter 1).

People-Processing Activities

In most cases, people-processing businesses have to locate the processing activity where customers live, work, or shop. This means that typical people-processing services—such as airline, hotel, restaurant, and car rental—need to maintain facilities around the world. In a few cases, specialized services, such as high-quality or advanced medical services, may be able to attract customers to travel to them. For example, some top hospitals in the United States and Britain are able to attract patients from Latin America and the Middle East, respectively.

Lenovo's Global Network

Lenovo Group has developed an effective strategy for locating operations on a global scale. Instead of having a centralized headquarters in one country, the company has operational hubs closely linked and aligned with customers' demands. Although Lenovo's core consumer market in China is largely transaction based, the company has a high amount of emerging market sales from large businesses and organizations in which long-term customer relationships are critical.[43] Segmenting the market into transaction and relationship business models allows the firm to customize the level of service in the overall business model. In fact, this ability to customize will be critical as the regionalized nature of China's rural market becomes even more of Lenovo's overall expansion strategy.[44]

Lenovo's organizational structure has globalized every aspect of the value chain. Global scaling is an underlying tenet of the company's strategy to maintain profitable growth. Unlike many other competitors, Lenovo owns and operates all of its own manufacturing facilities, eliminating the risk that contracted manufacturers could emerge in the future as competitors. Despite an extremely lean operation, the "worldsourcing" operating model[45] with decentralized hubs is backed by a diverse strategic imperative.

However, the company is not driven by exploiting differences in country costs. Rather, it is a holistic approach that takes into account the significance of customer relationships, innovation, and total quality management. Based on the need to integrate Lenovo's PC manufacturing operations and IBM's PC division after the merging of the two companies, Lenovo's operating model uses SAP's enterprise software to standardize its operations and centralize the company's purchasing data to evaluate performance.[46]

Possession-Processing Activities

Location needs for possession-processing activities depend on the ratio of service value to transportation cost. For example, it is increasingly more cost-effective to fly airplanes to a few specialized service centers rather than maintain service centers all over the world. Companies, such as Singapore Airlines, now do major business in servicing other airlines' planes at their domestic hubs. In contrast, the servicing of passenger automobiles continues to be a highly local, subnational industry.

Information-Based Activities

Most information-based services are easy to locate globally. In many cases, such as pure information services, no local physical presence may be needed at all. In other cases, information services that also have a physical component (e.g., the provision of currency or traveler's checks) or require specialized delivery equipment (e.g., pay-per-view entertainment) will need some local physical presence, provided by the company itself or by local partners.

Future Locations of Service Facilities[47]

In the future, we shall see a greater distinction between services that require an on-site "factory" in each country and those that require only a delivery system. By definition, all people-processing services that do not require customers to travel outside their home country for service delivery will require on-site operations in each country. The same will be true of any possession-processing service that cannot readily transport the object in question to another location for servicing. In these instances, managers may find that the best way to achieve global consistency in the core product is to create easily replicable service concepts, backed by clear standards, that allow for either franchises or country managers to clone the original core product in a new setting.

Information-based services offer management greater flexibility to split the back office and front office, with opportunities to centralize the former on a global or regional basis. Production can thus take place in one location (or just a few), yielding economies of scale and access to global expertise, while delivery remains local. Banking, insurance, and other financial service products lend themselves well to delivery through electronic channels. Many forms of news, information, and entertainment can also be delivered worldwide through public or private networks. Key issues in globalization include the constraints imposed by language, culture, and government regulations.

Global Location of Service Value Chain[48]

Different service elements can be sourced from different locations. The physical supplies needed for certain types of service delivery (such as food for hotels, fuel for transport vehicles, or spare parts for repair jobs) are often shipped from one country for consumption in another. The same is sometimes true for imported labor. But some companies, like McDonald's, choose to build up a network of local suppliers and to train host country nationals for local jobs as quickly as possible.[49]

As noted earlier, information-based services can be produced in one part of the world and delivered through electronic channels for consumption elsewhere. Indeed, information technology is a key globalization driver for such services. In the financial sector, for instance, offerings are now being pieced together from elements created in many different countries. Unlike physical goods, the logistics of service "assembly" and delivery tend to be much simpler once the necessary infrastructure and network are in place. Further, a majority of supplementary services (such as billing, payment, consultation, and advice) are information-dependent and can potentially be delivered from remote locations. In theory, a global company could centralize its billing on a global basis, using postal or electronic distribution channels to deliver the bills to customers, suitably converted to the relevant currency.

Similarly, information, consultation, order-taking/reservations, and many aspects of problem solving and payment could all be handled through electronic channels, ranging from in-person communication via telephone to remote communication via social networking tools. So long as service personnel skilled in the appropriate languages are available, many such service elements could be delivered from almost anywhere. Recent patterns of immigration in a country may create a comparative advantage in multilingual capabilities. By contrast, hospitality and safekeeping will always have to be provided locally, because they are responsive to the physical presence of customers and their possessions.

Like manufacturers, service firms should be looking for opportunities to exploit differences in national comparative advantages as they seek to build more efficient value chains. Significant economies may be gained by centralizing "information hubs" on a global basis, as FedEx does in Memphis. Through outsourcing, firms can also reduce the need for large fixed-cost investments. Taking advantage of favorable labor costs and exchange rates, a growing number of service-based businesses have identified key back-office

Sony Ericsson Joint Venture's Reverse Supply Chain System

The reverse supply chain, or the return, disposal, and repair of products, presents unique challenges to a globally competitive firm. Many telecommunication device manufacturers designing and marketing consumer electronics find reverse supply chain issues are a neglected portion of their business. Specifically, the cell phone industry has very short product life cycles and margins are very thin. The production and distribution of goods to consumers is typically a higher priority than replacing defective products. However, optimizing every point of operational cost is critical to maintaining competitiveness in this industry.

The Sony Ericsson joint venture found that the optimization of the reverse supply chain required the attention of logistics and repair specialists. To resolve this issue, the organization specified mobile phone repairs to be done in Mexico and received logistics support from the Supply Chain Solutions (SCS) division of UPS.[50] The basis for this decision was to maximize the expertise each entity had to offer. For the Mexican repair operations, the goal was reduced cost. Meanwhile, the SCS of UPS was part of the project based on its expertise in supply chain management.

Based on repair volume and customer diversity, the repair firm could not keep parts on site. Therefore, UPS handled the warehousing of returned phones and parts in a distribution facility in El Paso, Texas. Sony Ericsson was not required to possess any of the inventory involved. Instead, the joint venture managed the operation through Enterprise Resource Planning (ERP) software. Globalizing the reverse supply chain was a cost-effective solution for the company, but the cross-border logistical expertise required with both UPS and the ERP system provided Sony Ericsson with a point of differentiation deemed too difficult to consider by competitors. This provided the groundwork needed to develop a top-rate reverse logistics supply chain. To accomplish this and remain competitive in an industry known for rapid competitive adaptation, Sony Ericsson set continuous improvement goals focusing on both integrated processes and localized operations.[51] The result has been a more effective and efficient reverse logistics system aligned with marketplace needs.

activities that can be conducted more cheaply but without loss of quality in a different country from where their customers are located. As indicated with Ericsson and its reverse supply chain, this is happening with front-office and customer-interface elements, too, as companies build global reservation and customer service systems that are networked around the world.

LOCATING INDIVIDUAL ACTIVITIES

Thinking in terms of a global value-added chain makes it clear that a global strategy can be applied to different links of the chain. Some elements of the chain can be geographically concentrated while others are duplicated and dispersed. So how should each element of the value-added chain be located in a global strategy? The next sections discuss how to configure the elements whose location is most affected by globalization drivers.

Global Financing

This book concerns global strategy at the business rather than the corporate level. So issues like financing, a corporate function, are not really within the scope of this work. But one issue worth highlighting is how the financing task should differ between companies pursuing multilocal strategies and those pursuing global strategies. In particular, the finance function for global strategy needs to match *global* competitors' costs of capital, not just those of competitors in each national market.[52] Such matching requires in the first place that the company have a good understanding of global competitors' true cost of capital. That task is not so easy, as witnessed by debate in the 1980s and 1990s on whether Japanese firms had, on average, a lower cost of capital than Western companies.[53] In fact, this issue lingered for many years—particularly since Japan's interest rate has been extremely low since the mid-1990s. Though driven by the sustained economic downturn of the Japanese economy, this nonetheless impacts the cost of capital required by Japanese firms vis-à-vis their competitors.

Companies that aspire to be global in operations are finding that they must also be global in their approach to financing.[54] High domestic costs and international competition are forcing many companies to borrow at the lowest cost of capital. Therefore they must tap global equity markets, which are increasingly interconnected and open to international firms. Global financing, however, has led to increased complexity of financing. Financial derivatives, hedging, and the volatility of many financial markets are among those risks that create tension between headquarters and their subsidiaries. As a result, global firms have tended to centralize these financing responsibilities, ensuring control over such risky endeavors as hedging. Japan's Sony has gone one step further. In 2001, it became the world's first large multinational company to move its treasury and foreign currency operations to a different country from that of its headquarters. Sony planned to move this operation to London, in the hope of saving 6 or 7 billion yen a year in commission payments to market intermediaries.[55] This allowed Sony to reduce the impact of currency fluctuations in subsequent years in its worldwide operations. In fact, such a move freed Sony to take a more localized approach in its sourcing and manufacturing to optimize performance.[56]

Overall, a global approach to financial management "requires creating and sustaining financial management platforms and practices that minimize the firm's real after-tax cost of capital, diversify capital sources, minimize financial risks, and realize savings through globalization."[57] Issues to do with the management, rather than the location, of global financing will be discussed in Chapter 8.

Global Research and Development

In parallel with the notion of global products, the essence of a global strategy for R&D is that it be conducted to serve the entire global market rather than individual countries. Most multinational companies have historically run their R&D operation to stress serving either the home market or individual foreign markets, rather than the global market as a whole.[58] Global excellence in R&D means being able to access new knowledge and capabilities anywhere in the world and being able to develop globally appealing products and services that can be produced on a globally competitive basis.

In terms of accessing knowledge, multinational companies historically have concentrated their R&D activities in their home countries, thereby greatly reducing their ability to access overseas knowledge and innovation. This mattered less when the creation of new knowledge was the near monopoly of North America, Western Europe, and Japan (Kenichi Ohmae's triad economies),[59] also the home bases of most multinationals. But the exponential rise in technology and knowledge creation has created a global diaspora of expertise. Global companies now need to access knowledge and development capabilities not just in triad nations but also in emerging economies such as China, India, and Brazil. Several routes exist: physically setting up R&D overseas but keeping these units plugged into the global network, by electronic means constantly and in person sometimes; hiring scientists and technologists from overseas; or frequent visits to and other contacts with countries that are sources of innovation.

The location and management of the R&D activity can have a major effect on how well it serves such a global function. Many executives consider that the output of R&D activity serves end markets best when the activity is also located in those markets.[60] But a global strategy for R&D needs to balance this need with several others:

- Global R&D needs to tap into sources of knowledge and information wherever they might be located on the globe.
- Global R&D needs to transmit that knowledge back to the central R&D management wherever that might be.
- The central management function needs to ensure that this knowledge is used as appropriate.
- There has to be a process for allocating priorities on a global basis of strategic need rather than of proximity. Otherwise, the R&D staff are likely to favor the projects of the managers they see regularly rather than those of distant foreigners.
- The global R&D activity has to be able to develop global products with the capability for customization for major markets.

All of these tasks have to be performed while balancing the need to achieve critical mass and economies of scale, which varies by industry. Analysis of the industry's globalization drivers helps determine how best to locate and manage the R&D activity to meet these needs.

To meet the above needs, multinational companies have developed multiple approaches to R&D configuration:[61]

- *Home base model*—one country location for all technology development
- *Multiple home bases*—one country location for each technology or business, but not always the same country
- *Worldwide lead center*—one center in a dispersed network identified as the core location for specific business technology and responsible for managing dispersed technology management units worldwide
- *Regional bases*—one center in each region
- *Regional technology headquarters*—one regional center designated as the lead center for the region, managing a regionally dispersed network of centers and coordinating with other regional headquarters
- *Hetararchy*—lead centers chosen on a project-by-project basis.

EFFECTS OF MARKET GLOBALIZATION DRIVERS ON GLOBAL R&D   A number of market globalization drivers affect where R&D should be located and how it should be managed. *Common customer needs* make it less necessary to locate R&D in multiple countries, so favoring concentration to achieve scale benefits. The presence of *global customers* encourages companies to place some of their R&D activities close to their most important global customers. The existence of important *lead countries* strongly encourages companies to locate at least some of their R&D activities in those countries.

As a minimum, companies should locate in lead countries a scanning function to gather information on developments. A recurring theme found in the research conducted for this book was the need for American companies to locate some R&D activity in Japan. Many of these companies face strong Japanese global competitors and are also very weak in the Japanese market. R&D presence in Japan would help them to better understand the sources of their Japanese competitors' technical capabilities, as well as to improve their ability to serve the Japanese market, and perhaps global markets also.

Emerging economies can also be lead markets for R&D. As indicated by the emergence of China as an Asian R&D powerhouse,[62] there is little doubt that Japan's preeminence in the region is challenged by recent macroeconomic trends. More specifically, conditions in China have facilitated process and product innovation in the solar energy[63] and biotechnology[64] sectors to support this regional R&D shift. Additionally, countries such as India with an established presence in pharmaceuticals[65] also can become a lead market for medical devices specifically geared to disparate, rural communities.[66] Taken together, emerging economies offer unique opportunities for R&D to establish new markets regionally as well as worldwide.

EFFECTS OF COST GLOBALIZATION DRIVERS ON GLOBAL R&D Cost is easily the most important globalization driver in affecting the location of R&D activities. R&D activity seems, in most industries, to need a large amount of expensive equipment and many scientists to work in close collaboration to achieve any significant results. So companies have traditionally favored concentrating the activity. In addition, the high cost of R&D makes the international duplication of facilities very difficult. Increasingly, however, the need to locate R&D in globally strategic countries and the spreading availability of R&D skills are encouraging companies to spread their R&D efforts and to find creative ways to maintain a globally integrated network of R&D workers. As Texas Instruments proved, locating R&D in strategically important countries (e.g., India) and integrating them in a cohesive network can position a company well for strategic moves in the future.[67] In fact, computer and telecommunications technology is also making it more possible to have geographically dispersed R&D. As part of its computer utilization program, Dow Chemical's R&D activities in its U.S. and Europe centers are integrated through use of software and hardware programs shared throughout the Dow global network. This allowed Dow to develop new R&D initiatives focusing on environmental topics,[68] but also set the stage for the company to construct a technology research laboratory in China.[69]

EFFECTS OF GOVERNMENT GLOBALIZATION DRIVERS ON GLOBAL R&D While government trade policies—through tariffs, quotas, and local content rules—may force multinational companies to manufacture locally, government regulation can have a less direct effect on R&D. Companies may sometimes find it necessary to locate in particular countries in order to better understand the technical specifications and regulations. For example, the drug approval process is so complex that having a local R&D presence can help companies deal with the process more successfully. Governments are also eager for technology transfer into their countries. So a local R&D facility that operates as part of a global network can be used to enhance relations and bargaining power with host governments.

EFFECTS OF COMPETITIVE GLOBALIZATION DRIVERS ON GLOBAL R&D   As with other global strategy levers, companies need to be concerned if their competitors pursue a globally more astute strategy for R&D. In particular, companies that conduct their R&D primarily at home may well need to reciprocate when foreign competitors set up R&D on their territory. Lastly, companies may find acquisitions of competitors particularly helpful in strengthening their global R&D, both as a way of obtaining technical expertise and as a way of enhancing the scale of R&D operations.

Global Purchasing and Sourcing

Using a global strategy for purchasing is the mirror image of catering to global customers. A globally centralized and integrated approach to purchasing can ensure that the business has access to the best possible materials and components as well as the best possible prices. Whether to incur the costs and additional management requirements of global purchasing depends on the specific potential benefits. For example, Singer Furniture found its own offshore sourcing to be inefficient and unable to exploit the potential for sourcing economies. So it contracted with another company, IMX, to be its exclusive agent for overseas purchasing. IMX used its own global network to find low-cost sourcing opportunities that lower purchasing and shipping costs of Singer goods. In addition, Singer benefited from the increased purchasing clout and economies of scale from sharing this activity with another company. Based on its general sewing products and appliances, the company diversified on an international scale into a company not only emphasizing furniture, but also became an intermediary for many interior and home design products.[70]

The automotive industry has probably gone the furthest in the use of global sourcing. For example, the European Ford Escort, which was designed to be a world car and wound up as a pan-European model, sourced components from 15 different countries: the United Kingdom and Germany, where it is final-assembled, as well as Norway, Sweden, Denmark, Belgium, the Netherlands, France, Austria, Switzerland, Italy, Spain, the United States, Canada, and Japan.[71] Jose Ignacio Lopez led global cost-cutting efforts in procurement at General Motors and then at Volkswagen. Breaking from traditional relationships, Lopez put suppliers through rigorous rounds of bidding, demanding increased supplier efficiencies and lower prices.

The Internet further accelerated the trend toward global procurement. The three major U.S. automobile companies combined to create a joint purchasing on-line tool, ANX (Automotive Exchange Network), where potential suppliers can access these companies' requirements. Such initiatives allow automobile manufacturers to leverage purchasing and sourcing capabilities to develop products with a global appeal. In fact, Ford,[72] General Motors,[73] and Mercedes[74] have marketed so-called global car concepts, but Nissan is furthest along with its Sunny product already in the marketplace.[75]

Global sourcing has also been enabled by the emergence of global air cargo companies that provide end-to-end logistics services and delivery anywhere in the world. After constructing global networks in the 1990s, the four major companies (DHL, FedEx, UPS, and TNT) now operate in more than 200 countries.[76] This was clearly an indication of the extent to which global purchasing and sourcing became a part of everyday life and business two decades later.

Global Production

Production and manufacturing cover a large number of activities, including the development of product and process technology, the building of production capacity and plant facilities, maintaining the manufacturing information system, managing materials and inbound and outbound logistics, maintaining quality and reliability standards, planning production, and managing the actual production operations. Typically, most of these activities need to be performed in close proximity to each other, so that location decisions tend to cover these activities as a package. Nevertheless, to the extent that a particular activity can be separated from the others, the location strategy for it can be different.

Global sourcing and production have to reconcile several conflicting objectives: cost, productivity, quality, reliability, protection of expertise, and trade barriers. So there is seldom a single sourcing and production configuration that can maximize all of these objectives, but they can be optimized. In 2001, hourly labor costs ranged from over US $25 an hour in Germany to under 25 cents in Indonesia, or a ratio of more than 100 to 1. By 2007, average hourly labor costs in Germany were more competitive at $21.50 per hour[77] in comparison to China's less than $1 rate.[78] However, the comparative labor costs in countries such as Indonesia[79] still made the prospect of global sourcing and production important to multinational corporations.

With such large differences, even companies in non-labor-intensive industries need to seriously think about where to locate activities. Furthermore, companies should not be put off by the low *average* productivity in low-cost economies. These figures include all the unmodernized, often state-owned, companies. The whole point is to achieve higher levels of productivity by making investments and transferring technology and expertise.

There are many arguments for and against foreign manufacturing, some of which were covered in the discussion of offshore manufacturing. Reasons for foreign manufacturing include enhancing customer relations outside the home country; getting closer to markets; gaining access to local, immobile factors of production and technological resources; reducing transportation costs; avoiding tariff and nontariff barriers; satisfying some demands of and gaining benefits from local governments; hedging against country-specific risks and preempting competition.[80] This author assumes that the reader already understands these issues or can learn about them elsewhere[81] and concentrates instead on the issue of how to configure a global manufacturing network in the sense defined earlier.

Cost globalization drivers constitute the key reason for using global manufacturing, with government drivers also important, and market and competitive drivers less so.

EFFECTS OF COST DRIVERS ON GLOBAL PRODUCTION   Probably the most important cost driver for global manufacturing is the nature of *scale economies*. As discussed earlier, globally centralized manufacturing is favored to the extent that the minimum efficient scale is greater than the volume the firm can sell in individual national markets. In fact, if local and regional production initiatives fail, many companies consolidate manufacturing facilities to regain the scale economies lost. Steep *learning and experience effects* also favor global manufacturing in order to move down the curve faster. So it is no coincidence that competitors in the semiconductor industry, well known for its steep experience effects, primarily use globally centralized manufacturing.

Having *favorable logistics* is also a critical requirement for global manufacturing to work. Shipping costs must not be so great as to offset the cost savings from centralization. But creativity can sometimes be applied to reduce transportation barriers. An American manufacturer of medical sterilization equipment manufactured in its local markets because the product, with its large sterilization chamber, was too bulky to be shipped economically. But this manufacturing strategy left the company operating below full capacity in each of its minimum efficient scale plants. Eventually the company hit on the solution of centralizing in the United States manufacture of the sterilizing controls, which constituted the more valuable part of the product, shipping these high-value controls, using local suppliers to provide the low-value sterilizing chambers, and then conducting final assembly in the local countries. Similarly, Gettinger, a subsidiary of Electrolux, the Swedish appliance manufacturer, set up in several countries local manufacturing of the bulky appliance shells. Some products, however, such as explosive chemicals, face other, more difficult, logistical barriers.

Differences in country costs also favor the use of global manufacturing by making it worthwhile to locate in specific countries. Particularly when looking to exploit low labor costs companies need to consider what percentage of total costs (both purchases and value added) is accounted for by labor costs and the differences in labor productivity between countries. Differences in tax rates also provide another source of differences in country costs. Using a global manufacturing network, rather than duplicated multilocal facilities or a single exporting facility, offers two ways to reduce taxes. First, the selective location of manufacturing facilities, inherent in global strategy, allows the company to pick countries with low (either official or negotiated) tax rates. Second, the transshipment of raw materials, and intermediate and final products, within a global manufacturing network provides opportunities to set transfer prices and subsidiary remittances so as to minimize total tax liability.

Some researchers argue that in most manufacturing industries, labor costs have been outweighed by market access, quality control, timely delivery, and responsiveness to customers as determinants of global competitiveness. Therefore, global site selections might hinge on the cooperation, flexibility, and trainability of the labor force rather than on its cost.[82]

EFFECTS OF GOVERNMENT DRIVERS ON GLOBAL PRODUCTION   Whether an industry has *favorable trade policies* greatly affects the potential for global manufacturing. In essence, greater protectionism reduces the ability to operate with a global manufacturing network.[83] Ironically, while mature industries with their more stable product and process designs suit themselves to global manufacturing, protectionism is often more prevalent in such industries also, both because local production has had time to spread and because jobs lost to imports cannot be readily re-created. Many trade barriers are now falling, which is one of the major drivers spurring companies to investigate global manufacturing. The global network can also be used to circumvent or reduce the impact of trade barriers such as through the judicious use of local content. By assembling and conducting some manufacturing operations in Britain, Japanese automobile manufacturers were able to get their vehicles certified as European origin even though a very high percentage of the content is originally imported from Japan. The Goodyear Tire Company wanted to strengthen its production base in the global tire industry by setting up a manufacturing subsidiary in South Korea. But Goodyear faced stiff government regulations against its move. Only by agreeing to become an exporting plant was Goodyear able to win government approval for the ownership that the company wanted. Similarly, China, India, and many other countries often require high percentages of local manufacturing. From the host country government perspective, the reasoning for this is obvious: to increase employment and provide future manufacturing opportunities.

Compatible technical standards also make it easier to use global manufacturing, by reducing the need for running different product lines. So the task of a centralized manufacturing plant is simplified.

EFFECTS OF MARKET DRIVERS ON GLOBAL PRODUCTION   Product designs that are changing rapidly to meet changing market needs tend to require a close linkage between marketers, designers, and manufacturing. So the stable product designs that dominate in the mature stage of the product life cycle should make it easier to use global manufacturing, provided *common customer needs* across countries also apply. Furthermore, the cost savings from global manufacturing are most needed in mature industries where customers use precise, hard criteria based on product price performance relationships in their purchasing decisions.[84] It is no coincidence that maturity in the U.S. and European automobile and consumer electronics markets coincided with dominance by Japanese manufacturers using globally centralized manufacturing.

An additional market driver affecting global manufacturing is the country-of-origin effect discussed earlier. A dilemma that companies face in locating production facilities is that many low-cost countries do not have a high reputation for quality. One solution may be to use quality control managers from countries that have high reputations for quality, such as Germany or Japan, and to ensure that potential customers know about this fact. There is the apocryphal story that in the 1950s a town in Japan changed its name to Usa in order to be able to label products manufactured there as "Made in USA." In another example of how the preferred countries of origin have changed over time, nineteenth-century German toolmakers used to imitate the Sheffield (England) trademark. To minimize the negative connotations of manufacturing in a country with a poor image, Façonnable, a French clothing producer, sells garments and accessories while marketing that its products are "Designed in France, Made in China." Another example is Apple's iPad. The iPad is labeled as "Designed by Apple, Assembled in China."

EFFECTS OF COMPETITIVE DRIVERS ON GLOBAL PRODUCTION   As with the use of the other global strategy levers, global manufacturing may be mandated by competitive actions. If the industry has characteristics favoring global manufacturing, competitors that move first will gain scale, experience, or other advantages that can keep them ahead of slower movers. So in such industries firms need to match or preempt their *competitors' use of global manufacturing*.

ADDITIONAL FACTORS   Each factory can also have a different role in a global network. That role then affects the degree of integration needed as well as the sophistication and content of the support activities that should be located at the factory.[85] These roles include getting access to low-cost production factors, using local technological resources, and gaining proximity to local markets. Furthermore, for each of those roles, a factory can play more passive or active roles within the global network. Integration of the different factories within a global network is becoming increasingly important. In a multicountry study of international manufacturing, managers at several U.S. multinational corporations reported that their primary challenge in coming years is integrating their existing global operations to perform as a single system rather than as islands of manufacturing and technological capabilities.[86] Though technological advances facilitate corporate integration, this problem is an ongoing challenge.

In addition, some specific characteristics of a company's manufacturing process may make it easier to shift from a situation of duplicated independent plants to one of an interdependent global network. One characteristic is that the plants should have manufacturing processes that are more or less similar. A second characteristic is that the pattern of material that flows between plants and warehouses should be relatively simple. A third characteristic is that manufacturing configurations should be relatively simple.[87]

ROLE OF FLEXIBLE MANUFACTURING AND PRODUCTION   As mentioned in Chapter 4, the advent of computer-based "flexible manufacturing" (using computer-aided manufacturing—the CAM in CAD/CAM) redefined the notion of globally standardized products.[88] Flexible manufacturing is an important option that needs to be factored into global manufacturing strategy.[89] In particular, the use of flexible manufacturing interacts with both the use of globally standardized products and the use of geographically concentrated manufacturing.

In terms of market globalization drivers, the presence of *common customer needs* favors product standardization and the subsequent manufacturing concentration to produce those products. But flexible manufacturing allows more scope for producing customized variants of a core global product. So even in industries where customer needs are not that common, a business with a flexible manufacturing capability can design a standardized global core that it then customizes, in a centralized manufacturing facility, for different national or regional markets. Markets at an earlier stage of the product life cycle face greater variety in product design, which would usually prevent the use of globally standardized products. But, again, a flexible manufacturing capability may allow earlier use of standardized core global products and concentrated manufacturing. In terms of cost globalization drivers, high *economies of scale* favor concentrated manufacturing but have conflicting effects on the need to use flexible manufacturing. On the one hand, companies will not be able to support many minimum efficient scale plants, so having the flexibility to produce many different products in each plant will be an advantage. On the other hand, by their nature, flexible manufacturing techniques tend to reduce the gains from large-scale production.

Some experts believe that flexible manufacturing can be used to increase product variety without increasing costs.[90] But some increase in cost seems typically necessary. For example, Panasonic, the Japanese electronics company, makes customized, hand-built bicycle models to individual order. With few employees devoted to the product and a design software, its small factory has produced over 11 million variations on nearly 20 models in about 200 color patterns and almost any size. Customers can be fitted as for a made-to-measure suit before any production begins. Though no longer offered in the United States, the finished bicycles can sell for a considerable premium compared to standard bicycles. But it might be argued that these customized bicycles are based on a standardized core set of parts and designs. Furthermore, the large price differential over the mass production models limits the share of the market that can be obtained by the customized products.

MANAGING INTERDEPENDENCE BETWEEN BUSINESSES   Although not a central theme of this book, interdependence among different businesses within a company has implications for activity location. Many companies share activities across different businesses, and such sharing often takes place in several countries. For example, in many paper-based companies, different businesses share upstream pulp-processing facilities. Or different businesses in a company may share a distribution system or sales force as in many consumer packaged goods companies. In these cases, problems arise when one business requires a more globalized strategy in a shared activity than does another business. Two businesses in the same company may share two activities in their value-added chains, such as purchasing and manufacturing. But one business should have a primarily global strategy while the other business should not. So the first business should ideally have globally centralized manufacturing of standardized global products, while the second business needs locally adapted products and could use local manufacturing also. But the economics are such that both businesses' production costs are lower when they share centralized manufacturing facilities. So a possible compromise solution would be to allocate one corner of the factory to work on customizing products for the second business. In addition, any extra costs that the second business incurs because of having to accommodate the first business's need for centralized production, such as for transportation of finished goods, should be ameliorated by giving some break in the transfer price to local subsidiaries.

Global Distribution and Logistics

Global logistics embody the challenge for global companies to be able to deliver their intermediate and final products anywhere in the world in a cost-effective and timely manner. The solution can seldom be one single distribution hub, but again a network of hubs, exemplified by the systems of the global delivery companies, such as FedEx, DHL, and UPS. Another issue is whether to use a globally common distribution system or a differentiated one. Coca-Cola has achieved great success by replacing local distribution systems with its effective and efficient standardized distribution methods.[91] In Japan, it achieved a 70 percent market share in its category by displacing the country's traditional seven-layer distribution system.

Most of the issues in the location of distribution activities relate to classic marketing and internationalization concerns. Logistical factors become doubly important in an international context. But globalization drivers can also change how these factors apply. In particular, changes in government globalization drivers can redefine the optimal configuration of a global distribution system. The advent of the single European market provided the most dramatic application of this effect. The removal of border controls allowed distribution managers to redraw the maps that show time from their distribution centers to various delivery points. Maps that had been contorted by the time taken for trucks to pass frontier controls now show smooth concentric circles instead. As a result, distribution centers have been consolidated and centralized, as with manufacturing sites. Intel reduced shipping costs by at least 7 percent by consolidating its worldwide freight expenditures with four transportation firms. As a result, from its 14 manufacturing sites around the world, Intel improved on-time delivery performance into the high 90th percentile and significantly improved the level of service that Intel is able to provide its customers.

BENETTON'S GLOBAL DISTRIBUTION STRATEGY Creative thinking along the global value-added chain can produce highly effective global distribution. Benetton provides one of the best examples of a global distribution strategy. From a single computerized warehouse in Treviso, Italy, Benetton ships its products all over the world directly to the independent, but contractually tied, retail stores that sell its clothing. This distribution centralization is made possible, in part, by Benetton's use of just-in-time ordering. Benetton makes no garment until it is ordered by one of its stores. So an innovative approach in its order-taking and manufacturing value-added activities has allowed global strategic advantage to be attained via the distribution element of the value chain. Similar initiatives have been implemented by competitors such as Zara, Gap, and Hennes & Mauritz who also now operate in a more competitive market.[92]

Global Service

The last activity in the value chain, customer service, usually, by its nature, has to be performed locally. Even so, some aspects such as information and communication systems can be centralized. Furthermore, providing a uniform standard of service provides assurance to global customers—whether organizations or individuals. At the same time, differences in both culture and custom particularly affect what customers may expect in different countries. On weekends in Japan medical equipment company sales representatives have been known to wash the cars of the doctors that they call on! As a sign of their commitment to service, these representatives may even collect their customers' children from school.

Global success in service now requires the availability of consistent, effective, timely, and convenient customer service around the world on demand. Customers today require service anytime, anywhere. As the world's leading global retail bank Citibank goes a bit further. Its global motto has been that customers can do business with it "anytime, anywhere, any way." To support this, Citibank invested hugely in the 1990s in both physical infrastructure, such as branches and ATMs, and technological systems to make real on its boast. More recently, Citibank has built on this and positions itself as a company that "never sleeps."

Success also requires building close customer relationships through customer service and knowledge sharing. Hewlett-Packard (HP) is a global leader in computer-based customer support services for its customers. It maintains a globally standardized set of services that range from site design to systems integration to remote diagnostics. This global standardization includes seamless service at any hour of the day or night from anywhere in the world.[93] To provide this, HP maintains a global chain of customer response centers integrated into a global network. Diners' Club uses information technology to provide global services to customers as a means to maintain a competitive edge in the credit card industry. To satisfy the needs of its corporate customers, Diners' Club created Global Vision, a software program that tracks transactions and account balances and reports multiple currencies and summarizes them into a master currency. Global

Vision, therefore, enables customers around the world to see their transactions in local and foreign currencies in a streamlined system that is user-friendly and responsive to customer demand.[94]

Global companies also need to be sensitive to cross-cultural customer service issues. Infowavz, an Indian company that provides outsourced customer support services primarily over the Internet, gives American names to its Mumbai-based staff and trains them in colloquial American English. Other global service operations provide pop-up menus with weather and local news items, such as sports results, so that service staff can make small talk with callers.

GUIDELINES FOR LOCATING GLOBAL ACTIVITIES

An effective global network can locate activities to achieve the benefits of cost reduction, increased competitive leverage, and so on. At the same time this network must be able to serve the key needs of local markets around the world. The following guidelines summarize the key issues on this topic:

- In locating global activities, managers should free up their thinking by starting with the "zero-based" assumption that their business has no activities located anywhere in the world. Then ask what the ideal pattern of location would be. Only then should managers bring back into consideration the reality of where the business's activities are actually located now, and what it would cost (in the broadest sense) to relocate activities.
- Different activities have differing needs for global centralization, local dispersion, or some combination in between.
- The ideal pattern of location changes with circumstances and the evolution of the business.
- The best pattern of location usually allows for some duplication in order to provide flexibility and safeguards against disruption.
- Coordination of geographically dispersed activities can substitute in some cases for global centralization.
- Managers should consider both strategic advantage and comparative (country-based) advantage in locating activities to maximize competitive advantage.
- Some activities, particularly R&D, need to have presence in globally strategic countries.

Discussion and Research Questions

1. What is the difference between a multilocal and a global approach to locating value-adding activities?
2. What is the difference between strategic and comparative bases of advantage?
3. Select one company or business and trace how it has developed its strategic and comparative bases of advantage over time.
4. What parts of its value chain should an American manufacturer of pharmaceuticals consider relocating, and where, in light of the North American Free Trade Agreement? Would your answer be different for an alternative energy start-up?
5. Select one company or business and describe how the location of its value-adding activities has shifted over time.
6. Which aspects of service businesses are most suited to global centralization?

Notes

1. Michael Porter calls these choices configuration (location) and coordination, and he provides a four-cell typology of types of international strategy: high foreign investment with extensive coordination, country-centered strategy, export-based strategy, and purest global strategy. While these types provide helpful summaries, this author's approach views location and coordination choices as providing a continuum rather than discrete choices. Furthermore, the location and coordination of activities constitute only one each of the five global strategy dimensions and the four organization dimensions. See Michael E. Porter, "Competition in Global Industries: A Conceptual Framework," in Michael Porter, Ed., *Competition in Global Industries* (Boston, MA: Harvard Business School Press, 1986), and Porter, "Changing Patterns of International Competition," *California Management Review*, Vol. 28, No. 2, Winter 1986, pp. 9–40. For an in-depth discussion of the role of value-adding activities in competitive strategy, see Michael E. Porter, *Competitive Advantage* (New York: The Free Press, 1985).

2. Both Prahalad and Doz (1987) and Bartlett and Ghoshal (1989) advocate the use of a global network in which subsidiaries and the center specialize in different activities. See C. K. Prahalad and Yves L. Doz, *The Multinational Mission: Balancing Local Demands and Global Vision* (New York: The Free Press, 1987), and Christopher A. Bartlett and Sumantra Ghoshal, *Managing Across Borders: The Transnational Solution* (Boston, MA: Harvard Business School Press, 1989). See also Nitin Nohria, Sumantra Ghoshal (contributor), and Cedric Crocker (editor), *The Differentiated Network: Organizing Multinational Corporations for Value Creation* (San Francisco: Jossey-Bass Business and Management Series, 1997).

3. Thomas C. Lawton, "Exploding the Value Chain," research presentation at Judge Institute of Management Studies, University of Cambridge, February 3, 2000.

4. See Mari Kondo and George S. Yip, Chapter 16, "Regional Groupings—ASEAN, AFTA, APEC, Etc.," in George S. Yip, Ed., *Asian Advantage* (Reading, MA: Addison-Wesley, 1998), and *Asian Advantage: Updated—After the Crisis* (Cambridge, MA: Perseus Books, 2000).

5. See, for example, Rudiger Dornbush, Stanley Fisher, and Paul A. Samuelson, "Comparative Advantage, Trade and Payments in a Ricardian Model with a Continuum of Goods," *American Economic Review*, Vol. 67, December 1977, pp. 823–39.

6. For a discussion of the ethical issues in manufacturing in poor countries, see Christopher Avery, *Business and Human Rights in a Time of Change* (London: Amnesty International Publications, 2000).

7. Sarah Skidmore, "Nike Finds Major Labor Violations at Malaysian Factory," *USA Today*, August 1, 2008, http://www.usatoday.com/money/industries/retail/2008-08-01-nike-malaysia-labor-violations_N.htm.

8. Jeremiah Marquez, "China Will Look into Report of Cadmium in Childrens' Jewelry," *USA Today*, January 12, 2010, http://www.usatoday.com/news/health/2010-01-10-childrens-jewelry-probe_N.htm.

9. See Levi Strauss' company Web site, http://www.levistrauss.com.

10. "How Green Is My Sneaker?" *The Wall Street Journal*, July 21, 2010, http://online.wsj.com/article/SB10001424052748703724104575379621448311224.html.

11. James Epstein-Reeves, "The Parents of CSR: Nike and Kathie Lee Gifford," *The CSR Blog*, June 8, 2010, http://blogs.forbes.com/csr/2010/06/08/the-parents-of-csr-nike-and-kathie-lee-gifford.

12. There is extensive literature on the country-of-origin effect. See, for example, Johny K. Johansson, "Determinants and Effects of 'Made in' Labels," *International Marketing Review*, Vol. 6, No. 1, Spring 1989, pp. 47–58.

13. For a guide to these fundamental issues in internationalization see, for example, Michael R. Czinkota, Ilkka A. Ronkainen, and Michael Moffett, *International Business*, update 2000 (Harcourt, 2000), and Beamish, Morrison, Rosenzweig, and Inkpen, *International Management: Text and Cases*, 4th ed. (New York: Irwin McGraw-Hill, 2000).

14. "2011 Global R&D Funding Forecast," *R&D Magazine*, December 2010, http://www.rdmag.com.

15. There are many sources of advice on evaluating FDI. See, for example, Franklin R. Root, *Entry Strategies for International Markets* (San Francisco: Jossey Bass, 1994), Chapter 5, on which this list is based. Root also characterizes four kinds of risk in FDI—general instability risk, ownership (expropriation) risk, operations risk, and transfer risk. See also Stephen J. Kobrin, *Managing Political Risk Assessment* (Berkeley: University of California Press, 1982).

16. But Porter has challenged this traditional notion by espousing a concept of the competitive advantage of nations that includes factor conditions, demand conditions, related and supporting industries, and firm strategy, structure, and rivalry. See Michael E. Porter, *The Competitive Advantage of Nations* (New York: The Free Press, 1990).

17. Some strategists now argue that time is a critical source of competitive advantage. See George Stalk, Jr., and Thomas M. Hout, *Competing Against Time* (New York: The Free Press, 1990).

18. See Porter's discussion of the role of firm strategy, structure, and rivalry in spurring performance improvement in Michael E. Porter, *The Competitive Advantage of Nations* (New York: The Free Press, 1990).

19. "China's Total Manufacturing Costs Are Now Only 6% Below Those of American Factories," *IndustryWeek,* May 21, 2009, http://www.industryweek.com/articles/china_loses_low-cost_manufacturing_crown_to_india_mexico_19194.aspx.

20. Rafael Rivero and Sara Miller Llana, "Is Mexico the New China?" *The Christian Science Monitor,* September 11, 2008, http://www.csmonitor.com/2008/0911/p01s02-woam.html.

21. Sara Miller Llana, "Mexico Prepares for (Ford) Fiesta," *The Christian Science Monitor,* June 2, 2008, http://www.csmonitor.com/World/Americas/2008/0602/p06s02-woam.html.

22. "Automotive Manufacturing Industry," August 4, 2010, *U.S. Commercial Service,* http://www.buyusa.gov/mexico/en/automotive_manufacturing.html.

23. This analysis is based on Abraham M. George and C. William Schroth, "Managing Foreign Exchange for Competitive Advantage," *Sloan Management Review,* Winter 1991, pp. 105–16.

24. Lynn Thomasson and Rita Nazareth, "Caterpillar Beating Komatsu as Dow Soars on Dollar," *Bloomberg,* November 23, 2009, http://www.bloomberg.com/apps/news?pid=newsarchive&sid=aFu70bm9zvsc.

25. James R. Hagerty and Bob Tita, "Caterpillar to Buy Bucyrus," *Wall Street Journal,* November 16, 2010, http://online.wsj.com/article/SB10001424052748703326204575616223898424894.html.

26. See also W. Carl Kester and Timothy A. Luehrman, "Are We Feeling More Competitive Yet? The Exchange Rate Gambit?" *Sloan Management Review,* Winter 1989, pp. 19–28.

27. Richard Blackden and Louise Armitstead, "Japan Crisis Prompts First Joint Currency Intervention Since 2000 Amid Threat to Global Recovery," *The Telegraph,* March 18, 2011, http://www.telegraph.co.uk/finance/currency/8389699/Japan-crisis-prompts-first-joint-currency-intervention-since-2000-amid-threat-to-global-recovery.html.

28. See Donald R. Lessard, "Finance and Global Competition: Exploiting Financial Scope and Coping with Volatile Exchange Rates," in Michael E. Porter, Ed., *Competition in Global Industries* (Boston, MA: Harvard Business School Press, 1986).

29. See Marcus C. Bogue III and Elwood S. Buffa, *Corporate Strategic Analysis* (New York: The Free Press, 1986), pp. 69–74 and 93.

30. These three options are suggested by Bruce Kogut, "Designing Global Strategies: Profiting from Operational Flexibility," *Sloan Management Review,* Fall 1985, pp. 27–38.

31. See also Bruce Kogut, "Designing Global Strategies: Comparative and Competitive Value-Added Chains," *Sloan Management Review,* Summer 1985, pp. 27–38.

32. Paul Sonne, "To Wash Hands of Palm Oil Unilever Embraces Algae," *Wall Street Journal,* September 7, 2010, http://online.wsj.com/article/SB10001424052748703720004575477531661393258.html.

33. Gerrit Jeelof, "Global Strategies of Philips," *European Management Journal,* Vol. 7, No. 1, 1989, pp. 84–91.

34. Dataquest, reported in Clyde V. Prestowitz, Jr., *Trading Places* (New York: Basic Books, 1988), pp. 144–5, and also from a private communication with a (U.S.) Semiconductor Association spokesman, March 8, 1991.

35. Daisuke Wakabayashi, "One Goal: 10 Quadrillion Calculations," *Wall Street Journal,* October 4, 2010, http://online.wsj.com/article/SB10001424052748704029304575525463311543150.html.

36. See Kogut, "Designing Global Strategies: Profiting from Operational Flexibility."

37. The need to choose between low-cost and differentiation strategies, suggested by Michael E. Porter, *Competitive Strategy: Techniques for Analyzing Industries and Competitors* (New York: The Free Press, 1980), has been challenged in a number of studies. See, for example, Roderick E. White, "Generic Business Strategies, Organizational Context and Performance: An Empirical Investigation," *Strategic Management Journal,* Vol. 7, 1986, pp. 217–31.

38. "Simplifying Philips," *The Economist,* June 10, 2004, http://www.economist.com/node/2747544.

39. "Wireless Incorporated," *The Economist,* April 26, 2007, http://www.economist.com/node/9032014.

40. "The Printed World," *The Economist,* February 10, 2011, http://www.economist.com/node/18114221.

41. See, for example, Constantinos C. Markides and Norman Berg, "Manufacturing Offshore Is Bad Business," *Harvard Business Review,* September–October 1988, pp. 113–20.

42. Markides and Berg, "Manufacturing Offshore Is Bad Business," cite Hitachi, which made microprocessors for Motorola, introducing its own 32-bit microprocessor; Toshiba, which acted as a supplier of copying machines to 3M, now promoting its own brand name; and Daewoo, while still a subcontractor to U.S. companies, now selling its own personal computer. See also Anthony Leung and George S. Yip, "Enter the Global Original Equipment Manufacturer: A New Type of Multinational Company," Working Paper, London Business School, October 31, 2000.

43. Lenovo Group's 2007/2008 Annual Report, http://www.pc.ibm.com/ww/lenovo/pdf/07_08/Lenovo_2007-08_Annual_Report_Final_E.pdf.

44. Joel Backaler, "China's Homegrown Success Stories," *Forbes,* September 12, 2010, http://blogs.forbes.com/china/2010/09/12/chinas-homegrown-success-stories/.

45. William J. Amelio, "Worldsource or Perish," *Forbes,* August 17, 2007, http://www.forbes.com/2007/08/16/lenovo-world-sourcing-oped-cx_wja_0817lenovo.html.

46. See SAP's Web site, http://www.sap.com/germany/about/investor/reports/gb2006/files/pdf/en/SAP_AR06_Customers.pdf.

47. This section is drawn from Christopher H. Lovelock and George S. Yip, "Developing Global Strategies for Service Businesses,"*California Management Review,* Vol. 38, No. 2, Winter 1996, pp. 65–86.

48. This section is drawn from Lovelock and Yip, "Developing Global Strategies for Service Businesses."

49. Andrew Server, "McDonald's Conquers the World," *Fortune,* 1994.

50. Robert J. Bowman, "Looking Backward: Sony Ericsson Takes on Challenge of Reverse Logistics," *Supply Chain Brain,* May 1, 2006, http://www.supplychainbrain.com/content/industry-verticals/high-tech-electronics/single-article-page/article/looking-backward-sony-ericsson-takes-on-challenge-of-reverse-logistics/.

51. Eric M. Hemming, "Comprehensive Thinking Drives Reverse Logistics Success at Sony Ericsson," *Reverse Logistics Magazine,* August/September 2007, http://www.rlmagazine.com/edition07p25.php.

52. See Donald R. Lessard, "Finance and Global Competition: Exploiting Financial Scope and Coping with Volatile Exchange Rates," in Michael E. Porter, Ed., *Competition in Global Industries* (Boston: Harvard Business School Press, 1986).

53. See George N. Hatsopoulos, "High Cost of Capital: Handicap of American Industry," report sponsored by the American Business Conference and Thermo-Electron Corporation, April 1983, and Carliss Y. Baldwin, "The Capital Factor: Competing for Capital in a Global Environment," in Michael E. Porter, Ed., *Competition in Global Industries* (Boston, MA: Harvard Business School Press, 1986).

54. "A Global Approach to Financing," *The Financial Post,* November 11, 1997.

55. Katherine Griffiths, "London Chosen for Sony's $25 Billion Forex Operations," *The Independent,* June 5, 2001, http://www.independent.co.uk/news/business/news/london-chosen-for-sonys-25bn-forex-operations-672888.html.

56. Sony 20-F Report filed with Securities and Exchange Commission on June 23, 2009.

57. Deloitte & Touche, *Leaders in Innovative Globalization Program,* report, London, 1998.

58. Jack N. Behrman and William A. Fischer, "Transnational Corporations: Market Orientations and R&D Abroad," *Columbia Journal of World Business,* Fall 1980, pp. 55–60.

59. Kenichi Ohmae, *Triad Power: The Coming Shape of Global Competition* (New York: Free Press, 1985).

60. Robert Ronstadt and Robert J. Kramer, "Getting the Most Out of Innovation Abroad," *Harvard Business Review,* March–April 1982, pp. 94–9.

61. D. Eleanor Westney, "Research on the Global Management of Technology Development," *Business Review,* Vol. 46, No. 1, August 1998, pp. 1–21.

62. Gautam Naik, "China Surpasses Japan in R&D as Powers Shift," *Wall Street Journal,* December 13, 2010, http://online.wsj.com/article/SB10001424052748703734204576019713917682354.html.

63. Jason Dean, Andrew Browne, and Shai Oster, "China's 'State Capitalism' Sparks a Global Backlash," *Wall Street Journal,* November 16, 2010, http://online.wsj.com/article/SB10001424052748703514904575602731006315198.html.

64. Emily Veach, "Administering Drugs with Nanoneedles," *Wall Street Journal,* September 21, 2010, http://online.wsj.com/article/SB10001424052748703989304575503650437706596.html.

65. "India: Bigger Pharma," *Businessweek,* April 18, 2005, http://www.businessweek.com/magazine/content/05_16/b3929068.htm.

66. Gujan Bagla and Atul Goel, "Innovation from India: The Next Big Wave," *Businessweek,* February 11, 2009, http://www.businessweek.com/globalbiz/content/feb2009/gb20090211_273997.htm.

67. Shelley Singh, "Texas Instruments: Growth with Work Centering Around Low Cost Innovation," *The Economic Times,* September 3, 2010, http://articles.economictimes.indiatimes.com/2010-09-03/news/27576230_1_ti-india-chip-design-texas-instruments.

68. "Dow Reaches for a Greener Future," *Businessweek,* May 1, 2003, http://online.wsj.com/article/SB10001424052748703989304575503650437706596.html.

69. Rob Atkinson and Devon Swezey, "America's Green Innovation Problem," *Bloomberg Businessweek,* May 3, 2010, http://www.businessweek.com/innovate/content/apr2010/id20100420_110955.htm.

70. See Singer's corporate Web site, http://www.singer.com.

71. See Peter Dicken, *Global Shift: Industrial Change in a Turbulent World* (London: Harper and Row, 1986), p. 304.

72. Matthew Dolan, "Ford's Little Fiesta Strives to Be 'Global' Car," *Wall Street Journal,* December 3, 2009, http://online.wsj.com/article/SB10001424052748704107104574569971206679140.html.

73. Rumman Ahmed, "GM India to Be Ready to Develop New Car by 2012," *Wall Street Journal,* January 11, 2010, http://online.wsj.com/article/SB10001424052748703652104574651733741238254.html.

74. Norihiko Shirouzu, "Mercedes Mines China for Global Car Designs," *Wall Street Journal,* Octover 27, 2009, http://online.wsj.com/article/SB10001424052748703816204574485300957544432.html.

75. Tim Beissmann, "Nissan Sunny Global Small Car Coming to Australia," *Car Advice,* December 20, 2010, http://www.caradvice.com.au/95851/nissan-sunny-global-small-car-coming-to-australia/.

76. Lawton, "Exploding the Value Chain."

77. "Germany Becoming More Competitive," *Der Spiegel,* April 22, 2008, http://www.spiegel.de/international/business/0,1518,549003,00.html.

78. Keith Bradsher, "Investors Seek Asian Options to Costly China," *New York Times,* June 18, 2008, http://www.nytimes.com/2008/06/18/business/worldbusiness/18invest.html.

79. Chris Devonshire-Ellis, "China Now Has Third Highest Labor Costs in Emerging Asia," *China Briefing,* January 19, 2011, http://www.china-briefing.com/news/2011/01/19/china-near-top-of-the-list-for-wage-overheads-in-emerging-asia.html.

80. See M. Therese Flaherty "Coordinating International Manufacturing and Technology" in Porter, Ed., *Competition in Global Industries,* and Kasra Ferdows, "Mapping International Factory Networks," in Kasra Ferdows, Ed., *Managing International Manufacturing* (Amsterdam: Elsevier, North Holland, 1989).

81. See, for example, William H. Davidson, *Global Strategic Management* (New York: John Wiley & Sons, 1982), Chapter 5, and Wickham Skinner, *Manufacturing: The Formidable Weapon* (New York: Wiley, 1985).

82. See Kasra Ferdows et al., *The Internationalization of U.S. Manufacturing: Causes and Consequences* (Washington, DC: National Academy Press, 1990), pp. 23–4.

83. National trade policies are, of course, an enormous topic. For guidance see, for example,

Raymond Vernon and Louis T. Wells, Jr., *Manager in the International Economy* (Upper Saddle River, NJ: Prentice Hall, 1986), and Michael R. Czinkota, Ilkka A. Ronkainen, and Michael Moffett, *International Business,* update 2000 (New York: Harcourt, 2000).

84. Yves L. Doz, "Managing Manufacturing Rationalization Within Multinational Companies," *Columbia Journal of World Business,* Fall 1978, pp. 82–94.

85. This section is based on Ferdows, "Mapping International Networks."

86. Kasra Ferdows et al., *The Internationalization of U.S. Manufacturing: Causes and Consequences* (Washington, DC: National Academy Press, 1990), p. 30.

87. Flaherty, "Coordinating International Manufacturing and Technology."

88. A survey study found flexibility to be an important concern of Japanese manufacturers. See Arnoud de Meyer, Jinichiro Nakane, Jeffrey Miller, and Kasra Ferdows, "Flexibility: The Next Competitive Battle—The Manufacturing Futures Survey," *Strategic Management Journal,* Vol. 10, 1989, pp. 135–44.

89. For reviews of flexible manufacturing, see Joel D. Goldhar and Mariann Jelinek, "Computer Integrated Flexible Manufacturing: Organizational, Economic, and Strategic Implications," *Interfaces,* Vol. 15, May–June 1985, pp. 94–105, and Ramachandran Jaikumar, "Postindustrial Manufacturing," *Harvard Business Review,* November–December 1986, pp. 69–76.

90. James C. Abegglen and George Stalk, Jr., *Kaisha: The Japanese Corporation* (New York: Basic Books, 1985), pp. 89–90.

91. Kenichi Ohmae, *The Evolving Global Economy: Making Sense of the New World Order* (Boston, MA: Harvard Business School Press, 1995).

92. Armorel Kenna, "Gap to Open First Italian Store, Taking on Zara, H&M in Milan," *Bloomberg Businessweek,* November 19, 2010, http://www.businessweek.com/news/2010-11-19/gap-to-open-first-italian-store-taking-on-zara-h-m-in-milan.html.

93. Lovelock and Yip, "Developing Global Strategies for Service Businesses."

94. Stanley B. Lemons, "Diners Club International's Global Marketing Strategy," The Anderson School at UCLA, June 6, 1996.

CHAPTER 6

Creating Global Marketing

Global marketing constitutes the fourth global strategy lever that companies can use to globalize their strategy. A worldwide business uses global marketing when it takes the same or similar approach or content for one or more elements of the marketing mix, that is, the same or similar brand names, advertising, and so on, in different countries. Multinational companies increasingly use global marketing and have been highly successful—Nestlé with its common brand name applied to many products in all countries, Citibank with its global advertising themes, Hewlett-Packard (HP) with its global account management programs, and Xerox with its global leasing policies. But *global marketing is not about standardizing the marketing process.* Standardizing the way in which country subsidiaries analyze markets and develop marketing plans is merely good multinational practice—a way of transferring skills and setting high standards for the marketing function.[1]

Global marketing and selling means striving for the appropriate balance of global uniformity and local adaptation in all elements of the marketing mix, but with a probable bias in favor of uniformity unless a good case can be made for local exceptions. This means casting aside the previous conventional wisdom that companies should globally standardize the marketing process but not the marketing content. Global excellence in marketing now means looking for uniformity. For example, Unilever has recognized that marketing too many different brands around the world hampers it. In 1999 it began an initiative to reduce its number of brands from over 1,600 to about 400 and to emphasize a dozen or so global brands. This allowed Unilever to focus its efforts such that the company's top 20 brands provided 70 percent of its sales in 2010. Diageo's United Distillers Vintners unit now focuses on nine "global power brands." Research on global marketing shows that different elements of the mix need to have different degrees of global uniformity, with brand names and packaging needing the most uniformity; pricing, advertising, and distribution moderate uniformity; and selling and promotion the least.[2] Germany's Beiersdorf, the producer and marketer of the Nivea brand, provides an excellent example of global marketing that maintains tight and effective worldwide consistency. But companies can go too far. In the late 1990s British Airways (BA) made an attempt to further reposition itself as a global rather than just a British airline by replacing the national flag on the tails of its planes with art designs from around the world. Domestic opposition mounted, and the designs were dubbed "global graffiti." BA ended this experiment after just a few years. Instead, the airline returned to its British positioning and has maintained it even during the 2011 merger with Spanish carrier Iberia Airlines.[3]

Every element of the marketing mix—product design, product and brand positioning, brand name, packaging, pricing, advertising strategy, advertising execution, promotion, and distribution—is a candidate for globalization. As with other global strategy levers, the use of global marketing can be flexible. A business can make some elements of the marketing mix more global and others less so. Within each element, some parts can be globally uniform and others not. For example, a "global" pack design may have a common logo and illustration in all countries, but a different background color in some countries. So both marketing as a whole and each individual marketing element can be global to a greater or lesser extent in its *content*.[4]

Global marketing can also vary in its geographic *coverage*. Few global marketing programs can realistically apply to all of the worldwide market. A marketing element can be global without being 100 percent uniform in content or coverage. Exhibit 6-1 illustrates a possibly typical pattern. In this hypothetical example, packaging is highly uniform in both content and coverage, pricing is highly uniform in a small number of countries, while the global promotion program has a great deal of local variation and is applied to a small number of countries only. The benefits of global marketing (and other global strategy levers) can be realized without total uniformity. A mostly uniform marketing approach that covers the major markets accounting for, say, 80 percent of revenues

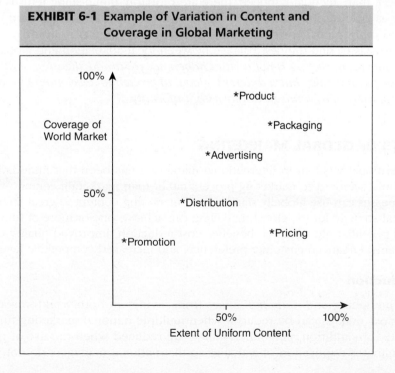

EXHIBIT 6-1 Example of Variation in Content and Coverage in Global Marketing

EXHIBIT 6-2 Net Benefits versus Degree of Uniformity

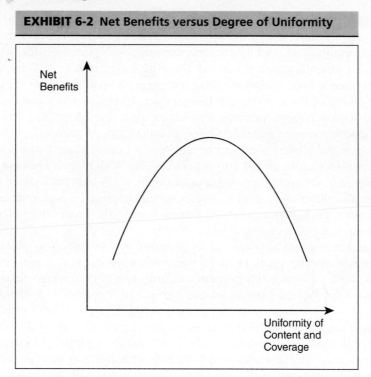

may be more than adequate. Indeed, there are probably diminishing returns to extreme uniformity as illustrated in Exhibit 6-2. The net benefits can rapidly decline if global marketing (and other global) programs are pushed to extremes of uniformity. The key in global strategy is to find the best balance between local adaptation and global standardization. *So global marketing is not a blind adherence to standardization of all marketing elements for its own sake, but a different, global approach to developing marketing strategy and programs that blends flexibility with uniformity.*

BENEFITS OF GLOBAL MARKETING

The conventional wisdom in international marketing has been that multinational companies should standardize marketing process rather than marketing content.[5] But worldwide businesses can use globally standardized marketing content to great effect. Like the other global strategy levers, global marketing can achieve one or more of four major categories of potential globalization benefits: cost reduction, improved quality of products and programs, enhanced customer preference, and increased competitive leverage.

Cost Reduction

In global marketing *cost reduction* arises from savings in both workforce and materials. Personnel outlays can be reduced when multiple national marketing functions are consolidated. In addition, personnel outlays are reduced when the use of global marketing eliminates duplication of activities so that national managers do not waste time reinventing each other's wheels. Materials costs are saved in producing global advertisements and commercials (which can represent up to 10 percent or more of the total advertising budget) and producing promotional materials and packaging print. (Savings from standardized packaging go well beyond the marketing sphere into that of inventory costs. Each packaging variant creates an additional stockkeeping unit. With typical inventory carrying costs at 20 percent of sales, any reduction in inventory can have dramatic effects on the profit margin.) As global and regional media—such as satellite television, multicountry programs, and international journals—increase in scope, global marketing can achieve additional cost savings by mounting multicountry campaigns through these vehicles. For example, EC Television, a subsidiary of the Interpublic Group (one of the largest multinational advertising agency concerns), created a pan-European soap opera, action-adventure series, and variety show. The rise of CNN, MTV, Asia's Star TV, and others as global or regional television networks has greatly increased the opportunities for global advertising.

Cost savings can also translate into improved program effectiveness by allowing more money and resources to be put into a smaller number of programs. More lavish advertising executions can be afforded for a single global campaign than for multiple national ones. BA was able to afford very spectacular, and expensive, special effects for its highly memorable "Manhattan Landing" global television commercial (in which Manhattan skyscrapers were shown landing on an English village).

Enhanced Customer Preference

Global marketing helps build global recognition that can *enhance customer preference* through reinforcement. For many products and services, their buyers, whether consumers or members of organizations, travel, get transferred, or become exposed to multicountry media. So, a uniform marketing message—whether communicated through the brand name, packaging, or advertising—reinforces their awareness, knowledge, and attitudes of the product or service. Anyone who has seen a billboard for a global product in a remote part of the world (such as a Coca-Cola advertisement at the Great Wall of China) will know the feeling of reinforcement such an experience provides. Many global consulting firms choose airports as their locale for global advertising messages.

Improved Program Effectiveness

Much of the previous debate on global marketing has identified cost savings and increased recognition as the primary benefits and reduced program effectiveness as a major drawback. But a strong case can be made that *improved program effectiveness is often the greatest benefit of global marketing. Good ideas in marketing are scarce.* So a globalization program that overcomes local objections to allow the geographic spread of a good marketing idea can often raise the average effectiveness of programs around the world. Of course, objections are not couched as "not-invented-here" (often the real problem) but as "you-don't-understand-we-are-different" (the most common argument). In addition, globalization of some elements of the marketing mix, for example, the positioning strategy, would free up national managers' time to improve other elements, such as trade relations.

Exhibit 6-3 illustrates how global marketing can improve program effectiveness. Left on their own to develop, say, an advertising campaign, the businesses in different

EXHIBIT 6-3 Gains and Losses of Global Marketing Programs

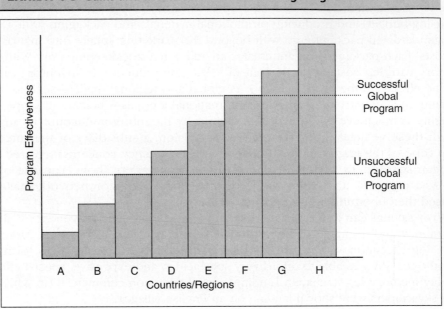

countries will achieve different levels of program effectiveness. So, as in Exhibit 6-3, there will be a wide range of effectiveness. But a global program can raise the average level of effectiveness. The two dashed lines in the exhibit show that the key in global marketing is to select a program that is *more* effective than the average of all the countries rather than to select one that is on average less effective. Exhibit 6-3 also shows that some loss in effectiveness is incurred even in the case of the successful global program—in countries G and H. In that case, why not let G and H opt out of the global program? First, the countries that will produce the better programs may not be known before the event, but only after letting each country duplicate the development effort. Second, allowing some countries to opt out may reduce the willingness of the others to use the global program.

Increased Competitive Leverage

Global marketing can *increase competitive leverage* in two ways. By focusing resources into a smaller number of programs, global marketing can magnify the competitive power of marketing efforts. While larger competitors may have the resources to develop different high-quality programs for each country, a smaller competitor may not. As indicated in the Dyson example, using global marketing then allows the smaller competitor to lessen its disadvantage. But perhaps the most important competitive benefit is that global marketing can get the entire organization behind one idea. Avis rental car created a global advertising and promotion campaign ("We try harder because we're number 2") that communicated in single-minded fashion not only to customers but to employees as well.[6] As a result the entire organization pulled together to deliver on the global promise, not just in marketing but also in all other activities.

Design at Dyson Leads to Global Success

In an increasingly competitive global marketplace, oftentimes consumers not only demand reductions in cost, but also demand the products they buy work better and are more pleasing to use. So-called designed objects are big business, and products that can differentiate themselves through marketing and design can command a premium in the marketplace. One of Europe's fastest growing companies, Dyson, demonstrates the power of marketing a product with superior design.[7] Its products are so elegantly designed that they have been exhibited in modern art museums around the world.

The company takes the name of its founder and CEO, James Dyson, a British inventor who patented the design of an innovative vacuum cleaner. The design has been the lifelong project of the company's charismatic leader, who envisioned the idea in 1978 when he observed a large conical-shaped dust evacuation device in a sawmill. Dyson spent five years developing his patented constant suction vacuum and another two searching for a company to license his technology. In 1993 a Japanese firm paid him royalties to sell a premium vacuum cleaner called the G-Force. Consumers found the product so extraordinary that they

were willing to pay $2,000 to own one.[8] James Dyson used the royalties from the G-Force's sales to found his own company that sells his product globally. Eighty percent of the company's sales are outside of the United Kingdom. The company moved production from Britain to Malaysia in 2002 to cut manufacturing costs, but continues its strategy of selling innovative products by investing heavily in its home-based research and development facility in England.

In fact, Dyson has continued as an innovation design advocate in the United Kingdom. Based on his successes over the last two decades, the James Dyson Award was established to encourage product design, industrial design, and engineering university students to solve everyday problems in the developed or developing world.[9] Additionally, Dyson has maintained that the development of capabilities related to design and invention are critical for long-term competitiveness.[10] As such, even in an international marketplace with well-known floor care brands such as Electrolux, LG, and Samsung, the humble origins of Dyson show how a small competitor can still be successful on a global scale with a properly defined problem and solution.

DRAWBACKS OF GLOBAL MARKETING

As with the other global strategy levers, global marketing can seem to run against the conventional wisdom of tailoring for local markets. The annals of international marketing overflow with horror stories arising from insufficient adaptation. For example, Pepsi-Cola once translated its advertising slogan "Come alive with the Pepsi generation" into Chinese for the Taiwan market. The selling pitch became "Come alive! You're the Pepsi generation!"[11] But amusing though such stories may be, they are mistakes of *international* marketing rather than of *global* marketing. These mistakes occur through poor or inadequate adaptation *after* a marketing program has been created for one country. But global marketing is not about forcing a domestic program onto the international subsidiaries. Instead, a global marketing program should be designed from the start with the needs of major target countries in mind. This last approach has its own dangers. In particular, programs designed for the global market run the risk of overaveraging or aiming for the lowest common denominator.[12] In addition, potential users of global marketing need to review the specific industry globalization drivers applying to their industry.

WHEN TO USE GLOBAL MARKETING

Industry globalization potential affects when to use global marketing. Market globalization drivers, not surprisingly, provide the strongest impetus for global marketing, while cost, government, and competitive globalization each have some effect also.

Market Globalization Drivers for Global Marketing

All of the individual market globalization drivers have major effects on the potential for using global marketing.

COMMON CUSTOMER NEEDS The more common customer needs are across countries, the more opportunity there is for marketing to customers in the same way around the world. The same types of appeals and promises can be made. Some marketing-related determinants of common customer needs include the similarity of the stage of market development and market segmentation and the role of psychological appeals.

GLOBAL CUSTOMERS AND CHANNELS The presence of global customers requires a globally coordinated marketing effort, so that the business makes either the same claims, promises, or terms of trade around the world or knows when and why these differ. A recent study found that global customers particularly want global consistency in service quality and performance, global contracts, uniform terms of trade, and global pricing.[13]

TRANSFERABLE MARKETING When marketing is globally transferable, it allows the use of the same marketing approaches and content around the world. A key determinant of marketing transferability is the extent to which usage of the product or service is rooted in national traditions. So, for example, the marketing of household cleaning products is rooted in traditional concepts of the role of homemaking. As these roles (or the concept of these roles) mostly differ from country to country, there is little transferability of those marketing elements, such as advertising, that depend most on these roles. In essence, there is not yet a concept of the "global homemaker"—almost a contradiction in terms. In contrast, products and services with little national culture attached to them tend to allow transferable marketing. Most industrial products and services fall in this category, as do many newer consumer products and services, such as fast food and credit cards.

Cost Globalization Drivers for Global Marketing

The more expensive it is to develop marketing programs and to produce them, the greater the incentive to use global marketing that avoids national duplication. The cost of marketing programs and production (e.g., television commercials) is probably a function both of individual company approaches and of the industry as a whole—as lavish productions by one competitor spur others to match them. Not surprisingly, it is some of the most expensive to produce advertising that gets used globally—like Coca-Cola's mountaintop commercial of the 1970s, BA's "Manhattan Landing" in the 1980s, and Citibank's global branding commercials in the 1990s.

Government Globalization Drivers for Global Marketing

Whether governments set *common marketing regulations* in this industry significantly affects the use of global marketing. Each element of the marketing mix can be subject to special regulation by a government in an important market. Advertising content is probably the most heavily and differently regulated marketing element. For example, comparative advertising is not allowed in several European countries.

Competitive Globalization Drivers for Global Marketing

As with each of the other global strategy levers, it can be important to match or preempt competitors in their use of global marketing. Being the first to use global branding is probably one of the most effective ways to get a first mover marketing advantage relative to competitors. Perrier's partial rebound in global markets, after its contamination problem in 1990, was due in large part to the preeminent position it occupied as the first global mineral water brand. However, Perrier recovered and maintains its position as a leading bottled water brand. Andersen Consulting's aggressive use of globally standardized and ubiquitous advertising helped cement its claim to be the world's leading systems integration consulting firm. In its new guise as Accenture, the firm continues this competitive strategy.

HOW TO USE GLOBAL MARKETING

Having reviewed when to use global marketing, this section discusses how to use global marketing for each element of the marketing mix. Each of the individual marketing elements has special considerations in globalization. These can be summarized as shown later.

We have already discussed global products in Chapter 4 and global distribution in Chapter 5. But each of the other marketing elements needs attention. *Also, both the global marketing of service businesses and the effects of the Internet on global marketing are so intertwined with issues affecting individual elements of the marketing mix that we will discuss them under each element later.*

Global Positioning

Positioning is the act of designing the company's product and marketing mix to fit a given place in the customer's mind, usually with regard to competitive offerings.[14] A common global positioning can both strengthen the effectiveness of marketing programs and increase competitive leverage. It can strengthen program effectiveness by providing a positioning that is tried and tested in many countries, and this provides the basis for commonality in other marketing elements. A common global positioning can increase competitive leverage by putting all of the resources of the business behind developing assets and qualities (such as superior reliability in the case of Volkswagen or Toyota cars or easy replacement in the case of American Express traveler's checks or credit cards) to support that positioning. By positioning itself with highly visible sporting events and well-known athletes, this is seen very readily in Nike's marketing strategy.

Nike as a Preeminent Brand in Global Sports

One of Nike's key global marketing strategies has simply been to position products in a way that allows maximum exposure to consumers. The message from commercials, advertisements, and sporting events is that Nike is one of the world's largest sports apparel and equipment manufacturing companies. However, it took a lot of strategy and effort for Nike to gain such breadth of exposure. One of the ways Nike has achieved its position is through endorsement deals with superstar athletes such as Michael Jordan, Lebron James, and Ronaldinho.[15] These superstar athletes are known by consumers in many areas of the world through sporting events such as the Olympics and the soccer World Cup.

Nike uses worldwide sporting events to its advantage from a marketing standpoint. For example, in the 2004 Olympics in Athens, fifty gold medals were awarded to Nike-sponsored athletes, many of whom were wearing newly designed shoes made specifically for the Olympics.[16] In the 2008 Olympics in Beijing, Nike competed primarily with global sporting goods company Adidas for athlete endorsements. Nike managed to sign 22 of China's 28 sports federations to wear its apparel during competition.[17] Even athletes with personal endorsements from other athletic companies, like Adidas, wore Nike gear during the games. This indicates the ubiquitous nature of Nike's successful global positioning strategy.

However, to accomplish this, Nike understood that superior assets and qualities were required for acceptance on such a wide scale. Thus, the company's standing is the result of unique and consistent performance over a very long period of time. Without the ability to develop and position its offerings with convincing differentiation to common users as well as competitive athletes, Nike would not be a preeminent brand in sports.

The head of global marketing in a major household products business considers brand positioning, rather than the brand name itself, to be the most important marketing element to be globalized. If a global brand positioning succeeded in several countries, then managers in other countries would "stop monkeying around" with the formula. In addition, more effort could be devoted to implementation. On the other hand, differences in the business's competitive position, purchase motivation (e.g., psychological appeals, ego involvement), and use/consumption patterns may argue for differing positions. For example, Volvo is positioned as a fairly unsophisticated automotive brand with high market share in Sweden, but it is positioned further upscale elsewhere in Europe. Many other automobile manufacturers, however, do position their marques, particularly luxury ones, the same way globally.

Companies that use a common positioning often find that they can make a large part of the marketing mix globally uniform. For example, M&M Mars was so confident of the similarities between the European and U.S. markets that it introduced two of its European brands, Bounty and Balisto, into the United States without any prior test marketing, based on the European positioning. The company used the same packaging for the two brands, and advertising for the brands was similar. Packaging across markets was for the most part standardized. The company's slogan "melts in your mouth, not in your hands" is also used successfully across markets.[18] The company used the same slogan to introduce M&M candies in Mexico.

GLOBAL POSITIONING ON THE INTERNET In many ways, a company's Web site constitute its positioning in cyberspace. For example, is the Web site cluttered and busy or is it

Marketing Element	Major Considerations in Globalization
Products	Commonality of customer needs and usage and of national technical standards
Positioning	Similarity of business's competitive position, purchase motivation (e.g., psychological appeals, ego involvement), and use/consumption patterns
Brand name	Global acceptance/prestige of home country of brand name; importance of having a name that means something; ease of pronunciation
Packaging design	Amount of information that needs to be communicated; similarity of distribution conditions (e.g., importance of display appeal); need for differentiation from local competitors; similarity of usage patterns and measurement systems; acceptability of multilanguage labeling
Absolute pricing	Similarity of market price levels, laws, role of price, business's delivered cost position
Relative pricing	Similarity of business's competitive position, delivered costs, and market objectives
Advertising strategy	Similarity of business's competitive position and market objectives, stage of product life cycle, and buying motivation
Advertising execution	Universality of images, situations, and characters to be used; global recognizability of personalities; need for differentiation from local competitors
Advertising media	Availability of desired media; lack of restrictions on use
Sales promotion	Lack of legal and customary restrictions; similarity of incentive effect
Selling approach	Similarity of channel structure and customer buying methods and behavior
Sales personnel	Importance of technical expertise; acceptability of foreigners
Distribution	Similarity of distribution structure and business's relationship with channels
Customer service	Similarity of customer need and support infrastructure (e.g., toll-free phone service)

cool and sophisticated? Is it the same around the world or is it very different? Does it use just one language or many?

THE USE OF LANGUAGE   The choice of languages makes a very powerful positioning statement. Staying with just the home country language sends a strong message, probably an unfavorable one. International marketers, pre-Internet, generally translated to the local language, unless there were special reasons, such as favorable country-of-origin effects, to use a foreign language. On the Internet, the ubiquity of English allows many English-language companies to build up significant international business with English-only Web sites. For example, Amazon stayed English-only for its first three years, until it added a German Web site in 1998. Retailers realized that, sooner rather than later, e-marketers had to build fully fluent foreign language Web sites, not necessarily for their biggest foreign markets but for the biggest foreign markets for whom the e-marketer's home language is not accessible for a large proportion of the target audience. In addition to its German offering, now Amazon has full functionality in Chinese, French, Italian, and Japanese as well.

The advent of Web translation software for both Web creators and Web users will reduce the problems of language.[19] But companies probably want to control the translation rather than rely on third-party software translating for their users. Automatic translations will not be able to avoid the translation mistakes common in international marketing and in machine translators.

THE COUNTRY-OF-ORIGIN ISSUE A critical issue in global positioning is the country of origin that the company wants to adopt.[20] Following the concept of lead countries (discussed in Chapter 2), a company may want to position itself or its products or brands as coming from a country other than the home base. Even though Qantas has continued its successful usage of the air carrier's Australian tradition, some companies find it increasingly hard to identify a single home base anyway (e.g., ABB, DaimlerChrysler, and other products of multicountry mergers). Britain has a commercial image that greatly lags reality. Consequently, many British companies have tried to hide their British origins, particularly by dropping the "British" in their names and switching to initials that start with "B" (from British Airways to BA, from British Petroleum to BP, from British Oxygen to BOC, etc.). Perhaps, the Italian clothing company Benetton has gone the furthest in positioning itself as global without a distinct national origin. Its theme of "The United Colors of Benetton" and its supporting advertising say to its customers that wearing Benetton clothes makes them a part of a global culture. This is in distinct contrast to the many American consumer companies that trade on promoting Americana.

BACKLASH AGAINST GLOBALIZATION Being too strongly positioned as a global company, especially for consumer products and services, now invites attention from antiglobalization protesters and rioters. It is no coincidence that McDonald's has become the favorite target of antiglobal violence. Similarly, by positioning itself as the global car for conspicuous consumption, BMW's cars also attract more than their share of street attacks. Critics of global capitalism have also targeted other companies such as Nike, Shell, Wal-Mart, and Microsoft.[21]

Global Brand Names

Using a globally uniform brand name provides the easiest way of building global recognition.[22] In 1990 Mars, Inc., changed the name of its Marathon product, in the United Kingdom and other countries, to Snickers, an American name. In the United Kingdom, Mars, Inc., went so far as to run a television commercial (featuring a frustrated Australian tourist) that explained the name change in terms of preventing confusion for traveling consumers. Rather than become an obsolete concept, this allowed the company to re-brand the Marathon concept as a health-conscious energy bar nearly two decades later in certain markets.[23]

Furthermore, the possibility of combination names such as a globally standard umbrella name combined with a local product name provides flexibility. The Eveready Battery Company, a division of Ralston-Purina, consolidated its various national brand

Qantas as an Australian Icon

While some companies attempt to rid themselves of a country-of-origin association, the Australian airline Qantas embraces its Australian roots and uses its cultural heritage to market itself globally to its consumers. Since World War II, Qantas has used a logo associating the airline with a quintessential Australian symbol: the kangaroo.[24] More recently, the koala became a very noticeable component of the company's advertising strategy from 1967 to 1990.[25] In fact, the concept of a frugal koala campaigning for Qantas in selected international markets was revisited in the company's marketing strategy in 1999.

However, perhaps the most compelling and enduring message Qantas has developed to date is its "I Still Call Australia Home" campaign. Based on the 1980 song by Peter Allen, the airline developed advertising and commercials around this concept in 1998.[26] The commercials throughout the campaign have pictured locations from all over the world, including the Eiffel Tower in Paris, Temple of Poseidon in Greece, Ninnaji Temple in Kyoto, Lincoln Memorial in Washington, DC, and other noticeable landmarks worldwide. Even though the campaign displays many international locations, the nostalgia for Australia is captured typically by a child or children's choir singing "I Still Call Australia Home" themes.

However, since Australia is significantly far away from many of the company's destinations, Qantas prides itself on being the pioneer of long haul travel. Despite offering flights to many disparate locations, the airline still maintains its Australian tradition. Inspired by Australia's natural colors, some of the company's planes have displayed Aboriginal and non-aboriginal imagery. As a result, the designs are recognized as being uniquely Australian and continue the synonymous association of Qantas as an Australian icon.

---

names—such as Ucar, Wonder, and Mazda—into one global name, Energizer, for its premium batteries. This move was partly necessitated by the fact that its major competitor, Duracell, already operated with one global brand. Whirlpool has created a three-tier branding structure to accommodate its various acquisitions in Europe.[27] The three brands are Bauknecht, featuring premium German engineering at the top; Whirlpool in the middle market; and Ignis at the budget level. In this process, Whirlpool also gradually dropped the Philips brand name that it acquired in Europe.

VOLKSWAGEN'S NAME ADAPTATIONS   Volkswagen has a model name series that denotes winds—Golf (Gulf wind), Scirocco (the hot wind from North Africa), and Passat (trade wind)—but made a highly successfully switch of the Golf to Rabbit for the U.S. market, which made for a much better fit with the youthful segment that was the target in the United States. Similarly, in the 1980s Volkswagen renamed its Santana line as Quantum for the American market, perhaps to avoid connotations of the General Santa Anna who captured the Alamo. But Volkswagen tries to mostly use the same model names around the world, because it views the car-buying public as very mobile.

The desirability of a global brand name depends in part on the global acceptance or prestige of the home country of the brand name, the importance of having a name that means something, and the ease of pronunciation. Its tongue-twisting name (for Japanese) caused Baskin-Robbins to use in Japan the name "31 Ice Cream" in English with the same logo that it uses in the United States, the "31" referring to the number of flavors sold. Brand names that mean something may need to be translated in order to perform the positioning task for which they were designed. Thus, Unilever's Close

Up toothpaste became for some years Très Près (Very Close) in France but retained its positioning (promotion of social confidence). Having established the brand in France, Unilever was later able to switch back to Close Up in its drive for global branding. In some cases, companies adopt a foreign brand name that would never be used in its home country; witness the Nissan Cedric, which is sold in Japan, but certainly not in the United Kingdom or the United States.

In many product and service categories, the preeminence of producers from particular countries encourages customers to prefer brand names indicating origin from that country. With the rise in prestige of Japanese products, companies like Toyota moved in the 1980s to model names with Japanese rather than American connotations—like Celica, Corolla, and Camry. In the 1990s, Nokia, the Finnish mobile phone company, was initially happy to be mistaken for Japanese. Having achieved preeminence in its category, Nokia now boasts its Finnish origins.

Many companies have overcome company or brand names not designed for easy worldwide pronunciation (e.g., Nestlé, being pronounced "NES-sull" by many in Britain), but few have designed a global brand name from scratch. An exception was Unilever's Omo brand of detergent, which was designed to be easily pronounced in any language. But Unilever never backed this up with global positioning. So Omo continues to be among the world's least consistent global brands.

DATSUN'S SWITCH TO NISSAN   Perhaps the biggest mistake in failing to use a global brand name comes, interestingly, from a Japanese company—Nissan. When Nissan first exported its automobiles, it used the name Datsun. After many years of establishing the name in the United States and elsewhere outside Japan, Nissan dropped the Datsun name in the early 1980s and went to the company name.[28] The goal of the worldwide name change, as stated by the Nissan Management Council, was to create a unified international image for the company. Before the change, Nissan had been the largest Japanese automobile importer into the United States. Ever since the change it has lagged both Toyota and Honda in share of the U.S. market. While a string of relatively weak Nissan products bears the brunt of the blame, the name change must also have played a major role in the decline.

Companies, particularly in Europe, are now adapting their names to globalize them. The second largest dairy cooperative in Europe, Mejeriselskabet Denmark, changed its name in the late 1980s to MD Foods and its packaging colors from red and white (as in the Danish flag) to green and yellow. The change was intended to underscore the international reach of its business and the fact that it sells much more than just dairy products. This changed image also helped make MD Foods much more attractive to job applicants. With a change in name and image came a change in organization design to coordinate production and marketing. Multiple subsidiaries in other countries were combined as a result. Interestingly, in another case, it was the marketers of an American product with purely domestic ambitions that created the fictitious, Scandinavian-sounding name Häagen-Dazs.

VALUE OF GLOBAL BRANDS   In recent years companies have begun to put financial values on their brands. Not surprisingly, the most valuable brands in the world are those that cross borders, even if they are not fully global. For example, the brand, Coca-Cola, has been valued at over $70 billion, and another 34 brands at a minimum of $10 billion each.[29]

GLOBAL BRANDING FOR SERVICE BUSINESSES Because of their greater global variability in makeup and quality, service businesses need stronger global brands. Such brands will reinforce customer expectations and experiences and, just as important, act as a motivator for employees. The minimum-wage worker for McDonald's or UPS in some developing country knows that he or she is expected to live up to the global standards represented by the brand.

GLOBAL BRAND NAMES ON THE INTERNET The Internet mandates globally uniform brand names, at least at the umbrella level (e.g., FedEx) and perhaps even at the sub-brand or product level (e.g., FedEx International Priority). Although local customers may stay mostly within national sites, it is very easy to stray. Becoming an international customer requires a few clicks, not a cross-border journey. So companies will find it increasingly difficult to maintain national variations in brand and sub-brand names. FedEx used to keep different brand names in different countries. But now, it uses all globally common names.

The Internet also makes it easier to build global branding and recognition, particularly for Web names with the right connotations. Google began as a very small start-up company in the late 1990s. However, the brand name's mathematical origins provided the search company a point of differentiation, legitimacy, and integrity vis-à-vis competitors. Google's success led to a highly successful initial stock offering in 2004, during which the company built its market capitalization to $24 billion. By the end of 2010, Google's market value had grown more than eight-fold.

REQUIREMENTS TO BE A GLOBAL BRAND In summary, a global brand needs several features:

- A broad geographic reach, that is, availability on most continents and in most countries
- A mostly uniform image and positioning worldwide
- Perception by consumers as global

MAKING THE CHANGE Because of history many companies, particularly in packaged goods, find themselves stuck with a wide variety of brand and product names that have little justification in real differences between countries. The brand management system encourages innovation, so that left to their own devices, national brand managers are liable to convert a "Boggo" brand into Bloggo, Bloxxo, and Bingo, making it far more difficult to use global packaging and advertising. A vice president of global marketing in a large American multinational consumer packaged goods business viewed ease of internal communication as an additional benefit of global brands. This company has a category of "federal charter brand" that is designated to be controlled by the center, with power as the absolute court of last resort. Only very large and important brands are accorded this status.

In implementing a change to global branding, managers need to consider the following:

- *Market issues*—what will happen to customer and trade loyalty, sales, and market share?
- *Disposal issues*—can regional or local brands be disposed of at a reasonable price and in a way that does not create future competitive problems?
- *Internal barriers*—are there internal constituencies that will block or hinder this move?

Global Value of Top 35 Brands

Company	Country of Origin
1. Coca-Cola	United States
2. IBM	United States
3. Microsoft	United States
4. Google	United States
5. GE	United States
6. McDonald's	United States
7. Intel	United States
8. Nokia	Finland
9. Disney	United States
10. Hewlett Packard	United States
11. Toyota	Japan
12. Mercedes-Benz	Germany
13. Gillette	United States
14. Cisco	United States
15. BMW	Germany
16. Louis Vuitton	France
17. Apple	United States
18. Marlboro	United States
19. Samsung	South Korea
20. Honda	Japan
21. H&M	Sweden
22. Oracle	United States
23. Pepsi	United States
24. American Express	United States
25. Nike	United States
26. SAP	Germany
27. Nescafé	Switzerland
28. IKEA	Sweden
29. J.P. Morgan	United States
30. Budweiser	United States
31. UPS	United States
32. HSBC	United Kingdom
33. Canon	Japan
34. Sony	Japan
35. Kellogg's	United States

Source: Adapted from Interbrand's Best Global Brands 2010, http://www.interbrand.com/en/best-global-brands/best-global-brands-2008/best-global-brands-2010.aspx.

(This study seemed biased against some very well-known brands that may not have high esteem. In specific, many energy-related brands are under-represented or absent.)[30] This study includes economic profit, brand role, and brand strength in its valuation of global brands. It is comprised of both company- and customer-focused measures. More specialized buyer groups would doubtless have identified other global brands that were relevant to them.

Global Packaging

The ability to use global packaging depends on several factors:

- Amount of information that needs to be communicated; the similarity of distribution conditions (e.g., importance of display appeal)
- Need for differentiation from local competitors
- Similarity of usage patterns and measurement systems
- Acceptability of multilanguage labeling

Gillette has achieved highly uniform packaging for its shaving products by substituting visual graphics for most of the wording that would otherwise be there. Furthermore, Gillette's use of consistent color, logo, and graphics provides a powerful umbrella image that makes it easy to introduce changes and new products with minimal disruption.

In the 1980s, 3M discovered that its segmented approach to the markets for magnetic tape products was inefficient. Because there were similar features in all markets, 3M decided to introduce a new global brand identity and packaging for the magnetic products line, developing a global marketing strategy. The new identity was designed to be used uniformly for all of the division's products in all markets and all countries. 3M developed a global advertising program that emphasized the logo and took advantage of the global transferability of the packaging. The new global marketing program boosted volume and market share, and the uniform packaging and design reduced the cost of marketing. In addition, the uniform marketing package exposure achieved quick customer recognition of 3M products.

Many companies have allowed unnecessary differences in their packaging. In the late 1980s a major New Zealand–based forest products company updated its corporate logo—a lion's head—that was printed on all its packaging, but in North America only! So customers, many of whom were global, saw a modern lion in North America and a traditional one elsewhere. Other companies simply fail to identify their products consistently. The management of a major manufacturer of textile tubes belatedly realized that many of its products lacked any corporate identification at all. The company had to make rapid efforts to correct that lapse. Many Japanese companies, particularly newly internationalizing ones, converted their corporate logos from the Japanese *kanji* characters to more globally recognizable versions. Fuji Bank, for example, now uses a stylized image of Mount Fuji for its logo and spells out its name in English. As shown in the MUJI example, some companies can be very successful at parlaying a Japanese identity worldwide.

But many customers seem to dislike packaging that signals foreign origin. Even multilanguage labeling has its potential pitfalls—companies selling in a particular country need to avoid adding the languages of those other countries that might trigger prejudice or connotations of poor quality—"If this is used in Country X then it can't be very good." In contrast, Zara, the highly successful Spanish fashion retailer, takes multicountry labeling to extremes. Each item of clothing in its stores carries labels that show up to a dozen national flags. Zara's labels were simplified after the introduction of euro notes and coins in 2002.

Differences in national culture have a surprising effect on labeling. In Germany and Japan, customers expect products to perform to high standards but do not expect performance beyond the stated level. So if a product is labeled as being able to bear 1,000 kilograms it will do that and no more. In America standards can be lower, but customers also

Muji as the Brandless Brand

Japanese consumer durables retailer Ryohin Kei-kaku is known around the world as MUJI, the company whose global marketing and branding strategy is to have none at all. The company markets products which are minimalistically designed and devoid of branding. As consumers around the world become increasingly concerned with issues of sustainability and conspicuous consumption, the company has ironically found a niche in selling the sustainable "un-brand" concept to so-called post-materialist consumers.[31] These consumers tend to ignore strategies of traditional marketing campaigns. The company's rapid expansion beginning in 1991 to the United Kingdom demonstrated that, although MUJI's customers may be a niche in the marketplace, the retailer was addressing an unaddressed need nonetheless.[32]

Instead of attempting to price competitively relative to rivals, MUJI differentiates itself based on consumer emotion and self-expression.[33] The company understands its target market well and realizes that an informed consumer understands the quality trade-offs often inherent in a good that is merely price competitive. Since the goods sold at MUJI are devoid of trendy brands requiring constant renewal and enhancement, the shelf life of many of the company's retail offerings is significantly longer than competitors'. The company seeks to attribute a timeless, highly individualized quality that enables the goods sold to endure and become a part of consumers' lives.[34]

Still, decisions related to the expansion of product lines are related to the company's core values and philosophy to maintain consistency with retail consumers.[35] Although MUJI operates on a global scale, with over 200 facilities in 21 countries, the company keeps strict oversight on every aspect of its supply network to ensure MUJI's offerings are high quality, affordably priced, and appealing to the values of conscious customers. As a result, the "brandless brand" concept introduced and supported internationally by MUJI for two decades has succeeded in its alterative approach to global branding and value delivery.

expect a lot more leeway in performance beyond standards.[36] So in the United States, labeling needs to allow for overloading or overdosage or else expect a lot of complaints and lawsuits. In Germany and Japan, the same policy would mean understating what the product can do, thus putting it at a competitive disadvantage.

GLOBAL PACKAGING ON THE INTERNET   While physical packages do not travel through the Internet, pictures of them are often displayed on Web sites. Companies need to think out a deliberate policy as to whether they wish to facilitate or discourage cross-border recognition or comparison. The knee-jerk reaction may be that we do not want our customers comparing prices and items across our different national Web sites. But then customers may migrate to competitors' sites that make comparison easy. In 1980, some strategists advised companies to keep their customers as ignorant as possible.[37] In 2000, it was insulting to try to keep Internet-savvy customers ignorant. By 2010, the emergence of wikis, blogs, and social networks made these traditional strategies futile at the least and detrimental at the worst.[38] The competition and customers are no longer down the street or in the next town or country, but a few clicks away.

Global Pricing

Global pricing can bring the benefits of consistency with global customers and distribution channels and the avoidance of "gray market" parallel importation or "transshipment."[39] Multinational companies often find themselves charging the same price to global customers without good justification. An international vice president of sales and distribution found that his company sometimes quoted the same customer different prices and availability in different countries, while finding it very difficult to explain why.

Charging the same absolute price can be very difficult because of inherent international differences in market price levels, laws, and the role of price, as well as differences in the business's market position and delivered costs. One regional area of exception may be the European Union. The single European market eliminated many government-based sources of price differences, such as tariffs and taxes, within at least the Euro-based European Union (EU) countries. Such Euro policy also encouraged buyers to cross borders. However, in the context of differences in market price levels in the other more than 200 countries worldwide, headquarters managers need to know the prices variables in different countries. But surprisingly few companies have sufficient information about their worldwide pricing variables to make decisions on global strategy.

Another way to have global pricing is to charge the same prices *relative* to competitors in each market. Using uniform relative pricing helps provide a consistent positioning in the market. Its viability depends on the similarity of the business's competitive position, delivered costs, and market objectives. Most commonly, it seems to be luxury products that manage to have pricing consistency, probably because being expensive is an essential part of what they offer.

GLOBAL PRICING FOR SERVICE BUSINESSES   Manufacturing businesses increasingly need to charge globally uniform prices to provide consistency with global customers and distribution channels and to avoid "gray market" parallel importation or "transshipment." In contrast, the lack of inventories in many service businesses means that such firms need worry less about using global pricing. It is relatively difficult to buy a service in one country and to resell it in another.

McDonald's prices certainly vary, so much so that *The Economist* magazine uses a "McDonald's Big Mac Price Index" to compare the cost of living in major business cities around the world. In the case of multinational customers as opposed to individuals, however, even service businesses need to avoid charging different prices in different countries to the same customer without good justification. DHL, the express delivery company, manages to maintain significant disparities across regions, but only where the company faces little competition, such as in many African markets.

GLOBAL PRICING ON THE INTERNET   The Internet provides a major driver for global pricing in two ways. The Internet makes it far easier for potential customers to check prices for the same product or service in different countries. Price-oriented search engines also facilitate this process. So multinational companies now have to work even harder at justifying cross-border price differences. Knowing that customers will compare across a supplier's national Web sites, suppliers should provide explicit explanations on their Web sites for price differences. For example, an American supplier's Japanese Web site, which shows a higher price for Japan, might state that X amount of the price is for freight, customs charges, and the like, from the United States.

Global Advertising

Global advertising has received more attention and publicity than any other aspect of global marketing, probably because of its visibility. Essentially, global advertising can be used at three levels:

- ***Same copy strategy***—the brand is positioned in the same way making the same claims. Colgate toothpaste has long used the globally common claim of protection against cavities. Using a common copy strategy depends on worldwide similarity of the business's competitive position and market objectives and similarity of the stage of market development and buying motivations.
- ***Same script***—the advertising uses the same script in different countries, while the actual execution is different. Using a common script depends on the universality of the images chosen and of the situations and characters to be used, and also the need for differentiation from local competitors. Coca-Cola has often taken this second approach of a common script, as in its famous "little-boy-gives-Coke-to-sports-hero" campaign. In America, the hero was Mean Joe Green of the Pittsburgh Steelers football team; in Latin America, Diego Maradona, the Argentine soccer superstar; and in Thailand, a local soccer star named Niwat. Rarely can the same personality be used, although IBM did this with its Charlie Chaplin campaign.
- ***Identical advertisement***—where each country uses the same commercial or advertisement with only the voices or text translated. Coca-Cola used this approach very successfully in its Italian hilltop chorale commercial in which youngsters from around the world stood together singing that they wanted to give the world a Coke.

As already mentioned, Saatchi & Saatchi's "Manhattan Landing" commercial for BA is probably the most famous piece of global advertising. But Benetton, the highly successful Italian clothing manufacturer, has probably produced the most courageous examples. Benetton has run a globally uniform "Colors of Benetton" advertising campaign that features interracial harmony as a central theme. Some of its global images backfired in the United States when American audiences saw racist stereotypes rather than harmonious integration (a black wrist and a white wrist handcuffed together and a white baby feeding at a black breast). Levi Strauss has used a mixture of all three levels of advertising uniformity. Its advertising strategy used a common positioning stressing the all-American heritage of its jeans. An Indonesian television commercial showed teenagers in Levis cruising around Dubuque, Iowa, in 1960s convertibles. In Japan, Levi's used James Dean, the 1950s American film star, as the centerpiece in virtually all its advertising. Some of Levi's advertising execution was uniform too: In most advertisements for Levi's 501 button-fly jeans the dialogue was in English.

Ironically, the one type of advertising that cannot be used worldwide is one that stresses the country of origin. By definition, such a claim usually has little benefit at home, unless the company is making patriotic as opposed to benefit claims. For example, Volkswagen greatly boosted its advertising awareness in the U.S. market with its *Fahrvergnügen* (joy of driving) campaign that directly played on the image of German cars as having superior handling and drivability. Neither the claim nor the attention-grabbing German-language headline would have worked at home. Audi followed suit with its advertising slogan of *Forsprung dürch Technik*. Similarly, BA's longtime use in U.S. advertising of an actor embodying the stereotypical Englishman would have done nothing for British audiences. BA's later global advertising evolved to avoid British references. One commercial featured different nationalities of people meeting each other, brought together by BA. Another featured a group of hundreds of people of all ethnicities, forming one face that then morphed into a picture of Earth from space—about as global as one can get in the use of people in advertising.

Being able to use the same advertising media worldwide depends on the availability of the desired media and on the lack of restrictions on the content of the advertising. The existence of national media with global reach forces advertisers to be consistent. In many industrial and scientific fields, journals published in one country have very wide circulation. A manufacturer of chemical and process equipment advertises in industry journals that have worldwide circulation and had to stop its European subsidiaries from running in these journals advertisements that differed from the global positioning.

Taking a totally uniform advertising approach can limit competitive flexibility. So some companies increasingly use two campaigns—a globally uniform one setting out the main theme, and local campaigns for tactical purposes—while using local campaigns to address particular local communication needs.

GLOBAL ADVERTISING FOR SERVICE BUSINESSES   Global advertising works equally for goods-based and service-based businesses. Whether to use it depends on such industry globalization drivers as common customer needs and the salience of global customers or global channels. Travel-related services can obviously benefit from global advertising, although the communications task may vary by country. A solution is the dual campaign, one for global themes and one for local messages. For many years, BA has used a succession of dramatic global advertising campaigns to establish its position as "The World's Favorite Airline" (backed up by significant improvements in service quality since privatization). At the same time, BA provides a smaller budget for local campaigns that focus on schedules, prices, and promotion of special tour packages. Singapore Airlines has achieved significant advertising impact with its temporally and globally consistent theme of the "Singapore Girl," a highly successful way of personalizing and differentiating a commodity service.

While most services are not physically packaged, staff uniforms and the layout and decor of facilities can be considered part of the package. Global consistency can bring significant benefits. Singapore Airlines has maintained the same uniform for its stewardesses for four decades. The *sarong kebaya,* designed by Paris couturier Pierre Balmain, makes the Singapore Airlines stewardess globally recognizable, unlike those of most other airlines. And like McDonald's, Citibank designs its new retail branches to look and operate in the same way around the world.

GLOBAL ADVERTISING ON THE INTERNET   Companies that sell over the Internet (e.g., book and travel sellers) and those that only present or advertise themselves on it (e.g., automakers) face different international challenges, while those who do both (e.g., airlines) face both challenges. The global advertising challenge for e-sellers is to either find e-copy (graphics, words, and click structure) that is equally compelling for all target nationalities and countries or find simple ways to customize. For example, Amazon.com simply changes the books featured on its home page in each country site. In addition, a side bar on the home pages lists the top 100 books sold on that country's Amazon site—a very simple and automatic method of local customization.

The global advertising challenge for e-advertisers is to find ways to convert their traditional media copy to accessible and relevant e-copy. Some companies offer the ability to download TV commercials or magazine stills, but only for those used in the country of the Web site address. Would globally minded users also want to access advertising from other countries without having to separately enter each country's Web site for the company?

TRANSLATION AND NATIONAL STYLE ON THE INTERNET   Internet advertising obviously needs to be in a language understood by the recipient. But translation may not be enough. Like traditional advertising, Internet ads may need to be adapted for national styles. Pioneering Web users and eBusiness customers to date have tended to be younger (the generation that grew up with personal computers), and for these "Netizens" an Internet style has overridden national styles. A 1999 study comparing Korean and American Web advertising found differences only in the informativeness of advertising messages, not in creative strategy or technological level.[40] But as e-commerce reaches into older and more traditional segments of populations, national culture and style will become more important. Two issues seem prominent: the degree of busyness and clutter and the degree of formality in addressing users.

Much has been debated about the pros and cons of global advertising in traditional media. The Internet provides a uniquely global medium that marketers may well wish to use to try out global advertising. They can still run national advertising in traditional media.

Global Sales Promotion

The tactical and short-term nature of sales promotion makes it probably the least likely candidate for globalization. Globalizing promotion probably makes sense on an opportunistic basis only—encouraging other countries to adopt a campaign or device successful elsewhere. Even then, barriers may arise from legal and customary restrictions and differences in how buyers react to promotional incentives. Countries vary particularly in the kinds of promotion they allow. In Europe, Great Britain, Ireland, Spain, Portugal, and Greece permit virtually every type of promotion, while Germany, Norway, and Switzerland forbid or restrict most types.

Trade shows provide an important exception to the desirability of globalizing promotions. In many industries they act as major communication and selling opportunities. More relevant to global strategy, they are often frequented by global customers. So it becomes important for a company to coordinate its trade show efforts around the world. Sharing trade show materials like booths and exhibits can save money.

The extent to which headquarters should be involved in local promotion strategies depends in part on whether local, regional, or global brands are involved.[41] For a global brand the center should define an overall promotional strategy that has guidelines for the relative emphasis on sales promotion versus media activity, for the relative weight of consumer and trade promotions, and for the role of price deals versus value-added offers. This central coordination will then help protect the integrity of the brand across national markets, particularly important in the case of promotion, which can easily destroy a brand franchise if misused. For global brands, the center should also encourage the cross-fertilization of promotional ideas and facilitate information transfer, particularly about successes and failures in promotional activities. For regional brands, the objectives can be more modest. The target should be brand harmonization rather than standardization, and the center's optimum role may be to encourage cross-fertilization of ideas. Lastly, for local brands, the center's task should be that of information transfer only. But effective transfer will help ensure that local managers benefit from the broader collective wisdom of the worldwide business.

GLOBAL PROMOTION AND SELLING ON THE INTERNET   International promotion and selling generally need the most local adaptation as they usually take place in the country, involve dealing with local buyers, and make country-specific offers. Increasingly, multinational companies treat these more tactical or below-the-line marketing activities more locally and treat the more strategic or above-the-line activities, such as positioning and advertising, more globally. The same holds true on the Internet. E-marketers can use the old above- and below-the line distinction literally on the Internet. The upper (higher) pages, or even the upper parts of pages, can be used for more global, strategic presentations and messages; while the lower (deeper) pages and parts can be used for more local, tactical messages. The tree structure of the Web lends itself perfectly to such an approach. For example, BA has a common first page for both the United Kingdom and the United States, while later pages offer specific and different promotions for the two countries.

Global Selling

Global selling can involve using a uniform selling approach, global account or customer management, or a centralized sales force. Using a *uniform selling approach* can bring the usual multinational benefits of ensuring best practice and high standards of behavior. Doing so depends on the similarity of channel structure and customer buying methods and behavior. Successful selling approaches can often be easily globalized, as IBM did with its highly trained sales personnel and systematic methods, and as Avon Products did with its use of part-timers calling on friends and neighbors. A uniform selling approach can be useful in industries where global customers or global channels are important.

USING GLOBAL ACCOUNT MANAGEMENT CAN PROVIDE A HIGHLY EFFECTIVE WAY OF SERVING GLOBAL CUSTOMERS   Global account managers (GAMs) can perform similar functions to those of national account managers, and companies need to be concerned with analogous issues, including how to select global accounts; how to manage them; how to develop, manage, and evaluate GAMs; how to organize a structure for global account management; and where to locate global account management in the organization.[42]

GAMs have to deal with customer demands such as for the following:[43]

- A single point of contact
- Global coordination of resources for serving customers
- Globally uniform prices
- Globally uniform terms of trade
- Global standardization of products and services
- Global consistency in service quality and performance
- Service in markets in which the supplier has no operations

In response to such demands, suppliers are implementing global customer management programs that include the following:

- GAMs and support staff
- Global revenue and profit measures
- Global reporting processes
- Global customer information systems
- Global personnel evaluation
- Global incentives and compensation
- Global customer councils or panels

While national account managers typically control their accounts, the geographic scope of global account management makes such control much more difficult and perhaps politically hazardous. A GAM can probably be more effective by merely coordinating the selling efforts of national sales forces and acting as the one interface with the customer at its head office. So in almost all cases the GAM should be located in the home country of the global customer.

One manager may be able to wear two hats—as a national sales executive and as a GAM. The GAM position is particularly vulnerable to turf battles and jealousy: National sales managers tend to resent interference with their local customers. If one manager becomes the GAM, he or she may get little cooperation. But if several national sales managers are assigned global account responsibilities, then they all have to cooperate with each other. Global account management certainly brings the benefit of speaking to a customer with one voice and avoiding having subsidiaries compete with one another for a customer's business. But companies also need to recognize the risks involved in global account management. Customers may use the centralized contact to demand that the lowest national price become the global price (or, more generally, that the most favorable national terms of trade become the global terms). An effective GAM will have good justification of international differences in prices and terms. In particular, this manager needs to know *all* the prices and terms being offered by his or her company in different countries.

Many multinational companies are adopting global account management or global customer management programs. These include technology companies such as ABB, IBM, HP, and Xerox; banks such as Bank of America, Citibank, HSBC, and Standard Chartered; most major advertising agencies; and many consumer companies for dealing with their retail customers. The trend in the advertising business toward global account management was perhaps the major factor behind the top 10 international agency networks increasing their share of global advertising in the 1990s. In 1994, this was visible when IBM's new CEO, Louis Gerstner, initiated the firing of over 40 different agencies around the world and consolidated the company's entire $400 to $500 million account at one top 10 global agency, Ogilvy & Mather Worldwide. Still, this trend continued in the realm of new media as well. In 2011, Unilever indicates its intention to develop deeper relationships with fewer digital agencies worldwide.[44]

Another way of globalizing selling is to use a *centralized sales force,* probably based at a number of regional head offices, rather than one global head office, because of the extensive travel required. In addition to the logistical issues, companies using global or regional selling need to worry about customer acceptance of foreign sales representatives. Sales specialists with technical expertise are usually quite acceptable, in contrast to foreign regular sales representatives responsible for the ongoing customer relationship. Customers would be much more willing to accept foreigners in the latter role.

WHERE TO USE GLOBAL MARKETING

A global marketing program need not be applied to every country. In general, a company can derive greater benefits by applying global marketing to larger countries, because all categories of benefits—cost reduction, improved program effectiveness, enhanced customer preference, and increased competitive leverage—will be larger. On the other hand, larger markets tend to be more demanding of local adaptation than smaller ones. Customers in smaller countries are more used to products and programs not being adapted for them and are typically subject to more cultural influence from larger neighbors. In contrast, customers in larger countries are somewhat spoiled by the importance of their market. Canadian customers are probably more willing to accept foreign products and programs than American customers, Dutch customers more than German ones, Belgians more than the French, and Koreans more than the Japanese. So companies face a trade-off in terms of whether to globalize in larger or in smaller markets. One way to solve this dilemma is to design core global products and programs more for the needs of larger countries than of smaller ones.

CONDUCTING GLOBAL MARKET RESEARCH

Global marketing presents a special difficulty in market research. Good marketing practice requires that most new marketing programs undergo some research to test their likely effectiveness. The potential pitfalls of translation (in its widest sense—linguistic, cultural, institutional, and so on) in international marketing make research doubly important. But global marketing also carries great dangers of doing too much research or doing the wrong kind of research.[45] In particular, testing a global program head-to-head against a best local program may result in the local programs winning many of the contests. But exhaustive market research cannot necessarily examine the strategic benefits of a unified global approach.

The potential danger of excessive research is illustrated dramatically by the experience of Marlboro's world-famous cowboy advertising campaign—probably one of the most widely recognized icons in the history of advertising. A senior executive at Philip Morris, the marketer of Marlboro, has commented that too much national research would have prevented the cowboy campaign from being adopted globally. National market research would probably have identified a boxer as the best symbol in Britain, a bullfighter in Spain, a cyclist in France, and a sumo wrestler in Japan. The power of the common global identity would then have never been achieved.

In essence, if there are good strategic reasons for global marketing, market research should be used to discover how to make a global program work better (and to avoid pitfalls in linguistic and cultural translation) rather than to pit it against each possible local program. If such head-to-head tests are conducted, the company-wide benefits of global marketing mean that the global program need not achieve parity with the local alternatives in order to justify adoption. So executives might set some achievement benchmark, such as the global program achieving 90 percent as much favorable purchase intention as the local program, in countries accounting for 80 percent of worldwide volume.

Using global marketing also allows managers to compare market research results from different countries. Provided the global marketing programs have a large enough common core, findings in one country can usefully be studied in other countries. Similarly, global market research can be used in experiments to find the best core global programs. Conducting global market research has become more feasible as suppliers of marketing information like A. C. Nielsen and newer vendors themselves globalize. Nielsen now offers a global information service that provides headquarters executives in multinational companies with a cross-country summary of the detailed data supplied to national subsidiaries. Another supplier, International Ratings Services, has begun to offer a subscription service that tracks the performance of specific U.S. television shows overseas. The service translates and standardizes ratings from over 20 countries and is aimed at movie studios and independent producers selling television shows abroad.

COLLECTING GLOBAL MARKETING INFORMATION

Collecting marketing information from most of the countries in which the business participates and might participate is essential for the ability to create global marketing programs. Such information is not the monthly sales and activity tracking data that the national companies collect for operating purposes. Instead, this global marketing information should be strategically oriented and needs to be collected periodically only, probably once a year. The country subsidiaries should be asked to provide information on the business and the largest local competitors as well as all global competitors designated by headquarters management. These designated competitors should include all key actual and potential global competitors. All countries should report on these competitors, however small the latter may be locally. Without such a directive, a complete worldwide picture of such global competitors would not be built up. A 5 percent market share in a single country for a local or regional competitor is typically trivial but may mean much more for a global competitor. For example, the global competitor may be in the process of creating a base for further expansion into that or neighboring markets. Similarly, tracking worldwide share changes over time for these global competitors will help identify the direction of their efforts, and possible threats and opportunities. The information reported from each country for the business and its competitors should include the following:

- Market share
- Products and sizes offered
- Brand names
- New product introductions
- Prices
- Advertising and promotion expenditures
- Advertising positioning and claims
- Product quality
- Customer satisfaction
- Distribution methods and penetration
- Delivered costs
- Estimated profitability

ORGANIZING FOR GLOBAL MARKETING

Global marketing raises some special issues for organization and management. In addition to GAMs, the other key organization element that can help implement global marketing is the use of global product or brand managers. Beginning in the 1980s Unilever, L'Oreal (the French cosmetics company), and Beiersdorf (a major German manufacturer of household products) all added European brand managers responsible for coordinating the strategy of brand groups that cut across countries. Many other companies have since added similar roles. At the same time, national marketing managers need to participate in the process of developing global marketing.[46]

Advertising agencies can play a helpful role in helping companies implement global marketing. Most companies seem to use too many advertising agencies around the world to allow for easy coordination of global advertising. As part of its globalization drive, Black & Decker (B&D) consolidated its worldwide advertising in 1986. From the previous 20 or more advertising agencies around the world, B&D selected two principal agencies to coordinate worldwide advertising. (Packaging and distribution were also harmonized around the world. B&D has similarly styled multilingual packages available at retail outlets.[47]) Saatchi & Saatchi played a major role in helping BA's corporate management convince its country subsidiaries to adopt the Manhattan Landing commercial, often reluctantly. The results seemed worthwhile. Tracking studies showed increases in unaided awareness and recall of BA in almost all of the 20 countries using the campaign, especially in the United States.[48] Clearly, only the larger agencies with wide global networks can perform such a function. But potential clients of such agencies need to look a bit closer to see how well the global network is integrated.

In addition to experience with global accounts, factors affecting an agency's global integration capability include the following:

- A network grown internally over time rather than put together from acquisition
- Fully owned subsidiaries rather than affiliates
- Frequent exchange of managers and staff between country subsidiaries

A rule of thumb that can help encourage the adoption of global marketing is to charge subsidiaries extra for products and programs that need to be different from the global standard or that require more than some minimum level of adaptation. When asked to pay a premium, national managers often realize that perhaps they do not need that "essential" local version after all.

A GLOBAL CONSUMER MARKETING SUCCESS STORY

The Kuschelweich/Robijn/Bamseline/Cajoline/Coccolino/Mimosin/Yumos/Snuggle/Fofo/Fafa/Pomi/Baubau/Huggie Brand

Unilever's creation of a new worldwide fabric softener product provides an illuminating example of the flexible and successful use of global marketing.[49] Perhaps the most interesting aspect of this strategy is its use of globally standardized positioning, global advertising, and many other globally standardized marketing elements, but a different brand name in each country. In the early 1970s, Unilever trailed Procter & Gamble in the fabric conditioner category in most countries. In 1970, Sunlicht, Unilever's German household products subsidiary, introduced a new product that was targeted at the economy end of the fabric softener market. To offset the negative quality implications of its claims of economy, Sunlicht devised two elements to connote softness—the key benefit desired by users. These two elements were "Kuschelweich," which means enfolded in softness in German, and a picture of a teddy bear on the bottle. The bear was just a symbol of softness and had no active role in the advertising. Sunlicht's success with the new product encouraged Unilever in France to introduce a similar product. But the French company changed the name to Cajoline, which has connotations of softness in French, and adapted the advertising by bringing the teddy bear on the bottle to life in a television commercial, so that it became a more active symbol of quality and softness. Success in France then led to adoption by many other countries. In each case the local Unilever subsidiary kept the positioning of economy and softness, changed the brand name to something indicating softness in the local language, but used virtually the same advertising with little change except for redubbing the voiceover. In Taiwan and Korea a scientific-style magnified close-up of fabric strands was added in the commercials to appeal to the desire of customers in those countries for scientific proof. The bottle was kept virtually identical in all countries, except for a few in which the base color was changed to provide more contrast with local competition.

By 1990 Unilever marketed the teddy bear brand as Kuschelweich in Germany, Robijn in Belgium and the Netherlands, Bamseline in Denmark, Cajoline in France, Coccolino in Italy, Mimosin in Spain, Yumos in Turkey, Snuggle in the United States, Fofo in Brazil, Fafa in Japan, Pomi in South Korea, Baubau in Taiwan, and Huggie in Australia. But in every country, the same teddy bear provided the brand identity and positioning. Only in the United Kingdom where there was already a strong Unilever brand, Comfort, was the new product not launched. Unilever considered the product a great success. Its worldwide introduction boosted Unilever's share of the category to the number one rank in many countries and second in many others. Purchased from Unilever in 2008, Sun Products continues to market Snuggle with the trademark teddy bear in the United States and Canada.[50]

Lintas: Worldwide, one of the major advertising agencies used worldwide by Unilever, played a key role in developing and adapting this global marketing effort. Lintas helped develop the positioning and advertising strategy as well as creating the actual advertising. Lintas set up a European account team coordinated through its Paris office and its international head office in London. Eventually creative work was also performed in New York, Tokyo, and Sydney. Unilever's use of Lintas for the product in almost all countries (except in South Korea, where a local agency accepted guidance from Lintas) made it much more possible to maintain and improve on the common marketing program. Lintas's coordination also saved a great deal of money in advertising production costs. Most of the television commercials in different countries used a large amount of common footage—helped greatly by the absence of human characters in the advertising.

This story has several lessons:

- Global companies need to seize on a big marketing idea—in this case, using a teddy bear to symbolize softness and to build brand identity in fabric care—and promote its widespread adoption.
- Such global marketing can be highly flexible. Only the marketing elements that can benefit from standardization should be standardized, and local adaptations to a core strategy can, and should, be allowed.

- Industry globalization drivers help to identify which elements should be standardized and which should not. In particular, the fact that consumers do not buy fabric softener when away from home negated any need for a common name. So the company standardized the meaning of the brand name rather than the name itself.
- A highly successful program was developed by a number of countries building on each other's efforts.
- Encouragement from head office, the involvement of some lead countries, and the participation of a global advertising agency all contributed to the rapid and successful worldwide adoption of the program.

A GLOBAL BUSINESS-TO-BUSINESS MARKETING SUCCESS STORY

Hewlett-Packard's Use of Global Account Management

HP's use of global account management illustrates successful use of global marketing in the business-to-business environment.[51]

Globalization Drivers Affecting the Computer Systems Industry

In the late 1980s and early 1990s, marketing within the computer systems industry was evolving toward a more customer-focused approach. First, in a strengthening of the *global customers* driver, customers' demands for more consistent worldwide service and support as well as increased standardization drove hardware producers into complex and occasionally secret alliances.

Second, *fast-changing technology* caused the old mode of centralized mainframes with massive headquarters support teams to rapidly evolve to the new mode of decentralized, networked computer systems linking divisions around the world. With this evolution, vendors are required to be more than just suppliers. Multinational customers demand that vendors be strategic partners who demonstrate an understanding of specific international business needs and deploy these solutions on a global basis without compromising customer satisfaction.

Third, another aspect of fast-changing technology and also reflecting the globalization driver of *high product development costs,* time to market and continuous innovation played a critical role in the computer systems industry. In 1993, more than half of HP's revenues stemmed from products less than two years old. Rapid technological changes, such as improvements in computing power combined with a continuous decline in the cost of memory, force firms to reevaluate their relationships with customers and suppliers as well as their practices regarding the use of strategic alliances.

Fourth, alternative channels of distribution—such as dealers, two-tier suppliers, systems integrators, or resellers—were prevalent throughout the computer systems industry and continue to grow. In 1980, approximately 80 percent of HP's customers purchased their computer equipment directly from HP. Today, dealer outlets represent all but a few percentage points of desktop sales. HP needed to identify a strategy to capture these alternative channels, many of them *global channels* or *regional channels,* and to maximize the opportunities they present.

Fifth, HP faced difficulties in building a *global organization.* It needed to develop a global program that promoted synergy and coordination across all three major field operations: the Americas, Asia Pacific, and Europe. Within HP's national sales program, coordination barriers existed across geographic regions, posing a major constraint in providing consistent service and developing new business. HP's performance measurement system was based on product quotas per region, and no incentives existed for managers to pursue or coordinate business outside their regions (i.e., on a global basis). In one instance, this lack of coordination led to HP's Australian subsidiary inadvertently establishing a new worldwide low price for a major customer. The Australian account manager had given a special discount without realizing that this would trigger a clause in HP's worldwide contract with the account.

HP's Organizational Response

In 1991, HP implemented a global account management pilot program for its largest division, the Computer Systems Organization (CSO). The program, initiated for six accounts, was extremely well received by customers, has since grown to over 30 accounts and is currently being diffused across other product divisions within HP. The company's focus was to provide direct customer support for key global accounts and, in doing so, has changed all four aspects of its organization: *structure, management processes, people,* and *culture.* The main components of HP's global account management program involve coordination along global lines—balancing geographic, product, and customer strategies; refining the worldwide sales organization structure to match multinational customer requirements; empowering and rewarding GAMs; capturing alternative channels and opportunities; measuring and tracking all performance variables on a global basis; restructuring the headquarters account program; formalizing an account assigned executive (AAE) program; and selecting the right global accounts.[52]

Coordinating on Global Lines: Balancing Geographic, Product, and Customer Focus

To address the demand for more consistent worldwide service and support, the program established a global distribution channel by introducing the GAM. GAMs are located near the customer headquarters, are responsible for and directly manage HP's relationship with the global account, and serve as the focal channel of distribution for the global account. GAMs' responsibilities involve (1) worldwide customer sales, support, and satisfaction; (2) ensuring that HP is perceived as one company at all customer locations; (3) working with HP's senior management to ensure HP is organized and resourced to service opportunities identified in the global account; and (4) establishing a close working rapport with the senior corporate executives assigned to support the account.

HP also defined a new organizational structure for the program based on a dual reporting system. GAMs report to the country/region and industry manager and to a field operations global accounts sales manager who is responsible for all global accounts business within a particular field operation. The global accounts sales manager for the field operation reports to the field operations manager and to the head of the global accounts program. The global account headquarters staff report directly to the GAM, while district sales managers and sales representatives dual report to the GAM and the local area sales manager. The dual reporting structure is critical to the overall program success, reinforces geographic responsibilities for the sales force, and empowers the GAM to make decisions independent of geography and to manage his or her sales team to satisfy customer needs.

GAMs are evaluated on the worldwide performance of the global account, while country managers are evaluated on the worldwide performance of global accounts head-quartered in their country and overall country performance. This approach provides incentives to country managers to coordinate and cooperate with the GAMs.

Empowering GAMs

To empower managers and ensure the appropriate vision, GAMs are responsible for the growth and health of the entire account including all sales and expense metrics. GAMs set revenue and cost targets that are reviewed at annual quota setting meetings. Once the targets are agreed upon, individual account targets are established such that the collective sum of these targets supports the total program objectives. This flexibility allows success in one global account to directly support another and is essential to program effectiveness.

Measuring Performance

An essential element of HP's program involves measuring performance on a global account basis rather than a product or geographic basis. The GAM program defines a worldwide measurement system aimed at understanding the full costs associated with implementing the global account program for any major account and providing a tracking mechanism for global account performance. Two metrics form the basis for the measurement system: (1) the selling cost envelope (SCE) and (2) the account-specific field selling cost (FSC) models. The SCE measures all selling costs associated with obtaining a list order. The FSC involves identifying all costs associated with worldwide implementation of the global account sales team and supporting programs. GAMs are responsible for identifying the FSC and the SCE.

The FSC and SCE estimations enable HP to determine if an account merits the use of a full-time or half-time GAM. In addition, GAMs are responsible for identifying the level of support needed for an account, such as the appropriate sales staff level including whether the account affords a full-time or half-time headquarters account manager (HAM). The intent is to institute a program that allows global account sales quotas and expense targets to be compiled by country, and held separately within that country, so that quotas or expenses are less likely to move in or out of the global accounts channel to other channels. The program also establishes clear cost and revenue objectives for the global accounts channel. The metric system defined as part of the GAM program assists HP in measuring performance by account rather than by product or region.

Setting Quotas

GAMs are also responsible for setting an overall sales objective for the upcoming year through detailed analyses of account quota by country and, in turn, country quota by product line. In order to ensure that the process provides a profitable investment for HP, GAMs are required to meet a specific objective that tracks worldwide FSCs and discount expenses. In addition, global account quotas and the nonglobal account quotas are combined to form the country and industry quotas. Country and industry managers maintain the global quotas and funding separate from their other accounts.

Restructuring Headquarters Activities

The global program also redefined HP's headquarters account management program. The mission of this latter, preexisting program and its HAMs is to "champion the critical needs and significant opportunities of the global account within HP headquarters and to establish HP as a strategic vendor of Cooperative Computing Systems through long-term sales growth and customer satisfaction."[53] HAMs dual report to the GAM and the CSO product division headquarters and assume global responsibility and ownership. HAMs are also responsible for global account development, issue resolution and customer satisfaction, strategic deal ownership and management, and sales and marketing goal congruence. The HAMs provide a focused channel for product divisions, a strategic partner for AAEs, and are advocates for the customer at HP headquarters as well as the main representatives for the GAM.

To support the program, HP enlisted the aid of high-level executives, including the CEO, as AAEs. The purpose of the AAE program is to define and encourage the active involvement of key HP executives in current or target major accounts that are considered crucial to HP's long-term success. One example of this approach is the implementation of an Integrated Bid Desk. As a result of a thorough analysis of customer concerns in the marketplace, the initiative reduced pricing for global accounts from two weeks to one day.[54] Customers have come to appreciate the establishment of a focal point at HP headquarters (the HAM) to represent their interests, as well as the connection to upper management through the AAE program.

Effects on Strategy

HP's global account management program resulted in more use of each global strategy lever. First, HP moved to more *globally uniform marketing,* particularly for pricing and other terms of sale. Second, the program involved a more consistent offering such that clients received *globally standardized products and services.* Third, selecting the right global accounts involved better use of *global market (and industry) participation.* Global accounts are selected based on specific industries where HP has the potential to be the most successful over the long term. Critical dimensions of account selection involve the analysis of several parameters including long-range projections of industry segment performance, evolving business conditions and needs within those segments, and HP's ability to deliver solutions for those business problems. Global accounts must also have a serious open systems client/server commitment to HP, demands consistent with worldwide sales and support programs, annual HP computer sales plus service revenue greater than $10 million, significant computer sales across two or three field operations, and be in a globally strategic industry segment. In addition, the account should provide HP with an opportunity to develop a defensible position as a strategic supplier.

Fourth, the program integrated a product focus with a customer focus and facilitated consistent sales and support across regions and countries, in effect changing HP's *location of value-adding activities.* In addition, the restructuring of the worldwide sales force eliminated coordination barriers that existed across geographic regions. By focusing on the global channel, the program assisted HP in capturing all order activity including indirect sales (through value-added resellers). HP positioned the global channel to operate more efficiently than other channels due to the benefits of global sales leverage and economies of scale.

Fifth, the GAM program differentiated HP from its main competitors—IBM, Sun, and Digital—improving its *global competitive position*. Resultant competitive benefits included providing one face to the customer, sharing of best practices with the customer as well as across accounts, improving alternative channels development, empowering the GAMs and HAMs to pursue business development opportunities that would otherwise have been missed, encouraging coordination and value-added activity across geographies, and establishing a global position in the marketplace.

GUIDELINES FOR CREATING GLOBAL MARKETING

In many ways marketing is the most difficult strategic element to globalize. Differences between countries are often greatest in the customer attitudes and behavior that marketers try to influence. Furthermore, many of the benefits of global marketing can be subtler than for the other elements of global strategy. At the same time, using global marketing can integrate the worldwide efforts of an organization in a more visible and powerful way than any other. The following key guidelines should be considered:

- Marketing can be, and sometimes should be, uniform in its content as well as its process.
- Each element of the marketing mix has its own unique opportunities and limitations in global uniformity.
- Managers should seek to push the limits of their imagination in devising global marketing programs. They should not be constrained by conventional wisdom about national preferences and prejudices.
- Testing global marketing programs against national alternatives requires care to avoid both underestimating and overestimating nationalistic reactions.
- National marketing managers need to remember that they have been trained to look for local differences. Creating successful global marketing requires a reorientation to look for similarities.

Discussion and Research Questions

1. What is the difference between a multilocal and a global approach to marketing?
2. Select a company or business and describe which aspects of its marketing mix are local, and which global.
3. How should a company go about developing a global segmentation strategy?
4. Which elements of the marketing mix are the easiest to make global, and which are the hardest?
5. When should a company use a global brand name, and when should it use different local names?

6. Identify a global advertising campaign not described in this chapter. What makes this campaign effective, and why?
7. What are the benefits and drawbacks of global account management?
8. What is different about global marketing for service businesses?
9. How can global marketers make effective use of the Internet and the Web?

Notes

1. Some researchers have focused on a standardized marketing process as the key attribute of global marketing. See discussion by Pradeep A. Rau and John F. Preble, "Standardization of Marketing Strategy by Multinationals," *International Marketing Review,* Autumn 1987, pp. 18–28.

2. George S. Yip, "Patterns and Determinants of Global Marketing," *Journal of Marketing Management,* Vol. 13, 1997, pp. 153–64.

3. See "British Airways Trades for Last Time Ahead of Iberia Merger," *The Guardian,* January 20, 2011, http://www.guardian.co.uk/business/2011/jan/20/british-airways-trades-last-time-merger.

4. Keegan (1989) identified five combinations of product and promotion adaptation—straight extension, communication adaptation, product adaptation, dual adaptation, and product invention—but there are many more combinations possible when each element of the marketing mix is considered. See Warren J. Keegan, *Multinational Marketing Management,* 4th ed. (Upper Saddle River, NJ: Prentice Hall, 1989), pp. 378–81.

5. See Ralph Z. Sorenson and Ulrich E. Wiechmann, "How Multinationals View Marketing Standardization," *Harvard Business Review,* May–June 1975, pp. 38–45, and Pradeep A. Rau and John F. Preble, "Standardization of Marketing Strategy by Multinationals,"*International Marketing Review,* Autumn 1987, pp. 18–28.

6. This example comes from a DDB Worldwide story on Wikipedia (http://en.wikipedia.org/wiki/DDB_Worldwide).

7. "James Dyson: Business Whirlwind," *BBC News,* February 5, 2002, http://news.bbc.co.uk/2/hi/business/1802155.stm.

8. "Suck It and See: The Hazards of Being an Entrepreneur," *The Economist,* February 1, 2007, http://www.economist.com/node/8582349.

9. "Clean Water Bottle Wins UK Leg of James Dyson Award," *BBC News,* August 3, 2010, http://www.bbc.co.uk/news/technology-10858815.

10. Hannah Richardson, "Lack of Top Researchers Could Harm UK PLC, Dyson Warns," *BBC News,* February 15, 2011, http://www.bbc.co.uk/news/education-12464204.

11. This example comes from Wikipedia's page on the Pepsi Generation (http://en.wikipedia.org/wiki/Pepsi_Generation).

12. For further discussion of the barriers to global marketing, see Robert D. Buzzell, "Can You Standardize Multinational Marketing?"*Harvard Business Review,* November–December 1968, pp. 102–13; Susan P. Douglas and Yoram Wind, "The Myth of Globalization," *Columbia Journal of World Business,* Vol. 22, No. 4, Winter 1987, pp. 19–29; and Kamran Kashani, "Beware the Pitfalls of Global Marketing," *Harvard Business Review,* September–October 1989, pp. 91–8. See also Subhash C. Jain, "Standardization of International Marketing Strategy: Some Research Hypotheses," *Journal of Marketing,* Vol. 53, January 1989, pp. 70–9, for a review of some of the conceptual research issues in global marketing, and Susan P. Douglas and C. Samuel Craig, "Evolution of Global Marketing Strategy: Scale, Scope and Synergy," *Columbia Journal of World Business,* Fall 1989, pp. 47–57, for a review of the evolution of global marketing strategy.

13. David B. Montgomery and George S. Yip, "The Challenge of Global Customer Management," *Marketing Management,* Vol. 9, No. 4, Winter 2000, pp. 22–9.

14. Philip Kotler, *Marketing Management,* 5th ed. (Upper Saddle River, NJ: Prentice Hall, 1984), p. 272.

15. "Nike's Marketing Strategy," Cornell Info 2040—Networks, April 22, 2008, http://expertvoices.nsdl.org/cornell-info204/2008/04/22/nikes-marketing-strategy/

16. Stanley Holmes and Aaron Bernstein, "The New Nike," *Businessweek,* September 20, 2004, http://www.businessweek.com/magazine/content/04_38/b3900001_mz001.htm.

17. Van Riper, Tom, "Nike vs. Adidas—Let the Games Begin," *MSNBC,* July 15, 2008, http://www.msnbc.msn.com/id/25690584/.

18. This example comes from Joel Glenn Brenner, *The Emperors of Chocolate: Inside the Secret World of Hershey and Mars,* (1999), p. 172.

19. Various programs are being developed, including those from Everymail.com, Slangsoft.com, and Worldpoint.com.

20. There is an extensive literature on country-of-origin effects. See, for example, Johny K. Johansson, "Determinants and Effects of the Use of 'Made in' Labels," *International Marketing Review,* Vol. 6, No. 1, 1989, pp. 47–58.

21. See Naomi Klein, *No Logo* (London: Flamingo, 2001).

22. D. A. Aaker and Joachimsthaler, "The Lure of Global Branding," *Harvard Business Review,* November–December 1999, pp. 137–44.

23. See the Snickers Marathon Web site at http://www.snickersmarathon.com/.

24. http://www.qantas.com.au/travel/airlines/history-kangaroo-symbol/global/en.

25. Greg Johnson, *Los Angeles Times,* March 25, 1999, http://articles.latimes.com/1999/mar/25/business/fi-20801.

26. "Qantas: I Still Call Australia Home," *STW Group,* http://www.stwgroup.com.au/what-works/GetWhatWorksPost.aspx?id=317.

27. John A. Quelch, "Global Brands: Taking Stock," *Business Strategy Review,* Vol. 10, No. 1, 1999, pp. 1–14.

28. In mid-1981, Nissan announced it would gradually phase out the Datsun brand in favor of the Nissan name worldwide. In the United States, the first model to bear the transition name (Datsun by Nissan) was the 1981 Maxima 810 (also the first export model to have a partly nonnumeric name). In 1982, the Nissan Stanza was introduced, and by 1985 all U.S. models and all U.S. dealers bore the Nissan name exclusively.

29. Interbrand's Best Global Brands 2010, http://www.interbrand.com/en/best-global-brands/best-global-brands-2008/best-global-brands-2010.aspx.

30. Suzanne Vranica, "Public Relations Learned the Hard Way," *Wall Street Journal,* December 29, 2010, http://online.wsj.com/article/SB10001424052970204685004576046302759708050.html.

31. David Aaker, "Muji: The No-Brand Brand," *Marketing News,* January 30, 2010, p. 13, http://www.marketingpower.com/ResourceLibrary/Publications/MarketingNews/2010/1_30_10/Aaker.pdf.

32. Fiona Rattray, "Your Life in Their Hands," *The Observer,* September 18, 2005, http://www.guardian.co.uk/lifeandstyle/2005/sep/18/fashion.shopping.

33. David Aaker, "Muji: The No-Brand Brand," *Marketing News,* January 30, 2010, p. 13, http://www.marketingpower.com/ResourceLibrary/Publications/MarketingNews/2010/1_30_10/Aaker.pdf.

34. David Teather, "The Makings of a Brand Leader," *The Observer,* July 12, 2009, http://www.guardian.co.uk/media/2009/jul/12/wolff-olins-olympics-2012-logo.

35. See MUJI Europe Web site at http://www.muji.eu/pages/about.asp.

36. Michael Czinkota and Ilkka Ronkainen, *International Marketing,* 2nd ed. (Chicago: Dryden Press, 1990), p. 270.

37. Michael E. Porter, *Competitive Strategy: Techniques for Analyzing Industries and Competitors* (New York: The Free Press, 1980).

38. Gerald C. Kane, Robert G. Fichman, John Gallaugher, and John Glaser, "Community Relations 2.0," *Harvard Business Review,* November 2009, pp. 45–50.

39. Gray market activity refers to the legal importation of genuine goods into a country by intermediaries other than the authorized distributors. See S. Tamer and J. Sikora, "How Multinationals Can Cope with Gray Market Imports," Working Paper No. 87–109 (Cambridge, MA: Marketing Science Institute, 1987).

40. Kyu-Won, Chang-Hoan Cho, and John D. Leckenby, "A Comparative Analysis of Korean and U.S. Web Advertising," paper presented to 1999 Annual Conference American Academy of Advertising, Albuquerque, New Mexico (uts.cc.utexas.edu/~kwoh/3A/99AAA.html).

41. This paragraph is based on Kamran Kashani and John A. Quelch, "Can Sales Promotion Go Global?" *Business Horizons,* Vol. 33, No. 3, May–June 1990, pp. 37–43.

42. This list is based on Kotler's (*Marketing Management,* p. 683) discussion of national account management.

43. Montgomery and Yip, *The Challenge of Global Customer Management.* For a full review of global account management see George S. Yip and Audrey Bink, *Managing Global Customers: An Integrated Approach* (Oxford, England: Oxford University Press, 2007); George S. Yip and Audrey Bink, "Managing Global Accounts," *Harvard Business Review,* Vol. 85, No. 9, September 2007, pp. 102–11; and George S. Yip, G. Tomas

M. Hult, and Audrey Bink, "Static Triangular Sim-ulation as a Methodology for Strategic Manage-ment Research," in David J. Ketchen and Donald D. Bergh, Eds., *Research Methodology in Strategy and Management,* Vol. 4 (Oxford, United King-dom: Elsevier Jai, 2007), pp. 121–60.

44. "Keith Weed: Unilever Wants to Work with Fewer Digital Shops, More Closely," *Adver-tisingAge,* March 8, 2011, http://adage.com/article/special-report-4as-conference/unilever-work-fewer-digital-agencies/149285/.

45. For a discussion of the problems in translating market survey instruments, and a guide to con-ducting international market research, see Susan P. Douglas and C. Samuel Craig, *International Marketing Research* (Upper Saddle River, NJ: Prentice Hall, 1983), pp. 186–90.

46. Solberg 2000, "Standardisation or Adaptation of the International Marketing Mix: The Role of the Local Subsidiary/Representative,"*Journal of International Marketing,* Vol. 8, No. 1, pp. 78–98.

47. Laurence J. Farley, "Going Global: Choices and Challenges," *Journal of Business Strategy,* Vol. 1, Winter 1986, pp. 67–70.

48. See John A. Quelch. "British Airways: Teaching Note," No. 5-587-016 (Boston: Harvard Business School, 1987).

49. We thank Michael Bowman of Lintas: Worldwide for making the details of the Unilever teddy bear brand history available to us.

50. Tom Hals, "Snuggle Takes on Care Bears in Brawl Over Logos," Reuters, May 26, 2010, http://www.reuters.com/article/2010/05/26/us-sunproducts-usnonwovens-bears-idUS-TRE64P4T420100526.

51. This example on HP is drawn from George S. Yip and Tammy L. Madsen, "Global Account Management: The New Frontier in Relation-ship Marketing," *International Marketing Re-view,* Vol. 13, No. 3, pp. 24–42, special issue on Global Marketing Implementation, 1996.

52. Greg Mirhan, "Advantage: Hewlett-Packard," *Global Executive,* March/April 1993, pp. 10–13.

53. Ibid.

54. Peter Burrow, "HP's Ultimate Team Player," *Businessweek,* January 30, 2006, www.businessweek.com/magazine/content/06_05/b3969071.htm.

CHAPTER 7

Making Global Competitive Moves

Making globally integrated competitive moves constitutes the fifth of the global strategy levers that a company can use to globalize strategy. In many ways it is the most difficult of the five levers to use, because its consequences are often less visible than developing and implementing activities associated with the other global strategy levers (e.g., globally standardized products, globally uniform marketing). At the same time, not making globally integrated competitive moves can undermine the advantages built up in individual countries and weaken a company's worldwide position as is the case with Apple and Microsoft.

KEY FEATURES OF GLOBAL COMPETITIVE MOVES

The Apple and Microsoft story illustrates how the last (and most often forgotten) global strategy lever, globally integrated competitive moves, can be highly effective. A global strategy approach to competitive moves means integrating competitive moves across countries or regions rather than making moves one country or region at a time. Integrated competitive moves also affect all of the other global strategy levers of global market participation, global products, global activity location, and global marketing, typically needing to be used in conjunction with one or more of the other global strategy levers.

Global competitive moves have several aspects:

- Cross-area subsidization within the same business
- Use of counterparries in countries or regions
- Globally coordinated sequence of moves
- Targeting of actual and potential global competitors
- Developing plans for each competitor
- Preemptive use of global strategy

These types of moves can be described as follows:

Type of Move	Definition
Cross-area subsidization	Using profits from one country or region in which a business participates to subsidize competitive actions in another country or region
Counterparry	Defending against a competitive attack in one country or region by countering in another country or region
Globally coordinated sequence of moves	Simultaneous or planned sequence in which competitive moves are made in different countries or regions in the same business
Targeting of global competitors	Identifying actual and potential global competitors and selecting an overall posture—attack, avoidance, cooperation, or acquisition—for each
Developing competitor plans	Analyzing strengths, weaknesses, opportunities, and threats for each global competitor in each major country or region, and developing a competitive plan of action for each country/region-competitor combination
Preemptive use of global strategy	Being the first competitor to make use of a particular element of global strategy—global market participation, global products, global activity location, and global marketing

Cross-Subsidization of Countries and Regions

Being willing and able to subsidize across countries or regions within the same business is perhaps the key requirement of a global strategy. As described in Chapters 3–6 covering global strategy levers, the overall use of these global strategy levers, such as global products and global marketing, can provide a worldwide platform of competitive advantage. But this advantage cannot be fully exploited unless global resources can be selectively focused on points of competitive pressure or opportunity. In other words, the worldwide business needs to practice cross-subsidization of countries or regions. This cross-subsidization should not apply to the same areas all the time but to different areas of the world as needed.[1] Global managers should view portfolio roles as long-term postures that may be modified to meet short-term competitive pressures and opportunities. An area—country of region—designated for a maintenance role may need temporary extra spending, subsidized by the rest of the world, to fend off a competitive thrust.

Counterparry

Counterparry represents a special case of cross-subsidization in which an attack by a competitor in one country or region is countered by a response in another.[2] Such a counterparry has the intention of retaliating where the competitor can be hurt most. In practice, the effectiveness of counterparry depends both on cooperation among countries or regions in the business using it and on the competitor receiving and understanding the signal.[3] Counterparry is most easily understood when two home countries are involved—a business attacked in its home country retaliates in the home country of the attacker.

Apple and Microsoft

The rivalry between Apple Inc. and Microsoft Corporation has been going on since the companies first formed (Apple in 1976 and Microsoft in 1975), and the superiority of each one's products is constantly the source of heated debate among global consumers. While Microsoft has traditionally dominated the market, Apple has still had its share of devoted followers. And with the iPod (2001), iPhone (2007), and iPad (2010) introductions by Apple in the 2000s, the competition that had tilted heavily in favor of Microsoft became fierce again. Apple still sells large quantities of Macintosh computers, but the global leverage reaped by the branding of the iPod, iPhone, and iPad products has stretched the competitive moves by the company vis-à-vis Microsoft to new heights.

In 2001, to expand its markets and attempt to increase its market share, Apple introduced iTunes and the iPod. These two products were originally able to operate only on Macintosh operating systems, but quickly made their way to Microsoft operating systems. Apple also decided to open Apple stores, which significantly aided in boosting its sales. To counter the attack, Microsoft introduced multiple portable video and audio players including the Windows Portable Media Centers and Zune. However, even with these counterattacks by Microsoft, Apple has been able to maintain its portable audio player market share dominance, although the Microsoft Zune is gaining in popularity.

In 2007, Apple introduced the iPhone—a totally new product for the company that had positive disruptive effects on the cell phone marketplace. Interestingly, when Microsoft first introduced the idea of a smart phone, experts derided it as a losing proposition. This all changed when Apple introduced the iPhone! Some point to the lack of the single-vision product at Microsoft, whereas Apple has relied heavily on Steve Jobs' input throughout the 2000s to introduce its line of "i" products. The result often is lack of pizzazz and bland, but often great, Microsoft products. The market share war in the cell phone industry spans far beyond Apple and Microsoft, with Google's introduction of the Android in 2008 being the most recent disruptive player in the market (and with Blackberry, Nokia, and Palm still going strong).

In 2010, Apple introduced the iPad as a tablet computer-inspired gadget, some would say a larger version of the iPhone without the phone capability! Going back a few years, at the *Wall Street Journal's* All Things Digital conference in 2007, Apple CEO Steve Jobs and Microsoft founder Bill Gates debated the future of computing and the notion of a tablet computer. Bill Gates said that he "believes in the tablet form factor," with the idea that a person would first buy the smart phone and then eventually buy the tablet. Steve Jobs said nothing on that topic at the time and instead simply developed and revealed it three years later! Why didn't Microsoft follow through on Gates's ideas? Making competitive moves at the right time in the right place had both a first-mover advantage for Apple and the effect of upholding the "pizzazz" aspect of the company vis-à-vis Microsoft.

In the 1990s, Microsoft seemed impregnable with a strong basis for competitive advantage—its high-quality, worldwide name recognition and distribution system—and had also globalized this strategy successfully. Microsoft had widespread global market participation, a globally standardized product line, and an efficient and concentrated activity chain. But Microsoft's global strategy had a number of potentially serious flaws, perhaps the most critical being not making appropriate global competitive moves vis-à-vis Apple. For the most part, Microsoft has opted to defend against Apple's challenge in the same countries in which it was attacked instead of implementing a counterparry move. A better strategy would have been to make globally integrated competitive moves coupled with developing truly innovative products wanted by the consumers instead of playing it safe with its product introductions (or lagging in introducing such new products).

Such a scenario has been seen in the "cola wars" between Coca-Cola and Pepsi for several decades. To make a counterparry effective, a business typically needs to have a large enough presence in key countries, particularly the home countries of global competitors, to provide a base for the counterattack.

Globally Coordinated Sequence of Moves

Globally integrated competitive strategy also requires that competitive moves, such as price changes and the introduction of new products or programs, be coordinated across countries or regions in their timing. This does not necessarily mean that they take place at the same time, only that there be a planned sequence to the moves. Why does this matter? First, competitive moves use resources and also usually spur competitor responses that may require even more resources in counterresponse. So the timing of competitive moves in each country or region needs to be planned to make best use of available resources.

A business with a global strategy would usually find it difficult to sustain a price war in several world regions simultaneously, especially if the contest is with different competitors in each country or region. Second, *a major benefit of global strategy is being able to apply experience from one country or region to another.*[4] *The experience gained and transferred is most useful when the right countries, usually within one region, make the first moves.* For example, entering markets in the right sequence can enhance the competitive advantages that build up with experience. Making a move on a tough market before the business is ready for it can damage long-term global prospects and not just performance in the specific market entered. Historically, Japanese companies were particularly successful in sequencing this very important type of competitive move—market entry. However, with the advantages that can be reaped by the global knowledge economy, sophisticated supply chain systems, and demanding global consumers, the need to better understand and implement competitive moves is becoming critical to the success of global strategy-oriented companies.

Targeting of Global Competitors

Actual and potential global competitors need to be identified and a worldwide competitive strategy developed for each one. A global competitor has significant market share in two or more major world regions and uses some elements of global strategy. So a potential global competitor for a business can be either a multinational company already competing in some of the same markets as the business that does not now use a global strategy but may do so or a multinational that already uses a global strategy but is not yet competing in the same markets as the business. *Targeting one competitor in many countries is likely to bring greater long-term gains than targeting several competitors in a few countries because opposition should be weaker in the former case.* But a multilocal approach to competitive strategy typically results in the latter pattern, because each local management team selects its most troublesome local competitor. Similarly, the most dangerous global competitors may not receive the highest priority unless a global view is taken of them. For example, a competitor with a strong number two position in many markets may be globally more dangerous than other competitors with leading positions in only a few markets.

The strengths and weaknesses of each targeted competitor need to be analyzed. In addition, their current and potential use of global strategy needs to be evaluated. An overall posture needs to be decided on for each competitor. Key choices include the following:

- Attack
- Avoid direct competition
- Cooperate
- Acquire

In *attacking a global competitor,* the business must develop a global plan rather than leave local management to develop separate plans. At the same time, local management must be involved in the formulation of the plans. Key decisions include which product lines and customers of the competitor to target, and the selection and timing of countries for offensive moves. While a simultaneous attack on many fronts has more chance of overwhelming a competitor, it also makes it more likely that the competitor will recognize the severity of the threat and retaliate correspondingly. Instead, a sequential, but coordinated, plan of attack may lull the competitor into a pattern of country-by-country surrenders, none crucial in itself, but accumulating to an irreversible loss of position.

Avoiding direct competition with a global competitor can require as much planning and forethought as attack. Retreating into multilocal protected niches offers the simplest way to avoid confrontation with global competitors. But such a strategy depends on the long-term sustainability of the conditions, external or internal to the business, that allow protection from global competition. Under this approach, management at the company's headquarters can do little to help the local businesses as they develop their own niches. A globally coordinated approach to avoiding competition may hold better hope of sustainability. To take such an approach requires predicting the likely expansion paths of global competitors in terms of products, customers, and geographic markets. It also requires prediction of how competitors will develop their sources of competitive advantage, such as in proprietary technology. Then the business needs to decide on which of these competitor expansion paths it can afford to get out of the way, and on which of these paths it has to dig in. For example, the business may be able to identify product lines, customers, and geographic markets that are less crucial than others and may be prepared to give ground there in order to better defend the remaining higher priority products, customers, and markets.

Cooperating with competitors via international joint ventures and alliances became highly popular in the latter part of the last century and is still popular in certain industries (e.g., car manufacturers BMW, Mercedes, and Porsche using the same retail dealerships in many countries). All joint ventures need to achieve some match between what each partner has to offer and what each partner will give up. In the specific context of global strategy, as opposed to corporate and competitive strategy in general, a key decision is the choice of geographic markets that will be made part of the joint venture. A joint venture can provide both defensive capabilities and offensive opportunities in the markets covered. But, at the same time, a joint venture can limit growth potential and, as argued in Chapter 3, reduces the degree to which the business is able to operate a truly integrated global strategy. For example, a worldwide business that operates as a self-contained globally integrated system rather than relying on joint venture partners will find it much easier to achieve the coordination and agreement needed to make a sequence of globally integrated competitive moves. Making globally integrated competitive moves typically requires self-sacrifice and cross-subsidization by geographic entities. That is difficult enough to achieve among fully owned internal subsidiaries but becomes even more complex with external partners. Another potential drawback is the argument that joint ventures serve as a crutch that discourages companies from developing their own capabilities.[5]

Acquiring competitors is the most effective means of eliminating competition, in particular as the acquisitions target influential competitors. In the global context, acquisition can bring the added benefit of filling out geographic coverage. So in selecting acquisition candidates, managers should apply a global strategic perspective in seeking those companies that can strengthen the company's position in key countries, as well as the other usual acquisition criteria in acquisitions (and mergers). Other things being equal, acquirers should be willing to pay a higher premium for acquisitions that improve their geographic balance, improve their position in key countries, or strengthen other aspects of their global strategy.

Developing Country-Competitor Plans

The targets for individual global competitors can be further developed into plans for individual country/region-competitor combinations. To make these plans, it is first necessary to understand the strategic position of each global competitor in each country or region. Doing so requires conducting the usual type of analysis of strengths, weaknesses, opportunities, and threats. Exhibit 7-1 provides an illustrative example of the summary output of such an analysis.

Following this analysis of country/region-competitor strategic positions, plans can then be developed for each country/region-competitor combination. In particular a target needs to be set for each combination. These overall targets can include several possibilities, for example,

- Attack
- Defend

EXHIBIT 7-1 Strategies for Country/Region-Competitor Combinations: Illustrative Example

| | Region | | | |
Competitor	North America	South America	Europe	Far East
Copeland, Inc.	Defend	Opportunistic attack	Avoid direct competition	All-out attack
Westminster PLC	All-out attack	All-out attack	All-out attack	All-out attack
Schumann AG	Opportunistic attack	Defend	Avoid direct competition	Preempt entry
Tokugawa K.K.	Defend	Defend	Defend	Defend

McDonald's Competitive Moves—Good or Bad?

McDonald's has always been known for its burgers and fries, but by adding baristas and espresso machines, the restaurant is now in competition with Starbucks, the global coffee chain. This move may seem like a smart idea from McDonald's standpoint, but any number of factors could lead to the demise of the McCafé. The reason for this is different thoughts come to consumers' minds when thinking about Starbucks and McDonald's. The two stores even serve different types of customers and attract different demographics. Starbucks attracts more female customers than McDonald's, and while McDonald's dominates the 18- to 34-year-old group, Starbucks dominates the 35 to 44 age group. Not only that, Starbucks and McDonald's attract people with different income levels, with Starbucks attracting people whose household income is more than $60,000 and McDonald's attracting people whose household income is less than $60,000.

McDonald's may be able to succeed in its strategy to attack Starbucks by offering cheaper alternatives to the normally expensive Starbucks coffee. For example, McDonald's has used advertisements directly attacking expensive Starbucks coffee with billboards pointing out the very expensive prices of Starbucks's coffee with catchy slogans. As such, McDonald's is hoping normal Starbucks customers who are looking for ways to save money might change their daily routine to include McDonald's coffee instead of Starbucks.

- Avoid direct competition
- Stay out
- Preempt
- Cooperate
- Acquire

Exhibit 7-2 provides an illustrative example of a set of targets for one business. Presenting all country/region-competitor combinations together helps make it clear whether or not the business is being too ambitious. For example, Exhibit 7-2 shows that the business has targeted one competitor, Westminster PLC, for all-out attack throughout the globe. For another competitor, Tokugawa K.K., the strategy is to hold defensively in all parts of the globe. Third, there is a selective strategy for Copeland, Inc., and Schumann AG that varies by region. As such, Exhibit 7-2 clearly shows an example of set targets for this particular business.

Preemptive Use of Global Strategy

Great advantages accrue for the first company in an industry that uses a global strategy. For global market participation, the first company to build a network of strong positions in all of the globally strategic countries (or regions) gains a preemptive advantage, as well as boosting scale advantage. For global products, the first company to introduce a globally standardized product can reap the advantage of setting industry standards and customer expectations and preferences. For activity location, the first company to build a global network of optimally concentrated and located activities reaps early cost and quality advantages that competitors should find difficult to match. For global marketing, the first company to promote global brands and global advertising can build image and preference leads that are difficult to dislodge.

EXHIBIT 7-2 Situation Analysis for Country/Region-Competitor Combinations: Illustrative Example

Competitor	Region			
	North America	South America	Europe	Far East
Copeland, Inc.	Market leader	Weak products and distribution slipping share	Increasing share, strong product line	Recent entrant, trying to build position
Westminster PLC	Market follower	Overpriced products	Market leader in some countries but slipping share	Share is holding steady but not reinvesting much
Schumann AG	Market follower, some weak product lines	Market leader, building position further	Market leader in some countries gaining share in others	Not yet present
Tokugawa K.K.	Small share but growing fast	Strong number two in market	Strong number two in most countries, share growing fast	Market leader with strong product lines and customer relationships

GLOBAL COMPETITIVE MOVES FOR SERVICE BUSINESSES

Service businesses need to make globally integrated competitive moves as much as product-based businesses. But the key feature of such moves, cross-country coordination, can be both easier and more difficult. Coordination can be easier for those service businesses that reproduce a strong core formula around the word. In such businesses, corporate headquarters plays a continuing role in monitoring the strategies of overseas units. Examples include franchising restaurants and hotels. But the prevalence of franchising in services, and its concomitant dispersion of ownership, makes global coordination much harder. Until they changed their international ownership structures, the major accounting and professional services firms (e.g., Deloitte Touche Tohmatsu, Ernst & Young, KPMG, and PwC), for example, operated on global basis mostly as quasi-franchises, with little sharing of ownership or profits across countries. Coordination may also be less necessary where both production and consumption occur locally, and central support plays a minor role. In contrast, manufacturing companies with factories serving multiple country markets find it essential to coordinate their different country strategies.

BENEFITS AND DRAWBACKS

The key benefit of globally integrated competitive moves lies in magnifying the resources available in any single country or region for competitive actions by leveraging the global resources of a business. So head office managers can design competitive strategies that involve the power of multiple moves, while local managers can call on help beyond that available in just their own markets. In addition, taking a globally integrated approach to competitive moves simply provides more options in attack and

Dell's Competitive Position

Dell Computer began as a simple college dorm room-based business. Since its inception, the company has reshaped traditional practices of the personal computer industry. One innovative component of the company's strategy is its emphasis on lean manufacturing and just-in-time principles. The company sources on a global scale and consolidates purchasing in its Texas-based headquarters to increase its buying power. Suppliers are required to hold inventory ownership at separate facilities located next to Dell's regional manufacturing centers. Due to the company's strong influence on the trends of the market, suppliers must often comply with Dell's demands. The only exception to this rule is Intel, a firm that, like Dell, makes its own rules in the industry. While other competitor PC manufacturers have outsourced manufacturing entirely, Dell continues to keep final assembly within the company. Strategic sourcing, something that Dell does best, could not be executed to the same extent if the firm outsourced manufacturing to a third party. Additionally, sourcing globally of large components with unfavorable logistics is not as strategic as locating manufacturing regionally and sourcing printed circuit boards and other components with favorable logistics globally. These strategies provide a unique competitive position for Dell in the global marketplace.[6]

PwC's Global Flexibility and Adaptability

Global accounting firm PricewaterhouseCoopers has a unique organizational structure. It is composed of local independent member firms that are all members of the larger organization. Part of this organization is due to strong government regionalization drivers in the accounting services industry, as well as in most other industries in which PwC operates. Practicing accountancy is often legally restricted to firms that are owned in part locally. To access these markets, PwC's disparate structure is a necessity. Despite the independence of PwC's members, the firm applies globally standardized practices for training employees, as well as providing quality, consistent professional services to customers. The nature of accounting services allows PwC to be competitive and deploy services around the globe with fewer barriers to entry than most firms that sell products. Advancements in the global standardization of accounting language such as the International Financial Reporting Standards (IFRS) mean that PwC's professional services need less adaptation to satisfy the demands of local markets. As an example, PwC provides its services to more than 400 of the Fortune Global 500 companies. The company's culture also contributes to its ability to deploy services on a global scale, serving more than 100 countries.

defense. Such an approach also helps managers to see country or region linkages so that they recognize the competitive interdependence of markets. That way the business can avoid the piecemeal, country-by-country conquest that has been the fate of many industries. Furthermore, managers taking a globally integrated approach to competitive moves are more likely to spot the preemptive actions that need to be taken—such as Wal-Mart's monopolizing location in rural areas and Coca-Cola's or Pepsi's dominance in global food markets.[7]

On the other hand, integrating competitive moves can have drawbacks also. It can mean sacrificing revenues, profits, or competitive position in individual countries, particularly likely when the subsidiary in one country is asked to attack a global competitor in order to send a signal or to divert that competitor's resources from another country. The manager of the sacrificing subsidiary may be reluctant to perform such a selfless role for the global benefit of the organization, particularly if the local market is constructed as a strategic business unit of the global company (i.e., a profit center). Overcoming such reluctance for the benefit of the overall company requires a performance evaluation and reward management system that encourages rather than discourages global cooperation.

CHOOSING THE SPEED OF GLOBALIZATION

As part of their global competitive moves, companies can choose whether to try to speed up or slow down the pace of globalization. In some industries and product categories, a diversified multinational company may be already well entrenched in multiple local markets with locally tailored offerings. In those industries, the company may want to avoid moves to greater global standardization as that would reduce its existing localization advantages and make it easier for new competitors to enter with global offerings. On the other hand, where a company is late or behind multilocal competitors, its best strategy would be to speed up globalization by playing a standardization game.

For example, Unilever enjoys a dominant multilocal position around the world in many food and other consumer product categories. In these categories Unilever tries to hold on to its advantages of local differentiation. On the other hand, because the company was late into the ice cream category, it chose a global approach as a way of challenging already established rivals. Obviously, the prospects for such moves depend on industry globalization drivers, but most industries offer some scope for strategic choice.

Some companies may have little choice. Many of the younger, technology-based companies do not have a long history of local adaptation. For them, the only game is to be as global as possible. Even a company with a moderately long history, such as Hewlett-Packard, needs to play a global and not a multilocal game. At the extreme, Microsoft is relatively young as a multinational and does not even try to play a multilocal game. Perhaps the most distinctive aspect of Microsoft's international approach is that *it seeks to adapt the world to its global strategy rather than the other way around.*

Successful global companies transfer their competitive advantages quickly and effectively around the world. Global transfer of critical capabilities and advantages is probably the single biggest factor in the success of overseas subsidiaries and hence the overall global strategy.[8]

GUIDELINES FOR MAKING GLOBAL COMPETITIVE MOVES

Perhaps the ultimate test of a total global strategy is whether a worldwide business can make globally integrated competitive moves. Some guidelines help managers to perform this difficult task:

- Global competitive moves require coordination and agreement among country and/or regional managers. In some cases it also requires country and/or region sacrifices for the sake of the worldwide business.
- Not making global competitive moves can be particularly damaging in the long term for a business's worldwide competitive position.

• It is critical for senior management to design and implement a system to both recognize the need for globally integrated competitive moves and achieve cooperation among different countries and regions.

Discussion and Research Questions

1. What is the difference between a multilocal and a global approach to making competitive moves?
2. Describe a competitive action or series of actions by a company that you think particularly exemplifies a global competitive move.
3. What should be the response of a company when a foreign competitor is dumping in that company's home market? Would your answer differ if the foreign competitor were (a) an exporter producing only in its home country or (b) a multinational company with production and sales around the world?
4. What organizational mechanisms are needed to allow a company to make effective global competitive moves?
5. What is different about global competitive moves for service businesses?

Notes

1. It is in the area of cross-subsidization, and also coordinated moves, that global strategy comes closest to military strategy. In the latter arena, concentration of forces at selected points to outnumber the enemy is perhaps the key maxim (or "get there fastest with the mostest," as one American general once said). For a more general discussion of analogies between business and military strategy, see Philip Kotler and Ravi Singh, "Marketing Warfare in the 1980s," *Journal of Business Strategy,* Vol. 1, No. 3, Winter 1981.
2. See Michael E. Porter, "Changing Patterns of International Competition," *California Management Review,* Vol. 28, No. 2, Winter 1986, pp. 9–40.
3. See Michael E. Porter, *Competitive Strategy: Techniques for Analyzing Industries and Competitors* (New York: Free Press, 1980), Chapter 4, and A. Michael Spence, "Entry, Capacity, Investment and Oligopolistic Pricing," *Bell Journal of Economics,* Vol. 8, Autumn 1977, pp. 534–44, on the role of signaling in competitive strategy.
4. Sumantra Ghoshal, "Global Strategy: An Organizing Framework," *Strategic Management Journal,* Vol. 8, No. 5, September–October 1987, pp. 425–40, characterizes the ability to learn and adapt as one of the three key objectives in global strategy, the other two being achieving efficiency and managing risk. See also Christopher A. Bartlett and Sumantra Ghoshal, *Managing Across Borders: The Transnational Solution* (Boston, MA: Harvard Business School Press, 1989), on how to organize for global learning.
5. As argued by Michael E. Porter, *The Competitive Advantage of Nations* (New York: The Free Press, 1990).
6. This example is based on Kenneth L. Kraemer and Jason Dedrick, "Dell Computer: Organization of a Global Production Network," December 1, 2002. *Center for Research on Information Technology and Organizations. Globalization of I.T.* Paper 255, http://repositories.cdlib.org/crito/globalization/255.
7. Hao Ma, "Creation and Preemption for Competitive Advantage," *Management Decision,* Vol. 37, No. 3, 1999, pp. 259–66.
8. Henry P. Conn and George S. Yip, "Global Transfer of Critical Capabilities," *Business Horizons,* Vol. 40, No. 1, January–February 1997, pp. 22–31.

CHAPTER 8

Building the Global Organization

Organization factors form the third corner of the globalization triangle, along with industry globalization drivers and global strategy levers. They affect what the nature of global strategy should be as well as the effectiveness of its implementation. Here we focus on how the nature of the organization—its structure, management processes, people, and culture—affects the use of global strategy levers and the ability to implement global strategy. The chapter describes these organization factors in depth and discusses how to build a global organization.[1] Key issues in global organization include how to achieve balance between autonomy and integration. Subsidiaries need autonomy in order to adapt to their local environment. But the business as a whole needs integration to implement global strategy.[2] Global organizations need to achieve both integration and autonomy while fostering the increasingly important tasks of learning and knowledge transfer.[3] Being able to transfer knowledge from one country to another provides a key source of advantage for multinational companies (MNCs).[4]

Many companies are struggling to achieve a globally integrated organization that retains the capability for local flexibility and responsiveness.[5] Very few companies have achieved a totally satisfactory solution, but a few have created highly successful elements in the global organization and management puzzle. In fact, organization provides the vehicle by which strategy can be formulated and implemented. The nature of the organization also affects the kind of strategy that can be developed. This is particularly true of global strategy. An organization of highly autonomous national business units, in which the managers from different countries seldom meet, with little transfer of personnel or information between countries, and with a nationalistic culture, is scarcely likely to be able to formulate a global strategy in the first place, let alone implement it. Such an organization may well believe that it does not need a global strategy—because it is not exposed to the information that might show otherwise.

Building the kind of company capable of formulating and implementing total global strategy is not easy. The task is achievable if managers break it down into digestible pieces and if they relate changes in organization to the specific changes needed in global strategy. A workable approach to global organization has two key requirements. First, it is no use announcing that the company needs a "global organization" without specifying the details of that organization. So managers need to view a global organization as comprising several factors and several elements within each factor. The second key requirement is to recognize that specific elements of global organization affect the ability to use specific elements of global strategy. For example, having a separate international division (an element of organization structure) makes it very difficult to design global products. So managers need to take an *elemental* approach to designing the global organization. The advantage of this elemental approach is that managers can make small changes that can build up over time[6] and can change one aspect of organization when blocked in another. Reorganizing the structure can be politically difficult, while less drastic changes in management process may meet less resistance. Changes in some elements can reduce the barriers to more major changes.

Four factors and their individual elements determine the crucial organization forces that affect a company's ability to formulate and implement global strategy:

- *Organization structure* comprises the reporting relationships in a business—the "boxes and lines."
- *Management processes* comprise the activities such as planning and budgeting that make the business run.
- *People* comprise the human resources of the worldwide business and include both managers and all other employees.
- *Culture* comprises the values and rules that guide behavior in a corporation.

Each of these factors directly affects the others and the use of global strategy. Each operates powerfully in different ways. A common mistake, in implementing *any* strategy, is to ignore one or more of them, particularly the less tangible ones such as culture. A blockage in even one dimension of organization can severely cramp the ability to think and behave globally. Exhibit 8-1 lists the key factors and their key elements.

Each organization factor and its elements have distinct effects on the use of each of the five global strategy levers. For example, having centralized global authority allows a more global approach to market participation—by allowing countries to be chosen more on the basis of global strategic importance and less on the basis of which regional manager has more political power. Centralized global authority also helps the development of global products, helps make global choices on the location of activities, and makes it easier to develop global marketing and to make global competitive moves.

The organization and management requirements of a global business can also be contrasted with those of a multilocal or export-based business. For these different businesses, each organization factor needs to stress different features. A *global* business needs some form of centralized global authority. But a *multilocal* business does better with dispersed national authority that allows each country to make its own decisions in adapting to local conditions. Lastly, an *export-based* business also needs centralized authority but one that takes the viewpoint of the home country business rather than that of the entire worldwide business. Exhibit 8-2 summarizes the desired organization features for each type of geographic strategy.

But, as in global strategy levers, companies need not adopt every global organization approach. Managers should select those global organization elements that seem the most helpful in achieving their global strategy objectives. Furthermore, as change is

EXHIBIT 8-1 Elements of Global Organization

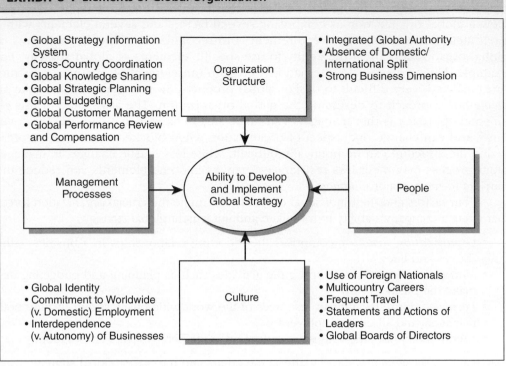

usually necessary, managers should select those changes that they think their organization is capable of making. And, if the company cannot make the needed organization changes, it should not even try to have a global strategy.

ORGANIZATION STRUCTURE

The first organization factor, organization structure, has the most obvious and direct, although not necessarily the most important, effect on global strategy.[7] Changes in organization structure (and, therefore, lines of reporting) send the clearest signals, which can be good or bad. So such changes need to be used with caution. In some cases, changes in other, less direct, aspects of organization, such as management processes, may need to be made first to pave the way for changes in structure.

Integration of Global Authority

One of the most effective ways to develop and implement a global strategy is to integrate or centralize authority so that all units of the same business around the world report to a common *global sector head*. Surprisingly few companies do this. Instead, they are tied for historical reasons to a strong country-based organization structure where the main line of authority runs by country rather than by business. In some businesses, however, particularly vertically integrated ones in raw-material processing industries such as chemicals or pulp and paper, it can be very difficult to carve out stand-alone lines of business in each country. Each factory, for example, may serve several businesses both inside and

EXHIBIT 8-2 Desired Organization Features for Types of Geographic Strategies

Geographic Scope	Organization Structure	Management Processes	People	Culture
Global	Centralized global authority	Extensive coordination processes	Multicountry careers	Global identity
	No domestic–international split	Global sharing of technology	Foreign nationals in home and third countries	Interdependence
	Strong geographic dimension relative to business and function	Global strategy information system	Extensive travel	
		Global strategic planning, budgets, performance review, and compensation		
Multilocal	Dispersed national authority	Transfer of technology from headquarters out	Professional expatriates	Multinational identity
	No domestic–international split	National information systems	Nationals run local businesses	Autonomy
	Strong geographic dimension relative to business and function	National strategic planning, budgets, performance review, and compensation	Limited travel	
Export-Based	Centralized home country control	Direction not coordination	Home country nationals run local marketing subsidiaries	Home country culture
	Separate domestic and international divisions	One-way information flow to headquarters		
	May have strong functional dimension	No technology transfer focus on sales targets		

outside the country in which the factory is located. In such cases, an alternative structural solution is to appoint *global business directors* who operate across the functional and geographic organizations.

The roles and responsibilities for such global business directors can include the following:

- Taking profit accountability for individual lines of business
- Coordinating all functions affecting these lines

- Developing a strategic plan and financial budgets in cooperation with the functions and regions
- Working with the functions and regions to implement the strategic plan
- Contributing to the design, creation, and maintenance of global strategy, marketing, and financial information systems
- Contributing to performance evaluations for functional and regional managers
- Traveling frequently

Another way of centralizing global authority is to have *global heads of individual functions* or value-adding activities. These heads can have either direct line authority over the function or a staff-like coordination responsibility. Functional heads can be very effective. The corporate head of global marketing in a major household products company viewed his role as partly to explain why ideas had failed in other countries. He would often say to a national manager, "You know more about your country than I do. I know more about the rest of the world. This strategy you propose has been tried in eight other countries. It failed in seven and here is why. Now let's examine your idea." But having real power can also be elusive. Companies sometimes delude themselves that they have created global authority by giving responsibility for global integration to an executive. The head of business planning in a large computer equipment business commented that while his business had one global product head "on paper," the latter had no real control and, therefore, little effect on global strategy.

Absence of Domestic–International Split

A common structural barrier to global strategy is the presence of an organization split between a domestic and an international division.[8] Typically, the international division oversees a group of highly autonomous country subsidiaries, each of which manages several distinct businesses. A global strategy for any one of these businesses can then be fully coordinated only at the level of the CEO's office. Until the 1990s, this split was very common among U.S. firms, partly for historical reasons and partly because of the enormous size of the U.S. market. Ironically, some European multinationals with small domestic markets separated out not their home market but the U.S. market. As a result they found it difficult to get their U.S. subsidiaries to cooperate in the development and implementation of global strategy. In one major European company, the heads of worldwide business sectors had to go "cap-in-hand to New York" to solicit support for their worldwide strategies. Afterward, this company strengthened the business sectors' direct authority over American operations.

Many American companies have separate international divisions and domestic divisions. In fact, some U.S. firms have disbanded international divisions. A major financial service company has shifted to three regions for the whole world. Its business head viewed this eliminating of the U.S. divisions, and consequent breaking down of regional barriers, as one of the company's greatest successes in globalizing strategy. The benefits included better allocation of resources and the recognition that business lost in one country need not necessarily be replaced in the same country, but can be recouped elsewhere. The head of international sales and distribution for a leading U.S. industrial controls business has viewed its domestic–international split as the biggest obstacle to global strategy. The head of another business complains that its heavily regional organization discourages global strategy by restricting the flow of information and technology.

The head of marketing in the international division of a food and beverages business commented that the original advantage of having a separate international division was in building up a power base. But now, with a global brand fighting a global competitor, the business needs to use its U.S. profits to subsidize international efforts, and the current structure does not allow that.

Business Dimension Stronger than Geographic Dimension

Issues of central control affect the global strategy capability of a worldwide business. But most worldwide businesses are part of MNCs that operate multiple businesses. The need to manage across both countries and businesses adds to the complexity of the challenge. Most MNCs have evolved a form of organization structure that combines business and geographic as well as functional dimensions.[9] In the 1990s, this approach has evolved into a global network, sometimes called the "transnational" company.[10] However, even by a full decade and a half later, corporations were still having trouble adapting post–World War II organizational structures with the realities of wired economic conditions.[11]

Unilever's global integration has been provided by a team of "coordinators" at the head office responsible for business sectors such as detergents and foods (the latter coordination split at one time into Foods I, Foods II, and Foods III). These coordination executives have mostly held senior country and regional general management positions. Its archrival, Procter & Gamble (P&G), was slow to take a similar approach. In the 1980s P&G adopted an integrated structure, first in Europe and then worldwide. A brand manager now reported both to his or her country manager and to a category manager. This change helped the company react more quickly to global competition.[12] At the same time some observers criticized P&G's use of European product managers for slowing the European launch of its Pampers brand of disposable diapers. In particular the change in reporting structure may have made national managers less interested in supporting Pampers. But, if true, that problem does not demonstrate the weakness of global organization or global marketing but of inadequate change in *all* the elements of global organization. P&G should also have changed the management evaluation and incentive process to support the new strategy. By the mid-1990s, P&G went beyond Unilever in globalizing its management structure by reorganizing away from a geographically dominated structure to seven global business units. Furthermore, P&G located the headquarters of some of these business units outside the United States. For example, the global management of the detergents business moved to Brussels. As a result, executives with broad experience were developed to provide a wider set of capabilities to manage the company both in the short term and in the long term.[13]

Dow Chemical has used a three-dimensional (function, business, and geography) management framework since the 1960s to cope with its plants in over 30 countries and its 1,800 different products. After many changes, Dow settled on a flexible approach in which, depending on the nature and needs of a business sector, one of the three dimensions of the management framework is chosen to carry more weight than the other two. Lastly, perhaps most important is that regardless of the organization structure, managers should think in an integrated fashion.[14] While doing this ensures accountability across the organization, it also encourages managers to think differently and develop distinct and competitive ideas otherwise not possible in a traditional corporate structure.[15]

In a company pursuing a global strategy, the extent of integration within businesses needs to be very strong. At the same time, integration within each country is important to coordinate the activities of the different businesses and to be able to present a common front to host governments, suppliers, channels, customers, and community groups. In theory, strong integration along both business and country dimensions should be possible. In practice, the two efforts often conflict. Exhibit 8-3 illustrates some possible combinations of geographic and business integration. The situation in the top left box, "Fragmented Multilocal Strategies," illustrates the case of extreme global fragmentation, in which there is no organization structure integrating either businesses within a country or countries within a business. Senior executives in many large and small American MNCs characterize (with embarrassment) their company that way.

The situation in the top right box, "Integrated Country Strategies," illustrates a historically very common form of multinational organization in which a country manager has great powers over all the businesses in his or her country. This form of integration was particularly popular in the early days of multinational expansion when communications and travel were far more difficult than today. European companies, with their heritage of colonial administration, probably developed the country manager role to its highest degree of power. The country managers of India in a British multinational company used to "rule like a rajah." Many corporate executives have complained of national and regional "fiefdoms" run by these highly independent country managers. Even Roger Enrico, who persuaded Michael Jackson to sing and dance for Pepsi-Cola, could not control the head of PepsiCo in Latin America.[16] Still, Coca-Cola found some success with this approach in its re-development of an overall corporate strategy.

EHIBIT 8-3 Different Corporate Approaches to Worldwide Strategy

Coca-Cola's Balance of Global and Local Strategies

In the mid-1990s, Coca-Cola took a unique position by saying it was planning to eliminate borders and start operating under a "think global, act global" mentality. This new way of thinking led to reorganization of the company. Soon, Coca-Cola generated 77 percent of its profits from outside the United States. In fact, the new strategy involved considerably high standardization in many areas of the world. Unfortunately, this strategy was short lived as Coca-Cola's earnings suffered considerably.[17]

To combat this, Coca-Cola changed its strategy again to a more local approach. However, this strategy did not work any better than the pure global strategy.[18] The company found out that, to be successful, it must find a balance between thinking completely globally and completely locally.[19] This shift has forced the company to examine some of its most profitable markets, such as Japan, and shift to focusing on promising markets for success.

As such, Coca-Cola was able to lower costs by modernizing its bottling operations and upgrading logistics and distribution to target rural areas more effectively in emerging markets.[20] The result was higher demand in countries such as Brazil, China, and India to drive profitability.[21] Though Coca-Cola has undergone considerable marketplace pressures in China,[22] the company's multi-product offensive strategy in India is an indication of Coca-Cola's continued success with its new balanced strategy.[23]

However, the need for global strategy and improvement in communications causes many companies to reduce the role of the country manager. *In one sense, the country manager has been made obsolete by the fax machine and the Internet.* In a major American financial service business the role of the country manager has changed a great deal. The country manager used to run the business in the country but is now more the titular head who represents the parent company in the country. It seems, however, that there will always be one role for the country manager. The Swiss chief financial officer of a European multinational said that his company would always need country managers, because "governments need one man to go after to put in jail"! On the other hand, the opening up in the 1990s of many emerging economies re-created the need for country managers in those markets.

The bottom left box, "Integrated Business Global Strategies," illustrates the situation in which the organization structure provides strong global integration within each business across countries but provides little integration across businesses within each country. Only in the bottom right box, "Integrated Corporate Global Strategy," does the structure provide integration across both dimensions. When executives are asked which diagram best represents their corporation, few select this last box, but almost all say that their company is headed that way. Philips, the giant Dutch manufacturer of electrical products, provides an instructive example of a company that long had a much more powerful geographic dimension than a business one but is now striving hard to tilt the managerial framework toward the business dimension. Because of the Dutch colonial heritage and because the head office was cut off from the subsidiaries during World War II, the latter grew to operate very independently. But under global attack from Japanese electronics manufacturers in the 1980s, and facing the integration of Europe, Philips found that it needed a global rather than a multinational organization.[24] In addition, IBM's recent efforts at becoming a globally integrated enterprise are illustrative of the investments required for accomplishing an integrated global strategy.

IBM's Globally Integrated Enterprise

Samuel J. Palmisano, the president and CEO of IBM, wrote an essay in 2006 on the globally integrated enterprise.[25] The essay encompassed the idea that companies are working in a global environment as the competitive marketplace continues to grow. In it, Palmisano indicated that corporations needed to move away from their models as multinational corporations to global ones. Advancing a doctrine for executives to consider, he noted that in the past, corporations would set up facilities close to their customers to meet their needs. However, with companies constructing over 60,000 manufacturing facilities in China from 2000 to 2003 to serve a global customer base, that trend has changed.

Indeed, the speed and intensity of global competition is no longer what it once was.[26] Strategies can be developed in a more decentralized fashion. Market knowledge can become irrelevant if not linked to a compelling corporate message. Also, market power no longer resides in a command-and-control structure instead requiring the application of skills deemed minimal in a static international marketplace.

Since much of IBM's business provides information systems to its customers, the company needed to follow the trend set by global companies. Palmisano made major investments at IBM in team development and capabilities in emerging markets.[27] In doing this, the company's goal was to make itself more integrated such that it was considered, in many aspects of the company, to be truly global.[28] This created conditions for considerable growth in countries such as Brazil, China, India, and Russia.[29] As a result, IBM had transformed itself into a dynamic organization able to identify and capitalize on market opportunities—key attributes required for continued competitiveness.

Lastly, companies need not adopt just one of the four modes depicted in Exhibit 8-4. A mixture can be best, allowing some businesses (those in industries with low globalization potential) to be managed on a country-by-country basis, some countries (those with high barriers to trade) to operate independently with extensive control over the businesses in them, and other countries and businesses to be part of global integration. This idea is summarized in Exhibit 8-4, which shows that the organizational logic has to match the strategic logic.

Designating Strategic Leaders

A less direct approach to globalization than changing the organization structure is to assign to a specific country the lead role in developing a product and to see to that product's spread into other countries and to its adaptation.[30] Thus some responsibilities are diverted from the other countries to the country acting as the strategic leader. One of the most effective ways of using this approach is to assign strategic leadership responsibility for different products to a number of different countries. In that way, each country has to cooperate with the others, and none is singled out. Assigning lead roles to subsidiaries helps to compensate them for the way in which global strategy reduces their scope and autonomy. Some researchers argue that subsidiaries can play a new role by bidding for "global mandates" to perform either internal roles (such as becoming a global regional activity center) or external roles (such as working with global customers).[31]

National Differences in Global Organization

MNCs from the three major business regions of the world—the United States, Europe, and Japan—tend to have differing organization structures and therefore face differing globalization challenges.[32] Because of the small size of their home markets and because

EXHIBIT 8-4 Match of Organizational and Strategic Logic

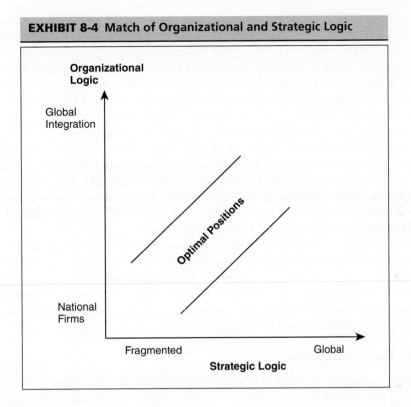

of their nations' overseas empires, European companies were typically the most advanced in multinationalization whether measured by the percentage of their sales outside their home country or by their use of managers of different nationalities. More important, European multinationals—such as Unilever, Philips, and Nestlé—have probably given more autonomy to their foreign subsidiaries than have American or Japanese multi nationals. Many European multinationals face, therefore, a greater need to reduce multilocal autonomy and increase global integration.

Because of the huge size of their home market, American companies were somewhat slower to go international than were comparable European and Japanese companies. From the 1980s there was increased pressure to internationalize because of increased foreign competition, slower growing domestic markets, and the new public recognition of America's trading problems. Although indirect, the last factor powerfully affected the attention paid to international business by corporate stakeholders (such as share owners, boards of directors, and employees) and, therefore, the attention of senior management. The size of the American domestic market has also created an issue that is more typical for American multinationals—the organizational and psychological division between the home country and other countries. Separate domestic and international organizations are common in American multinationals but rarer in European ones.[33] As a result American companies pursuing global integration face the dual challenge of confronting not just local country autonomy but domestic–international divisions as well.

Most Japanese companies operated until the late 1980s/early 1990s as exporters rather than as multinationals. Although they typically used an international division, the export emphasis of their businesses allowed very close links between their domestic and international businesses. Their rising domestic costs, plus the threat of protectionism in their foreign markets, spurred an increasing relocation of their production activities to the countries of their markets. Japanese companies faced the task of learning how to operate as MNCs and to build the needed organization structure. In terms of global strategy, they faced a challenge opposite to that for American and European companies. Japanese companies have generally been highly effective in operating with an integrated global strategy. However, they faced the task of retaining that global integration while allowing the local autonomy needed to operate as multinationals. The challenges related to attaining this balance were tested anew with the infrastructure disruptions Japan experienced recently. Based on the natural and economic conditions of 2011, Japanese automakers were required to keep assembly facilities closed due to electricity conservation measures such as rolling blackouts.[34] This, in turn, impacted worldwide sales for products in especially high demand (e.g., Honda's Fit and Toyota's Prius).

As multinationals arise from other economies—especially Korea, the rest of Asia, and Latin America—they all face the same issue of transition from national focus to a global one. By virtue of their relative lateness in internationalization, most of these companies will be able to bypass or accelerate through some of the earlier forms of international organization, such as multilocal, autonomous subsidiaries, and reach quickly for effective forms of global organization.

Potential for Cost Savings

Reorganizing along global rather than multilocal lines can produce major cost savings by reducing the extent to which activities are duplicated in multiple countries (as discussed in Chapter 5). The traditional way to cut costs in reorganization is to eliminate *horizontal* layers by cutting the number of levels in a company. Reorganization along global lines provides a *vertical* option for cost cutting, such as by eliminating 9 out of 12 manufacturing sites in different countries. But companies need to beware of reorganizing globally just for the sake of cost savings. The reorganization must also make sense strategically, relative to industry globalization drivers and the type of global strategy needed.

MANAGEMENT PROCESSES

While organization structure has a very direct effect on management behavior, it is management processes that power the system. The appropriate processes and systems can even substitute to some extent for the appropriate structure. These processes and systems include the global strategy information system, cross-country coordination, global strategic planning, global budgeting, and global performance review and compensation.

Global Strategy Information System

Information systems comprise the data that are collected, analyzed, stored, and communicated as well as the methods for performing those activities. Information systems go beyond hardware and software. Having information about the world is a minimum requirement for being able to formulate and implement a global strategy. Information needs to be specified at a global level as well as at regional and national levels. So the system needs to contain information about *global* market share as well as national market

Embraer's Technological Supplier Relationships

Embraer is the third largest aircraft manufacturer in the world behind Boeing and Airbus. The company's strategy has been to deliver significant competitive advantages and to find a niche in the marketplace. The firm is headquartered in Brazil. However, in 2006, 95 percent of its total sales were located outside of the country.[35] In fact, with joint ventures in China and manufacturing plants in Portugal and the United States, Embraer is busy establishing itself as a globally focused company.[36]

Embraer's specialty is in the market segment for airplanes of up to 120 seats. With the increase in global aviation, the marketplace increasingly demands more flexible regional aviation. This is a particular niche that is not well suited for aircraft from Boeing and Airbus. As such, the company has leveraged the technological expertise of Brazil's universities to facilitate research and development (R&D) in a mutually beneficial relationship that allows the company to minimize the risk of wasted R&D expenditures while at the same time providing universities with highly applicable engineering research.

Paramount to Embraer's success in a capital-intensive global industry has been the management of risks through contracted partnerships with global suppliers.[37] High-level suppliers make investments in the design, research, and development of products to supply to the company, and in turn they receive the advantage of having a preferred and longer-term relationship with the company. Sophisticated technology such as CAD/CAM and CATIA links engineering suppliers around the globe into the company's integrated knowledge network. Although the company heavily sources its supply chain on a global scale, many risk-sharing partners have invested in facilities near the company's base in São José dos Campos. This creates a streamlined organization of companies to remain competitive and respond to marketplace demand.

---

share, and so on. A useful test for managers is to ask whether the system has information about the company's global share of a particular customer's business. The system also needs to regularly collect strategic information in a common format for easy comparison. Information needs to be communicated to headquarters in a method that is as easy as possible for subsidiary managers. The information needs to be processed and analyzed for global strategy implications. *Perhaps most important, headquarters need to disseminate its findings back to the countries so that they do not view the home country as a black hole, sucking in information but giving nothing in return.*

Information technology—enterprise resource planning (ERP) systems such as SAP, the Internet, and CRMs (customer relationship management systems)—makes it easier to maintain a global strategy and remain competitive. Dow Chemical globally interconnected the different parts of its organization by implementing SAP R/2. By installing this ERP by SAP throughout the world, Owens-Corning transformed its organization from a decentralized company into a centralized, global one. Many companies use CRMs to collect and manage information about their national and multinational customers to share and use information across borders both internally and externally. In fact, as Embraer has proven, other technology-based tools can be used with considerable success across supplier relationships.

However, the term "system" needs to be interpreted loosely and need not be equated with computers. Many companies have foundered in their initial attempts at building global strategy information systems by getting sidetracked into developing complex computer-based data entry and retrieval systems that never became usable. They forgot that the more difficult task in global information is getting the data in the first place. The way in which information gets sent by the subsidiaries should be made as simple as possible. A medium-sized industrial equipment company has developed a one-page form on which national sales representatives can report competitive intelligence. A major chemical company has done quite well by keeping its information on paper, updating with hand notations as needed. The company has also found that subsidiary managers are much more willing to fax information in fairly casual formats than to enter data into a computer terminal. One major international advertising agency used to collect global information by sending a senior executive traveling around the world. He would "beat the information out of the national managers." Today leading agencies use technological advances instead: National offices conduct their local advertising via the Internet so that all facets of the business can see what is being done for a given client around the world.

Cross-Country Coordination

Creating cross-country coordination mechanisms provides a way to make up for the lack of direct reporting structure, although its use seems limited to date. The lack of coordination can bring drastic consequences. In defending an advertising claim, a drug manufacturer argued with the U.S. Federal Drug Administration that the recommended dosage of *two* tablets for its full strength analgesic product provided the maximum possible benefit. The regulatory agency accepted this argument until it discovered a television commercial by the same company in Canada recommending *three* tablets for severe symptoms. An industrial company frequently got into trouble with its global customers because businesses in different countries did not share their plans on pricing changes. In one instance, the business in France offered a temporary price reduction on a product line sold to a global customer that also bought from the United States. The customer then switched its purchases from the United States to France and shipped the product across the Atlantic—the price cut more than covering the additional transportation cost and duty.

Cross-country coordination mechanisms range from sharing of information—the least coercive—to setting direct requirements—the most coercive:

- Countries can *share information* about their strategic and operating plans. That alerts headquarters and other countries about opportunities and the possibility of conflicts.
- Countries can be required to *negotiate* their plans with headquarters and other countries that might be affected.
- Countries can be required to *clear* their plans with headquarters and other countries.
- Headquarters or some coordination group may *direct* countries to take certain actions. For example, all countries may be required to launch a particular new product. Giving direct orders verges on changing the organization structure to direct reporting. So management needs to be particularly cautious in setting down the path of directing countries' actions.

While informing, negotiating, clearing, and directing represent critical functions in cross-country coordination, their effectiveness is limited unless they are based on more than paper being shuffled around the globe. Processes directly involving managers can greatly enhance cross-country coordination. The least formal approach is to have regular *global meetings*. Holding global groups and forums allows exchange of information and building of relationships across countries. This in turn makes it easier for country nationals to gain an understanding of whether the differences they perceive between their home country and others are real or imagined. It also facilitates the development of common products and the coordination of marketing approaches. While these meetings can be costly in travel time and expense, ways can be found to reduce such costs. For example, management training programs can be set up to double as global forums if participants are drawn from geographically mixed locations.

A more formal, and increasingly adopted, approach is to set up *global teams* (or regional, e.g., European teams). These teams can take responsibility for specific programs or for all of the global strategy. A French manufacturer of security devices uses councils of country managers, with different countries playing the lead role for different products. While this approach is time consuming, the company has found that this reliance on line managers makes it easier for various countries to accept the input of other countries, and thus for global approaches to be pursued by all.[38]

In setting up the coordination process, top management needs to set a balance between doing too much and too little at the start. On the one hand, it is very tempting to appoint a powerful coordinator or even "czar." But such an appointment can immediately stimulate resistance from subsidiary managers who feel threatened by the new appointment. On the other hand, setting up a coordination committee with a weak leader where the real power lies with subsidiary managers can lead to little action.[39]

Going further, a business can appoint *global product managers* or *global account managers*. Although adding such managers might be viewed as a change in organization structure, their roles are typically more that of coordination. In both cases the global product managers or global account managers perform similar roles on a global (or regional) scale to those performed by their national equivalents.

Global Knowledge Sharing

Many argue that the main source of competitive advantage for MNCs is being able to share knowledge and learn across their geographic subsidiaries. To benefit from global innovation, creativity, and superior customer service, vital knowledge and information from any part of the company should be systematically captured and made accessible in real time to all parts of the company around the world.[40] Being able to transfer knowledge can also be the most important determinant of subsidiary success.[41] However, as indicated in Sony's attempts to share knowledge through joint ventures, research to date shows the great difficulty in managing and transferring knowledge.[42]

Global Strategic Planning

MNCs and their subsidiaries are now quite skilled at developing *corporate* and *national* strategic plans.[48] But most have yet to develop *global* strategic plans that integrate the strategies of the same business in different countries, let alone integrating strategies across multiple worldwide businesses. Too often, strategic plans are developed separately for each country and then summed to add up the numbers. But no real strategic integration has been planned. Failure to plan across countries makes it difficult to understand the business's competitive position worldwide and difficult to develop integrated strategic responses to competitors who do plan on a global basis.[49] This makes it difficult to design and implement global programs that need the cooperation of several countries.

The Sony's Joint Ventures to Share Knowledge

In industries that require large investments in production facilities with high-technology tools, former competitors often find that forming joint ventures is the only way to achieve efficient production. Since the amount of capital required for such innovative manufacturing facilities is considerable, sharing the burden with competitors can become a necessity. In fact, two industries adopting this model in the past have manufactured automobile and electronic goods. Although joint ventures appear as the most effective solution to streamline production and cut costs, results can vary. Often, competitors have difficulty differentiating their products with consumers after manufacturing has been completed for two different companies at the same factory.

Still, in 2004, Sony and Samsung, two of the largest manufacturers of LCD panels, formed S-LCD Corporation.[43] After production started, Sony found that its products had little competitive advantage when the core component, the panel, came from the same facility as Samsung's. Nonetheless, the facility allowed Sony to gain market share and lower production costs. In fact,

the competitive rivalry in the LCD market continued through the end of the decade, with Samsung's leading global market share at 22 percent and Sony placing second at 16.7 percent.[44]

However, to increase the company's market position against Samsung, Sony formed another joint venture in 2008 with competitor Sharp to build the world's first facility committed to its 10th-generation glass substrate panel modules. This time, however, Sony announced that it planned to use the factory to make its own panel modules and avoid the problems related to the joint venture with Samsung.[45] Still, after problems prolonged the development of the manufacturing facility,[46] Sony decided to outsource more from alterative partnerships to support its current operations.[47] As such, Sony has sought to share manufacturing knowledge with a variety of partners to keep it competitive. However, though global market share has improved for the company since before its joint venture with Samsung, the implementation of more recent initiatives is planned to make a considerable impact in the marketplace.

Ideally, there should be a global strategic planning process that involves the senior management from key countries and regions. Such a process would fit in with the corporate and national strategic planning cycles. Whether the global strategic planning process should precede or follow the national planning processes is less important than that it should be done at all. (Extensive research on formal strategic planning has shown that it needs to use a multilevel and multistage process. Agreement needs to be sought between levels—corporate, business, and function—at each of three stages—objective setting, program formulation, and budgeting—in contrast to a one-stage process in which the corporate level sets objectives and the business in turn responds with a complete plan that is a *fait accompli*.[50] For global strategic planning, a similar process can be used that involves corporate, global, and national levels.)

A key benefit of any strategic planning process is that it brings in the views of those who might not otherwise be heard. Such a benefit doubly applies in global strategic planning: It brings in the views of units that may be geographically distant but strategically critical. As the head of a multinational computer equipment business said, "Having a global strategic planning process helps give the 'outlanders' some say."

Having a formal global strategic plan provides a way to put teeth into cross-country coordination processes. Instead of coordinating with no particular end objective, managers in the different countries have to work together in producing the global plan.

A global strategic plan needs to contain the usual plan information expressed at a global level. But, in addition, the global plan needs to contain strategies and programs that cut across countries and are, thus, inherently difficult to formulate without a cross-country planning effort.

Global Budgeting

Having global strategies and programs implies having global budgets to implement them. Adding up the country budgets into a global total for each product line provides a first step in global resource allocation.[51] Surprisingly few companies do this thoroughly. Many companies do not even know how much profit they make worldwide in a particular business. Typically, the profit contribution is spread across many national and regional accounts. Most alarming is that many managers believe that the global numbers are readily available only to find otherwise when asked to produce them.

Beyond knowing the global numbers, companies need to do three other, difficult, things:

• First, companies need to be able to transfer resources from one country to another in order to be able to subsidize across countries. Such strategic subsidization is a crucial requirement of global strategy. But the accounting system frequently interferes with such efforts. For example, many companies set transfer prices rigidly. So, these companies cannot provide lower prices to countries that need them in order to strengthen their competitive position as part of the global strategy. If making a strategic move means incurring red ink, then many subsidiary managers will decline the invitation to participate in the global strategy. Some companies have found ways to have *flexible transfer pricing*—particularly where there is the opportunity to reduce taxes. Flexible transfer pricing includes the use of different margins and allows for different rates at which capital equipment is amortized.[52] So why not be flexible for the sake of global competitiveness? *Companies should not allow their accounting systems to prevent them from having a global strategy.*

• The second difficult accounting task is to cost out these activities in a globally neutral way. For example, as one executive put it, the French subsidiary should not be charged a low price for raw materials just because the plant it buys from happens to be in France. Thus the global budgeting process needs to provide for *geographically neutral costs* as the base point. These prices can then be adjusted as strategically necessary.

• The third difficult accounting task is to have *global budgets* that are available only for global programs. Typically, budgets are controlled by national and regional managers with limited amounts left to corporate. The drive against overhead has made large corporate budgets highly unpopular. But budgets for global programs do not provide for overhead. Instead, they can fund strategically vital activities, such as developing global products or subsidizing attacks on global competitors. Such activities are typically difficult for individual countries, or even regions, to undertake. Global budgets can provide a pot of money or "war chest" that managers with ideas for global activities can apply for. But protecting global budgets can be very difficult. Executives in one division of a diversified *Fortune* 500 company were worried that if they created a global budget for strategic contingencies, the money would be appropriated by corporate "the next day."

At its most extreme a global accounting system would charge companies the same cost for materials and products regardless of where they were shipped from. One of the largest companies in the world, a U.S.-based chemical company, is attempting to use such a transfer price approach. But the company has found its cost accounting system so inflexible that it has to make adjustments by hand in the businesses taking this approach. Executives at this company estimate that it will probably take them five to seven years to change the accounting system.

Global Customer Management

As discussed in Chapters 2 and 6, managing customers on a global basis has become increasingly necessary. Being able to do so effectively is in many ways a real test of a global company. It means that the company has to be able to deploy its resources and processes to serve global customers on an integrated and coordinate basis around the world. As discussed in Chapter 6, HP's global account management program required changes in all aspects of its organization.

Global key account (GKA) management plays a critical part in ABB's integrated organization system. Each global account is managed by a GKA executive, supported by a GKA team. Each team member represents its business area, company, or country. The team concerns itself with such issues as the global structure for dealing with the customer, major investments needed to serve the customer across regions and businesses, increasing sales potential, and running a centrally coordinated decision process.[53]

Global Performance Review and Compensation

The last and, in many ways, most important global management process involves the way in which managers are evaluated and rewarded. Getting these systems to support global strategy can go a long way to offsetting deficiencies in the other systems. If the financial reporting system cannot be changed, managers can still be motivated to undertake loss-incurring strategic actions if they are evaluated and rewarded appropriately. So, rewards, especially bonuses, need to be set in a way that reinforces the company's global objectives. If not, the global strategy never takes off. For example, an electronics manufacturer decided to start penetrating the international market by introducing a new product through its strongest division. The division head's bonus was based on the current year's worldwide sales, with no distinction between domestic and international sales. Because increasing his domestic sales was a lot easier—and had a much quicker payoff—than trying to open up new international markets, the division head did not worry much about his international sales. Predictably, the firm's market penetration strategy failed.

Most companies seem to have a long way to go. The head of international marketing and sales for an industrial controls business viewed the lack of global performance review as a major problem. To help remedy this defect, the company moved to basing a portion of incentive compensation for global team members on worldwide achievement. The head of business planning for a computer equipment company found that the difficulty of getting product managers to think globally was exacerbated by the lack of global reward systems. So it was all too common to not take the global job requirements as seriously as the domestic ones. Indeed, this executive believed that the product managers would like to be measured on a global basis and were willing to take their chances on that. In the same business, the director of international strategic planning also viewed the lack of global compensation as a major weak spot.

The last example shows the importance of rewarding those with global responsibility for global performance. Going further, companies also need to find ways to reward managers for performance in geographic areas *beyond their immediate control,* but that are influenced by their actions. Country managers need to be rewarded not just on the basis of their country's performance but on that of their region or the world. Thus, the French country manager needs to be given incentive to help and cooperate with the German country manager, and the German with the Italian. Performance review and compensation should depend not just on a manager's performance in his or her own region but on the performance of the rest of business globally, evaluations by global business managers, evaluations by managers of other regions, and the achievement of global objectives (e.g., the introduction of particular products into region, implementation of a global program, or creation of an information system to report back to headquarters).

Getting Global Cooperation

Each of the methods just described has the common aim of getting global cooperation. Each company has to find what works best for a particular business at a particular time. Typically, using multiple methods reinforces the benefits, as shown in the following example. Even as entrepreneurial a business as the music and recording industry has some need for global strategy. A leading multinational music company uses three different approaches for globalizing its programs. First, the company uses direction, by insisting on global adoption in the case of new albums by already established international recording stars. In the case of real superstars, the insistence is unspoken. National managers just know that they will get into serious trouble if they do not adopt the album. In other cases, a committee of regional heads agrees on artists and albums as global priorities, which all countries must then introduce. Unfortunately, getting agreement is seldom easy. Second, individual countries ("exporters") use flexible budgets to set up inducements for other countries ("importers") to adopt their national stars, by paying for such expenses as airfare and other tour and promotional expenses that would normally be the responsibility of the importers. Third, the company simply relies on voluntary adoption in other cases. This last approach has had its failures. When asked, each national manager was able to cite instances in which other countries incorrectly failed to adopt one of his or her artists or had waited too long, thereby missing the boat in this fast-changing business.

PEOPLE

Global strategy can be implemented only by the people in the organization. Developing managers and other members of the organization to think and behave globally requires many of the policies used by successful MNCs, but it also needs to go beyond that. In particular, the "United Nations" model of multinational management has favored having local nationals take over all positions in their countries. But in the extreme, such an approach reduces the benefit from executives having experience in many countries. The ideal human resource policy for global strategy provides a mix of different national backgrounds represented in the management of each country's business. And in further violation of the United Nations spirit of equality, it is executives from globally strategic countries who should be favored for global careers. It is more important to spread their experience globally from these key countries than that of executives from strategically marginal countries. So while it might be easier to move a native of Liechtenstein around the world, it might help the global strategy more to move someone from Japan.

In the early stages of internationalization, companies tend to rely on expatriates, while in the multilocal stage, companies aim to have as many local managers as possible. The global stage requires a balance of global, regional, and national managers. A global network can be operated if many members have had international experience and also have many interpersonal connections and shared experiences. Furthermore, individuals can take different roles at different stages of their career or family life cycle. Global companies need to invest in building a portfolio of needed capabilities, not just in technical or business terms but in terms of language and cultural capabilities and types of international experience. Japanese and Korean companies may find it difficult to incorporate foreign nationals into their management systems, but they also invest heavily in preparing their own nationals for foreign assignments. Samsung puts executives through a global expert program which includes sending them abroad for one year as a part of its Human Resources Development Center. Statoil, the Norwegian oil company, finds that many of its international opportunities lie in Central Asia. Few Norwegians speak the languages of Kazakh or Uzbek! Perhaps it should fund students in Norwegian schools to learn these languages.

The development of global leaders requires the creation of an environment that fosters and promotes cooperation across borders, free exchange of information, and the development of creative managers capable of functioning effectively anywhere in the world.[54] Necessary programs include the following:

- Establishing successful leadership development programs for global organizations
- Empowering managers with the flexibility and creativity to transform and apply best practices on a global scale
- Strong commitment to recognizing, hiring, developing, and nurturing managers with the greatest global leadership potential
- Maintaining practices to encourage managers to boost global awareness, multicultural, and multilinguistic skills

Use of Foreign Nationals

High-potential foreign nationals need to gain experience not just in their home country but at headquarters and in other countries. This practice has three benefits. It broadens the pool of talent available for executive positions, it visibly shows the commitment of top management to internationalization, and it gives talented individuals an irreplaceable development opportunity. U.S. companies have been slow to do this, particularly at the most senior ranks. Promoting foreigners, and using staff from various countries, has often paid off.

A packaged goods manufacturer undertook some years ago to move its European staff from country to country. As such, of 15 staff working at headquarters, seven were French, three were English, three were German, and two were Italian. The company credits this practice, among others, for its remarkable turnaround. It can be particularly helpful to move national managers to headquarters early in their careers. The plastics division of a major chemical company implemented a plan for moving foreign executives to headquarters early in their careers, placing them in market manager positions. These positions were ideal as they provide broad strategic exposure to the business in the home country but did not have direct selling responsibility, which typically poses the greatest cultural barriers. Companies should also use non–home country nationals not just at headquarters but in other countries as well. Indeed, companies should ideally never use the term "foreign national" or even "home country." American companies could refer to "non-U.S. nationals"; Japanese companies to "non-Japanese nationals" rather than to "gaijins," and so on.

A global company also needs to have the courage and common sense to override local objections to foreigners. National managers are often nervous about bringing foreigners into their country. One of the more extreme examples concerns an American multinational professional services company. Its senior European managers recently held a meeting to select a new country manager for the Netherlands. When a Spanish manager was suggested, the Dutch executive present objected that Spain used to rule the Netherlands, so a Spaniard would not be welcome. Surprised, an American executive asked when that rule was. The Dutchman replied, "About four hundred years ago, but the Spanish are still very much resented." This objection was overruled, and the Spanish manager was appointed without subsequent problems.

Multicountry Careers

Making work experience in different countries a necessity for progression, rather than a hindrance, is another important step that helps a company become truly global. An electronics manufacturer decided to make a major push into Japan, but a middle-level executive offered a transfer there was loathe to take it. He was concerned whether there would be a job for him when he came back. As he put it, "The road to the executive suite lies through Chicago, not Osaka." In contrast, Jacques Maisonrouge, the former head of IBM World Trade (then IBM's international arm), initiated a policy that no executive could rise to a general manager position without having taken a foreign assignment beforehand. Using home country nationals overseas has been a very common practice. Increasing costs of relocation and the problems of moving dual-career couples have made this more difficult. But companies need to take a longer term view of the benefits from such placements. Companies have to be willing to pay the cost of transferring executives around the world. A senior executive in a large American multinational company did not see the flaw in his company's position that it would pay American executives transferred overseas the higher of the American or local rate, but had trouble getting Swiss executives to come to the United States because of the lower American pay.

In fact, ABB implemented many innovative global human resource management (HRM) practices.[55] All employees were required to read a short booklet that outlined company objectives and values. In addition, English was made the company language and a small headquarters staff supervised the entire organization. An executive committee with members from different regions of the world and a select number of global managers supported the thin core. The global managers were required to be experienced and willing to move with their families. Their responsibilities included the transfer of expertise around the world, the task of keeping the organization closely bound together, and the continuous communication to leadership of different perspectives from the field.

To encourage multicountry careers, companies may need to set tough rules such as the following:

- No advancement occurs beyond a certain level without two years outside the home country of the national.
- Transfers occur at an early stage of a manager's career.
- A target of all positions at a certain level and above held by nonnationals is set at 10 percent.
- The best performers get transferred overseas.
- Transferees are guaranteed a position back home, but its level depends on performance overseas.
- Veterans of foreign assignments get job preference.
- The human resources department tracks and takes responsibility for the careers of overseas transferees.

Using foreign nationals and multicountry careers has the important additional benefit of gradually creating a group of subsidiary managers who are likely to be more sympathetic to global strategy. As managers gain multicountry experience, they are less likely to focus on the unique differences of the particular country in which they operate and more able to appreciate the benefits of also looking for global commonality. This greater sympathy for global strategy becomes more important as the role of subsidiary managers changes with globalization—from that of running their own show to that of integrating into a larger global effort.[56]

Frequent Travel

Senior managers must spend a large amount of time in foreign countries. The CEO of a large grocery products company spends half his time outside the United States—a visible demonstration of the importance and commitment of the company to its international operations. Also important, senior managers should spend more of their time in the strategically important countries rather than in countries with operational difficulties but that are not important in the global strategy. Such countries represent black holes for senior management time.

Statements and Actions of Leaders

The senior management of a company that wants to globalize its strategy needs to constantly restate that intention and to act in accordance with it. Otherwise, the rank and file will not believe that the globalization strategy is for real. One test among many is the prominence given to international operations in formal communications such as the chairman's letter in the annual report or statements to stock analysts.

Global Boards of Directors

Another increasingly important test of globalization is the extent to which the board of directors has been globalized. A global company must have a board that reflects its global operations. Excellence in global governance and leadership means getting the best top executives and board members from anywhere in the world. Few of even the largest MNCs have representation of all continents on their boards, even though nonexecutive directors provide an easy source of such expertise. Companies that cannot quickly change their legal boards are instituting global advisory boards as a first step at tapping into a broader global base of advice. Japanese companies have found it particularly hard to change their boards. Sony has been an exception to the rule. The company has heavily recruited non-Japanese, added outside directors to its board, and created regional boards that include local nationals. In fact, after considerable time spent in its U.S. operations, Sony named Welsh-born Howard Stringer its CEO and president in 2009.[57]

CULTURE

Culture is the most subtle aspect of organization, but it can play a formidable role in helping or hindering a global strategy.

Global Identity

A strong national identity can hinder the willingness and ability to design global products and programs. It can also create a "them or us" split among employees. One firm was making a strong global push, and yet many of its corporate executives wore national flag pins! European companies are generally well in advance of both American and Japanese firms in adopting a global identity. Having multiple national identities—a different one in each country—is more international than having just the identity of the home country, but it is not global. Instead a truly global culture would transcend the nationality of the home and other countries.[58] At the same time, each national business still needs to be rooted in its local culture, or at least some of the executives, depending on their jobs, need such roots. Building a global identity is helped if nationalistic displays are avoided. Similarly, it helps if important meetings are not always held in the home country. Having foreign nationals on the corporate board also helps foster a global identity as well as bringing the substantive knowledge of these board members. In the words of one executive, "We need to be sensitive to national cultures, but not paralyzed by them."

Partly to help foster a global identity, P&G now seeks to instill a global perspective in all of its employees. P&G wants to establish the mindset of seeing the world as the company's marketplace. To do so, P&G is cultivating two attitudes in its people. The first is to search for ideas that can be applied to its business around the world. The second is to find reapplications for good ideas that have already been developed. In 1990, P&G made another major commitment to globalization when the company appointed as its new chief executive the head of its international division—jumping him over a more senior executive in the U.S. business. As evidence of P&G's global perspective, its Febreze brand performed well in North America, Europe, and Japan to become the company's fourth brand with over $1 billion in sales.[59] This provides clear indication of P&G's commitment to a global approach to market development and performance.

Commitment to Worldwide Not Domestic Employment

Many companies view their domestic employees as somehow more important than their foreign employees and are much more committed to preserving domestic employment than to developing employment regardless of location. This often leads them to decide to keep expensive manufacturing operations in the home country rather than relocate them in lower cost countries—thereby putting them at a competitive cost disadvantage and threatening their overall competitive position. Of course, there may be good defensive reasons for maintaining higher cost facilities in the home country. But cultural bias should not be one of them.

Interdependence of Businesses

A culture of local business autonomy, when carried too far, can also be a barrier to globalization. The culture needs to balance the celebration of autonomy with the recognition of interdependence. Achieving such a balance is not easy. Country managers are masters at ignoring directives from the head office. Like Admiral Nelson at the Battle of Copenhagen, they delight in putting the telescope to their blind eye. Top management can help foster a sense of country interdependence by educating staff in each country, particularly the home country, about achievements of operations in other countries.

Matching Culture to Globalization Needs

Companies pursuing global strategy need to develop not just a generally favorable culture but also specific cultural characteristics to support specific strategies. A large manufacturing company's culture included the following characteristics:

- A high degree of responsiveness to customers' requests for product tailoring
- A strong emphasis on letting every business and every country be highly autonomous
- A desire for 100 percent control over foreign operations
- A commitment to preserving domestic employment

Not surprisingly, the company found it very difficult to implement a global strategy. Senior management was able to understand its difficulties more clearly only after it spelled out the cultural change implications in global strategy. Specifically, the CEO came to realize that rapidly implementing a pure global strategy would require an organizational revolution. In contrast, a culturally less risky option would be to make a series of incremental changes in both strategy and organization, leading to a mixed strategy of globalization and national responsiveness. The CEO also considered an explicit rejection of globalization, which would require a conscious decision to build on the company's existing organizational and cultural characteristics to develop a pure national responsiveness strategy. Thinking through these cultural implications helped the company to make fundamental and realistic choices rather than assuming the unavoidable dominance of strategy over organization and of globalization over national responsiveness. Aided by this analysis, the company chose the second, mixed option of incremental change and has had satisfying results to date.

MINIMIZING THE DRAWBACKS OF GLOBAL ORGANIZATION

Globalization can incur organizational as well as strategic drawbacks. Costs may rise because of increased coordination, reporting requirements, and even added staff. Globalization can also reduce management effectiveness in individual countries if overcentralization hurts local motivation and morale. But some approaches can minimize these problems. Costs can be held down if new global functions replace rather than add to national functions. When a manufacturer of chemical and refining process equipment reorganized its separate European businesses into one, the company was able to eliminate some of the general management and administrative support positions. Those savings more than paid for the positions related to the new office of the general manager for Europe.

Political infighting can be minimized if global responsibilities are shared by many executives, each of whom retains some national (regional) roles. The "two hat" approach is particularly helpful. For example, the general manager of one country takes on the role of global marketing chief, while the general manager of another country becomes the global manufacturing chief. So each executive has to cooperate with the other. Resentment of headquarters can be assuaged if lead responsibilities get spread around the world. Thus different countries can be given the lead for different strategic thrusts.[60] Companies may even go so far as to relocate business headquarters out of the home country. Lastly, headquarters executives should try to be psychologically equidistant from any part of the world, making decisions on the basis of strategic advantage rather than emotional attachment.[61]

COMBINING STRATEGIC AND ORGANIZATIONAL ANALYSIS

In sum, the four organization factors—organization structure, management processes, people, and culture—play a key role in facilitating or hindering a company's move toward globalization. For example, take a company with a strong structural split between domestic and international activities, management processes that are country-driven rather than business-driven, people who work primarily in their home countries, and a parochial culture. Implementing global strategy in the company is likely to prove exceedingly difficult. If the analysis of industry globalization drivers has shown that such strategies are necessary for market, cost, or competitive reasons, top managers need to make a tough choice. Either they undertake a major change effort aimed at making the internal environment better adapted to the strategic moves the company needs to make, or they have to decide that the profound organizational changes needed to adopt a global strategy are too risky and that the company should avoid globalization and compete based on its existing organizational strengths.

This chapter ends with two examples of how to combine the analysis of all three elements in the globalization triangle: industry globalization drivers, global strategy levers, and global organization capability. The examples come from the experiences of two companies, both of them multi-billion-dollar multinationals. One company, disguised as TransElectronics, is a U.S.-based concern operating in many aspects of electronics. The other company, disguised as Persona, is a European-based manufacturer and marketer of consumer packaged goods. The two companies provide different views of the challenge of global strategy. TransElectronics is still developing as a fully multinational company and faces the challenge of accelerating that process to become a global competitor. Persona, on the other hand, has long been thoroughly multinational, with many highly autonomous companies operating around the world. Its challenge is to temper some aspects of that multinational autonomy in order to compete more effectively on a global basis.

Transforming TransElectronics

The communications sector of TransElectronics had one division, Electron, based in the United States, that sold "transcramblers" against fierce European and Japanese competition. A major market, Japan, closed until recently to foreign competition, was beginning to open through a combination of TransElectronics' efforts and U.S. government pressure on Japanese trade barriers. So developing a global strategy for transcramblers was a high priority for TransElectronics. A complication was that Electron was not a stand-alone business unit: Other units had related responsibilities. As will be described, this split of responsibilities was one of the major barriers to Electron's implementation of a global strategy.

ANALYZING INDUSTRY GLOBALIZATION POTENTIAL   Electron's managers were unsure as to how much potential for globalization there was in the transcrambler industry. A step-by-step analysis made this much clearer. First, *market* drivers pushed for globalization: There were few differences among countries in what they wanted from transcramblers. On the other hand, few global customers existed: National public sector telecommunications companies (PTTs) accounted for a large part of the market in each country. *Cost* drivers also strongly pushed for globalization: There were substantial scale economies and learning effects; sourcing efficiencies could be gained by consolidating manufacturing; and Electron's labor costs—a significant part of the product's total cost—were much lower in Puerto Rico and Taiwan than they were in the United States. *Government* drivers favored globalization: The privatization of some national PTTs was opening up previously closed markets, and products were becoming more standardized in Europe around a common format. An offsetting factor was local content requirements in many countries. Lastly, *competitive* forces were also pushing for globalization: Electron's major competitors (European and Japanese) took a global product approach with fewer price levels and with minimum product customization. The competitors had also largely centralized their manufacturing activities in just one or two countries each. In summary, strong external forces pushed the transcrambler industry to globalization. Not only was globalization already high, but it was likely to continue increasing.

EVALUATING USE OF GLOBAL STRATEGY   The Electron managers next evaluated how much the business actually used global strategy. Electron was quite global in its *market participation*—its sales split among countries closely matched that of the industry. Electron's *product line* was highly standardized—in fact, more than its executives realized. Electron's R&D and purchasing *activities* were specialized in the United States, but much of its manufacturing was dispersed across the United States, Puerto Rico, Taiwan, and Europe. *Marketing* was primarily done in the United States. Selling, distribution, and service were by necessity done locally, but were not at all coordinated across countries. Electron's competitors were all much more centralized and coordinated. The product positioning of transcramblers was consistent across countries, as was that of Electron's competitors. If anything, TransElectronics' marketing policies were too uniform, with a rigid pricing policy that did not allow Electron to adapt to the wide variations in price across countries. As a result, Electron did not use price as a strategic weapon. Lastly, Electron did not integrate its *competitive moves* across countries, but, fortunately, neither did its competitors.

From the previous analyses, the Electron managers concluded that their extent of globalization was significantly lower than the industry potential, and lower than that of their competitors. The industry potential for globalization was steadily increasing. It was clear that Electron had a strong need to develop a more global strategy than it had been pursuing. The next issue was whether Electron would be able to implement such a strategy.

EVALUATING ORGANIZATIONAL CAPABILITY   Having understood the strategic changes needed, the Electron managers now had to understand the organization factors that might affect implementation. They diagnosed that TransElectronics' *organization structure* worked in two major ways against a global strategy. First, TransElectronics operated with a strong domestic–international split within each sector. Second, worldwide responsibilities for Electron's business were scattered throughout the organization. The Electron division itself had responsibility for some product development, some manufacturing, and some marketing. Other divisions in the United States and overseas shared these responsibilities. Selling was the responsibility of both local non-U.S. countries and in the United States of a totally separate distribution group for the entire communications sector. In effect, there was no manager below the sector head who had global authority over transcramblers.

Management processes did not help global strategy much. The budget process worked against a global approach, in that the Electron division budgeted only a total number for overseas sales, without country targets. The International Group in the communications sector set country quotas for the entire sector, without product quotas or product-by-country quotas. The strategic planning process did not help either: The Electron Division and the International Group developed separate plans simultaneously. In terms of compensation, there were no international components in the bonus formula for domestic managers. In addition, Electron's strategic information systems provided only spotty coverage of key markets and key competitors.

TransElectronics' use of *people* worked against a global approach. There were few foreign nationals in the United States at either corporate or divisional levels. There were many foreign nationals overseas, but these were mostly in their home countries, and there was little movement between international and domestic jobs. In particular, the U.S. divisions were reluctant to give up people, and overseas assignments were not seen as being a desirable career track.

Lastly, TransElectronics' corporate *culture* worked against a global view in both obvious and subtle ways. At the obvious level, TransElectronics was very much an American company with a "them-and-us" mentality. Indeed, the CEO had made speeches calling for increased trade barriers against Japanese firms. More subtly, TransElectronics had a very strong culture of being responsive to customer requests for product tailoring, born of a heritage of selling exclusively to a very small number of automotive customers. This culture worked strongly against attempts to standardize globally.

So, TransElectronics clearly had a very low organizational ability to develop a global strategy for transcramblers. It had certainly experienced many difficulties in its fitful attempts at doing so.

CHANGES NEEDED   The globalization analysis, just described, convinced the Electron managers that the most important business changes they had to make were to exploit more opportunities for product standardization and to specialize somewhat more as to where different activities (particularly manufacturing) were conducted. More widespread changes were needed in terms of management and organization. While many aspects of these needed to change, the most implementable change was in terms of management process. TransElectronics adopted for the transcrambler business a global strategic planning process and globally based evaluation and compensation. These relatively modest changes would pave the way for future acceptance of the more radical changes needed in organization structure, people, and culture.

Repositioning Persona

Persona had operating companies around the world that sold many kinds of personal care as well as other household products. The global strategy analysis was conducted for one particular product, "hairfloss," that was sold worldwide.

ANALYZING INDUSTRY GLOBALIZATION POTENTIAL Persona's managers had always assumed that there were major differences in customer needs and trade practices across countries, such that the hairfloss category did not have much globalization potential. But the systematic globalization analysis revealed some surprises. *Market* drivers pushed strongly for globalization: Market needs were very much the same around the world within income categories—higher income countries were earlier users of the new variants and ingredients that were introduced every few years. Brand names and advertising were also widely transferable: Some competitors used just one major brand name around the world and essentially the same advertising campaign. *Cost* drivers were less important, given that product costs were only about 25 percent of total costs, economies of scale were low, and price was not a major basis of competition. Also the low value-to-weight ratio of hairfloss made it uneconomical to ship it far. Nonetheless, there was some centralized manufacturing on a multicountry regional basis in parts of Europe, Southeast Asia, and Africa.

Government drivers did not particularly favor globalization. In Europe, however, the increasing importance of multicountry media, particularly satellite television with wide reception, and of the European Community pushed for regional, if not global, approaches. It was *competitive* behavior that was the major force pushing the industry to globalization. Persona faced three major worldwide competitors, multinationals like itself. Two of these competitors took a much more standardized approach than Persona: They concentrated their resources behind the same one or two brands of hairfloss in each country. In contrast, Persona tended to market three or four brands in each country, and furthermore, these brands were different among major countries. Persona's competitors were also quick to transfer successful innovations from one country to the next, while Persona's brand fragmentation hindered its efforts. This global fragmentation seemed to be a major reason behind Persona's slipping share and profitability.

Persona concluded that there were strong external forces pushing the hairfloss industry toward globalization—at least to the extent of requiring coordinated regional operations—and this push toward globalization was likely to increase in the future.

EVALUATING USE OF GLOBAL STRATEGY Although Persona had plenty of market and competitive information from virtually all the countries in which it operated, its managers did not make much use of that information to evaluate its global, as opposed to national, strategies. Using this information for global purposes revealed a new view of the worldwide hairfloss business. Persona's *global market participation* was very strong: It sold hairfloss in markets that accounted for almost 90 percent of worldwide category volume. Its largest competitor participated in almost 100 percent. Persona's hairfloss *product line* was quite highly standardized around half a dozen variants. Persona generally marketed a larger number of variants in wealthier countries, but the variants were still basically the same across countries. Like most consumer packaged-goods multinationals, Persona practiced very little specialization of *activities* by country: It fielded a full business operation in most countries. In terms of *global marketing,* Persona was severely lacking because of its multiple brands, multiple product positionings, and multiple advertising campaigns. Lastly, Persona did not do much to integrate its competitive moves across countries, although it had recently begun to experiment with such attempts. Overall, Persona's actual extent of globalization was somewhat lower than that of its competitors.

While Persona's worldwide hairfloss strategy was quite global in some respects, it was the lack of global marketing that was the biggest problem. The key variables that Persona could operate on were brand name and positioning. First, to increase local marketing muscle, Persona needed to reduce the number of brands in each country to two. Second, to achieve the benefits of global market uniformity, they had three broad alternatives:

- A different brand but common positioning for each product variant in each country
- A common regional brand and positioning
- A common global brand and positioning

Because Persona already had strong brand names around the world that it did not want to abandon, and because a common positioning would achieve most of the benefits of uniformity, the company concluded that the second alternative was best. The next issue was whether Persona would be able to implement such a strategy.

EVALUATING ORGANIZATIONAL CAPABILITY   The Persona managers conducting the globalization analysis were the most discouraged by what they found about organization capability. Persona's *organization structure* made it very difficult to develop and implement a global strategy. Persona operated with a strong geographic structure that was overlaid with a worldwide product direction function at corporate. This function, however, had advisory rather than direct authority over the individual country-businesses. Furthermore, the direction function did not include the United States. *Management processes* were of limited help. The budget and compensation systems worked against global strategy: These were done on a strictly local basis, although aggregated geographically. But there was no mechanism to encourage local participation in a worldwide effort. A strategic plan was developed globally, but local acceptance was voluntary. Persona did, however, have an excellent strategic information system. Each year the subsidiaries provided detailed and accurate data for products, markets, and competitors. For example, Persona knew how much each global competitor spent on advertising on each product category in each country and even had fairly accurate estimates of each competitor's profitability in each country. Persona also scored highly on the global capability of its people. Managers were drawn from all over the world, and transfers both among countries and to and from corporate were common. Culture was really the biggest organization barrier. Persona had a very strong culture of giving autonomy to its local managers. Although corporate increasingly wanted to give direct orders on strategy, the firm was loathe to risk the possible loss of local accountability and commitment. So, like TransElectronics, Persona also had a low organizational capacity for global strategy, but for somewhat different reasons.

CHANGES NEEDED   As a result of the globalization analysis, Persona managers realized that the most important business changes they had to make in hairfloss were to reduce the number of brands in each country and develop a common brand by region and common positioning for each major product variant. Organizationally, it was too huge a disruption to change the structure. What was needed was a greater willingness by corporates to push for countries to adopt a global approach. A first step was a directive that all countries should launch the new "high-gloss" variant within a six-month period. Persona hoped that a successful experience of common action would start moving the culture toward greater acceptance of global strategies.

GUIDELINES FOR BUILDING THE GLOBAL ORGANIZATION

In building the global organization, managers should keep in mind the following guidelines:

- A global strategy cannot succeed in the face of organization barriers and resistance.
- Different aspects of organization—whether organization structure, management processes, people, or culture—will be more difficult to globalize depending on the history and circumstances of the company. Managers may find it best to work on the most easily changed aspects first, in order to prepare the way for the more difficult changes.
- As with the elements of global strategy, different aspects of organization can have different levels of being global.
- But globalization will not work fully unless all aspects of organization complement each other to support the desired global strategy.
- Changing the organization, particularly toward globalization, can take a great deal of time. Senior management needs to instill a sense of urgency to drive toward the desired changes.

Concluding Thoughts

Global strategy in the twenty-first century sets very tough challenges for companies. They need to be globally excellent in nearly every activity and find the right balance of global, regional, and national solutions. This concept is best summed up in the philosophy at Beiersdorf: "As global as possible, as local as necessary." The global company does not have to be everywhere, but it has the capability to go anywhere, deploy any assets, and access any resources, and it maximizes profits on a global basis. Now global companies also need to do it all instantaneously. And if they do not do all this, their competitors will. Globalization means there is no place to hide.

Discussion and Research Questions

1. What are the key elements of a global organization?
2. What are the ways in which organization structure can be used to implement global strategy?
3. What are the ways in which management processes can be used to implement global strategy?
4. What are the ways in which human resource policies can be used to implement global strategy?

5. What are the ways in which culture can be used to implement global strategy?
6. Select one company that has made significant changes in its organization in order to globalize. Describe and critique the changes this company has made.

Notes

1. This chapter is based in part on George S. Yip, Pierre M. Loewe, and Michael Y. Yoshino, "How to Take Your Company to the Global Market," *Columbia Journal of World Business,* Vol. 23, No. 4, Winter 1988, pp. 37–48. For a recent review of the academic literature on multinational organization, see D. Eleanor Westney and Srilata Zaheer, "The Multinational Enterprise as an Organization," in Alan M. Rugman and Thomas L. Brewer, Eds., *The Oxford Handbook of International Business* (Oxford, England: Oxford University Press, forthcoming 2001), Chapter 13, pp. 349–79.

2. A stream of work has described and characterized this dilemma as the integration-responsiveness grid. See C. K. Prahalad, "The Strategic Process in a Multinational Corporation," unpublished doctoral dissertation, Harvard Business School, 1975; C. K. Prahalad and Yves L. Doz, "An Approach to Strategic Control on MNCs," *Sloan Management Review,* Summer 1981, pp. 5–13; Yves L. Doz, Christopher A. Bartlett, and C. K. Prahalad, "Global Competitive Pressures vs. Host Country Demands: Managing Tensions in Multinational Corporations," *California Management Review,* Vol. 23, No. 3, 1981, pp. 63–74; C. K. Prahalad and Yves L. Doz, *The Multinational Mission: Balancing Local Demands and Global Vision* (New York: The Free Press, 1987).

3. The importance of global learning has been particularly stressed by Sumantra Ghoshal, "Global Strategy: An Organizing Framework," *Strategic Management Journal,* Vol. 8, No. 5, September–October 1987, pp. 425–40, and Christopher A. Bartlett and Sumantra Ghoshal, *Managing Across Borders: The Transnational Solution* (Boston, MA: Harvard Business School Press, 1989). See also Anil K. Gupta and Vijay Govindarajan, "Knowledge Flows Within Multinational Corporations," *Strategic Management Journal,* Vol. 21, No. 4, 2000, pp. 473–96; Karl Moore and Julian M. Birkinshaw, "Managing Knowledge in Global Service Firms: Centres of Excellence," *Academy of Management Executive,* December 1998, and Julian Birkinshaw, "Why Is Knowledge Management So Difficult?" *Business Strategy Review,* Vol. 12, No. 1, Spring 2001, pp. 11–18.

4. This view is particularly stressed in the literature on foreign direct investment, for example, John H. Dunning, "The Eclectic Paradigm of International Production: A Restatement and Some Possible Extensions," *Journal of International Business Studies,* Spring 1988, and on internalization theory, for example, Peter J. Buckley and Mark Casson, *The Future of the Multinational Enterprise* (New York: Holmes and Meier Publishers, Inc., 1976); Alan M. Rugman, *International Diversification and the Multinational Enterprise* (Lexington, MA: Lexington Books, D. C. Heath, 1979); and Peter J. Buckley, *The Theory of the Multinational Enterprise,* Acta Universitatis Upsaliensis, *Studia Oeconomiae Negotiorum* 26, Uppsala, Sweden, 1987. See also Henry P. Conn and George S. Yip, "Global Transfer of Critical Capabilities," *Business Horizons,* Vol. 40, No. 1, January–February 1997, pp. 22–31.

5. "The New Organisation," *The Economist,* January 19, 2006, http://www.economist.com/node/5380483.

6. This incremental approach to strategic change has been advocated by many management theorists. See, for example, C. E. Lindblom, *The Policy-Making Process* (Upper Saddle River, NJ: Prentice Hall, 1968); Henry Mintzberg, *The Nature of Managerial Work* (New York: Harper & Row, 1973); and James Brian Quinn, "Strategic Goals: Process and Politics," *Sloan Management Review,* Fall 1977, p. 22.

7. Much early research on MNC management has confirmed the critical role of formal organization structure in influencing both parent and subsidiary strategy. Clee and di Scipio (1959) and Clee and Sachtjen (1964) were among the first to point out the shortcomings of the international structures adopted by MNCs and to recommend the implementation of global organization structures. See G. H. Clee and A. di Scipio, "Creating a World Enterprise," *Harvard Business Review,* November–December 1959, pp. 77–89, and G. H. Clee and W. M. Sachtjen, "Organizing a Worldwide Business," *Harvard Business Review,* November–December 1964, pp. 55–67. Fouraker and Stopford (1968), Stopford and Wells (1972), and Franko (1976) conducted a

series of studies aimed at confirming Chandler's (1962) strategy-structure fit thesis with respect to international business, as did Egelhoff (1982, 1988) and Daniels, Pitts, and Tretter (1984). See Lawrence E. Fouraker and John M. Stopford, "Organization Structure and Multinational Strategy," *Administrative Science Quarterly,* Vol. 13, 1968, pp. 57–70; John M. Stopford and Louis T. Wells, Jr., *Managing the Multinational Enterprise* (New York: Basic Books, 1972); Larry G. Franko, *The European Multinationals* (Greenwich, CT: Greylock Press, 1976); Alfred D. Chandler, Jr., *Strategy and Structure* (Cambridge, MA: The MIT Press, 1962); William G. Egelhoff, "Strategy and Structure in Multinational Corporations: An Information Processing Approach," *Administrative Science Quarterly,* Vol. 27, 1982, pp. 435–58; ———, "Strategy and Structure in Multinational Corporations: A Revision of the Stopford and Wells Model," *Strategic Management Journal,* Vol. 9, 1988, pp. 1–14; J. D. Daniels, R. A. Pitts, and M. J. Tretter, "Strategy and Structure of U.S. Multinationals: An Exploratory Study," *Academy of Management Journal,* Vol. 27, 1984, pp. 292–307. But that stream of research focused on dimensions of international strategy (foreign product diversity and percent of foreign sales) that do not relate directly to global strategy. More directly relevant to the latter, Davidson and Haspeslagh (1982) examined the role of global product and global integration approaches and found that global product organizations had many disadvantages. (See William H. Davidson and Philippe Haspeslagh, "Shaping a Global Product Organization," *Harvard Business Review,* July–August 1982, pp. 125–32.)

Focusing on global strategy, Bartlett and Ghoshal (1987, 1989) argued for a network structure that facilitates global learning. See Christopher A. Bartlett and Sumantra Ghoshal "Managing Across Borders: New Strategic Requirements," *Sloan Management Review,* Summer 1987, pp. 7–17, and ———, *Managing Across Borders: The Transnational Solution* (Boston, MA: Harvard Business School Press, 1989). Ghoshal (1987) argued that the tendency of global strategy toward a centralized global authority, and the potential corresponding erosion of global learning benefits, is one of the "strategic trade-offs" associated with pursuing a global strategy. (See Sumantra Ghoshal, "Global Strategy: An Organizing Framework," *Strategic Management Journal,*

Vol. 8, No. 5, September–October 1987, pp. 425–40.)

8. In a study of 180 leading U.S.-based multinationals, the Harvard Multinational Enterprise Project found that 163 initially created a separate international division to manage foreign operations. See William H. Davidson, *Global Strategic Management* (New York: John Wiley & Sons, 1982), p. 274. This study covered the period up to 1979.

9. According to the stages theory of multinational organization design, many firms evolve through either a product-dominated or a geography-dominated structure toward some form of integrated organization (Stopford and Wells, *Managing the Multinational Enterprise*).

10. Bartlett and Ghoshal define the transnational as follows: "In contrast to the global model, the transnational mentality recognizes the importance of flexible and responsive country-level operations—hence the return of *national* into the terminology. And compared to the multinational approach, it provides for linking and coordinating those operations to retain competitive effectiveness and economic efficiency—as indicated by the prefix 'trans.' The resulting need for intensive organization-wide coordination and shared decision making implies that this is a much more sophisticated and subtle approach to MNC management." See Christopher A. Bartlett and Sumantra Ghoshal, *Text, Cases, and Readings in Cross-Border Management,* 3rd ed. (Boston: McGraw-Hill, 2000), p. 13. See also Nitin Nohria, Sumantra Ghoshal (contributor), and Cedric Crocker (editor),*The Differentiated Network: Organizing Multinational Corporations for Value Creation* (San Francisco: Jossey-Bass Business and Management Series, 1997).

11. "The New Organization," *The Economist,* January 19, 2006, http://www.economist.com/node/5380483.

12. "Perestroika in Soapland," *The Economist,* June 10, 1989, pp. 95–7.

13. "Thinking for a Living," *The Economist,* January 19, 2006, http://www.economist.com/node/5380450.

14. Christopher A. Bartlett and Sumantra Ghoshal, "Matrix Management; Not a Structure, a Frame of Mind," *Harvard Business Review,* July–August 1990, pp. 138–45.

15. Robert Simons, "Stress-Test Your Strategy: The 7 Questions to Ask," *Harvard Business Review,* Vol. 88, No. 11, November 2010, pp. 92–100.

16. See Roger Enrico and Jesse Kornbluth, *The Other Guy Blinked: How Pepsi Won the Cola Wars* (New York: Bantam Books, 1986).

17. "The Bubbles Pop," *The Economist,* April 22, 1999, http://www.economist.com/node/201344.

18. Pankaj Ghemawat, "Globalization: The Strategy of Differences," *Harvard Business School Working Knowledge,* November 10, 2003, http://hbswk.hbs.edu/item/3773.html.

19. Jessie Scanlon, "Coca-Cola: Building a Better Design Machine?" *Businessweek,* October 13, 2008, http://www.businessweek.com/innovate/content/oct2008/id20081013_466588.htm.

20. Pankaj Ghemawat, "Coca-Cola's Global Rethink," *Harvard Business Publishing,* October 1, 2007, http://blogs.harvardbusiness.org/ghemawat/2007/10/cocacolas_global_rethink.html.

21. "Coca-Cola Posts Strong Profit on Emerging-Market Sales," *New York Times,* February 9, 2010, http://www.nytimes.com/2010/02/10/business/10coke.html.

22. Bruce Einhorn, "Coke Committed to China Expansion," *Businessweek,* June 23, 2009, http://www.businessweek.com/globalbiz/content/jun2009/gb20090623_410186.htm.

23. Ratna Bhushan, "Coke Prepares Big Expansion in India," *Businessweek,* January 30, 2009, http://www.businessweek.com/globalbiz/content/jan2009/gb20090130_941843.htm.

24. See Gerrit Jeelof, "Global Strategies of Philips," *European Management Journal,* Vol. 7, No. 1, 1989, pp. 84–91, and Francis J. Aguilar and Michael Y. Yoshino, "The Philips Group: 1987," Case No. 9-388-050 (Boston: Harvard Business School, 1988).

25. Samuel J. Palmisano, "The Globally Integrated Enterprise," *Foreign Affairs,* May/June 2006.

26. Gary Hamel and Polly Labarre, "Inventing Management 2.0," *WSJ Blogs,* February 17, 2011, http://blogs.wsj.com/management/2011/02/17/inventing-management-20/.

27. See IBM's 2008 annual report.

28. Steve Hamm, "The World Is IBM's Classroom," *Businessweek,* March 12, 2009, http://www.businessweek.com/magazine/content/09_12/b4124056268652.htm.

29. Steve Hamm, "IBM's Global Hand," *Businessweek,* August 13, 2007, http://www.businessweek.com/technology/content/aug2007/tc20070810_700113.htm.

30. See also Roderick E. White and Thomas A. Poynter, "Strategies for Foreign-Owned Subsidiaries in Canada," *Business Quarterly,* Summer 1984, pp. 59–69, on the different strategic roles that national subsidiaries can play.

31. Julian Birkinshaw and Nick Fry, "Subsidiary Initiatives to Develop New Markets," *Sloan Management Review,* Vol. 39, No. 3, 1998, pp. 51–62.

32. See Johny K. Johansson and George S. Yip, "Exploiting Globalization Potential: U.S. and Japanese Strategies," *Strategic Management Journal,* Vol. 15, October 1994, pp. 579–601, and George S. Yip, Johan Roos, and Johny K. Johansson, "Effects of Nationality on Global Strategy," *Management International Review,* Vol. 37, No. 4, October–December 1997, pp. 365–84.

33. Most companies, whatever their nationality, begin their international activities with separate domestic and international organizations. But the typical pattern has been an evolution to a multinational form of organization in which the uniqueness of the domestic market disappears. American companies seem to be slower than European companies in making this transition.

34. Nick Bunkley, "Auto Plants in Japan Remain Closed as Companies Take Stock," *New York Times,* March 13, 2011, http://www.nytimes.com/2011/03/14/business/global/14auto.htm.

35. See Embraer's 2007 annual report.

36. "The Jet Set," *The Economist,* September 9, 2010, http://www.economist.com/node/16964074.

37. Paulo Figueiredo, Gutenberg Silveira, and Roberto Sbragia, "Risk Sharing Partnerships with Suppliers: The Case of Embraer," *Journal of Technology Management & Innovation,* 2008, Vol. 3, No. 1, pp. 27–37.

38. The author thanks Pierre M. Loewe of The MAC Group, San Francisco, for this example.

39. See Yves L. Doz, "Managing Manufacturing Rationalization Within Multinational Companies," *Columbia Journal of World Business,* Fall 1978, pp. 82–94.

40. Deloitte & Touche, *Leaders in Innovative Globalization Program,* report, London, 1998.

41. Henry P. Conn and George S. Yip, "Global Transfer of Critical Capabilities," *Business Horizons,* Vol. 40, No. 1, January–February 1997, pp. 22–31.

42. See Karl Moore and Julian M. Birkinshaw, "Managing Knowledge in Global Service Firms: Centres of Excellence," *Academy of Management Executive,* December 1998; Julian Birkinshaw, "Why Is Knowledge Management So Difficult?" *Business Strategy Review,* Vol. 12, No. 1, Spring 2001, pp. 11–18; and Johan Roos,

Georg von Krogh, and George S. Yip, "An Epistemology of Globalizing Firms," *International Business Review,* Vol. 3, No. 4, pp. 395–409, special issue on Organization's Knowledge, Knowledge Transfer, and Cooperative Strategies, November–December 1994.

43. See Sony press releases at corporate Web site, July 15, 2004, http://www.sony.net/SonyInfo/News/Press_Archive/200407/04-0715E/index.html.

44. Moon Ihlwan, "Sony and Samsung's Larger LCD Ambitions," *Businessweek,* June 4, 2009, http://www.businessweek.com/globalbiz/content/jun2009/gb2009064_729613.htm.

45. "Sony, Sharp Form JV for 10th-Gen LCD Fab," *Nikkei Electronics Asia,* April 2008, http://techon.nikkeibp.co.jp/article/HONSHI/20080327/149601/.

46. Adam Le, "Sony, Sharp Say LCD Venture's Output, Ownership Plans Unchanged," *Bloomberg Businessweek,* November 28, 2010, http://www.businessweek.com/news/2010-11-28/sony-sharp-say-lcd-venture-s-output-ownership-plans-unchanged.html.

47. Kanji Hall, "TV Giants Are Outsourcing More Manufacturing," *Businessweek,* July 9, 2009, http://www.businessweek.com/globalbiz/content/jul2009/gb2009079_881220.htm.

48. They have had plenty of help from both academics and consultants. For guides to strategic planning, see, for example, George A. Steiner, *Strategic Planning: What Every Manager Must Know* (New York: The Free Press, 1979); Peter Lorange, *Implementation of Strategic Planning* (Upper Saddle River, NJ.: Prentice Hall, 1982); and Arnoldo C. Hax and Nicolas S. Majluf, *Strategic Management: An Integrative Perspective* (Upper Saddle River, NJ: Prentice Hall, 1984).

49. C. K. Prahalad and Yves L. Doz, *The Multinational Mission: Balancing Local Demands and Global Vision* (New York: The Free Press, 1987), have argued for using global strategic planning. For a discussion of different types of global strategic planning, see Balaji S. Chakravarthy and Howard V. Perlmutter, "Strategic Planning for a Global Business,"*Columbia Journal of World Business,* Summer 1985, pp. 3–10, and David C. Shanks, "Strategic Planning for Global Competition," *Journal of Business Strategy,* Winter 1985, pp. 80–9.

50. See Richard F. Vancil and Peter Lorange, "Strategic Planning in Diversified Companies," *Harvard Business Review,* January–February 1975, and George S. Yip, "Who Needs Strategic Planning?" *The Journal of Business Strategy,* Vol. 6, No. 2, Fall 1985, pp. 30–42.

51. See the discussion of global management control in John J. Dyment, "Strategies and Management Controls for Global Corporations," *Journal of Business Strategy,* Spring 1987, pp. 20–6.

52. For an in-depth discussion see Robert G. Eccles, *The Transfer Pricing Decision* (Lexington, MA: Lexington Books, 1985), and Lorraine Eden, "Taxes, Transfer Pricing, and the Multinational Enterprise," in Alan M. Rugman and Thomas L. Brewer, Eds., *The Oxford Handbook of International Business,* Chapter 21, pp. 591–622.

53. Anton Fritschi, "Global Key Account Management bei ABB: Erfolg kennt keine (Lünder-) Grenzen," *Thexis,* Vol. 4, 1999, pp. 26–9.

54. Deloitte & Touche, *Leaders in Innovative Globalization Program.*

55. Ibid.

56. White and Poynter have written extensively on the role of subsidiary management. See Roderick E. White and Thomas E. Poynter, "Strategies for Foreign-Owned Subsidiaries in Canada," *Business Quarterly,* Summer 1984, pp. 59–69, and ———, "Organizing for Worldwide Advantage," in Christopher A. Bartlett, Yves L. Doz, and Gunnar Hedlund, Eds., *Managing the Global Firm* (London: Routledge, 1990).

57. "Game On," *The Economist,* March 5, 2009, http://www.economist.com/node/13234173.

58. See Howard V. Perlmutter, "The Tortuous Evolution of the Multinational Corporation," *Columbia Journal of World Business,* January–February 1969, pp. 9–18, for the distinction between ethnocentric (national), polycentric (multinational), and geocentric (global) corporate cultures.

59. Ellen Byron, "Febreze Joins P&G's $1 Billion Club," *Wall Street Journal,* March 9, 2011, http://online.wsj.com/article/SB20001424052748704076804576180683371307932.html.

60. For example, Bartlett and Ghoshal, *Managing Across Borders: The Transnational Solution* (p. 106), describe how Philips assigned responsibility for developing the teletext TV business to its UK subsidiary.

61. Kenichi Ohmae, *The Borderless World: Power and Strategy in the Interlinked Economy* (New York: Harper Business, 1990), p. 17.

CHAPTER 9

Regional Strategy

So far this book has focused on industry globalization drivers and global strategies that apply on a worldwide basis. But the same drivers and strategies also apply on a regional basis.[1] For example, as discussed in Chapter 2, there can be drivers and strategies that apply across the European Union (EU). Indeed, because regions (defined here as multi-country, rather than subcountry, areas) are smaller, the forces for regional integration in any given industry are usually stronger than that for global integration. The word "usually" is applied here, rather than "always," because some geographically contiguous regions can be so diverse (from the perspective of a particular industry) that it makes little sense to develop common strategies within that region. For example, Gillette groups its regions by socioeconomic/usage criteria and not geography. One of its regions encompasses Canada, the United States, Britain, Australia, and New Zealand.

REGIONAL STRATEGY IN THE CONTEXT OF GLOBAL STRATEGY

Regional strategies should be developed in the context of an overall global strategy:

- *Overall global strategy*. Before deciding whether and how to do business in a region of the world, a company needs to have a clear global strategy. As developed in earlier chapters, key elements of this strategy include the core business strategy, the competitive objectives for the business, and the extent to which the business will be operated as one integrated business or a looser collection of geographically independent units.
- *Regional strategy*. Next, a company needs to decide on the overall role of the region within the global strategy. Should the region be a source of growth, of profit, or of both? Should the region be primarily a source of supply or a locus of markets? Or should different countries play differing roles? In which Asian countries should the company do business?
- *Country strategy*. Having selected the countries in which to be involved, the company needs to develop a country strategy that includes the mode of entry, partner

selection, and the usual elements of a business strategy (what activities to conduct including what parts of the value chain to locate in the country, and how activities in the country will relate to those in the rest of the region and the world).

- *Country operations.* Lastly, the company has to be concerned with implementation at the operational level. Here the company has to deal with detailed matters such as how to adapt to local culture and business practices, how to develop the right kinds of contacts, how to find customers, and how to cope with the country's written and unwritten regulations.

DEFINING REGIONS

Regions are not synonymous with continents. An increasing number of regional organizations now provide some degree of macroeconomic and/or political integration for many countries. Broadly speaking, these entities, in increasing degrees of integration, are customs unions (e.g., European Community from 1965), border unions (e.g., the Schengen Agreement countries within the EU that have agreed to drop all border controls among themselves), monetary unions (e.g., the Euro zone), and political unions (a declared long-term objective of many leaders in the EU). Some countries belong to multiple regional entities, and many regions offer multiple organizations. For example, the United Kingdom belongs to most, but not all, aspects of the EU, NATO, the World Trade Organization, Group of Eight, and others. Asia-Pacific boasts a wide variety of trade entities: Association of South-East Asian Nations (ASEAN), Asia-Pacific Economic Cooperation (APEC), ASEAN Free Trade Area (AFTA), PECC, ANZERTA, among others.[2] The task of the multinational company (MNC) is to make the best use of these formal (e.g., trade pacts) similarities and integrating forces as well as others (e.g., culture, contiguity) to develop effective regional strategies analogous to the global strategies discussed in the rest of this book.

Regions can be defined in many ways depending on the purpose of the definition. For MNCs, geographic proximity is usually the default basis of definition, if only because of the extensive travel involved in running a global business. A region defined for strategic reasons is also easier to administer if it has geographic coherence or even if it just spans the same band of time zones. But, in addition, a region defined for the purposes of business strategy should have a high degree of commonality in as many as possible of the following other characteristics:

- Culture
- Physical environment
- History
- Language
- Way of doing business
- Form of government
- Institutional arrangements
- Cross-investment
- Intraregional trade
- Trade policies and agreements
- Economic performance and prospects
- Infrastructure, such as airline connections

Nissan's Multi-Regional Product Strategy

What could be considered Nissan's world car actually goes by different names, depending on the country or region in which it is sold. The Nissan Sunny, as it is called in Africa and the Middle East, goes by the name Almera in Europe, Bluebird Sylphy in Japan, and Sentra in North America. Nissan operates in four regions—the Americas, Europe, Asia/Oceania, and the Middle East/Africa—and designs automobiles to cater to the needs of the consumers in each market. This aspect of the company's product strategy allows for considerable flexibility not only across regions but also within regions.

For example, the Sunny comes with three engine options in the Middle East. One is a 1.3 liter engine with 92 horsepower, one is a 1.6 liter engine with 110 horsepower, and one is a 1.8 liter engine with 126 horsepower.[3] In fact, the success of the Sunny has led Nissan to introduce the automobile in China.[4] With this move, the company can support its operations for this world car strategy in other regions as well. However, low-power, high-efficiency options are sufficient for the Middle Eastern and Asia/Oceania markets, but in North America, where consumers want a more powerful car, and 2.5 liter engine is available, and the car is called the Sentra, instead of the Sunny. Thus, Nissan's strategy is a response to the tangible and less tangible characteristics of this product line. The result is that it makes Nissan more adaptable to the varied demands for its world car.

While taking geography into account, a region is also defined by less tangible characteristics. An MNC must consider all these characteristics to develop a successful long-term strategy. In fact, the Nissan example shows how variation in regional characteristics can influence precise product specifications in particular areas of the world.

EXAMPLES OF MAJOR REGIONS

A number of major regions are so frequently used by MNCs that they are worth noting here. They include the EU, Central and Eastern Europe, Asia-Pacific, North America, and Latin America.

European Union as a Region

From the viewpoint of MNCs, the EU provides the most clear-cut region in the world. Its membership and conditions are clearly defined, and it provides a number of increasingly integrated mechanisms. With the adoption of the Euro currency by most member states in 1999 (and Euro notes and coins in 2002), this region became even more integrated. Planned expansion eastward will probably reduce integration and homogeneity.

Central and Eastern Europe as a Region

The former members of the Soviet bloc other than the U.S.S.R. (the Baltic states, Poland, the Czech and Slovak Republics, Hungary, the Balkan states, Romania, and Bulgaria) shared many common experiences and became free of Soviet domination all at about the same time around 1990.[5] On the other hand, these economies have huge discrepancies in wealth and economic strength. But all are undergoing a rapid period of transition and opening to free markets and globalization, albeit at different speeds. Most of these states have also applied to join the EU. Consequently, most MNCs tend to treat them as one region, partly because few are large enough to merit stand-alone strategies.

In terms of social makeup (culture, history, religion, language, and ethnic groups), the region is diverse and varied. Many existing social divisions do not correspond to constructed political and geographic boundaries. For example, there is a large population of ethnic Hungarians in Romania and the former Yugoslavia, Slovaks in Hungary, and Ukrainians in the Slovak Republic and Poland. Throughout the region large minority groups co-exist within a shared geographical area.

The Former Soviet Union as a Region

Some companies include Russia and other former parts of the Soviet Union as part of an eastern European region. Others treat them separately. Arguments for the latter include the much longer history of communism (from 1917 to 1991 for Russia rather than from 1945 for central and eastern European nations) and/or a lower level of economic development and political stability. In addition, the sheer physical size and diversity of Russia make it almost a region unto itself.

The Middle East and Islamic Countries as a Region

The Middle East scarcely exists as an economic region. A common language, religion, and culture cover most of the territory from the Atlantic coast of Morocco to the Sultanate of Oman on the Arabian Sea. Beyond the Middle East, the Islamic religion stretches as far as Indonesia in the Pacific and as far north as Kazakhstan in the heart of the former Soviet Union. But the economies remain highly separated by high trade barriers. The exception perhaps is among the six members of the Gulf Cooperation Council where stronger economic integration includes lower trade barriers. So, MNCs face many limitations in how far they can apply regional strategies.

North America as a Region

Most MNCs have long grouped Canada and the United States together. Indeed, the north–south economic ties between Canada and the United States are in many ways stronger than the east–west ties within Canada, a function of the distribution of Canada's population in a string along its U.S. border. The advent of the North American Free Trade Agreement (NAFTA), with Mexico as a third member, increasingly pulled Mexico into closer economic alignment with its northern neighbors. Both Canada and Mexico now have over 80 percent of their trade with, and over 60 percent of their foreign direct investment (FDI) stocks in, the United States.[6] Several industries, such as automotive, increasingly operate on an integrated basis within NAFTA. Interestingly, geographic proximity has created a business region out of a group of very diverse countries, particularly in terms of the cultural and economic differences between Mexico and its neighbors.

Latin and South America as a Region

The countries of Latin and South America share a common language, Spanish (in all cases except for Brazil, whose native Portuguese is closely related to Spanish), a similar history and culture, and similar stages of economic development. On the other hand, attempts at trade and economic integration have met only limited success. Neither Mercosur (the pact among Argentina, Brazil, Paraguay, and Uruguay) nor the Andean Pact (Bolivia, Colombia, Ecuador, Peru, and Venezuela, Chile having withdrawn in 1977) has had a huge impact. Mexico has now moved into the North American orbit by joining NAFTA, and Chile is negotiating with NAFTA. But increasing liberalization and deregulation are creating more opportunities for MNCs to use integrated strategies in this region.

Africa as a Region

Most MNCs treat Africa as one region, although some split sub-Saharan Africa from the Arab countries of North Africa. The continent enjoys few trade pacts, but that is not of great relevance as few MNCs currently locate production activities on the continent. Most MNCs operate in Africa through a strategy of direct export. There are sufficient similarities in economic development and culture that in many cases companies are able to offer regionally standardized products and services. Furthermore, the low level of development of most markets means that those customers cannot indulge in preferences for national versions of foreign products. Most MNCs are waiting to see if the transformation of South Africa, combined with increasing democratization and liberalization in some other countries, can spill over to produce real growth on the continent.[7]

Asia-Pacific as a Region

Asia-Pacific is the largest, most populous, and most diverse of the regions commonly used by MNCs.[8] The region can encompass the countries and economies in the triangle from Japan to India to New Zealand, and it may sometimes extend beyond India to include Pakistan and contiguous countries. The trade policies in the region vary tremendously from nearly totally open markets in Hong Kong and Singapore to heavily controlled markets in Vietnam. But all these economies are moving in the direction of greater openness. Furthermore, there is rapid growth of many intraregion mechanisms to reduce trade barriers. Several regional institutions—particularly ASEAN and its AFTA program, APEC, and "growth triangles" or "growth polygons"—play increasingly important roles in fostering regional trade, although APEC includes countries on the other side of the Pacific.

Including Australia and New Zealand is somewhat of a stretch, but they exhibit a number of qualifying characteristics. Both have now deemphasized their British heritage and have committed themselves to becoming a part of Asia. Most important, they have opened their borders to immigration from Asia. One of the ASEAN leaders, the prime minister of Singapore, has made an open invitation for Australia to join ASEAN. So the links northward will continue to strengthen. Many Hong Kong entrepreneurs have emigrated to Australia and New Zealand, bringing these countries into the overseas Chinese network. In addition, a large number of Australian nationals and, to a lesser extent, New Zealanders have spread throughout Asia in the role of expatriate managers.

DIAGNOSING INDUSTRY REGIONALIZATION POTENTIAL

The industry globalization drivers framework described in Chapter 2 can be adapted to diagnose the opportunities for regional strategies, as opposed to either national or global strategies. The potential will vary from region to region. In some industries, some regions will be open to global strategies while other regions will be more hospitable to regional strategies. The EU, as the world's most integrated region, generally offers the most opportunities for regional strategies in most industries. A very interesting question is whether the EU will be able to nurture new pan-European companies that will evolve into global winners. Finland's Nokia is so far the most dramatic example of a company that used an initial European strategy to achieve global leadership (in mobile phone handsets). In contrast, most other Europe-based global companies achieved global scale before the advent of the EU.

Market Regionalization Drivers

Each market *globalization* driver can act as a market *regionalization* driver.

COMMON CUSTOMER NEEDS AND TASTES   The earlier list of potential regional commonalities (culture, history, etc.) can be strong drivers to create regionally common customer needs and tastes. Products and services that have strong cultural roots in their use can be candidates for cultural commonality. Companies should, of course, make use of any existing cultural commonalities, such as a traditional value for gold in Middle Eastern, Arab, and Indian cultures; for olive oil in the Mediterranean region; and for cream in Northern Europe. More interesting, companies can make use of growing regional identities to pioneer pan-regional products or services. The EU, in particular, offers many opportunities to get ahead of the curve. In particular, LG shows how Europe can be a test market to develop an overall global strategy. However, as increasing numbers of EU inhabitants, especially younger ones, include being European in their self-identity, savvy companies such as Benetton, Ikea, and Zara actively promote their European as opposed to national identities. Britain even has a popular television program called "Eurotrash." In addition, a growing sense and pride in being Asian supports emerging Asian media and fashion companies, such as Star TV and Shanghai Tang. As such, similarity in the physical environment (including climate) also provides many opportunities for regional offerings in categories as varied as housing, automobiles, clothing, and appliances.

REGIONAL CUSTOMERS AND CHANNELS   In many industries it is easier for regional rather than global customers and channels to emerge. Transportation, trade, or other barriers can prevent many customers and channels from going fully global. For example, most construction-related businesses tend to buy on a national or regional basis. In such industries, the existence of companies that operate around the world does not necessarily mean that they act as global customers. In general merchandise retailing, including supermarkets, companies have found it far easier to expand regionally than globally (because of the large need to adapt to local customer tastes and the limited transportability of bulky, low-value merchandise). But managers must be careful to recognize and treat differently *global* customers who make purchase decisions on a global basis, even if they get deliveries on a regional basis. Lastly, as discussed in Chapter 6, suppliers can convert multilocal customers into regional ones by changing the way in which they service the customers.

REGIONALLY TRANSFERABLE MARKETING   Most industries should offer more opportunities for regionally, rather than globally, transferable marketing. Transferability depends on an absence of inhibiting differences such as in culture, language, market and distribution

LG Develops European Test Market for Global Strategy

Sometimes focusing on one region as a test market can lead to a successful global strategy. For LG Electronics, that test market was Europe. In 2008, the company decided it was going to invest heavily in marketing in Europe in an attempt to map out its global strategy. LG chose Europe because of its diverse culture and competitive markets. It has also been known to be dynamic in its adoption of new technologies, making it an ideal test market for new products and designs.[9] Because of the diversity in Europe, LG was able to gauge what kinds of marketing strategies would be successful in other regions of the world. As such, the company's investment in the European market was seen as a make-or-break situation for its overall international marketing strategy.[10] However, the success of this strategy is noted in LG's continued introduction of new product concepts in the European market. In 2010, the company allied with British Sky

Broadcasting to introduce three-dimensional televisions to the UK market.[11] As a basis for further expansion in Europe as well as globally, identifying and aligning with key partners to enhance regional expertise for global use is key for LG's success.

This was not the first time LG launched a strategy in one region and then expanded it to other regions. In 2007, the company started a line of health-focused home appliances in Africa and the Middle East with the intent of expanding it globally.[12] By leveraging its position as a market leader in this region and unique health-conscious consumer concerns, LG has found the opportunity to not only introduce and test home appliances emphasizing consumer health and well-being in strategic countries such as the United Arab Emirates and South Africa, but also use the knowledge gained during this market expansion process to utilize in other regions later.

structures, legal restrictions, currency, and the norms for doing business. Fewer such barriers can exist within regions, although each region tends to offer different opportunities. The EU lacks legal and currency barriers (in most cases) and has falling cultural and distribution barriers to marketing transferability, but language barriers remain. In contrast, Latin America faces only limited language barriers (different versions of Spanish, and the difference between Spanish and Portuguese), limited cultural barriers, but many legal and distribution barriers to marketing transferability. In much of Asia, a converging lifestyle for the educated, younger elite is enabling English-language, American-style marketing in many industries.

REGIONAL LEAD COUNTRIES Lead countries can emerge, or be created, more easily on a regional rather than global basis. Japan has become a fashion leader for younger consumers in much of Asia, but much less so in the rest of the world. As indicated with Toyota's successful Lexus brand, the United States acts as a lifestyle leader for many consumers all over the world. However, the United States as a lead country is even more profound in Latin America, especially with lifestyles from Miami or Los Angeles. Western Europe, especially Germany, acts as a lead country for most of Central and eastern Europe. Interestingly, individual western European countries seem to resist taking the lead from anyone else. Indeed, European countries seem to have a number of "antilead" countries, at least as perceived by their cultural elites: for example, the United States for France, France for Britain, Spain for Portugal, and Sweden for Norway.

Acceptance of Lexus in United States Leads to Global Trend

To enter into the luxury-car market in the United States once dominated by German manufacturers, Japanese manufacturers found that marketing a luxury car abroad required considerably different strategies than those that were employed in Japan. Toyota entered the luxury-car market in America in 1989 not by selling luxury Toyotas, but by creating a separate luxury brand, Lexus, that could focus specifically on beating the market that Mercedes and BMW dominated. The creation of the brand in the United States was partially out of fear that American consumers were unwilling to spend luxury-car money on a vehicle with a mass-market brand, regardless of its quality. Lexus focused on superior service in its dealer networks and offered a product to compete with German full-size luxury cars, but at a significantly lower price point and cost of operation than its rivals. In 1990, the LS 400 sedan received top awards from the American automotive press and received the #1 award in

J.D. Power and Associates Initial Quality Study. Toyota's regional strategy paid off, but it is an important example of how a successful regional strategy can become a global strategy over time. Focusing on fulfilling untapped demand in a specific market can serve as a much lower risk test bed that, if successful, can become globally transferable.

In 2005, Lexus officially entered the Japanese domestic market by converting luxury Toyota models into Lexus models. Similar to the earlier emphasis in the United States, the focus again was to win back market share from German brands. However, success was limited in the Japanese luxury market. Only after the introduction of the ultra-luxury LS Lexus model was the move into Japan considered successful.[13] As such, Lexus was able to apply the expertise gained in the United States against its German competitors to different consumer preference conditions in the Japanese market.

Cost Regionalization Drivers

Most industry cost drivers can have strong regionalization effects.

REGIONAL SCALE ECONOMIES   In many industries, direct activities, such as production, achieve the minimum efficient scale at regional rather than global levels. For example, most automobile assembly plants can operate economically while serving regional-size markets, such as Europe or North America. Operating at a global scale can bring further cost reductions but not dramatically so, and often not enough to offset the other benefits of regional location (such as reducing the impact of tariffs). In contrast, some support activities, such as research and development (R&D) and information systems, typically continue to benefit from increasing scale. On the other hand, in most industries these support activities represent relatively small proportions of total costs.

REGIONAL EXPERIENCE CURVE   The experience curve effect is perhaps the only driver that always benefits significantly from expanding to global rather than regional scale. Assuming a constant decline in unit costs from increasing accumulated experience, there is no reason why the effect should stop at regional borders. But that assumption depends on not having to change the product that is being produced. Once a company shifts from global to regional products, a significant part of accumulated experience can be lost.

REGIONAL SOURCING EFFICIENCIES   Companies operating regional production sites can usually also benefit by sourcing regionally. But at the same time, they need to think about which supplies can best be sourced locally, nationally, regionally, or globally.

REGIONALLY FAVORABLE LOGISTICS   Transportation costs limit many industries to regional rather than global movement of products. Products with logistic costs that are high relative to prices and margins—such as steel, wood panels, and other bulky, heavy, or perishable items—impose a regional restriction on manufacturing. At the same time, the product designs could be global and the companies can operate globally. It is just the manufacturing stage of the value chain that has to stay regional. For example, the top three or four European steel companies operate mainly as regional producers and account for only about 10 percent of market share. In wood panels, top global firms, such as Portugal's Sonae Industria, hold only a small portion of global market share. In such logistically challenged industries, direct global competition occurs only in periods of severe excess supply or demand. Excess supply may drive some producers to export out of their region at marginal costs low enough to offset the additional transportation costs. Excess demand may generate prices and margins high enough to cover extraregional transport.

DIFFERENCES IN REGIONAL COSTS   Differences among regions in production or activity costs may become so great that some regions become prohibitively expensive and other regions possess a formidable advantage. In the production of consumer electronics, Western Europe has long since lost its viability, and North America except for Mexico has followed. South and Far East Asia have become dominant as location sites for production and support activities in many industries.

Government Regionalization Drivers

Most industry government drivers have even stronger effects at the regional level than at the global level.

FAVORABLE TRADE POLICIES   Regional trade arrangements continue to grow: the deepening and broadening of the EU; continuing expansion of NAFTA to cover more categories of trade; Mercosur in South America; U.S. proposals to create a free trade area of the Americas covering all of North and South America; the widening role of ASEAN; other emerging regional pacts; and special multicountry free trade zones such as the SIJORI growth triangle of Singapore, the Malaysian state of Johore Bahru, and the Riau Islands in Indonesia.[14] Within each region covered by special trade and investment arrangements, most industries will face more favorable trade policies. Negotiations with governments are also easier, as companies can go to the relevant regional body to argue their case for market, trade, or investment access. For example, from 1998, deregulation in the EU allowed any telephone company in the EU to offer services across national boundaries.[15] Resistance to change, however, may slow down the expected benefits of deregulation. Many countries are not adhering to market-opening rules. Thus for deregulation to take root in Europe's telecommunications market, regulators will play a large role in ensuring that the new rules are followed by all participating countries.

REGIONALLY COMPATIBLE TECHNICAL STANDARDS   As indicated in the Ikea example, regional pacts can also make technical standards more compatible within the region, thereby creating significant product and distribution opportunities. In mobile phones, Europe adopted the technology known as Global System for Mobile Communication (GSM) in 1987 and has used the common standard ever since. In the third generation (3G)

IKEA's Distribution Centers Adapt to Different Regional Standards

In a perfect world, globally compatible technical standards would eliminate the problems associated with conflicting standards, but in reality many needed global technical standards are either not fully implemented and influenced by legacy technology, or they simply do not exist. Sweden's global furniture company IKEA encountered technical road-blocks in its implementation of a standardized network of distribution centers (DCs) for its furniture to different regions around the globe. Existing international standards are not truly global; rather, they are an international agreement of regional standards. ISO Standard 6780 specifies multiple technical standards for three regions: North America, Europe, and Asia. This presents challenges when building a network of global distribution. To maximize the efficiency of a DC, every inch or millimeter of product must be optimized.

As a compromise, IKEA's standardized packaging system is designed to take into consideration the various regional pallet sizes and maximizes the utility of different and conflicting size pallets to accommodate an otherwise incompatible system. Sophisticated information systems ensure that 90 percent of the pallets in IKEA's DCs move in and out completely filled to maximize space and eliminate waste in the facility. Building an organization on a global level is much easier with recent developments in the scale and scope of technical standards. In fact, adapting to accommodate regional standards can make ordering pallets and sourcing compatible equipment easier by allowing for interchangeability across regions. In IKEA's case, building a coherent global supply chain must start with a careful consideration of regional compatibility.[16] By accomplishing this, the company is able to integrate its DCs effectively and seamlessly to remain competitive.

of cellular systems, Europe has also agreed to adopt a common standard. The United States, on the other hand, has three separate digital systems. For 3G, the United States appears intent on allowing for a multitude of incompatible digital standards. European compatibility has allowed European handset manufacturers such as Finland's Nokia and Sweden's Ericsson to become global leaders.

REGIONALLY COMMON MARKETING REGULATIONS Regional agreements that create common marketing regulations can have powerful implications in specific industries. For example, as already discussed in Chapter 2, the EU is developing a set of common rules to regulate marketing on the Internet.

REGIONAL GOVERNMENT-OWNED COMPETITORS AND CUSTOMERS Competitors and customers owned by national governments can cause enough problems for the global strategies of private MNCs. Those owned or supported by multicountry regional entities pose even larger problems. As yet, only Europe has produced a significant regionally owned competitor—Airbus. This consortium—supported by the French, German, British, and Spanish governments—has reached parity with Boeing in commercial aircraft. It may represent a forerunner of future regionally sponsored global competitors.

REGIONAL HOST GOVERNMENT CONCERNS Regional entities can be just as protectionist as national governments, and with even more power. The EU has used its greater influence again and again in bilateral trade disputes and in setting rules that affect the behavior of MNCs. Most recently, EU concerns about anticompetitive effects in *Europe* have stopped would-be mergers between *U.S.* companies, as in the case in 2001 of General Electric and Honeywell.

Competitive Regionalization Drivers

Regional groupings can create strong competitive effects within them and usually more quickly than effects from global competitors coming from outside a region.

REGIONAL EXPORTS AND IMPORTS   The main purpose of regional trade pacts is to increase intraregion trade relative to interregion trade. In 1997, intraregional exports were 49 percent of total exports in NAFTA, 53 percent in Asia, and 61 percent in the EU.[17] In consequence, MNCs face significant competition from within their own regions.

REGIONAL INTERDEPENDENCE OF COUNTRIES   A major consequence of regional groupings is for MNCs to create regional activity networks. Consequently, industries rapidly become regional rather than national, at least on the supply side.

REGIONALLY TRANSFERABLE COMPETITIVE ADVANTAGES   As discussed in Chapter 2, industries that depend on locally based advantages, such as local knowledge and local relationships, tend to be multilocal rather than global. But advantages can also be regionally based or extended to a regional level as a consequence of regional integration. Many European companies thought that their industries were inherently national until European integration revealed opportunities to transfer their advantages regionally. For example, many food categories, thought to be based on national tastes and hence advantages, have turned out to have broad regional appeal, allowing previously national European companies to go pan-European.

Summary

Analysis of industry regionalization drivers may show potential for regional strategies, especially for regional players. But larger MNCs may choose to stay with global strategies. Industries with strong regionalization drivers will not allow dominance by a small number of global firms. Global strategies are blocked from their full potential. For example, the car rental industry has sufficiently strong regionalization drivers that it allows for global, regional, and national players.

THE CASE OF THE EUROPEAN UNION

The EU provides an intriguing and highly important example of how industry globalization drivers can be analyzed for an entire region across all its industries.[18] The EU program increased the strength of all globalization (or Europeanization) drivers within the EU and also affected overall globalization drivers for any industry of which Europe is part of the world market.

Changes in EU Government Globalization Drivers

The legislation creating EU can be viewed as direct changes to each of the government globalization drivers in Europe:

- *Trade policies* were made fully favorable among all member countries by eliminating all tariff and nontariff barriers and all subsidies. "Mutual recognition," whereby (with few exceptions) products accepted for sale in any member country will have to be accepted by all member countries, represents a very powerful weapon against nontariff barriers. Consequently, Germany could no longer rely on its "beer-purity" laws to keep out British and other European beers.

- *Subsidies* were outlawed. When Mercedes wanted to set up a plant in Baden-Wurttemberg, the wealthiest state in Germany, the European Commission prevented the state government from offering a subsidy.
- *Technical standards* are becoming compatible through harmonization of each industry's standards, although each industry is proceeding at its own pace. The EU distinguishes between those areas where European harmonization is needed and those where mutual recognition of national standards is sufficient. The European Commission is restricting itself to laying down essential health and safety requirements that are obligatory in all member states.[19] Adoption by most EU member states of a common currency, the euro, from 1999 can be considered a special and very important case of harmonizing a technical standard. Conversion from national currencies to the euro in 2002 has made it far easier for consumers in participating countries (the so-called eurozone) to see cross-European price differences and has put pressure on many companies to reduce arbitrary, country-specific price differentials.
- *Marketing regulations* may, however, take somewhat longer to become compatible because of the strong cultural attitudes toward the role of advertising and other forms of promotion.
- *Government-owned competitors* can remain, but will lose much of their subsidy-based advantages when competing within the community.
- *Government-owned customers* will lose their ability to favor national suppliers at any rate. Given that public procurement now accounts for about 15 percent of the community's gross domestic product, this is a particularly powerful change.[20]

Changes in Competitive Globalization Drivers

EU increased the strength of each of the competitive globalization drivers. *Exports* and *imports* within the EC increased. By 1996, intra-EU exports accounted for 61 percent of all EU exports.[21] The number of *competitors from different (European) countries* in each single country increased. The large size of the integrated European market has also attracted more *competitors from different continents*. Both American and Japanese companies geared up to participate more in Europe. The competitive *interdependence of countries* also increases as companies build manufacturing and distribution networks that are continental in scope rather than national. By 1997, 41 percent of the stock of FDI was intra-EU.[22] But there has also been a surge of investment from outside the EU, with the United Kingdom as the largest recipient. As a result, competitive battles are becoming Europe-wide in scope. Lastly, *Europeanized competitors* are increasing in number and scope, as companies increasingly adopt pan-European strategies.

Changes in Market Globalization Drivers

Market drivers for globalization or Europeanization have increased. *Customer needs* and tastes are becoming more common across countries through exposure to other products. This is not to say that needs and tastes will reduce in number and variety. Rather, in most markets there is arising both a large "Euromass" segment and smaller national segments at the fringe, instead of the current largely separate national segments to one large European (global) segment with fringe national segments. *Europe-wide customers and channels* will increase in importance. Many previously national European retailers now operate throughout the continent, including France's Carrefour/Promodès and Intermarché, Germany's Metro and Rewe, and the Netherlands' Ahold.

Companies increasingly search the EU for suppliers. Distribution channels are already merging and forming alliances to provide pan-European coverage. *Transferable marketing* is increasingly becoming the norm, as buyers become increasingly exposed to multilanguage packaging (e.g., German sales representatives in France and vice versa) and to pan-European advertising created by pan-European marketing teams. Furthermore, *lead countries* now play a greater role with the freer movement of products and services. In the 1990s, London became the trend capital of not just Europe but the world. For example, the head of Ford's luxury-car group (which includes the Aston Martin, Jaguar, Land Rover, Lincoln, and Volvo marques) resides in London, as does the head of Switzerland's Richemont Group (owners of Montblanc pens and Cartier watches). This allows the opportunity for each company to understand and access high-end trend-conscious consumers otherwise improbable without such deliberate location.

Changes in Cost Globalization Drivers

Lastly, strengthening of cost globalization drivers is a major objective of EU. The potential for *European scale economies* greatly increases because the elimination of barriers to trade will allow the concentration of production, and the harmonization of standards enhances the potential for standardized products. Similarly, the increasing acceptability of pan-European products makes *experience curve* strategies more viable. One of the strongest cost drivers has been *favorable logistics* such as the elimination of frontier checks which speeds the flow of trucks from their previous average of 15 mph or so.[23] Combined with the elimination of tariff and nontariff barriers, these favorable logistics conditions now make *sourcing efficiencies* from centralized purchasing locations more achievable. In the short term, *differences in country costs* have been more significant in the absence of trade and logistical barriers, as companies find it easier to shift from high-cost to low-cost countries, such as Spain and Ireland. Additionally, the expansion to include Poland and other eastern European economies has brought many new locations of low-cost labor. In the longer term, these developments will push costs closer together. Companies now feel encouraged to invest in high-cost pan-European *product development* efforts because there will be larger markets for the results.

USING REGIONAL STRATEGIES

Each global strategy lever obviously can be used at the regional level as well or instead. Some researchers have cited the many difficulties of implementing global strategies and therefore favor regional solutions.[24]

Regional Market Participation

Expansion within a region has been the traditional first route for internationalizing companies, often on the basis of convenience and familiarity. Regional integration adds an extra dimension—perhaps the need to expand rapidly to all major markets in a region for both offensive and defensive reasons. A key question is whether a company needs to expand first within its region or hopscotch around to key markets around the globe. The answer depends on the relative strength of regionalization as opposed to globalization drivers, the potential benefits of first mover advantages, and the starting position of the company. For example, Nokia, then unknown outside Finland, had to first establish a position and reputation in Europe, where it was relatively easy to do so, before going global. In contrast, many already established European companies often target the U.S. market for new products before rolling out to the rest of Europe. The United States is a more important market for Ferrari cars than the rest of Europe outside Italy. Sweden's Hennes and Mauritz (H&M), a clothing retailer, is using European integration and convergence to expand into the rest of Europe from its Nordic and Germanic base.

Many industries have patterns of regional dominance. In the express delivery industry, FedEx dominates the Americas, while DHL does so for Europe, and TNT to a lesser extent for Asia-Pacific. Many companies struggle as they expand outside their home region. Wal-Mart has had to deal with being considered too "all-American" for the Latin American market despite its partnerships with important local store chains. Wal-Mart does not accept postdated checks, which are commonplace in Brazil, and its huge inventory has not been accepted well in Argentina, where customers care more about "creatively priced and promoted specials" than a large selection. Within its own region, the Jollibee chain of fast-food restaurants is successfully expanding beyond its home base of the Philippines. America's MTV is working hard to enter the Asian regional home market of Star TV's rival Channel [V].[25] MTV has started 24-hour service in some areas and launched Indian, Chinese, and Southeast Asian versions of its basic format. Each week MTV produces programs with local partners as well as importing the latest music from the United States.

Regional Products and Services

Designing regional rather than global products and services requires fewer complexities and is more appropriate when there are strong interregional differences in customer needs and tastes. For example, U.S. and Canadian drivers prefer wider, bigger cars than do Europeans and Asians, while in most emerging markets most customers can afford only basic versions of models sold in the developed world. Consequently, despite the large economies of scale in both R&D and production, many but not all mass-market automobile producers offer separate lines for different regions. It would be even better to develop global product platforms that can be adapted relatively easily for regional markets, as Honda has now done with its adjustable width platform. In the service sector, Club Med bends its philosophy of maximal standardization to cater to the North American market by offering greater comfort (including in-room phones and television sets) and fewer public announcements in French (a key part of its French ambience). Indeed, the brochures sent to North American clients exclude various Club Meds that are too basic or French for the tastes of these vacationers.

Managers also need to beware of overadapting to regional markets. At first glance, it might seem obvious that multinationals serving the emerging markets of Central and Eastern Europe need to make significant product adaptations. But a recent study found that most MNCs market globally standardized products quite successfully in that region.[26] On the other hand, managers must recognize the limits of regional standardization.

For example, continuing European diversity means that European hotel chains cannot push as far in pan-European standardization as can their U.S. competitors, who cater more for American customers.

Regional Activity Location

Many companies now build regionwide activity networks. Staying within a limited number of time zones and limited geographic distances, and within regional tariff barriers, such networks can be much easier to operate than global ones. Again, it is the relative strength of industry regionalization as opposed to globalization drivers that determines the optimum strategies. The automotive industry has many strong regionalization drivers as well as globalization ones.[27] Toyota spent $13.5 billion on global expansion through 2000 in an aggressive effort to become the first car manufacturer with major manufacturing hubs in the three major markets (North America, Europe, and Asia).[28] Toyota now has the ability to customize vehicles for regional markets. Such extensive coverage allows Toyota to react quickly to regional tastes, bypass regional trade barriers, and use regionally based suppliers to increase cost efficiencies. For example, a new plant in France allowed Toyota to bypass tariffs and locally produce Toyota's "Europe Car." In Asia, a local network of suppliers and assembly hubs permits Toyota to build sturdy, simply designed, low-priced cars that appeal to the Asian consumer.

ASEAN offers a "brand-to-brand complementation" (BBC) scheme whereby imports and exports of components or final products of the same brand (e.g., Toyota) are tariff free. Companies can benefit by production networks that have sites in different countries in the region specializing in particular components or production stages.

In logistics, European integration allows more and more companies to create centralized distribution systems, as has been done by both European and foreign companies.

Regional Marketing

Convergence of regional needs and tastes, growth of regional media and channels of distribution, and harmonization of regional marketing regulations all can make regional marketing feasible relative to multilocal marketing and much easier than global marketing. Again, European companies have the chance to pioneer with regional marketing.

Regional Competitive Moves

Strengthening competitive regionalization drivers, such as increased intraregional trade and the rise of regional competitors, spurs companies to pay attention to regional competitive moves. Such moves, relative to national or global ones, are particularly necessary when the weakening of a regional market position will have serious global repercussions. For example, Nokia's global success depends first on the maintenance of its European regional base, as do DHL's and Ikea's global positions.

Regional Strategy as a Partial or Temporary Solution

In many cases, the use of regional as opposed to global strategies should be viewed as partial or temporary solutions. A multiindustry study found that companies employing regional strategies had poorer performance than those using global strategies.[29] A recent examination of the automotive industry found that the more successful companies deployed regional strategies in the context of global strategies rather than implementing purely global strategies.[30] Industry drivers can also change. In the 1980s, the major appliance industry faced very strong regionalization drivers in Europe, favoring those companies that used regional rather than global strategies.[31] But by the 1990s, changes in the EU and in the industry seemed to strengthen industry globalization drivers and favor global strategies.[32]

REGIONAL ORGANIZATION AND MANAGEMENT

Each of the global organization structures and processes discussed in Chapter 8 can apply at the regional level. Decisions on these organizational issues should follow the analysis of the need for regional strategies and balance the strategic and organizational logic. Three critical issues arise in terms of regional organization structure—the autonomy of the regions and the role and location of the regional headquarters.

AUTONOMY OF REGIONS   MNCs need to decide how much autonomy each regional operation should have. This decision depends mainly on the integration of the region with the overall global strategy and also on the level of experience of the subsidiaries in the region and their managers.

ROLE OF REGIONAL HEADQUARTERS   As a company builds its presence in a region, the role of the regional headquarters needs to change. One researcher suggests that there are three evolving roles:[33]

- *Explorer:* exploit local opportunities, with limited self-contained operations and only an ambivalent commitment to the region.
- *Mover:* build regional presence through regional linkages and a strong regional headquarters, with a very high commitment to the region.
- *Consolidator:* run a balanced role for the region within the global portfolio, using global linkages and a reduced but still high commitment to the region.

LOCATION OF REGIONAL HEADQUARTERS   Often the most important issue is whether and where to have regional head offices. That decision inevitably has an influence on the emphasis placed within the region. Currently, in the Asia-Pacific region, the most popular cities for regional headquarters are Hong Kong, Singapore, Tokyo, and Sydney. Companies also shift their headquarters in a region as they change their priorities within the region.

GUIDELINES FOR DIAGNOSING REGIONALIZATION POTENTIAL AND DEVELOPING REGIONAL STRATEGIES

- Do not assume that industries are either regional or not regional. Instead, nearly every industry has regionalization potential in some aspects and not others.
- Different industry regionalization drivers can operate in different directions, some favoring regionalization and others making it difficult and inadvisable.
- Businesses can respond selectively to industry regionalization drivers, by regionalizing only those elements of strategy affected by favorable drivers.
- The level of regionalization potential changes over time.
- Regional strategies must be developed in the context of global and national strategies and may change over time.
- Regional trade agreements and blocs can be particularly important as a focus for regional strategies.

Discussion and Research Questions

1. Research and evaluate the different regional trade and trading bloc agreements—the EU, the NAFTA, Mercosur, ASEAN, APEC, and so on—in terms of how they affect global and regional strategies.

2. Select an industry and analyze its regionalization drivers as they were five years ago, as they are today, and as they are likely to be in five years' time.

3. How should a company decide when to use regional rather than global strategies?

4. What are the most globally successful companies from your region? How have these companies developed the capabilities for success over time?

Notes

1. This chapter draws on George S. Yip, *Asian Advantage: Key Strategies for Winning in the Asia-Pacific Region* (Reading, MA: Addison Wesley, 1998); *Updated Edition—After the Crisis* (Cambridge, MA: Perseus Publishing, 2000).

2. Mari Kondo and George S. Yip, "Regional Groups—ASEAN, AFTA, APEC, Etc.," in Yip, Ed., *Asian Advantage,* Chapter 16.

3. Mashfique H. Chowdhury, "2005 Nissan Sunny," Drive Arabia, http://www.drivearabia.com/nissan/nissansunny.html.

4. Tim Beissmann, "Nissan Sunny Global Small Car Coming to Australia," *Car Advice,* December 20, 2010, http://www.caradvice.com.au/95851/nissan-sunny-global-small-car-coming-to-australia/.

5. This section is drawn from Andrzej Kozminski, George S. Yip, and Anna M. Dempster, "Evaluating the Central and Eastern European Opportunity: Eastern Promise," in Andrzej K. Kozminski and George S. Yip, Eds., *Strategies for Central and Eastern Europe* (Basingstoke, England: Macmillan, 2000), Chapter 1, pp. 1–32.

6. Alan M. Rugman, *The End of Globalization* (London: Random House Business Books, 2000), Chapter 6, p. 96.

7. See also John A. Quelch and James E. Austin, "Should Multinationals Invest in Africa?" *Sloan Management Review,* Vol. 34, No. 3, Spring 1993, pp. 107–19.

8. See George S. Yip, *Asian Advantage: Key Strategies for Winning in the Asia-Pacific Region* (*Updated Edition—After the Crisis*) (Cambridge, MA: Perseus Publishing, 2000).

9. Ian Williams, "LG Shifts Business Focus to Europe," vnunet.com, June 26, 2008, http://www.vnunet.com/vnunet/news/2220096/lg-shifts-business-focus-europe.

10. Ben Furfie, "LG: 'Europe Critical to Global Success,'" *PCR,* June 25, 2008, http://www.pcr-online.biz/news/30075/LG-Europe-critical-to-global-success.

11. Kim Yoo-chul, "LG Seeks 3D Breakthrough in Europe," *Korea Times,* March 16, 2010, http://www.koreatimes.co.kr/www/news/tech/2010/04/133_62446.html.

12. LG Press Release, "LG Leads Health-Oriented Home Appliances Market," April 17, 2007, http://www.lg.com/us/press-release/article/lg-leads-health-oriented-home-appliances-market.jsp.

13. Viknesh Vijayenthiran, "Honda Delays Acura Introduction to Japan," *Motor Authority,* July 18, 2007, http://www.motorauthority.com/blog/1026938_honda-delays-acura-introduction-to-japan.

14. Kondo and Yip, "Regional Groups—ASEAN, AFTA, APEC, Etc."

15. Based on "In the Shark Pond," *The Economist,* January 1, 1998, pp. 59–60.

16. See Bob Trebilcock, Modern Materials Handling. "Ikea Thinks Global and Acts Local," February 1, 2008, http://www.mmh.com/article/CA6528805.html.

17. Based on Rugman, *The End of Globalization,* p. 116.

18. For a detailed explanation of Europe 1992, see, among others, Paolo Cecchini, *The European Challenge: 1992, The Benefits of a Single Market* (London, England: Wildwood House, 1988), and John A. Quelch, Robert D. Buzzell, and Eric R. Salama, *The Marketing Challenge of 1992* (Reading, MA: Addison-Wesley, 1990). For a quantification of how much EC 92 might improve business profitability, see George S. Yip, "A Performance Comparison of Continental and National Businesses in Europe," *International Marketing Review,* Vol. 8, No. 2, 1991, pp. 31–9.

19. See Chris C. Burggraeve, "Meeting Product Standards in the Single Market," *The Journal of European Business,* May/June 1990, pp. 22–6.

20. Speech by Peter Sutherland, former commissioner of the European Community, to the Planning Forum Conference on "The Challenge of Europe 1992," Boston, October 16, 1989.

21. International Monetary Fund, *Direction of Trade Statistics, 1999,* reported in Rugman, *The End of Globalization,* Figure 7.2, p. 116.

22. Rugman, *The End of Globalization,* Figure 7.4, p. 120.

23. Estimate by McKinsey & Company.

24. Allen J. Morrison and Kendall Roth, "The Regional Solution: An Alternative to Globalization," *Transnational Corporations,* Vol. 1, No. 2, 1992, pp. 32–55; A. J. David, Allen J. Morrison, David A. Ricks, and Kendall Roth, "Globalization Versus Regionalization: Which Way for the Multinational?" *Organizational Dynamics,* Vol. 19, No. 3, 1991, pp. 17–29.

25. "MTV Cranks Up the Volume in Asia," *Business Week,* June 23, 1998, p. 23.

26. Arnold Schuh, "Global Standardization as a Success Formula for Marketing in Central Eastern Europe?" *Journal of World Business,* Vol. 35, No. 2, Summer 2000, pp. 133–48.

27. Erik Schlie and George S. Yip, "Regional Follows Global: Strategy Mixes in the World Automotive Industry," *European Management Journal,* Vol. 18, No. 4, August 2000, pp. 343–54.

28. Adapted from "Toyota's Crusade," *Business Week,* April 7, 1997, pp. 104–14.

29. Henry P. Conn and George S. Yip, "Global Transfer of Critical Capabilities," *Business Horizons,* January–February 1997, Vol. 40, No. 1, pp. 22–31.

30. Schlie and Yip, "Regional Follows Global."

31. Charles W. F. Baden Fuller and John M. Stopford, "Globalization Frustrated: The Case of White Goods," *Strategic Management Journal,* Vol. 12, No. 7, 1991, pp. 493–507.

32. S. Segal-Horn, D. Asch, and V. Suneja, "The Globalization of the European White Goods Industry," *European Management Journal,* Vol. 16, No. 1, 1998, pp. 101–9.

33. Helmut Schütte, "Strategy and Organisation: Challenges for European MNCs in Asia," *European Management Journal,* Vol. 15, No. 4, August 1997, pp. 436–45.

CHAPTER 10

Measuring Industry Drivers, Strategy Levers, Organization Factors, and Regional Focus

The previous chapters have discussed globalization concepts without specifically explaining how to measure them. Being able to measure industry globalization drivers and global strategy levers greatly increases the usefulness of these concepts. Usable measures allow management to compare the globalization potential of different industries at the same time, of one industry over time, of the extent of globalization of different businesses within a company, and of a business and its competitors. Measures also facilitate implementation by making it clearer what needs to be changed and by how much. Instead of deciding to "increase the extent of global products," which is a very vague goal, it is far better to be able to decide to "increase the proportion of revenues in global products from 60 to 80 percent."

Good measures encourage implementation by exploiting the familiar idea that executives manage what is measured. So this chapter provides a series of practical measures of globalization. These measures have been developed and tested on over 50 American, European, and Japanese businesses and their executives in both research and consulting settings. However, users should feel free to adapt the measures suggested here and to develop their own. The important thing is to make some measurement.

Geographic Basis for Measurement

Measures can be made at both global and subglobal (e.g., regional) levels. Often, a global measure may be less useful than separate regional measures. For example, in measuring common customer needs, there may be significant commonality within regions (Europe, North America, etc.) but major differences among regions. So the commonality of customer needs should be measured at both levels—between countries within a region and between regions. Also, the definition of the world varies. The definition should usually exclude markets that are effectively closed to Western (and other market economy) multinational companies.

Who Should Do the Measuring

Because the measures of industry globalization and business global strategy cut across countries, it is important to receive input from representatives of the major regions or countries in a business. While one manager (or team) should be responsible for assembling and updating the measurements, he or she should involve managers from different geographic locations, as well as different functions, in developing and checking the measures. Chapter 8 described in detail how to assemble a global team to diagnose globalization potential and to develop global strategy.

MEASURING INDUSTRY GLOBALIZATION DRIVERS

Each of the four types of industry globalization drivers—market, cost, government, and competitive—differs in its nature. Thus, the measures for them vary. Many, but not all, of the measures can be quantified.

Summary of Globalization Measures

Driver	Measure
Market Drivers	
Common customer needs and tastes	Extent to which customer needs and tastes are common around the world
	Percentage (by cost) of the components of a global product or service that can be common worldwide
National global customers	Share of worldwide market sales to customers who search the world for vendors
Multinational global customers	Share of worldwide volume accounted for by customers who purchase or select centrally
Global channels	Share of worldwide volume accounted for by channels that purchase centrally
Transferable marketing	For each element, share of world market accounted for by countries where foreign element is acceptable
Lead countries	Number of countries that account for the most important product innovations
Cost Drivers	
Global scale economies	Percentage of world market needed for minimum efficient scale production or service operation
Steep experience effects	Percentage decrease in unit production costs with each doubling of accumulated capacity
Sourcing efficiencies	Potential percentage savings in purchase expenditures from making all purchases centrally
Favorable logistics	Transportation cost over a standard intercontinental route, excluding customs and duties, as a percentage of the selling price
Differences in country costs	Ratio of lowest to highest cost countries in the industry for (1) fully loaded hourly cost of the most common form of production labor and (2) total unit production cost

continued

Driver	Measure
High product development costs	Total cost of developing (but not marketing) a major new product or service, as a percentage of the expected lifetime sales of the product or service
Fast-changing technology	Market life of typical new product
Government Drivers	
Tariffs	Percentage of the pretariff selling price, averaged globally
Subsidies	Percentage of the presubsidy selling price, averaged globally
	Net percentage effect on selling prices of subsidized competitors
Nontariff barriers	Percentage of the world market that is blocked from imports
Compatible technical standards	Percentage, in cost, of the typical product that is in components that are technically compatible worldwide
Common marketing regulations	Proportion of the industry's worldwide marketing expenditures that are in activities allowed in every country
Government-owned competitors	Combined global market share of all government-owned competitors
Government-owned customers	Combined share of global industry purchases made by government-owned customers
Competitive Drivers	
Exports	Exports as a percentage of the world market
Imports	Imports as a percentage of the world market
Competitors from different continents	Number of continents that are the home of global competitors
Interdependent countries	Amount of volume sold in each country that is dependent on production facilities that supply more than one country, averaged across competitors
Competitors globalized	Extent to which competitors use global strategy levers
Transferable competitive advantage	Extent to which competitive advantages in the industry are transferable globally

Market Globalization Drivers

Measuring market globalization drivers requires making some qualitative judgments in addition to quantitative estimates.

COMMON CUSTOMER NEEDS DRIVER *Common customer needs and tastes* represent perhaps the most difficult driver to measure, because customer need in a product or service category is actually a bundle of different needs. For example, in a passenger automobile, safety is one kind of need and comfort is another kind. The only common yardstick is to measure the proportion of total cost accounted for, in a typical product, by the product or service components that satisfy each individual need. In an automobile, components such as brakes and caging provide safety, while components such as seating and shock absorbers provide comfort. If these safety and comfort components account for about 10 percent of the total cost of a typical vehicle, and if safety and comfort needs are the only ones to vary by country, then needs are 90 percent common. Of course, what customers consider a comfort need in one country may be considered a safety need in others (e.g., rust on automobiles is viewed as a safety hazard in Germany[1]). But such differences do not matter. What matters is the sum of the costs for all components that need to differ between countries.

This is evident in the Starbucks example as well. Even though there are many different population groups that drink coffee, sourcing and demand is relatively similar. In terms of sourcing, particular countries export unroasted coffee beans. However, providing additional value to the consumption of coffee, still other countries export roasted coffee beans on a large scale. That stated, demand for coffee is similar globally in that it is a consumer beverage. The tastes and trends differ internationally; the process and delivery of coffee for consumption is common.

An important consideration is to distinguish between changeable and unchangeable differences in country needs. Changeable needs arise from differences in customer tastes and preferences. For automobiles these changeable needs include styling and comfort. Unchangeable needs arise from legal, technical, or physical differences. For automobiles, unchangeable needs include the side on which the steering wheel is placed, emission control systems, heavy-duty batteries in cold countries, and air conditioning in hot ones. A manufacturer has to adapt its products to meet unchangeable needs but may be able to alter or offset changeable needs through marketing. Volkswagen used innovative advertising in the late 1960s and early 1970s in changing some American consumers' previous preference for large automobiles. Clearly, there are gray areas that fall somewhere between changeable and unchangeable needs. For example, the size of vehicles is affected both by preferences (a changeable factor) and by road and traffic conditions in a country (an unchangeable factor).

Managers using the type of measure just described usually find that customer needs are much more common than they might have seemed before applying the measure. Managers, particularly those with single-country responsibilities, tend to focus on the differences between countries, because it is the differences that require effort in adaptation. But when taking a global view, it is helpful to use this measure to get a better

The Influence of Starbucks in the Coffee Industry

Coffee is one of the world's most popular beverages, with over one-third of the population drinking it in some form. Many countries rely on coffee beans as one of their chief exports. In fact, it is estimated that 125 million people rely on coffee bean farming for their livelihood. Brazil is by far the largest exporter of coffee, followed by Vietnam and Colombia. However, these countries specialize in exporting green, or unroasted, coffee beans. Larger, more developed countries import these green coffee beans, roast them, and either distribute them within their country or export them. The top exporting country of roasted coffee beans is Italy, followed by Germany, Belgium, and the United States.[2] One example of a company that buys coffee beans is Starbucks. Starbucks purchased coffee from 25 countries around the world in 2007. Between October 2006 and September 2007, Starbucks purchased 352 million pounds of coffee. That accounted for 2.2 percent of the 16 billion pounds of total worldwide coffee production during that time period.[3] As such, this indicates the scope of Starbucks' operations in particular but also the coffee industry in general.

Large Banks Turn to Islamic Banking Practices

Islamic financial services were once ignored by globally competitive banks.[4] Many banks now know that they severely under-valued the potential of customized services for Muslim clientele. Standard and Poor's estimated the value of the Islamic banking market to be roughly $400 billion in 2006, but other estimates value the market at over $1.5 trillion. Western banks must make many changes to the way they do business in order to gain the approval of Islamic scholars and customers alike. In fact, the consumption of culturally and religiously questionable products can be forbidden under Islamic banking. For example, directly charging customers interest is forbidden. This presents challenges for banks, but accommodating for these challenges is necessary for banks to gain access to this growing market.

Within Islam, differing opinions between orthodox and liberal sects of the faith mean that banks often offer different financial services to customers in Saudi Arabia than they do in Indonesia. Some of the world's largest banks such as Citigroup, Goldman Sachs, and HSBC have entered the market. Many western banking firms once saw the sector as a barrier, or even a threat, to growth in countries with Muslim majorities. Even in western countries with Muslim minorities, openness to Islamic banking can be seen as undermining secular legal and financial systems.[5] However, related to a fast-growing world religion, Islamic banking and finance is a rapid growth segment in global financial services. In fact, some industry experts have indicated that openness to Islamic banking provides the opportunity to keep western countries competitive in the global marketplace.

understanding of the extent of commonality. This is specifically evident in the case of Islamic banking. Even though considerable differences exist concerning adherence to banking practices in Islamic areas of the world, commonality can be sought and established to develop a burgeoning market sector.

The measure can also be applied to separate product categories where there is more than one, and to separate features of an individual product. In the latter case the ratings of the separate features can be summed into a composite for the entire product.[6]

GLOBAL CUSTOMERS AND CHANNELS   There are two types of global customers: national and multinational. For industries that sell to organizations, the extent to which there are *national* global customers can be measured by the share of worldwide market sales to customers who search the world for vendors. The extent to which there are *multinational* global customers can be measured by the extent to which these customers buy or select centrally for global use. These multinational global customers may do all of the buying at one or a small number of central points or may make centrally major decisions such as the selection of vendors. An analogous measure is for regional customers. For industries that sell to consumers or individuals, the measure applies to purchases made outside the home country.

The extent to which there are *global channels* can be measured by the share of worldwide sales through channels of distribution that buy or select centrally. An analogous measure is for regional channels.

For both global customers and global channels, it may be worth repeating that mere multinationality does not qualify: The customers and channels have to make central purchase or selection decisions. Only then does the selling business need to respond with global programs for selling to and servicing these customers and channels.

TRANSFERABLE MARKETING Marketing transferability can be measured by analyzing the extent to which customers around the world accept or would accept a foreign element of the marketing mix (e.g., a foreign brand name or sales representative). This measure should be applied to all elements of the marketing mix—company name, brand name, packaging, advertising, promotion, and sales representatives. For company and brand names, being foreign means having a name that is generally recognized as being from another country, for example, McDonald's, in non–English-speaking countries or Louis Vuitton in non–French-speaking countries. For packaging, being foreign means using a nonlocal language for the pack copy, including multilanguage packs. For advertising, being foreign means not just using a foreign language (which is usually, but not always, undesirable) but also using recognizably foreign situations, scenery, or characters. To be more precise, transferable marketing can be measured for each marketing element by the share of the world market accounted for by countries where a foreign element is acceptable.

LEAD COUNTRIES Lead countries can be easily identified as those in which the most important product or process innovations occur. The measure can be made more precise by identifying the countries that accounted for the last 10 major innovations in the industry. In some industries the last 10 major innovations will have occurred over a short time span, such as one year or less. In other, slow-changing industries the time span may cover decades.

Cost Globalization Drivers

Cost globalization drivers are probably both the easiest and the most difficult to measure. They should be the easiest because they can be quantified. They can be the most difficult because most companies seem to collect little cost information that applies on a global basis. Yet, understanding the fundamental cost economics of a global business is critical for efforts to improve its global strategy.

GLOBAL ECONOMIES OF SCALE AND SCOPE Managers can measure global economies of scale by the share of the worldwide market needed to support a minimum efficient scale production or service operation. The extent of global economies of scope is usually more difficult to measure. It is indicated by the minimum global market share needed for a viable worldwide business. Global economies of scale or scope are typically significant when a global market share of 5 percent or more is needed to achieve the minimum efficient scale. In the passenger automobile business, the fifth and sixth largest global competitors, Nissan and Chrysler, had global market shares of only just over 5 percent in 1990. It can also be important to measure where in the value chain these scale economies occur.[7] In many industries, such as pharmaceuticals and electronics, it is in research and development rather than in manufacturing that world-scale economies occur.

STEEP EXPERIENCE EFFECTS The extent to which there are learning and experience effects is measured by the percentage decrease in unit production costs for each doubling of accumulated experience. This is the standard measure of the experience effect popularized by the Boston Consulting Group.[8]

SOURCING EFFICIENCIES Managers should keep in mind that the extent of sourcing efficiencies is more easily measured for an individual competitor within an industry than

Whirlpool's Global Supply Chain Optimization

When Whirlpool acquired competitor Maytag in 2005, the firm became the largest appliance company in the world. With this merger came many challenges to the firm's supply chain.[9] Changing market conditions had made location activities for both companies sub-optimal. Customers were changing as well. Shorter product life cycles, changing technology, and increasing wealth all contributed to an increase in the speed at which consumers shop for and purchase major appliances. Learning how to integrate the different ways by which both firms manufactured and distributed their products was an immediate logistical necessity. In fact, the potential benefits of strategic planning were hard to ignore. Whirlpool was able to reduce the number of stages in production and distribution by hiring logistics and supply chain management firm Penske Logistics to reduce operating costs by $60 million. Whirlpool finished the restructuring needed for a successful acquisition of Maytag by way of operations at fewer facilities. Still, by developing and implementing solutions related to the acquisition, the merged company was able to maintain and expand market share even amid these formidable challenges.

for the industry as a whole. The measure is the potential percentage savings in purchase expenditures from making all purchases centrally.

FAVORABLE LOGISTICS   The extent to which there are favorable logistics can be measured by the transportation cost over a standard intercontinental route in the particular industry, such as Tokyo to Chicago, or Chicago to Frankfurt, excluding customs and duties, as a percentage of the selling price. Transportation costs below 10 percent of the manufacturer selling price seem to be generally favorable for globalization. On the other hand, managers need to keep in mind that transportation, other logistical costs, and tariffs need to be related to margins and to the competitive price range. In general, the total transportation and tariff cost as a percentage of price needs to be at most half that of the competitive price range in most countries. That is, if the competitive price range is from 90 to 110 as an index, for a spread of 20 percent, transportation and tariff costs need to be no more than about 10 percent. For example, gourmet foods are globally competitive while basic foods are not, because the former's transportation cost is low relative to their price and the competitive price range. In addition, the availability of local products and trade barriers has a major influence on whether final products are shipped between countries.

That stated, large firms also merge to remain competitive. However, since the operations of many large companies are international at the very least and global at the very most, any major corporate merger has a profound influence on sourcing and logistics on a global scale. This is very evident in the Whirlpool example. Since processes required streamlining in many difference aspects of the business, support from outside the company was brought in to provide analysis to keep Whirlpool competitive.

DIFFERENCES IN COUNTRY COSTS   The extent to which there are differences in country costs is measured in two ways. Each involves a comparison between the highest cost country and the lowest cost country in which there is production in the industry. In addition, managers may find it necessary to include countries that are potential producers. One measure of the differences in country costs is to compare fully loaded hourly cost of the most common form of production labor in the industry. The other measure is more complete but also more difficult and may require making hypothetical estimates. It is to compare the total unit cost of production between the highest and lowest cost countries.

HIGH PRODUCT DEVELOPMENT COSTS The extent to which product development costs affect industry globalization potential is measured by the total cost of developing (but not marketing) a major new product or service as a percentage of the expected lifetime sales of the product or service. Both parts of this measure are difficult to estimate. Managers will need to make intelligent projections from past experience in most cases.

FAST-CHANGING TECHNOLOGY The rate of change of technology can be measured by the market life of typical new products. It can be particularly helpful to measure this over time to see if the pace of technology change is accelerating (as Philips did for the telecommunications industry—described in Chapter 2).

Government Globalization Drivers

Measuring government globalization drivers requires a good understanding of worldwide trade and other government policies and practices that affect a particular industry.

FAVORABLE TRADE POLICIES Managers can use several different measures of the extent to which trade policies are favorable to industry globalization:

Tariffs. The importance of tariffs is measured by their charge as a percentage of the pretariff selling price. Usually it is just the individual country tariffs that matter when making decisions about single country-markets. But when taking a global view, managers will find it helpful to calculate a single global number that represents the average worldwide extent of tariffs in a particular industry. A global average can be calculated by averaging tariffs across all countries, weighted by the share of the worldwide market accounted for by each country and adjusted for the universality of the tariff (i.e., a tariff may be levied against imports from some countries and not others). The latter adjustment can be made for each tariff-imposing country by weighting by the share of imports. For example, if France imposes a 10 percent tariff on electronics products from countries outside the European Community, and these countries account for 70 percent of electronics imports into France, the weighted tariff for France is 10 percent times 70 percent ($.10 \times .70$), which equals 7 percent.

Subsidies. The level of government subsidies is measured by their effect as a percentage of the selling price (including the full terms of sale such as financing and warranties). This effect is what matters to competitors rather than the effect on profitability. Estimating the effect on the selling price can be complicated, as subsidies are often in the form of a flat amount. It is their effect on the selling price that matters, not the total amount of the subsidy. For example, Airbus Industrie, the European aircraft consortium, is estimated to have received over $10 billion in subsidies from its start in 1970 to mid-1989, but to have delivered only 500 units over that period. If the full amount of the subsidy were allocated, the per aircraft amount would be $20 million, equivalent to about 50 percent of the average selling price. Even Boeing and McDonnell-Douglas, vociferous complainers about the Airbus subsidies, would not claim that their rival underprices by that amount.

More relevant is the much smaller percentage price discount, of the order of 10 to 20 percent, that Airbus Industrie has in effect offered to customers. As in the case of tariffs, it is useful to be able to calculate one global number. A global average can be calculated by averaging subsidies across all competitors weighted by their global market share.

Nontariff Barriers. The strength of quotas and other nontariff barriers is measured by the share of a country's market that is blocked from imports. For example, France's nontariff restrictions on Japanese automotive imports have restricted the latter's share to less than 5 percent. Without these restrictions Japan's share of the French automotive market might be closer to 20 percent (the level in the United Kingdom). The effect is, therefore, 15 percent. Local content requirements can be accounted for by using an analogous procedure to estimate the market value of the foreign content that is kept out. To calculate an overall global number, the national estimates should be summed and weighted by each country's market size as a percentage of the world total.

COMPATIBLE TECHNICAL STANDARDS Whether technical standards are globally compatible is measured by the percentage, in cost, of the typical product that is in technically compatible components worldwide. For example, in a television receiver, a large percentage of the product cost is in components that need to meet different technical specifications in different countries.

COMMON MARKETING REGULATIONS The degree to which there are common marketing regulations cannot be easily quantified. One approach is to estimate the proportion of the industry's worldwide marketing expenditures that are in activities allowed in every country. For example, in the cigarette industry, television advertising is banned in many, but not all, countries. So worldwide television advertising as a proportion of industry marketing expenditures accounted for by advertising in *any* medium is the measure of marketing regulations not being common.

GOVERNMENT-OWNED COMPETITORS AND CUSTOMERS The extent of government-owned competitors or customers can simply be measured by their combined global market share.

Competitive Globalization Drivers

Measuring competitive globalization drivers requires an effective global competitive intelligence system.

HIGH EXPORTS AND IMPORTS The level of exports and imports is simply measured by the sum of world exports and imports as a percentage of the world market size.

COMPETITORS FROM DIFFERENT CONTINENTS The extent to which there are competitors from different continents is measured by counting the number of continents that are the home of global competitors. A global competitor is a multinational business that has significant and extensive selling and/or production presence on more than one continent. The specifics of the latter definition will vary from industry to industry, but not its spirit.

INTERDEPENDENT COUNTRIES Whether countries are competitively interdependent can be measured by the degree to which individual competitors share activities within a global network. The key activity is production. For each competitor, the extent of sharing is measured by the amount of volume sold in each country that is dependent on production facilities that supply more than one country. For example, an American business may have 50 percent of its U.S. volume supplied from Taiwan and 30 percent of its volume in Italy also supplied from Taiwan. Summing up the total volume dependent on shared facilities and dividing by the competitor's global volume yields that competitor's country interdependence. For the industry as a whole, interdependence of countries is simply calculated by averaging across all competitors weighting by their global market share.

GLOBALIZED COMPETITORS   Managers can measure the globalization of competitors by first estimating the extent of globalization for each individual competitor, using the measures described later in this chapter for global strategy levers. To get the industry average, weight by each competitor's global market share.

TRANSFERABLE COMPETITIVE ADVANTAGE   Measures of the transferability of competitive advantage include how long it would take for companies in the industry to re-create advantages in new countries and how much it would cost to make the transfer.

MEASURING GLOBAL STRATEGY LEVERS

In addition to measuring the globalization potential of the industry in which a business participates, its managers also need to measure where the business is in terms of the use of global strategy levers. Only then can the managers know whether they are adequately exploiting the industry's globalization potential. In addition, it helps to make three kinds of comparisons:

- Comparative measurement over time helps to identify the speed and direction of change in the business's globalization strategy.
- Measurement of competitors' strategies helps to provide both a guide to what might be done in this business and an indication of competitive opportunities and threats.
- Comparing measurements for multiple businesses in the same company helps to set benchmarks for what each business should target in the use of global strategy levers.

Summary of Measures of Global Strategy Levers

Lever	Measure
Global Market Participation	
Global market share	Business's global volume (units or revenues) divided by the total volume of the worldwide market
Globally strategic market share	Business's volume in globally strategic country-markets only, divided by the total volume in those markets
Global share balance	Index of the worldwide business's geographic split of revenues compared with that of the worldwide market
Market Presence	
• Number of selling countries	Number of countries in which the worldwide business sells
• Global coverage	Share of global volume accounted for by the countries in which the worldwide business sells

continued

Lever	Measure
Global Products and Services	
Mix standardization	Percentage of worldwide revenues in a common product or service mix
Content standardization	Percentage of cost of product or service that is in standardized components
Global Location of Activities	
Concentration of individual	(1) Share of global spending on activity in the country with the most activity
	(2) Index of concentration across all countries
Concentration of entire value chain	Weighted average of the concentration indices of individual value activities
Global Marketing	
Comparative marketing intensity	Standard deviation of marketing intensity by country, for advertising, promotion, and selling
Marketing element uniformity	(1) Share of the business's worldwide revenues accounted for by the countries that have a uniform approach
	(2) Degree of similarity of each country's marketing element to that in a base country
Overall marketing uniformity	Score on each element weighted by each country's share of the business's worldwide revenues and by each element's importance
Global Competitive Moves	
Cross-area subsidization	How much profits are used from one country or region in which a business participates to subsidize competitive actions in another country or region
Counterparry	How often a business responds to a competitive attack in one country with a move in a different country
Globally coordinated sequence of moves	The number of countries involved in each sequence of moves
Targeting of global competitors	Identifying the number of global competitors in each world region and strategic country
Developing competitor plans	Number of competitive plans of action for each country/region-competitor combination relative to countries/regions of concern
Preemptive use of global strategy	The company's order of market entry in making use of a global strategy—global market participation, global products, global activity location, and global marketing

Global Market Participation

Global market participation can be measured in several ways. Each measure provides a different perspective on the extent of global market participation.

GLOBAL MARKET SHARE   *Global market share* is measured by the worldwide business's global volume (units or revenues) divided by the total volume of the worldwide market. Managers should also consider an important variant—*globally strategic market share*—measured by the worldwide business's volume in globally strategic country-markets only, divided by the total volume in those markets. *Globally strategic countries* can be identified simply by reviewing the key characteristics discussed earlier:

- Large source of revenues or profits
- Home market of global customers
- Home market of global competitors
- Significant market of global competitors
- Major source of industry innovation

GLOBAL SHARE BALANCE   *Global share balance* can be measured by managers in a number of ways. The simplest approach is to compare the percentage split of the worldwide business's revenues accounted for in each country with the percentage split of the world market accounted for in each country. A business with a "perfect" global share balance would have its percentages match the market's exactly. For example, if 30 percent of the world market were in the United States, 20 percent in Japan, and 50 percent in Europe, the business would have 30 percent of its revenues in the United States, 20 percent in Japan, and 50 percent in Europe.

To calculate the global share balance, count the business's split in each country only to the extent that it does not exceed the market's split in that country. Using the previously mentioned market split, if the business's split were 60 percent in the United States, 10 percent in Japan, and 30 percent in Europe, its global share balance would be 0.7 (30 percent United States + 10 percent Japan + 30 percent Europe). One way to think about this balance is that it represents the portion of the business's revenues that are in the right countries relative to the location of the worldwide market. An index value of 1.0 indicates that the worldwide business's sales are in perfect balance with the market's. An index value of 0 indicates the limiting case where 100 percent of the worldwide business's volume is in a country that accounts for 0 percent of the world market volume.[10]

MARKET PRESENCE   The extent of *market presence* can be measured by the *number of selling countries* (the number of countries in which the worldwide business sells) and by *global coverage*. The latter is the share of global volume (units or revenues) accounted for by the countries in which the worldwide business sells. This is not the same measure as the business's global market share.

Global Products and Services

As indicated in the smartphone industry, managers can measure the use of global products and services by examining the level of standardization across countries. This standardization needs to be measured at two levels: mix standardization and content standardization.

The Smartphone as a Global Product Offering

In the world of smartphones, Apple's iPhone is making considerable advances and continuously increasing its market share. However, it still has rivals in the global marketplace. In terms of global market share, Research in Motion's (RIM) BlackBerry share was almost double the iPhone's for the first quarter of 2009. In June 2009, Apple released an updated version of the iPhone called the iPhone 3GS. In its first weekend on the market, the new iPhone sold one million units, shattering analysts' sales forecasts by 25 to 50 percent.[11] This popularity put the iPhone on its way to threatening Blackberry's dominance of the smartphone market.

One reason for the BlackBerry's market power could be its availability. The Blackberry is sold in over 90 countries, and it can place and receive calls in more than 160 countries.[12] The iPhone is slightly less available, with sales occurring in over 80 countries.[13] Despite this geographic disadvantage, the iPhone still draws and satisfies users with its constantly improving technology and access to thousands of applications. Also, iPhone users are fervent supporters. Eighty-two percent of users say they are loyal to their iPhones, but 4 out of 10 BlackBerry and other smartphone users say they would switch to the iPhone.

MIX STANDARDIZATION A business may sell a different mix of product types or models in different countries. For example, Volvo does not sell its smaller automobiles in the United States. If these smaller models account for 30 percent of Volvo's worldwide automotive revenues, only 70 percent of its mix is global. Within this global mix, the products themselves have varying levels of standardization. So a complete measure of product or service standardization would read as follows: "This business sells a product (or service) mix that is 80 percent globally common. Of that common mix, products are 70 percent standardized in countries that account for 90 percent of world market volume."

CONTENT STANDARDIZATION Managers will find that measuring the extent of content standardization is complex because of the multidimensional nature of a product. Cost is the most common denominator and is, therefore, the best basis for measurement. Content standardization is measured by the percentage of the product's cost in components that are the same in each country. If the worldwide business sells more than one product, a composite measure can be used weighted by the worldwide sales volume of each product. An electronics business, part of an American multinational company, had a product line that was highly standardized—in fact, more than its executives realized. They initially thought that their product was not standard across countries, because 40 percent of the product cost was in a decoder that was different in each country. However, after further analysis, they discovered that within the decoder, only the software was unique. Furthermore, the software was embodied in purchased parts (masked ROMs). Therefore, there was no difference in the manufacturing process, only in the inventory to be kept. Also, the cost of developing the unique software was amortized over a large sales base. As a result, what initially appeared to be 40 percent nonstandard turned out to be only 3 percent nonstandard.

The foregoing measure may need to be adjusted for major countries only, or particular groups of countries. This adjustment is particularly necessary if the worldwide business sells a highly standardized product in some but not all countries. With the geographic adjustment the measure has two numbers, as follows: "The worldwide business sells products that are X percent standardized in countries that account for Y percent of world market volume." The product XY (X times Y) can be used if a single statistic is desired.

The measure cannot adequately handle all possibilities. For example, the statistic XY would be the same for a worldwide business with 90 percent standardization in countries accounting for 55 percent of worldwide volume and no standardization in the remaining countries, and for another worldwide business that also had a different standardized product for the remaining countries.

Global Location of Activities

As with the other global strategy levers, companies need to have an idea of where they are in their use of global activity location before they can decide whether and how to change it. Some useful measures include the following:

CONCENTRATION OF INDIVIDUAL ACTIVITY　Each activity should be analyzed in terms of how the geographic share of expenditure on that activity compares with the geographic share of the worldwide business's revenues. This can be done visually via comparative bar charts, numerically by comparing the percentage of the activity in key countries with the percentage of the world market or of the business's revenues in the same countries, or via concentration indices.[14] These comparisons then provide some of the basis for deciding whether the pattern of location is out of line with what it should be.

CONCENTRATION OF ENTIRE VALUE CHAIN　One measure can be developed for the concentration of the entire value-adding chain by using the weighted average of the concentration indices of individual value activities.

PRODUCTION LOCATION MATRIX　Managers can better understand their global strategy for production location by creating a matrix of where products are produced versus where they are sold. Such a matrix helps to identify the flow of products and also shows the extent of reliance on local manufacture. Exhibit 11-4 provides an example of such a matrix.

Global Marketing

Much of marketing is qualitative so that precise quantification of the extent of globalization will be difficult. But a number of measures can be applied to global marketing. These measures include the following:

COMPARATIVE MARKETING INTENSITY　This measures the degree to which spending on each element of the marketing mix—such as advertising, promotion, and selling—varies by country. It is measured by the standard deviation of the expenditure-to-sales ratios in each country for each marketing element.

MARKETING ELEMENT UNIFORMITY　This can be measured in two ways: (1) by the share of the business's worldwide revenues accounted for by the countries that have a uniform approach and (2) by the degree of similarity of each country's marketing element to that in a base country.

OVERALL MARKETING UNIFORMITY　Lastly, an overall measure of global marketing can be created by the similarity score on each element weighted by each country's share of the business's worldwide revenues and by each element's importance.

Global Competitive Moves

MEASURING GLOBAL COMPETITIVE MOVES   Six key types of global competitive moves were outlined in Chapter 7:

- Cross-area subsidization within the same business
- Use of counterparries in countries or regions
- Globally coordinated sequence of moves
- Targeting of actual and potential global competitors
- Developing plans for each competitor
- Preemptive use of global strategy

Each of these six key moves can be used to measure how much this global strategy lever is used by a business or by its competitors. But two of these features are more easily quantified than the others—the use of counterparries and the use of a globally coordinated sequence of moves. The use of counterparries can be measured by how often a business responds to a competitive attack in one country with a move in a different country. The use of a globally coordinated sequence of moves can be measured by the number of countries involved in each sequence of moves. The measures of the other levers are unique to individual companies and have to be developed in the context of each company. For illustration purposes, the following table addresses potential ways to measure each competitive move.

MEASURING GLOBAL ORGANIZATION

Measuring the extent to which management and organization help global strategy involves more subjectivity than measuring industry globalization potential and the use of global strategy levers. Because the effects of organization are so specific to individual companies, corporate managers might find it particularly helpful to measure global organization in their different worldwide businesses. They are likely to find that some elements are common across businesses, while others differ. Then they can investigate if these differences have helped or hurt the globalization efforts of each business. These measures are as follows.

Summary of Measures of Global Organization

Organization Element	Measure
Organization Structure	
One global head	Whether there is one person whose primary job is to be head of the worldwide business
International division	Whether there is an international division that does not contain the domestic business
Functional line heads	Whether there is a single head with line authority for each function
Functional staff heads	Whether there is a single staff coordinator for each function
Strength of business dimension	In a matrix structure, the strength of the business dimension relative to the geographic and functional dimensions
Management Processes	
Global strategic information system	Extent to which the business collects strategic information, such as market share and competitor data, from around the world in a consistent format on a regular basis

(continued)

continued

Organization Element	Measure
Cross-country coordination	Extent to which the business has processes for coordinating strategy across countries—*sharing information, negotiating plans, clearing plans with headquarters,* and *direction by headquarters*
	Frequency and extent of *global meetings*
	Number and extent of *global teams*
	Number of *global product managers* or *global account managers*
Global knowledge sharing	Extent to which a company shares knowledge and information across borders
Global strategic planning	Extent to which the business uses an effective strategic planning process that integrates across countries rather than just adding up the national plans
Global budgeting	Extent to which the business has global budgets that are used for global programs, as opposed to national budgets for national programs
Global customer management	Extent to which the business manages multinational customers on a globally integrated basis, including the percentage of revenues from customers managed this way
Global performance review and compensation	Extent to which senior managers are evaluated and compensated on the basis of global and not just regional or national performance; percentage of compensation tied to global performance
People	
Foreign nationals in home country	Percentage of senior managers in home country who are foreign nationals
Home country nationals in other countries	Percentage of senior managers in other countries who are home country nationals
Foreign nationals in other countries	Percentage of senior managers in other countries who are non–home country foreign nationals
Global boards of directors	Percentage of board that are not nationals of the home country; geographic coverage represented by board members
Culture	
Global culture	Extent to which corporate or business culture is global rather than national
Interdependent culture	Extent to which culture favors interdependence rather than autonomy

MEASURING REGIONAL FOCUS

Four integral drivers of regionalization were discussed in Chapter 9:

- Market regionalization
- Cost regionalization
- Government regionalization
- Competitive regionalization

Each of these four drivers can be measured to evaluate the extent to which a region is localized, regionalized, or globalized. By applying a detailed analysis of each and all regionalization drivers, a more precise understanding of the regional landscape can be achieved prior to entry into a specific market. In addition, a simultaneous evaluation of different regional markets can allow firms to evaluate particular regional opportunities for future strategic moves.

Summary of Measures of Regional Focus

Regionalization Driver	Measure
Market	Extent to which customer needs and tastes are similar in region
	Extent to which customers and channels have regionalized (rather than remaining localized or globalized)
	Extent to which marketing activities are transferable throughout region
	Extent to which lead countries influence other countries in region
Cost	Extent to which scale economies of direct activities (e.g., production) can be achieved in region
	Extent to which an experience curve has been achieved in the region
	Extent to which sourcing can be achieved effectively in the region
	Extent to which infrastructure conditions are favorable toward logistics in the region
	Extent to which production or activity costs vary in the region
Government	Extent to which favorable trade policies exist for trade in region
	Extent to which technical standards are compatible among countries in the region
	Extent to which common marketing regulations exist in the region
	Extent to which competitors and/or customers are owned by governments of countries in the region
	Extent to which region exerts its influence economically, politically, etc.
Competitive	Extent to which intraregional trade accounts for total exports and imports in the region
	Extent to which countries are interdependent politically, economically, etc.
	Extent to which competitive advantages are transferable from specific countries to the entire region

Discussion and Research Questions

1. What are the benefits of measuring globalization and global strategy?

2. Which industry globalization drivers are the easiest to measure, and which are the most difficult? What is the basis for your assertions?

3. How often and by whom should measures of globalization and global strategy be made?

4. Select one company and its product line. Describe how you would measure that product line's extent of global standardization. Also, how would you get the necessary information?

Notes

1. The author thanks Ed Davis, University of Virginia, for this example.
2. Daniel Workman, "Top Coffee Bean Exporters," August 4, 2007, http://internationaltrade.suite101.com/article.cfm/top_coffee_bean_exporters.
3. Starbucks Corporation 2007 Corporate Social Responsibility Fiscal 2007 Annual Report.
4. "Calling the Faithful," *The Economist,* December 7, 2006, http://www.economist.com/node/8382406?story_id=8382406.
5. "Sharia Calling," *The Economist,* November 12, 2009, http://www.economist.com/node/14859353?story_id=14859353.
6. The composite can be derived by weighting the individual features according to their share of product cost, as follows:

$$H_i = \Sigma S_j C_j$$

where
H_i = the homogeneity index of product i
S_j = the similarity score for feature j
C_j = the percentage of product i's cost accounted for by feature j

7. See Michael E. Porter, *Competitive Advantage* (New York: The Free Press, 1985).
8. See Arnoldo C. Hax and Nicolas S. Majluf, *Strategic Management: An Integrative Perspective* (Upper Saddle River, NJ: Prentice Hall, 1984), Chapter 6.
9. See Businessweek 24 Oct 2008. "The issue: Whirlpool cleans up its supply chain" http://www.businessweek.com/managing/content/oct2008/ca20081024_801808.htm.
10. This measure of global share balance can be somewhat tedious to calculate if there are a large number of countries. The same index can be developed more easily by applying a computer spreadsheet program to the following formula:

$$\text{Index} = 1 - \Sigma \left(|BS_i - MS_i| \right)/200$$

where
BS_i = the percentage share of the worldwide business's volume in country i
MS_i = the percentage share of the worldwide market's volume in country i
The index will range from 0 to 1.0 in value.

11. Jennifer LeClaire, "Apple's iPhone 3GS Sales Strong Even in a Recession," *NewsFactor Network*, June 23, 2009, http://www.newsfactor.com/story.xhtml?story_id=033001WSVZCI.
12. "The BlackBerry 8830 World Edition Smartphone Available in Verizon Wireless Communications Stores Today," Verizon Wireless Press Release, May 28, 2007, http://www.prnewswire.com/cgi-bin/stories.pl?ACCT=104&STORY=/www/story/05-28-2007/0004596834&EDATE.
13. "Apple Announces the New iPhone 3GS—The Fastest, Most Powerful iPhone Yet MEASURING REGIONALIZATION DRIVERS," Apple Press Release, June 8, 2009, http://www.apple.com/pr/library/2009/06/08iphone.html.
14. The following index for activity concentration can be used:

$$\text{Index} = \sqrt[2]{\Sigma S_i^2}$$

where S_i is the ith country's share of global expenditure on the activity.

CHAPTER 11

Conducting a Global Strategy Analysis

This last chapter provides a guide to the more practical aspects of applying the global strategy framework and conducting the necessary analyses. It also provides a number of forms that have proved useful in guiding executives through the analysis. One of the greatest challenges for the would-be global manager is acquiring the information that is needed both to formulate and to implement a global strategy. Surprisingly, many companies do not have complete and readily accessible information about the products and services they offer worldwide. Often, complete information by country exists only at the country level. Some companies even get trapped in a circular dilemma: They cannot collect information about a particular country because they do not participate in it, and they do not participate there because they do not have any information about the country.

WORKSTEPS

A global strategy analysis can range in effort from a one-day brainstorming exercise to a multimonth study. The analysis can also cover a strategic business unit, or even the entire company, or be restricted to a narrow range of issues, such as developing a global packaging design or a global sourcing policy. The following list (depicted in Exhibit 11-1) sets out the steps for a comprehensive effort:

- **A.** Assembling the global team
- **B.** Defining the business
- **C.** Identifying key markets
- **D.** Identifying key competitors
- **E.** Checking the core strategy
- **F.** Checking country selection
- **G.** Diagnosing industry globalization potential
- **H.** Evaluating current and potential use of global strategy levers
- **I.** Evaluating organization capability
- **J.** Developing global programs

EXHIBIT 11-1 Steps in Global Strategy Analysis

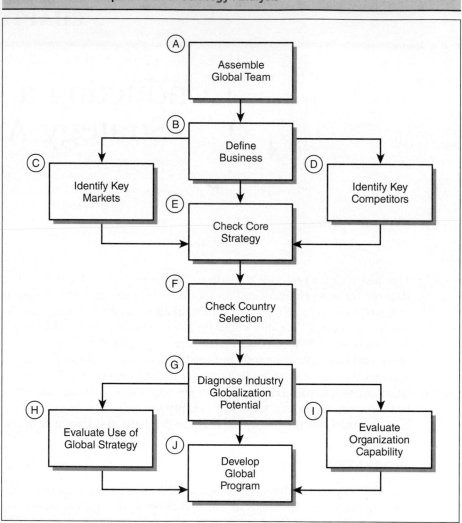

Also, as shown in Exhibit 11-1, feedback to earlier steps should be provided at each step. For example, discovering an opportunity to use global strategy at step H may generate a need to reconsider the core strategy checked earlier in step E.

A. ASSEMBLING THE GLOBAL TEAM

Involvement of managers from different functions and locations is absolutely crucial to the success of a global strategy. So selecting the team to participate in the global analysis is a key decision. The team needs to be selected from the following:

- Head of the worldwide business, if there is one
- Senior representatives from related businesses (that share facilities or staff)

- Senior corporate executive
- Heads of major regions/countries
- Heads of key functions

Ideally, the team should consist of no more than six to eight regular members. If choices have to be made, full geographic representation should be favored over full functional representation. In addition, the team needs support staff, such as from the planning function, or staff from the organization of the individual members. The invitation to join the global team should come from the highest possible level, ideally from the CEO. The inviter needs to stress the importance and relevance of the effort and indicate the hoped-for outcome. The team should have a leader, who should be the head of the worldwide business or the nearest equivalent.

Although perhaps obvious, the most difficult practical problem is often setting up a meeting schedule, so that should be done at the first meeting. Because each of the executives is likely to be extremely busy, it is better to establish a set schedule even though the work may not fit exactly. At least three meetings should be set up, between one and two months apart, perhaps piggybacking onto other events such as corporate planning meetings. It is also very helpful to move the location of the meeting around the world—anything to avoid the appearance of a head office/home country-driven project helps. In addition, rotating the location helps the team members to undertake the travel needed in a global business and allows local staff to participate.

The schedule should also allow enough time between meetings to collect and analyze information and to develop strategies and reports. Having new input greatly enhances what can be achieved in each meeting.

B. DEFINING THE BUSINESS

The leader of the global team needs to have a good idea of what business will be analyzed before he or she can assemble the global team, but developing a complete definition needs the input of the team. *Business definition is an important issue, because a global strategy analysis is often more effective by starting out with a piece of the business rather than with the entire business.* Experience with analyzing this part of the business can then be transferred to subsequent expanded efforts. Perhaps equally as important, the first global analysis needs to achieve usable results within a short time span, say, six months at the most. Classically, business definition has focused on the three dimensions of product (or service) function, technology employed, and customer groups served.[1] In the context of global strategy, the fourth dimension of geography must, of course, be added. Taking account of the geographic dimension will make it clearer which businesses face broader global issues and, therefore, have a greater need for global strategy. In addition, the team may wish to restrict the analysis to just one region, such as Europe or even a portion of a larger region (e.g., Scandinavia as a part of Europe). So, for example, a manufacturer of medical equipment may have several options in defining the business to study:

- The entire medical equipment division (and the industries in which it participates)
- The worldwide hospital equipment business
- The worldwide hospital radiography equipment business
- The European hospital radiography equipment business

Another concern is to define the business broadly enough to encompass competition from actual and potential substitutes.

C. IDENTIFYING KEY MARKETS

The global team cannot collect and analyze information about every country in which the business operates or might operate, because of both the time and effort needed for collection and the resultant information overload. One approach is to split the analysis into two levels, first by region and then by country within each region. The choice of regions is usually relatively easy—North America, South America, Europe, Far East, or Pacific Rim being the most common. However, companies are finding that these traditional regions are often either too large or too complex, resulting in the need to establish smaller regions for analysis (e.g., Southeast Asia, Eastern Europe). Matching the region definitions to the way in which the company is organized may not be the purest approach, but is usually the most practical for data gathering and for subsequent implementation. Some companies use unusual regional groupings. Gillette has organized a North Atlantic region, because of the similarity in income levels and lifestyle among the United States, Canada, and Western Europe. Citibank also has an unusual grouping for its global finance business—JENA, an acronym for Japan, Europe, North America, Australia, and New Zealand, in short, most of the developed world. When selecting countries within regions, the definition of a country is flexible, as described in Chapter 1. For example, a "country" can be Benelux or Scandinavia. As with regions, only the most important countries should be chosen. Criteria for country selection should include the largest country-markets, the countries in which the company has the largest businesses, and globally strategic countries.

Splitting the analysis into two levels—global and regional—reduces the number of geographic entities that need to be considered at one time. *It is surprisingly important to be able to view all key markets spread across one exhibit as a comparative chart.* Executives are able to generate new understanding and insight when they can compare and contrast across regions and countries. Furthermore, when the members of the global team view these comparative charts *together,* they stimulate each other in developing ideas. So a total of no more than 10 geographic entities plus "all other" and "total world (region)" columns should be used. At the country level, markets should be selected for analysis using the criteria in Chapter 3 on global market participation. The list should include the six or so largest markets in which the business participates, any other country-markets among the largest six in the world even if the business is not there, any other markets that are strategically important, and any other markets in which the worldwide business has its largest country-businesses. This combination will usually result in a list of 8 to 10 countries. In deciding on the "all other" category, the team needs to define the world. As stated in Chapter 1, the world market includes only country-markets that are accessible to multinational companies. Such accessible countries vary from industry to industry and also change over time. In some industries, it may be useful to add a column combining the countries that are not accessible to the business. Having such a column will give a better perspective on the total market and may help the global team avoid being blindsided by developments coming out of inaccessible countries.

The global team should then use the list of countries as the basis on which most of the information will be collected and displayed.

Information to be Collected for Each Region/Country

In conducting analysis of individual countries in order to make an entry decision, for example, a large amount of information needs to be collected (some of which will be identified in step F). But for this step of identifying key markets, much less information is needed. The following basic set of information needs to be known for each country-market:

- Market size in units and revenues
- Stage of product life cycle
- Number of global competitors
- Number of regionwide competitors
- Number of national or local competitors
- Percentage of country production (in the industry) exported
- Percentage of country consumption imported
- Local content requirement
- Labor cost
- Government share of customer purchases
- Tax rate for local and for foreign companies
- Percentage of foreign ownership allowed

COPING WITH EXCHANGE RATES   Currency exchange rates have a very crucial role in globalization decisions. To make data collection simple and to ease subsequent analysis, all data should be reported in the currency of the headquarters country at historical exchange rates, that is, using the same exchange rates that were applied by the local businesses when they reported to headquarters in each time period in the past. Typically, that means the annual average exchange rate for revenue and profit items and year-end exchange rates for balance sheet items. The key reason for converting to the home currency is that most owners or shareholders care about the worldwide business's contribution to revenues and profits in their home currency. Similarly, the key reason for using historical exchange rates is that for a globalization analysis, the need is to know how each country-business contributed to the total business. So, a depreciating local currency, for example, needs to be recognized for its impact on the role that the local business can play. (In contrast, evaluating the performance of local managers should generally be done using figures in their local currency.)

D. IDENTIFYING KEY COMPETITORS

Just as every country cannot be analyzed, neither can every competitor. So the global team needs to select the most important competitors to study. Competitors that need to be analyzed include the following:

- All global competitors, as defined by all competitors that have significant market presence in North America, Europe, and Asia and have at least a 5 percent global market share. (This definition may need to be adapted in industries where the key continents are different from those listed.)

EXHIBIT 11-2 Example Data Matrices for Analyzing Competitors

Markets / Competitors	N. America	S. America	Europe	Asia	All Others	Total
Our Company						
Competitor A						
Competitor B		Market Share %				
Competitor C		* 3 Years Ago				
Competitor D		* This Year				
Competitor E		* 3 Years in Future				
All Others						
Total						

Markets / Competitors	Germany	France	United Kingdom	Italy	All Others	Total
Our Company						
Competitor A						
Competitor B		Market Share %				
Competitor C		* 3 Years Ago				
Competitor D		* This Year				
Competitor E		* 3 Years in Future				
All Others						
Total						

Create Also for | Relative Prices | Relative Costs | Relative Quality |

- The largest competitors based in each lead country and major region, even if they are not global.
- Potential global competitors.

If possible, the list of all competitors should be kept to 10 or fewer.

The list of key competitors combines with the list of key markets to make a very powerful organizing framework for displaying and analyzing information. Exhibit 11-2 illustrates the different kinds of data matrices that are useful to develop for this market-competitor combination—such as global and European matrices for competitors' market share, relative prices, relative costs, and relative quality.[2]

E. CHECKING THE CORE STRATEGY

In conducting a global strategy analysis, it is common for the members of the global team either to not know what the business's core strategy is or, more commonly, to hold differing views on what it is. So the global team will find it very helpful to check its core business strategy early in the process. The best way to conduct this check is to have executives from both headquarters and each major region or country write down the core strategy. Doing so has two benefits. First, if the core business strategy is not already specified in some document, this procedure helps make explicit what may have been implicit. In addition, many statements of business strategy are typically less detailed than they should be and often consist of what Americans like to call "apple pie and motherhood" statements, such as "this business will profitably offer the highest quality products and provide the best value to our customers." Such statements can be very helpful in motivating organization members and reassuring shareholders but provide little strategic guidance. The essence of a strategy is that it makes choices, something that the previous example does not. After all, who would choose the opposite: "This business will unprofitably offer the poorest quality products and provide the worst value to our customers"? Andrall E. Pearson, then president of PepsiCo, very succinctly captured the importance of strategic choice when he said, "A strategy is something that someone else would not be stupid not to choose."[3] So managers should write out their core business strategy in some detail and in a format that makes choices explicit.

The statement of core strategy should include the following:

- Business definition
- Strategic thrust
- Financial targets
- Sources of competitive advantage
- Strategy elements
- Value-adding activities
- Competitive strategy

Exhibit A-1 provides forms that are useful for specifying the core strategy.

The second benefit of having each major region or country specify its view of the core business strategy is that differences among the regions and countries can then be identified.

F. CHECKING COUNTRY SELECTION

Country selection is one of the most important elements in both internationalization and globalization. It is also a decision for which analytical techniques can be particularly helpful. Traditional analytical approaches to selecting countries for entry have focused entirely on stand-alone attractiveness.[4] But managers need to consider the global strategic importance of a country. Of additional relevance is the potential for synergy between the business under consideration and sister businesses in each country. For example, a leading American forest products company finds that a key factor in deciding whether to expand a particular business into a new country is that business's potential for absorbing paper production capacity already in place in the country. So three sets of overall factors should determine country selection:

- Stand-alone attractiveness
- Global strategic importance
- Synergy

The global team should evaluate country selection using the following steps:

1. Identify countries/regions for analysis
2. Develop a list of subfactors for each of the three sets of overall factors
3. Assign weights to each subfactor
4. Rate each country/region on each subfactor
5. Combine the weights and ratings to arrive at a total score for each country or region
6. Adjust the total score for country risk

1. Identify Countries/Regions

The global team should identify all countries or regions in which the business already participates or might do so. Existing countries should be analyzed in order to help determine the level of effort that should be devoted to them and to provide a benchmark for evaluating new countries. It is particularly important to include countries that may be difficult to enter but that are globally strategic or potentially so.

2. Develop List of Subfactors

The global team should develop its own list of subfactors to assess each of the sets of factors. Such a list might include the following:

STAND-ALONE ATTRACTIVENESS OF COUNTRY/REGION

- Size of market
- Growth rate of market
- Barriers to entry
- Competitive situation
- Price levels
- Tax rates
- Macroeconomic conditions
- Political risk
- Cost of adaptation

GLOBAL STRATEGIC IMPORTANCE OF COUNTRY/REGION

- Home market of global customers
- Home market of global competitors
- Significant market of global competitors
- Major source of industry innovation
- Home of most demanding customers

SYNERGY WITH OTHER BUSINESSES IN COUNTRY/REGION

- Shares activities with other company businesses
- Uses upstream (e.g., raw material production) capacity

- Uses downstream (e.g., final assembly or distribution) capacity
- Proximity to other markets

For countries in which the business is not already present, *potential* synergy is what should be evaluated.

3. Assign Weights to Each Subfactor

The global team should next assign a weighting to each subfactor such that the total for all subfactors sums to 100 points. One approach is to first split the 100 points among the three overall factors of stand-alone attractiveness, global strategic importance, and synergy with other businesses. For example, these three overall factors might be assigned 40, 40, and 20 points respectively. Then the points for each overall factor can be split among the individual subfactors.

4. Rate Each Country/Region on Each Subfactor

The global team should then rate each country or region on each individual subfactor on a scale from 0 to 10. A practical way to do this is to set benchmarks by giving a rating of 10 to the country or countries with the strongest showing on each particular factor. For example, on the market size subfactor, the largest market can be assigned a score of 10 and all other countries scaled in proportion. In some other cases no country may qualify for the maximum score, so the global team needs to consider what would rate a maximum score and scale the countries accordingly. The exact approach used is not as important as the end result of differentiating among the countries on the various subfactors.

5. Combine the Subfactor Weights and Country Ratings

To arrive at a total rating for each country, the weights and ratings should be multiplied together and summed (and divided by 10 to get a total country rating that is out of 100).

6. Adjust for Country Risk

Finally the total country ratings should be adjusted for country risks such as political instability, the risk of expropriation, and the risk of currency devaluation. Traditionally, country risk has been included with other factors in evaluating stand-alone attractiveness, rather than being considered separately as done here.[5] This separate approach is preferable for three reasons. First, it separates the business factors from the political ones. For example, both Brazil and Japan are large markets that may be highly attractive in particular industries. But the level of country risk has been much higher in Brazil than in Japan. Mixing the two types of factors makes it difficult to recognize two fundamentally different sources of uncertainty that need to be managed in different ways. Second, risk can be viewed as a discount factor applied to expected returns from participating in a country. Third, country risk changes much more quickly than business attractiveness, as it did for China in 1989, the Middle East in 1990, Mexico in 1994, Russia and Indonesia in 1998, and Greece in the 2000s. Various services such as Political Risk Services provide relatively low-cost and comprehensive ratings of country risk.[6] The ratings provided by these services should be converted into a risk adjustment factor scored from 0 as hopelessly risky to 1.0 as no risk at all.

Using the Ratings

The resultant ratings should be used as one input to the decision on country selection and should not be used in a mechanistic way. The global team should solicit the input of managers familiar with the individual countries as well as use their own individual judgment. Although a lot of work, this kind of comprehensive analytical process can be helpful in dispelling myths or clearing up ignorance about the attractiveness of particular countries. The process can also force companies to recognize the importance of entering countries that have been avoided for their difficulty. In summary, the benefits of this technique include identifying relevant data, reducing complexity, encouraging a systematic approach, providing quantitative measurement, and complementing intuition. At the same time, users have to be cautious of its weaknesses, which include oversimplifying, requiring subjective evaluations, and needing modification for each application. Most important, this technique must not be used blindly.

G. DIAGNOSING INDUSTRY GLOBALIZATION POTENTIAL

Diagnosing industry globalization potential can best be done in two stages. In the first stage, the global team can make preliminary assessments through group discussion at one of its meetings, using the measures summarized in Chapter 10. These assessments should be written up so that they can be verified by country managers and staff in a second stage. A typical assessment might be as follows:

> The globalization driver of global customers rates a moderate score today and is increasing in strength. Global customers now account for about 20 percent, up about 5 percentage points from three years ago, and regionwide customers a further 35 percent, up about 10 points from three years ago. We expect both global and regionwide customers to increase their share of purchases. Showa K.K. behaves the most globally as a customer. In its last request for proposal, it required a bid with standard prices for each country. Duvall & Cie. is starting to behave as a global customer and now requires all products to be approved in Paris even though its local subsidiaries make their own purchase decisions. We are not sure what Schmidt AG is doing and want each country manager to report back with an assessment.

Next, the global team should identify how industry globalization drivers give rise to opportunities to use global strategy levers. For example, what does the diagnosis of global customers indicate for the use of global marketing such as global account management?

H. EVALUATING CURRENT AND POTENTIAL USE OF GLOBAL STRATEGY LEVERS

Identifying changes to be made in the use of global strategy levers requires a diagnosis of both their current and their potential use. There are three major sources of ideas for diagnosing the potential use of global strategy levers:

- Analysis of the potential benefits from using global strategy
- Analysis of the industry globalization drivers
- Analysis of what competitors are doing

EXHIBIT 11-3 Example Calculation of Potential Savings from Product Standardization

Reducing the number of products worldwide by 33% would save:	
	% of Sales
• Manufacturing	3% to 4%
• Inventory (14% of sales times 20% carrying cost)	2.8%
• Out-of-stock and orders not pushed from fear of out-of-stocks (10% of sales times 40% gross margin)	4.0%
Total	10% to 11%

These potential savings can be compared with a pretax margin of 8% and a media budget of 12%.

Various analytical and display techniques can help diagnose the individual global strategy levers, as explained next.

Global Market Participation

A key aspect of a global approach to market participation is the extent to which the business's revenues are in geographic balance with those of the market as a whole. It can be very helpful to depict graphically the global share balance to compare where the business has its revenues with the overall global market. A comparative bar chart might show, for example, that a business has far too much of its revenues concentrated in the United States and not nearly enough in Japan and that this imbalance will worsen in the next five years.

Global Products and Services

The key analysis needed for product standardization decisions is the calculation of potential cost savings. Potential cost savings from product standardization can be small for individual factors but can add up significantly. Exhibit 11-3 illustrates the type of analysis needed.

Global Activity Location

As with market participation, the analysis of activity location can be enhanced through the use of visual display. Working with an industrial supplies company, this author found one such display helped to highlight the dominance of Germany in research and development (R&D) and manufacturing relative to its share of the business's global revenues. The implications depend, of course, on the specific situation of the business. In this example, the business's high level of concentration helped to achieve economies of scale in R&D and manufacturing. But the business also suffered from a lack of R&D facilities in two of the most innovative markets—the United States and Japan.

The location of manufacturing is typically the most difficult issue in global strategy. It helps to start with a good understanding of where products are produced and where they are shipped. Exhibit 11-4 provides an example of a *production location matrix* that helps managers understand their current production location strategy. In Exhibit 11-4

EXHIBIT 11-4 Product Location Matrix

Units in Millions

Produced in \ Sold in	United States	Germany	France	United Kingdom	Japan	Brazil	Others	Total Units Produced
United States	1,320						230	1,550
France		380	250	210			130	970
Brazil						140		140
Taiwan					470		220	690
Total Units Sold	1,320	380	250	210	470	140	580	3,350

▨ = Produced and Sold in the Same Country

51% of Production is for Local Sale (United States, France, and Brazil = 1,710 Million Units out of 3,350 Million Total)

the shaded boxes indicate units that are sold in the country of production. So in this example, 51 percent of production is for local sale, which in most cases is probably greater than it should be under a globally integrated strategy.

Having evaluated each value-adding activity, the team should summarize the actual and target location of each activity in terms of whether it is, or should be, mostly local or mostly central. In addition, the team should decide on the nature of headquarters coordination and control needed for each activity (Exhibit 11-5).

Global Marketing

As with value-adding activities, it can be useful to summarize the actual and target use of global marketing. Exhibit 11-6 provides a format for summarizing conclusions on which marketing element to globalize and to what extent. It can provide a useful focus on the

EXHIBIT 11-5 Actual and Target Globalization by Activity

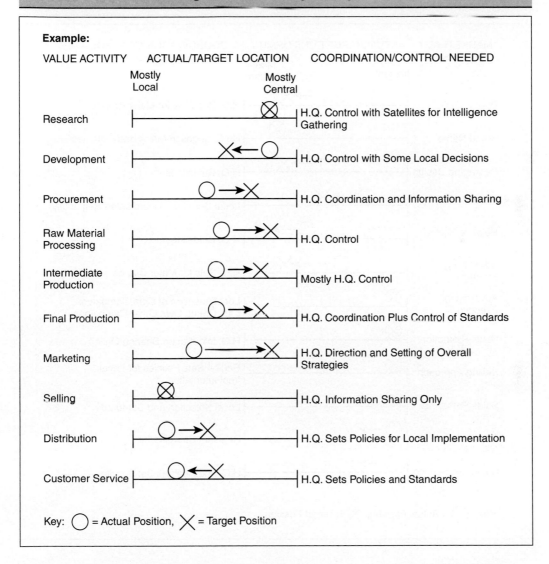

Example:

VALUE ACTIVITY   ACTUAL/TARGET LOCATION   COORDINATION/CONTROL NEEDED

Mostly   Mostly
Local   Central

Research — H.Q. Control with Satellites for Intelligence Gathering

Development — H.Q. Control with Some Local Decisions

Procurement — H.Q. Coordination and Information Sharing

Raw Material Processing — H.Q. Control

Intermediate Production — Mostly H.Q. Control

Final Production — H.Q. Coordination Plus Control of Standards

Marketing — H.Q. Direction and Setting of Overall Strategies

Selling — H.Q. Information Sharing Only

Distribution — H.Q. Sets Policies for Local Implementation

Customer Service — H.Q. Sets Policies and Standards

Key: ◯ = Actual Position, ✕ = Target Position

end objective of the analyses of industry globalization drivers, potential benefits of global strategy levers, and competitors' approaches.

The global team can also use a *relative price map* to deal with the one marketing element that is easy to quantify—pricing. Such a map shows the business's pricing in each country indexed relative to the home country (or any one reference country). This index can be constructed in a number of ways. The easiest way is if there exists a typical product that is sold in every country or region being analyzed. If no one product meets this criterion or if different products have different patterns of international pricing (e.g., one major product may be priced in Europe above the company's home country price,

EXHIBIT 11-6 Summary of Global Marketing Strategy

MARKETING ELEMENT	ACTUAL/TARGET UNIFORMITY	COORDINATION/CONTROL NEEDED
	Mostly Different — Mostly Uniform	
Positioning	○ → X	H.Q. Specifics for Major Brands
Brand Name	⊗	No Changes in Major Brand Names
Packaging Design	○ → X	H.Q. Guidelines
Absolute Pricing	○ → X	Local Decisions Coordinated Regionally
Relative Pricing	○ → X	H.Q. Guidelines
Advertising Strategy	○ → X	H.Q. Sets for Major Brands
Advertising Execution	⊗	Local Adaption of Core Campaigns, Plus Create Own Other Campaigns
Sales Promotion	⊗	H.Q. Information Sharing Only
Selling Approach	⊗	Region Sets Policies for Local Implementation
Sales Personnel	⊗	Local Selection and Standards
Distribution	○ → X	Regional Coordination
Customer Service	○ → X	H.Q. and Regions Set Policies

Key: ○ = Actual Position, X = Target Position

while another major product may be below the home country price), then the global team needs to create either a number of different charts or a single weighted composite.

Global Competitive Moves

Most companies have very poor information about their competitors' moves. If the information exists, it is usually scattered around the company with different people and in different countries. Historical information about competitors' moves is even scarcer. *But collecting and maintaining such information is crucial for understanding and predicting the pattern of competitors' global moves.*[7] For example, mapping the history of each major competitor's moves, as in Exhibit 11-7, helps to identify the extent to which they globally integrate their competitive moves. In the example in Exhibit 11-7, "Pudong International"

EXHIBIT 11-7 Map of a Competitor's Moves

Example:

COMPETITOR: Pudong International

Period / Market	N. America	S. America	Europe	Asia	Other
2012 Q1	▲ Raised Price on X79 Model				
2012 Q2			▲ Raised Price on X79 Model		
2012 Q3				▲ Raised Price on X79 Model	
2012 Q4					
2013 Q1		▲ Raised Price on X79 Model			▲ Raised Price on X79 Model
2013 Q2				◯ New Ad Campaign	
2013 Q3	▪ Introduced Z82 Line		▪ Introduced Z82 Line		
2013 Q4			◯ New Ad Campaign		
2014 Q1				▪ Introduced Z82 Line	
2014 Q2	◯ New Ad Campaign				
2014 Q3	▲ Raised Price on Z82 Line				▪ Introduced Z82 Line
2014 Q4			▲ Raised Price on Z82 Line		

Key: ▲ = Pricing Move   ▪ = Product Move   ◯ = Advertising Move

seems to make its price and product moves in North America first, closely followed by the other regions. In contrast, new advertising campaigns seem to start in Asia. It is also helpful to map the history of competitors' global responses to your business's moves.

Summary of Business and Competitors

Having evaluated the use of each individual global strategy lever and its elements, it is helpful to summarize the total use of global strategy by the business and its major competitors. The example in Exhibit 11-8 illustrates the position of the business and its three major competitors in terms of their use of each of the five global strategy levers.

EXHIBIT 11-8 Summary of Competitors' Use of Global Strategies

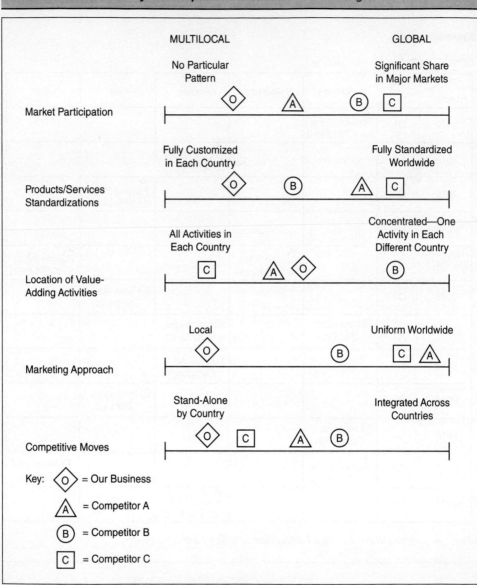

I. EVALUATING ORGANIZATION CAPABILITY

Organization and management factors make a crucial difference to how well global strategy can be developed and implemented. So it is also essential to evaluate the organization's capability for global strategy and to diagnose the necessary changes. Chapter 8 discussed each of the sets of factors and their individual elements to determine together the organization's capability for global strategy. The global team should systematically evaluate each of these factors and elements using the measures described in Chapter 10. Typically, the methodology for this step should include getting the views of both head-quarters and subsidiary managers through interviews, group discussions, and surveys. In this data-gathering process, the global team should not just collect information about problems (which managers are usually happy to talk about) but also find out about possible solutions, as well as test for reactions to solutions devised by the team. To help find the best solutions, the global team should try to discover how other effective companies in the same industry or comparable industries organize and manage for global strategy.

J. DEVELOPING GLOBAL PROGRAMS

The last task in a global strategy analysis is to specify plans for global programs in sufficient detail that they can take on a life of their own. In other words, this last step ensures the transition to implementation. The previous analyses will typically have identified a large number of global programs. For example, one company that conducted a global strategy analysis concluded with the following programs that needed to be implemented:

- Global Products
- Global Technology Management
- Global Materials Procurement
- Global Marketing Management
- Global Account Management
- Global Pricing
- Global Identification
- Global Trade Show Coordination
- Global Market Intelligence

To move to implementation, the company developed plans for each program. The following summary illustrates the plan for the global products program:

GLOBAL PRODUCTS PROGRAM

Product and process are so interlinked that we need to treat them together. Our ability to develop highly customized products for key customers is a key competitive advantage. At the same time global customers expect to be able to purchase consistent/uniform products wherever they operate sophisticated equipment. But consistent products require a consistent manufacturing process, which we do not have. There is now wide variation from region to region in our manufacturing approach, arising from a combination of raw material availability, equipment, customers' expectations, and local economic conditions. The result is that products are not as standardized as they could or should be.

Objective

Maintain and augment our competitive advantage of being able to provide consistent/uniform products around the world to those customers who require consistency. In addition, cut costs.

Overall Strategy

Increase standardization across countries by individual characteristics at tighter specifications that provide added value to customers. We will standardize only when the additional cost is low or is recoverable from customers.

Potential Benefits

- Cost savings for the company
- Improved quality or performance for the customer
- Increased barriers to competition
- Improved trust of the company by customer management
- Training efficiencies

Potential Disadvantages

- Possibly easier for customers to copy
- May be too expensive in many cases
- Impact on upstream product profitability and availability
- Customer perception of reduced flexibility

Implementation

1. Use the strategic account management programs in the various regions to develop an information base on the types of products required by key accounts throughout the world: type of equipment, product specifications, performance criteria, quality, and so on. This activity will be managed by the global marketing manager.
2. Develop a complete database on our manufacturing capabilities for sophisticated textile tubes worldwide. This activity will be managed by the global technical manager. An attachment shows a partial and preliminary analysis for the XYZ product and lists the key variations across countries.
3. Decide on which products and characteristics to standardize, and develop a cost–benefit analysis to justify each recommendation. This will be done jointly by the global marketing and technical managers.

   Next Steps: Complete analysis of worldwide capabilities for all high-end products

   Responsibility: John Poulenc and Maria Suzuki

   Timing: By end of June 2014

FURTHER STEPS

The global strategy analysis described in this chapter provides four concrete outputs:

- An assessment of how global an industry is today and is likely to become in the future
- An understanding of how global a company's approach is today, and how it compares to its competitors and to the industry potential for further globalization
- An identification of the organizational factors that will facilitate or hinder a move toward globalization
- A broad action plan, specifying strategic and organizational change priorities

The analysis in and of itself does not provide the details of a global competitive strategy. If its output has shown that adopting some form of global strategy is indeed desirable, the analysis needs to be followed by another effort aimed at developing a detailed total global and competitive strategy. Among the decisions that will need to be made are the definition of a competitive posture in various countries (i.e., in what part of the world should we compete on our own and in what part should we form alliances), the articulation of specific functional strategies (manufacturing, marketing, financial, etc.), and the adoption of organizational mechanisms aimed at reinforcing the strategic objectives sought.

SOME GUIDING IDEAS FOR IMPLEMENTING A TOTAL GLOBAL STRATEGY

In conducting a global strategy analysis and then globalizing a business's strategy, the reader may wish to keep in mind a number of guiding ideas that summarize the concepts in this book:

1. Do not assume that "it cannot happen here." Almost any industry has the potential for globalization and global competition.
2. Global industries are not born but are created by global companies. The rewards of globalization often go to the first movers.
3. Globalization requires a clear vision of the firm as a global competitor. It also requires a long-term time horizon and a commitment from top management.
4. Globalization is not all or nothing. A business can be global in some elements of its strategy and not in others.

Discussion and Research Question

1. Using the framework in this chapter, select a company and one of its worldwide businesses and conduct a complete global strategy analysis.

Notes

1. See Derek F. Abell, *Defining the Business: The Starting Point of Strategic Planning,* (Upper Saddle River, NJ: Prentice Hall, 1980).
2. Evaluating relative quality is a very difficult task. The PIMS program has developed some useful techniques. See Robert D. Buzzell and Bradley T. Gale, *The PIMS Principles: Linking Strategy to Performance* (New York: Free Press, 1987), Chapter 6.
3. He made this statement at a presentation at the Harvard Business School in 1982. See also George S. Yip, "Planning at Pepsi (B)," Case No. 9-583-051 (Boston: Harvard Business School, 1983).
4. For example, Franklin R. Root, *Entry Strategies for International Markets* (San Francisco: Jossey-Bass,

1994), provides a thorough method for scoring country attractiveness.
5. See Root, *Entry Strategies for International Markets* for a discussion of country risk.
6. Some observers have commented that the level of political risk varies by company. Companies with good ties to local power groups (such as via the prime minister's brother-in-law's cousin) face less risk of expropriation and other forms of risk affected by government actions.
7. There are now many guides on how to collect competitive intelligence. See, for example, Leonard Fuld, *Competitor Intelligence: How to Get It—How to Use It* (New York: John Wiley & Sons, 1985).

APPENDIX

Worksheets for Evaluating Core Strategy

BUSINESS _____

REGION/COUNTRY _____

Date Completed _____

1. BUSINESS DEFINITION

The essence of both business definition and strategy formulation is choice. By defining your business in a certain way, you are choosing to do some things and not others. Similarly a strategy involves selecting certain customer groups and not others, offering some types of products and not others, and so on. Mention any changes that you plan to make in your business definition, for example, shift from one type of customer to another type.

Customer Needs Addressed:

_____

Technologies Used:

_____

_____

Customer Segments Served:

_____

_____

Products Offered:

_____

_____

_____

Geographic Scope:

_____

(continued)

EXHIBIT A-1 (Continued)

2. STRATEGIC THRUST

State whether you are trying to grow, maintain, or shrink the size of this business and at what rate.

State your short-term performance priorities in terms of market share, revenues, and profitability.

Direction:

Rate:

Performance Priorities:

1st _____

2nd _____

3rd _____

3. FINANCIAL TARGETS

4. SOURCES OF COMPETITIVE ADVANTAGE

State your major sources of competitive advantage. These sources both must be important to customers and must give you a significant advantage over competitors. The following list provides categories of advantage: You need to add more detail to the ones you specify:

- Patents
- Research capability
- Development capability
- Product or service quality
- Alignment of offerings with critical needs of customers
- Breadth of product line
- Customer relationships
- Access to lower cost or more effective factors of production
- Location of manufacturing near customers or sources of supply
- Unique manufacturing technology
- Vertical integration
- Operating efficiency
- Access to distribution channels
- Physical distribution capability
- Marketing skills
- Reputation of company
- Strength of brand name
- Sales force effectiveness
- Technical support strength
- Customer service
- Government support or protection
- Size of business
- Superior financial resources
- Lower cost finance
- Cross-business synergy
- Corporate support

Describe in order of importance your most important sources of competitive advantage:

_____

_____

_____

EXHIBIT A-1 (Continued)

5. STRATEGY ELEMENTS

For each strategy element specify the nature of your strategy:

Technology:

_____

_____

Manufacturing:

_____

_____

Product Line:

_____

_____

_____

Pricing:

_____

_____

Selling Approach:

_____

_____

Marketing Communications:

_____

_____

Distribution:

_____

_____

Customer Service:

_____

_____

(continued)

EXHIBIT A-1 (Continued)

6. VALUE-ADDING ACTIVITIES

Specify the location of each value-adding activity in your business. Examples of value-adding activities include:

- Research
- Development
- Procurement
- Raw material processing
- Intermediate production/subassembly

- Final production/final assembly
- Marketing
- Selling
- Distribution
- Customer service

Activity   Location

_____   _____

_____   _____

_____   _____

_____   _____

_____   _____

_____   _____

_____   _____

_____   _____

_____   _____

_____   _____

7. COMPETITIVE STRATEGY

Identify your major competitors and specify your strategy versus each of them. Examples of competitive strategy are as follows:

- To keep competitor A as the second-choice vendor by maintaining closer relationships with our customers
- To be a fast follower of innovations by competitor B
- To avoid head-to-head price competition with competitor C
- To restrict competitor D to its current segment of customers
- To gain five points of share in the next three years from competitor E

Competitor   Strategy versus Competitor

_____   _____

_____   _____

_____   _____

_____   _____

_____   _____

_____   _____

BIBLIOGRAPHY

BOOKS

Abegglen, James C., and George Stalk, Jr. *Kaisha: The Japanese Corporation.* New York: Basic Books, 1985.

Abell, Derek F. *Defining the Business: The Starting Point of Strategic Planning.* Upper Saddle River, NJ: Prentice Hall, 1980.

Avery, Christopher. *Business and Human Rights in a Time of Change.* London: Amnesty International Publications, 2000.

Baden Fuller, C., C. P. Nicolaides, and J. Stopford. "National or Global? The Study of Company Strategies and the European Market for Major Appliances." *London Business School Centre for Business Strategy Working Paper Series,* No. 28, 1987.

Baldwin, Carliss Y. "The Capital Factor: Competing for Capital in a Global Environment." In Michael E. Porter, ed. *Competition in Global Industries.* Boston: Harvard Business School Press, 1986.

Bartlett, Christopher A. "Building and Managing the Transitional: The New Organisational Challenge." In Michael E. Porter, ed. *Competition in Global Industries.* Boston: Harvard Business School Press, 1986, pp. 367–404.

Bartlett, Christopher A., and Sumantra Ghoshal. *Managing Across Borders: The Transnational Solution.* Boston: Harvard Business School Press, 1989.

Bartlett, Christopher A., and Sumantra Ghoshal. *Text, Cases, and Readings in Cross-Border Management,* 3rd ed. Boston: McGraw-Hill, 2000.

Bartlett, Christopher A., Yves L. Doz, and Gunnar Hedlund, eds. *Managing the Global Firm.* London: Routledge, 1990.

Beamish, Paul, and J. Peter Killing, eds. *Cooperative Strategies.* Lanham, MD: Lexington Books, 1997.

Beamish, Paul W., J. Peter Killing, Donald J. Lecraw, and Harold Crookell. *International Management: Text and Cases.* Homewood, IL: Irwin, 1991.

Beamish, Paul W., Allen J. Morrison, Philip M. Rosenzweig, and Andrew C. Inkpen. *International Management: Text and Cases,* 4th ed. New York: Irwin McGraw-Hill, 2000.

Black, J. Stewart, and David Ulrich. "The New Frontier of Global HR." In Pat Joynt and Bob Morton, eds. *The Global HR Manager.* London: Institute of Personnel and Development, 1999, Chapter 2, pp. 12–38.

Brandenburger, Adam M., and Barry J. Nalebuff. *Coopetition.* New York: Currency Doubleday, 1996.

Buckley, Peter J., and Mark Casson. *The Future of the Multinational Enterprise.* New York: Holmes and Meier Publishers, Inc., 1976.

Buzzell, Robert D., and Bradley T. Gale. *The PIMS Principles: Linking Strategy to Performance.* New York: Free Press, 1987.

Cecchini, Paolo. *The European Challenge: 1992, the Benefits of a Single Market.* England: Wildwood House, 1988.

Chandler, Alfred D., Jr. *Strategy and Structure.* Cambridge, MA: The MIT Press, 1962.

Committe for the Study of the Causes and Consequences of the Internationalization of U.S. Manufacturing, Manufacturing Studies Board, Commission on Engineering and Technical Systems, National Research Council. *The Internationalization of U.S. Manufacturing: Causes and Consequences.* Washington, D.C.: National Academy Press, 1990.

Contractor, Farok J., and Peter Lorange. *Cooperative Strategies in International Business.* Lexington, MA: D.C. Heath and Company, 1988.

Cvar, Marquise R. "Case Studies in Global Competition: Patterns of Success and Failure." In Michael E. Porter, ed. *Competition in Global Industries.* Boston: Harvard Business School Press, pp. 483–516.

Czinkota, Michael R., Pietra Rivoli, and Ilkka A. Ronkainen. *International Business.* Chicago: The Dryden Press, 1989.

Czinkota, Michael R., Ilkka A. Ronkainen, and Michael Moffett. *International Business,* update 2000. New York: Harcourt, 2000.

Davidson, William H. *Global Strategic Management*. New York: John Wiley & Sons, 1982.

Davidson, William H., and José de la Torre. *Managing the Global Corporation: Case Studies in Strategy and Management*. New York: McGraw-Hill, 1989.

Deloitte & Touche, *Leaders in Innovative Globalization Program,* report, London, 1998.

Dicken, Peter. *Global Shift: Industrial Change in a Turbulent World*. London: Harper and Row, 1986.

Douglas, Susan P., and C. Samuel Craig. *International Marketing Research*. Upper Saddle River, NJ: Prentice Hall, 1983.

Doz, Yves L. *Government Control and Multinational Management*. New York: Praeger, 1979.

Eccles, Robert G. *The Transfer Pricing Decision*. Lexington, MA: Lexington Books, 1985.

Enrico, Roger, and Jesse Kornbluth. *The Other Guy Blinked: How Pepsi Won the Cola Wars*. New York: Bantam Books, 1986.

Evans, Philip, and Thomas S. Würster. *Blown to Bits: How the New Economics of Information Transforms Strategy*. Boston: Harvard Business School Press, 1999.

Ferdows, Kasra. "Mapping International Factory Networks." In Kasra Ferdows, ed. *Managing International Manufacturing*. Amsterdam: Elsevier Science Publishers (North Holland), 1989.

Flaherty, M. Therese. "Coordinating International Manufacturing and Technology." in Michael E. Porter, ed. *Competition in Global Industries*. Boston: Harvard Business School Press, 1986.

Franko, Larry G. *The European Multinationals*. Greenwich, CT: Greylock Press, 1976.

Franko, Larry G. "Organizational Structures and Multinational Strategies of Continental European Enterprises." In M. Ghertman and J. Leontiades, eds. *European Research in International Business*. Amsterdam: North Holland, 1978.

Fuld, Leonard. *Competitor Intelligence: How to Get It— How to Use It*. New York: John Wiley & Sons, 1985.

Ghemawat, Pankaj. *Commitment: The Dynamic of Strategy*. Boston: Harvard Business School Press, 1991.

Ghoshal, Sumantra, Christopher A. Bartlett, and D. Eleanor Westney, eds. *Organization Theory and the Multinational Corporation*. London: Macmillan, 1993.

Giddens, Anthony. *Runaway World: How Globalization Is Reshaping Our Lives*. New York: Routledge, 2000.

Grant, Robert M. *Contemporary Strategy Analysis*. Oxford, England: Blackwell Publishers, 1998.

Hamermesh, Richard G. *Making Strategy Work: How Senior Managers Produce Results*. New York: John Wiley & Sons, 1986.

Harrigan, Kathryn R. *Managing for Joint Venture Success*. Lexington, MA: Lexington Books, 1986.

Hatsopoulos, George N. "High Cost of Capital: Handicap of American Industry." Report sponsored by the American Business Conference and Thermo-Electron Corporation, April 1983.

Hax, Arnoldo C., and Nicolas S. Majluf. *Strategic Management: An Integrative Perspective*. Upper Saddle River, NJ: Prentice Hall, 1984.

Hertz, Noreena. *The Silent Takeover: Global Capitalism and the Death of Democracy*. London: William Heinemann, 2001.

Hofstede, Geert. *Culture's Consequences: International Differences in Work Related Values*. Beverly Hills, CA: Sage, 1984.

Keegan, Warren J. *Multinational Marketing Management,* 4th ed. Upper Saddle River, NJ: Prentice Hall, 1989.

Klein, Naomi. *No Logo*. London: Flamingo, 2001.

Kotler, Philip. *Marketing Management,* 5th ed. Upper Saddle River, NJ: Prentice Hall, 1984.

Kotler, Philip, Liam Fahey, and S. Jatusripitak. *The New Competition*. Upper Saddle River, NJ: Prentice Hall, 1985.

Kozminski, Andrzej K., and George S. Yip, eds. *Strategies for Central and Eastern Europe*. Basingstoke: Macmillan, 2000.

Kozminski, Andrzej K., George S. Yip, and Anna M. Dempster. "Evaluating the Central and Eastern European Opportunity: Eastern Promise." In Andrzej K. Kozminski and George S. Yip, eds. *Strategies for*

Central and Eastern Europe. Basingstoke: Macmillan, 2000.

Kyu-Won, Chang-Hoan Cho, and John D. Leckenby. "A Comparative Analysis of Korean and U.S. Web Advertising." Paper presented to 1999 Annual Conference American Academy of Advertising, Albuquerque, New Mexico (uts.cc.utexas.edu/~kwoh/3A/99AAA.html).

Lessard, Donald R. "Finance and Global Competition: Exploiting Financial Scope and Coping with Volatile Exchange Rates." In Michael E. Porter, ed. *Competition in Global Industries.* Boston: Harvard Business School Press, 1986.

Leung, Anthony, and George S. Yip. "Enter the Global Original Equipment Manufacturer: A New Type of Multinational Company," Working Paper, London Business School, October 31, 2000.

Lewis, Geoff. "Carlton & United Breweries." In Geoff Lewis and Peter Fitzroy, eds. *Cases in Australian Management.* Sydney: Prentice Hall, 1991.

Lindblom, Charles E. *The Policy-Making Process.* Upper Saddle River, NJ: Prentice Hall, 1968.

Lorange, Peter. *Implementation of Strategic Planning.* Upper Saddle River, NJ: Prentice Hall, 1982.

Malnight, Thomas W. "Toward a Model of Accelerating Organizational Change." In P. Christopher Early and Harbir Singh, eds. *Innovations in International and Cross-Cultural Management.* Thousand Oaks, CA: Sage, 2000, pp. 267–310.

Management Analysis Center/Paul J. Stonich, ed. *Implementing Strategy.* Cambridge, MA: Ballinger, 1982.

Markides, Constantinos C. *All the Right Moves.* Boston: Harvard Business School Press, 1999.

Mintzberg, Henry. *The Nature of Managerial Work.* New York: Harper & Row, 1973.

Morrison, Allen J. *Strategies in Global Industries: How U.S. Businesses Compete.* Westport, CT: Quorum Books, 1990.

Nohria, Nitin, Sumantra Ghoshal (contributor), and Cedric Crocker (editor). *The Differentiated Network: Organizing Multinational Corporations for Value Creation.* San Francisco: Jossey-Bass Business and Management Series, 1997.

Ohmae, Kenichi. *The Mind of the Strategist.* New York: McGraw-Hill, 1982.

Ohmae, Kenichi. *Triad Power: The Coming Shape of Global Competition.* New York: Free Press, 1985.

Ohmae, Kenichi. *The Borderless World: Power and Strategy in the Interlinked Economy.* New York: Harper Business, 1990.

Ouchi, William G. *Theory Z: How American Businesses Can Meet the Japanese Challenge.* Reading, MA: Addison-Wesley, 1981.

Pascale, Richard Tanner, and Anthony G. Athos. *The Art of Japanese Management: Applications for American Executives.* New York: Simon & Schuster, 1981.

Porter, Michael E. *Competitive Strategy: Techniques for Analyzing Industries and Competitors.* New York: Free Press, 1980.

Porter, Michael E. *Competitive Advantage: Creating and Sustaining Superior Performance.* New York: Free Press, 1985.

Porter, Michael E. "Competition in Global Industries: A Conceptual Framework." In Michael E. Porter, ed. *Competition in Global Industries.* Boston: Harvard Business School Press, 1986.

Porter, Michael E. *The Competitive Advantage of Nations.* New York: The Free Press, 1990.

Prahalad, C. K. "The Strategic Process in a Multinational Corporation." Unpublished doctoral dissertation, Harvard Business School, 1975.

Prahalad, C. K., and Yves L. Doz. *The Multinational Mission: Balancing Local Demands and Global Vision.* New York: Free Press, 1987.

Prestowitz, Clyde V., Jr. *Trading Places.* New York: Basic Books, 1988.

Quelch, John A., Robert D. Buzzell, and Eric R. Salama. *The Marketing Challenge of 1992,* Reading, MA: Addison-Wesley, 1990.

Root, Franklin R. *Entry Strategies for International Markets.* San Francisco, CA: Jossey-Bass, 1994.

Rugman, Alan M. *International Diversification and the Multinational Enterprise.* Lexington, MA: Lexington Books, D. C. Heath, 1979.

Rugman, Alan M. *The End of Globalization.* London: Random House Business Books, 2000.

Rumelt, Richard P., and Robin Wensley. "In Search of the Market Share Effect." *Proceedings*. Academy of Management Annual Meeting, pp. 2–6, 1981.

Segal-Horn, Susan, and John McGee. "Strategies to Cope with Retailer Buying Power." In L. Pellegrini and S. K. Reddy, eds. *Retail and Marketing Channels*. London: Routledge, 1989.

Singh, Kulwant, Joseph Putti, and George S. Yip. "Singapore—Regional Hub." In George S. Yip, ed. *Asian Advantage: Key Strategies for Winning in the Asia-Pacific Region (Updated Edition—After the Crisis)*. Cambridge, MA: Perseus Publishing, 2000, Chapter 7, pp. 155–79.

Skinner, Wickham. *Manufacturing: The Formidable Weapon*. New York: Wiley, 1985.

Steiner, George A. *Strategic Planning: What Every Manager Must Know*. New York: The Free Press, 1979.

Stopford, John M., and Louis T. Wells, Jr. *Managing the Multinational Enterprise*. New York: Basic Books, 1972.

Stopford, John M., and S. Strange, with J. S. Henley. *Rival States, Rival Firms: Competition for World Market Shares*. Cambridge: Cambridge University Press, 1991.

Takeuchi, Hirotaka, and Michael E. Porten. "Three Roles of International Marketing in Global Strategy." In Michael E. Porter, ed. *Competition in Global Industries*. Boston: Harvard Business School Press, 1986.

Tallman, Stephen B., and George S. Yip. "Strategy and the Multinational Enterprise." In Alan M. Rugman and Thomas L. Brewer, eds. *The Oxford Handbook of International Business*. Oxford, England: Oxford University Press, 2001, Chapter 12.

Treacy, Michael, and Fred Wiersema. *The Discipline of Market Leader*. Reading, MA: Addison-Wesley, 1995.

Vernon, Raymond. *Storm over the Multinationals*. Cambridge, MA: Harvard University Press, 1977.

Vernon, Raymond, and Louis T. Wells. *Manager in the International Economy*. Upper Saddle River, NJ: Prentice Hall, 1986.

Westney, D. Eleanor, and Srilata Zaheer. "Chapter 13: The Multinational Enterprise as an Organization." In Alan M. Rugman and Thomas L. Brewer, eds. *The Oxford Handbook of International Business*. Oxford, England: Oxford University Press, forthcoming 2001.

White, Roderick E., and Thomas A. Poynter. "Organizing for Worldwide Advantage." In Christopher A. Bartlett, Yves L. Doz, and Gunnar Hedlund, eds. *Managing the Global Firm*. London: Routledge, 1990.

Woo, Carolyn Y., and Karel Cool. "Porter's (1980) Generic Strategies: A Test of Performance and Functional Strategy Attributes." Working Paper, Purdue University, 1983.

Yip, George S. "An Integrated Approach to Global Competitive Strategy." In Roger Mansfield, ed. *Frontiers of Management Research and Practice*. London: Routledge, 1989.

Yip, George S. "Do American Business Use Global Strategy?" Working Paper No. 91-101, Cambridge, MA: Marketing Science Institute, January 1991.

Yip, George S. *Asian Advantage: Key Strategies for Winning in the Asia-Pacific Region*. Reading, MA: Addison-Wesley, 1998.

Yip, George S. *Asian Advantage: Key Strategies for Winning in the Asia-Pacific Region (Updated Edition—After the Crisis)*. Cambridge, MA: Perseus Publishing, 2000.

Yip, George S. "Bases of Competitive Advantage." In Stuart Crainer and Des Dearlove, eds. *Financial Times Handbook of Management,* 2nd ed. London: Financial Times/Prentice Hall, 2001a, pp. 253–63.

Yip, George S. "Global Strategy in the 21st Century." In Stuart Crainer and Des Dearlove, eds. *Financial Times Handbook of Management,* 2nd ed. London: Financial Times/Prentice Hall, 2001b, pp. 150–63.

Yip, George S. and Audrey Bink, *Managing Global Customers: An Integrated Approach,* Oxford, England: Oxford University Press, 2007.

Yoshino, M. Y. "Global Competition in a Salient Industry: The Case of Civil Aircraft Competition." In Michael E. Porter, ed. *Global Industries*. Boston: Harvard Business School Press, 1986, pp. 517–38.

Yoshino, Michael Y., and U. Srinivasa Rangan. *Strategic Alliances: An Entrepreneurial Approach to Globalization*. Boston: Harvard Business School Press, 1995.

JOURNALS

Aaker, David A., and Erich Joachimsthale. "The Lure of Global Branding." *Harvard Business Review,* November–December 1999, pp. 137–44.

Baden Fuller, Charles W. F., and John M. Stopford. "Globalization Frustrated: The Case of White Goods." *Strategic Management Journal,* Vol. 12, 1991, pp. 493–507.

Bartlett, Christopher A., and Sumantra Ghoshal. "Managing Across Borders: New Strategic Requirements." *Sloan Management Review,* Summer 1987, pp. 7–17.

Bartlett, Christopher A., and Sumantra Ghoshal. "Matrix Management: Not a Structure, a Frame of Mind." *Harvard Business Review,* July–August 1990, pp. 138–45.

Bartlett, Christopher A., and Sumantra Ghoshal. "What Is a Global Manager?" *Harvard Business Review,* September–October 1992, pp. 124–32.

Behrman, Jack N., and William A. Fischer. "Transnational Corporations: Market Orientations and R&D Abroad." *Columbia Journal of World Business,* Fall 1980, pp. 55–60.

Berkowitz, Marvin, and Krishna Mohan. "The Role of Global Procurement in the Value Chain of Japanese Steel." *Columbia Journal of World Business,* Winter 1987, pp. 97–110.

Biggart, Nicole Woolsey, and Mauro F. Guillen. "Developing Difference: Social Organization and the Rise of the Auto Industries of South Korea, Taiwan, Spain, and Argentina." *American Sociological Review,* Vol. 64, No. 5, 1999, pp. 722–47.

Birkinshaw, Julian. "Why Is Knowledge Management So Difficult?" *Business Strategy Review,* Vol. 12, No. 1, Spring 2001, pp. 11–18.

Birkinshaw, Julian, and Nick Fry. "Subsidiary Initiatives to Develop New Markets." *Sloan Management Review,* Vol. 39, No. 3, 1998, pp. 51–62.

Boddewyn, Jean J. J., Robin Soehl, and Jacques Picard. "Standardization in International Marketing: Is Ted Levitt in Fact Right?" *Business Horizons,* Vol. 29, November–December 1986, pp. 69–75.

Buckley, Peter J. "The Theory of the Multinational Enterprise." Acta Universitatis Upsaliensis. Uppsala, Sweden: *Studia Oeconomiae Negotiorum,* Vol. 26, 1987.

Burggraeve, Chris C. "Meeting Product Standards in the Single Market." *The Journal of European Business,* May–June 1990, pp. 22–6.

Buzzell, Robert D. "Can You Standardize Multinational Marketing?" *Harvard Business Review,* November–December 1968, pp. 102–13.

Buzzell, Robert D., Bradley T. Gale, and R. G. M. Sultan. "Market Share—A Key to Profitability." *Harvard Business Review,* January–February 1975, pp. 97–106.

Campa, José M., and Mauro F. Guillen. "The Internalization of Exports: Firm and Location-Specific Factors in a Middle-Income Country." *Management Science,* Vol. 45, No. 11, 1999, pp. 1463–78.

Chakravarthy, Balaji S., and Howard V. Perlmutter. "Strategic Planning for a Global Business." *Columbia Journal of World Business,* Summer 1985, pp. 3–10.

Clee, G. H., and A. di Scipio. "Creating a World Enterprise." *Harvard Business Review,* November–December 1959, pp. 77–89.

Clee, G. H., and W. M. Sachtjen. "Organizing a Worldwide Business." *Harvard Business Review,* November–December 1964, pp. 55–67.

Conn, Henry P., and George S. Yip. "Global Transfer of Critical Capabilities." *Business Horizons,* Vol. 40, No. 1, January–February 1997, pp. 22–31.

Craig, C. Samuel, and Susan. P. Douglas. "Configural Advantage in Global Markets." *Journal of International Marketing,* Vol. 8, No. 1, 1999, pp. 6–26.

Daniels, J. D., R. A. Pitts, and M. J. Tretter. "Strategy and Structure of U.S. Multinationals: An Exploratory Study." *Academy of Management Journal,* Vol. 27, 1984, pp. 292–307.

Das, Gurcharan. "Local Memoirs of a Global Manager." *Harvard Business Review,* March–April 1993, pp. 38–47.

Davidson, William H., and Philippe Haspeslagh. "Shaping a Global Product Organization." *Harvard Business Review,* July–August 1982, pp. 125–32.

de Meyer, Arnold, Jinichiro Nakane, Jeffrey Miller, and Kasra Ferdows. "Flexibility: The Next Competitive Battle—The Manufacturing Futures Survey." *Strategic Management Journal,* Vol. 10, 1989, pp. 135–44.

Dess, G., and P. Davis. "Porter's (1980) Generic Strategies as Determinants of Strategic Group Membership and Organizational Performance." *Academy of Management Journal,* Vol. 27, 1984, pp. 467–88.

Dornbush, Rudiger, Stanley Fisher, and Paul A. Samuelson. "Comparative Advantage, Trade and Payments in a Ricardian Model with a Continuum of Goods." *American Economic Review,* Vol. 67, December 1977, pp. 823–39.

Douglas, Susan P., and C. Samuel Craig. "Examining Performance of U.S. Multinationals in Foreign Markets." *Journal of International Business Studies,* Winter 1983, pp. 51–7.

Douglas, Susan P., and Yoram Wind. "The Myth of Globalization." *Columbia Journal of World Business,* Vol. 22, No. 4, Winter 1987, pp. 19–29.

Doz, Yves L. "Managing Manufacturing Rationalization Within Multinational Companies." *Columbia Journal of World Business,* Fall 1978, pp. 82–94.

Doz, Yves L., Christopher A. Bartlett, and C. K. Prahalad. "Global Competitive Pressures vs. Host Country Demands: Managing Tensions in Multinational Corporations." *California Management Review,* Vol. 23, No. 3, 1981, pp. 63–74.

Dunn, S. W. "Effect of National Identity on Multinational Promotional Strategy in Europe." *Journal of Marketing,* October 1976, pp. 50–7.

Dunning, John H. "The Eclectic Paradigm of International Production: A Restatement and Some Possible Extensions." *Journal of International Business Studies,* Spring 1988.

Dyment, John J. "Strategies and Management Controls for Global Corporations." *Journal of Business Strategy,* Spring 1987, pp. 20–6.

Egelhoff, William G. "Strategy and Structure in Multinational Corporations: An Information Processing Approach." *Administrative Science Quarterly,* Vol. 27, 1982, pp. 435–58.

Egelhoff, William G. "Patterns of Control in U.S., U.K. and European Multinational Corporations." *Journal of International Business Studies,* Fall 1984, pp. 73–83.

Egelhoff, William G. "Strategy and Structure in Multinational Corporations: A Revision of the Stopford and Wells Model." *Strategic Management Journal,* Vol. 9, 1988, pp. 1–14.

Farley, Laurence J. "Going Global: Choices and Challenges." *Journal of Business Strategy,* Vol. 1, Winter 1986, pp. 67–70.

Fouraker, Lawrence E., and John M. Stopford. "Organization Structure and Multinational Strategy." *Administrative Science Quarterly,* Vol. 13, 1968, pp. 57–70.

Frazee, Valerie. "Tearing Down Roadblocks." *Workforce,* Vol. 77, No. 2, February 1998, pp. 50–1.

George, Abraham M., and C. William Schroth. "Managing Foreign Exchange for Competitive Advantage." *Sloan Management Review,* Winter 1991, pp. 105–16.

Ghoshal, Sumantra. "Global Strategy: An Organizing Framework." *Strategic Management Journal,* Vol. 8, No. 5, September–October 1987, pp. 425–40.

Goldhar, Joel D., and Mariann Jelinek. "Computer Integrated Flexible Manufacturing: Organizational, Economic, and Strategic Implications." *Interfaces,* Vol. 15, May–June 1985, pp. 94–105.

Gupta, Anil K., and Vijay Govindarajan. "Knowledge Flows Within Multinational Corporations." *Strategic Management Journal,* Vol. 21, No. 4, 2000, pp. 473–96.

Hamel, Gary, and C. K. Prahalad. "Do You Really Have a Global Strategy?" *Harvard Business Review,* July–August 1985, pp. 139–48.

Haspeslagh, Philippe. "Portfolio Planning: Uses and Limits." *Harvard Business Review,* January–February 1982, pp. 58–73.

Hedlund, Gunnan. "The Hypermodern MNC: A Heterarchy?" *Human Resource Management,* Vol. 25, 1986, pp. 9–35.

Heenan, David A., and Calvin Reynolds. "ROP's: A Step Toward Global Human Resources Management." *California Management Review,* Vol. 18, No. 1, Fall 1975, pp. 5–9.

Henzler, Herbert, and Wilhelm Rall. "Facing Up to the Globalization Challenge." *The McKinsey Quarterly,* Winter 1986, pp. 52–68.

Hill, J. S., and R. R. Still. "Adapting Products to LDC Tastes." *Harvard Business Review,* March–April 1984, pp. 92–101.

Hirschey, Robert C., and Richard E. Caves. "Research and Transfer of Technology by Multinational Enterprises." *Oxford Bulletin of Economics and Statistics,* Vol. 43, No. 2, May 1981, pp. 115–30.

Hout, Thomas, Michael E. Porter, and Eileen Rudden. "How Global Companies Win Out." *Harvard Business Review,* September–October 1982, pp. 98–108.

Hrebiniak, Lawrence. "Implementing Global Strategies." *European Management Journal,* Vol. 10, No. 4, December 1992, pp. 392–403.

Hu, Yao-Su. "Global or Stateless Corporations Are National Firms with International Operations." *California Management Review,* Vol. 34, No. 2, Winter 1992, pp. 107–26.

Huszagh, Sandra M., Richard J. Fox, and Ellen Day. "Global Marketing: An Empirical Investigation." *Columbia Journal of World Business,* Twentieth Anniversary Issue, Vol. 20, No. 4, 1986, pp. 31–43.

Jaikumar, Ramchandran. "Postindustrial Manufacturing." *Harvard Business Review,* November–December 1986, pp. 69–76.

Jain, Subhash C. "Standardization of International Marketing Strategy: Some Research Hypotheses." *Journal of Marketing,* Vol. 53, January 1989, pp. 70–9.

Jatusripitak, Somkid, Liam Fahey, and Philip Kotler. "Strategic Global Marketing: Lessons from the Japanese." *Columbia Journal of World Business,* Spring 1985, pp. 47–53.

Jeelof, Gerrit. "Global Strategies of Philips." *European Management Journal,* Vol. 7, No. 1, 1989, pp. 84–91.

Johansson, Johny K. "Determinants and Effects of 'Made in' Labels." *International Marketing Review,* Vol. 6, No. 1, Spring 1989, pp. 47–58.

Johansson, Johny K, and George S. Yip. "Exploiting Globalization Potential: U.S. and Japanese Strategies." *Strategic Management Journal,* Vol. 15, October 1994, pp. 579–601.

Kacker, M. P. "Patterns of Marketing Adaptation in International Business." *Management International Review,* Vol. 12, issues 4–5, 1972, pp. 111–18.

Kacker, M. P. "Export Oriented Product Adaptation." *Management International Review,* Vol. 6, 1975, pp. 61–70.

Kanter, Rosabeth Moss. "Change in the Global Economy: An Interview with Rosabeth Moss Kanter." *European Management Journal,* Vol. 12, No. 1, 1994, pp. 1–9.

Kashani, Kamran. "Beware the Pitfalls of Global Marketing." *Harvard Business Review,* September–October 1989, pp. 91–8.

Kashani, Kamran, and John A. Quelch. "Can Sales Promotion Go Global?" *Business Horizons,* Vol. 33, No. 3, May–June 1990, pp. 37–43.

Kester, W. Carl, and Timothey A. Luehrman. "Are We Feeling More Competitive Yet? The Exchange Rate Gambit." *Sloan Management Review,* Winter 1989, pp. 19–28.

Kogut, Bruce. "Designing Global Strategies: Comparative and Competitive Value-Added Chains." *Sloan Management Review,* Summer 1985, pp. 27–38.

Kogut, Bruce. "Designing Global Strategies: Profiting from Operational Flexibility." *Sloan Management Review,* Fall 1985, pp. 27–38.

Kogut, Bruce. "Joint Ventures: Theoretical and Empirical Perspectives." *Strategic Management Journal,* Vol. 9, No. 4, July–August 1988, pp. 319–32.

Kogut, Bruce, and Nalin Kulatilaka. "Operating Flexibility, Global Manufacturing, and the Option Value of a Multinational Network." *Management Science,* Vol. 40, No. 1, January 1994, pp. 123–39

Kogut, B., and U. Zander. "Knowledge of the Firm and the Evolutionary Theory of the Multinational Corporation." *Journal of International Business Studies,* Vol. 24, No. 4, 1993, pp. 625–45.

Korine, Harry. "Fresenius AG: High Speed Globalization." *Business Strategy Review,* Vol. 11, No. 2, Summer 2000, pp. 47–57.

Kotabe, Masaaki, and Glenn S. Omura. "Sourcing Strategies of European and Japanese Multinationals: A Comparison." *Journal of International Business Studies,* Vol. 20, No. 1, Spring 1989, pp. 113–30.

Kotler, Philip, and Ravi Singh. "Marketing Warfare in the 1980s." *Journal of Business Strategy,* Vol. 1, No. 3, Winter 1981, pp. 30–41.

Lazer, W., and E. H. Shaw. "Global Marketing Management: At the Dawn of the New Millennium." *Journal of International Marketing,* Vol. 8, No. 1, 2000, pp. 65–77.

Levitt, Theodore. "The Globalization of Markets." *Harvard Business Review,* May–June 1983, pp. 92–102.

Lewis, Geoffrey, John Clark, and Bill Moss. "BHP Reorganizes for Global Competition." *Long Range Planning,* Vol. 21, No. 3, 1988, pp. 18–26.

Malnight, Thomas W. "Globalization of an Ethnocentric Firm: An Evolutionary Perspective." *Strategic Management Journal,* Vol. 16, No. 2, 1995, pp. 119–41.

Malnight, Thomas W. "The Transition from Decentralized to Network-Based MNC Structures: An Evolutionary Perspective." *Journal of International Business Studies,* Vol. 27, No. 1, 1996, pp. 43–66.

Markides, Constantinos C., and Norman Berg. "Manufacturing Offshore Is Bad Business." *Harvard Business Review,* September–October 1988, pp. 113–20.

Martinez, Jon I., and J. Carlos Jarillo. "The Evolution of Research on Coordination Mechanisms in Multinational Corporations." *Journal of International Business Studies,* Vol. 20, No. 3, Fall 1989, pp. 489–514.

Maruca, Regina Fazio. "The Right Way to Go Global: An Interview with Whirlpool CEO David Whitwam." *Harvard Business Review,* March–April 1994, pp. 135–45.

McCormick, Janice, and Nan Stone. "From National Champion to Global Competitor: An Interview with Thomson's Alain Gomez." *Harvard Business Review,* May–June 1990, pp. 127–35.

McGee, John F. "1992: Moves Americans Must Make." *Harvard Business Review,* May–June 1989, pp. 78–84.

Medina, J. F., and M. F. Duffy. "Standardization vs. Globalization: A New Perspective of Brand Strategies." *Journal of Product and Brand Management,* Vol. 7, No. 3, 1998, pp. 223–43.

Mirhan, Greg. "Advantage: Hewlett-Packard." *Global Executive,* March–April 1993, pp. 10–13.

Mitchell, Will, J. Myles Shaver, and Bernard Yeung. "Getting There in a Global Industry: Impacts on Performance of Changing International Presence." *Strategic Management Journal,* Vol. 13, 1992, pp. 419–32.

Montgomery, David B., and George S. Yip. "The Challenge of Global Customer Management." *Marketing Management,* Vol. 9, No. 4, Winter 2000, pp. 22–9.

Moore, Karl, and Julian M. Birkinshaw. "Managing Knowledge in Global Service Firms: Centres of Excellence." *Academy of Management Executive,* December 1998.

Morrison, Allen. J., David. A. Ricks, and Kendall Roth. "Globalization versus Regionalization: Which Way for the Multinational?"*Organizational Dynamics,* Vol. 19, No. 3, 1991, pp. 17–29.

Morrison, Allen J., and Kendall Roth. "The Regional Solution: An Alternative to Globalization." *Transnational Corporations,* Vol. 1, No. 2, 1992a, pp. 37–55.

Morrison, Allen J., and Kendall Roth. "A Taxonomy of Business-Level Strategies in Global Industries." *Strategic Management Journal,* Vol. 13, 1992b, pp. 399–418.

Motameni, R., and M. Shahrokhi. "Brand Equity Valuation: A Global Perspective." *Journal of Product and Brand Management,* Vol. 7, No. 4, 1998, pp. 275–90.

Murtha, Thomas P., Stefanie Ann Lenway, and Richard P. Bagozzi. "Global Mind-Sets and Cognitive Shift in a Complex Multinational Corporation." *Strategic Management Journal,* Vol. 2, No. 19, 1998, pp. 97–114.

Oliff, Michael D., and Donald A. Marchand. "Strategic Information Management in Global Manufacturing." *European Management Journal,* Vol. 9, No. 4, December 1991, pp. 361–71.

Perlmutter, Howard V. "The Tortuous Evolution of the Multinational Corporation." *Columbia Journal of World Business,* January–February 1969, pp. 9–18.

Pierson, Robert M. "R&D by Multinationals for Overseas Markets." *Research Management,* July 1978, pp. 19–22.

Porter, Michael E. "Changing Patterns of International Competition." *California Management Review,* Vol. 28, No. 2, Winter 1986, pp. 9–40.

Porter, Michael E. "New Global Strategies for Competitive Advantage." *Planning Review,* May–June 1990, pp. 4–14.

Prahalad, C. K., and Yves L. Doz. "An Approach to Strategic Control on MNCs." *Sloan Management Review,* Summer 1981, pp. 5–13.

Quelch, John A. "Global Brands: Taking Stock." *Business Strategy Review,* Vol. 10, No. 1, 1999, pp. 1–14.

Quelch, John A., and Edward J. Hoff. "Customizing Global Marketing." *Harvard Business Review,* May–June 1986, pp. 59–68.

Quelch, John A., and James E. Austin. "Should Multinationals Invest in Africa?" *Sloan Management Review,* Vol. 34, No. 3, Spring 1993, pp. 107–19.

Quinn, James Brian. "Strategic Goals: Process and Politics." *Sloan Management Review,* Fall 1977, p. 22.

Ramachandran, K., and George S. Yip. "It's Time to Globalise Now." *General Management Review* (Economic Times, India), Vol. 2, No. 1, 2000, pp. 40–7.

Rau, Pradeep A., and John F. Preble. "Standardization of Marketing Strategy by Multinationals." *International Marketing Review,* Autumn 1987, pp. 18–28.

Reeb, David M., Chuck C. Y. Kwok, and H. Young Baek. "Systematic Risk of the Multinational Corporation." *Journal of International Business Studies,* Vol. 29, 1998, pp. 263–80.

Ronstadt, Robert, and Robert J. Kramer. "Getting the Most Out of Innovation Abroad." *Harvard Business Review,* March–April 1982, pp. 94–9.

Roos, Johan, Georg von Krogh, and George S. Yip. "An Epistemology of Globalizing Firms." *International Business Review,* Vol. 3, No. 4, special issue on Organization's Knowledge, Knowledge Transfer and Cooperative Strategies, November–December 1994, pp. 395–409.

Rosen, Barry Nathan, Jean J. Boddewyn, and Ernst A. Louis. "Participation by U.S. Agencies in International Brand Advertising: An Empirical Study." *Journal of Advertising,* Vol. 17, No. 4, 1988, pp. 14–22.

Roth, Kendall, and Allen J. Morrison. "An Empirical Analysis of the Integration-Responsiveness Framework in Global Industries." *Journal of International Business Studies,* Vol. 21, No. 4, Fourth Quarter 1990, pp. 541–64.

Roth, Kendall, and David A. Ricks. "Goal Configuration in a Global Industry Context." *Strategic Management Journal,* Vol. 15, No. 2, February 1994, pp. 103–20.

Roth, Kendall, David M. Schwieger, and Allen J. Morrison. "Global Strategy Implementation at the Business Unit Level: Operational Capabilities and Administrative Mechanisms." *Journal of International Business Studies,* Third Quarter 1991, pp. 369–402.

Rugman, Alan M. "The Corporate Performance of U.S. and European Multinational Enterprises, 1970–79." *Management International Review,* Vol. 23, No. 2, 1983, pp. 4–14.

Samiee, Saeed, and Kendall Roth. "The Influence of Global Marketing Standardization on Performance." *Journal of Marketing,* Vol. 56, April 1992, pp. 1–17.

Schlie, Erik, and George S. Yip. "Regional Follows Global: Strategy Mixes in the World Automotive Industry." *European Management Journal,* Vol. 18, No. 4, August 2000, pp. 343–54.

Schuh, Arnold. "Global Standardization as a Success Formula for Marketing in Central Eastern Europe?" *Journal of World Business,* Vol. 35, No. 2, Summer 2000, pp. 133–48.

Schütte, Helmut. "Strategy and Organisation: Challenges for European MNCs in Asia." *European Management Journal,* Vol. 15, No. 4, August 1997, pp. 436–45.

Segal-Horn, S., D. Asch, and V. Suneja. "The Globalization of the European White Goods Industry." *European Management Journal,* Vol. 16, No. 1, 1998, pp. 101–9.

Shanks David C. "Strategic Planning for Global Competition." *Journal of Business Strategy,* Winter 1985, pp. 80–9.

Sölvell, Örjan, and Ivo Zanden. "Organisation of the Dynamic Multinational Enterprise: The Home-Based and the Heterarchical MNE." *International Studies of Management and Organization,* Vol. 25, No. 1/2, 1995, pp. 17–38.

Sorenson, Ralph Z., and Ulrich E. Wiechmann. "How Multinationals View Marketing Standardization." *Harvard Business Review,* May–June 1975, pp. 38–167.

Spence, A. Michael. "Industrial Organization and Competitive Advantage in Multinational Industries." *American Economic Review,* Vol. 74, No. 2, May 1984, pp. 356–60.

Spence, A. Michael. "Entry, Capacity, Investment and Oligopolistic Pricing." *Bell Journal of Economics,* Vol. 8, Autumn 1977, pp. 534–44.

Starr, Martin K. "Global Production and Operations Strategy." *Columbia Journal of World Business,* Winter 1984, pp. 17–22.

Taylor, William. "The Logic of Global Business: An Interview with ABB's Percy Barnevik." *Harvard Business Review,* Vol. 6, No. 2, March–April 1991, pp. 91–105.

Vancil, Richard F., and Peter Lorange. "Strategic Planning in Diversified Companies." *Harvard Business Review,* January–February 1975, pp. 81–90.

Vernon, Raymond. "The Product Cycle Hypothesis in a New International Environment." *Oxford Bulletin of Economics and Statistics,* Vol. 41, 1979, pp. 255–67.

Walters, Peter G. P. "International Marketing Policy: A Discussion of the Standardization Construct and Its Relevance for Corporate Policy." *Journal of International Business Studies,* Summer 1986, pp. 55–69.

Westney, D. Eleanor. "Research on the Global Management of Technology Development." *Business Review,* Vol. 46, No. 1, August 1998, pp. 1–21.

White, Roderick E. "Generic Business Strategies, Organizational Context and Performance: An Empirical Investigation." *Strategic Management Journal,* Vol. 7, 1986, pp. 217–31.

White, Roderick E., and Thomas A. Poynter. "Strategies for Foreign-Owned Subsidiaries in Canada." *Business Quarterly,* Summer 1984, pp. 59–69.

Yip, George S. "Gateways to Entry." *Harvard Business Review,* September–October 1982, pp. 85–92.

Yip, George S. "Who Needs Strategic Planning?" *The Journal of Business Strategy,* Vol. 6, No. 2, Fall 1985, pp. 30–42.

Yip, George S. "Global Strategy . . . In a World of Nations?" *Sloan Management Review,* Vol. 31, No. 1, Fall 1989, pp. 29–41.

Yip, George S. "A Performance Comparison of Continental and National Businesses in Europe." *International Marketing Review,* Vol. 8, No. 2, 1991, pp. 31–9.

Yip, George S. "Industry Drivers of Global Strategy and Organization." *The International Executive,* Vol. 36, No. 5, September–October 1994, pp. 529–56.

Yip, George S. "Global Strategy as a Factor in Japanese Success." *The International Executive,* special issue on Japan, Vol. 38, No. 1, January–February 1996, pp. 145–67.

Yip, George S. "Patterns and Determinants of Global Marketing." *Journal of Marketing Management,* Vol. 13, 1997, pp. 153–64.

Yip, George S., and Audrey Bink. "Managing Global Accounts," *Harvard Business Review,* Vol. 85, No. 9, September 2007, pp. 102–111.

Yip, George S., and George A. Coundouriotis. "Diagnosing Global Strategy Potential: The World Chocolate Confectionary Industry." *Planning Review,* January–February 1991, pp. 4–14.

Yip, George S., and Tammy L. Madsen. "Global Account Management: The New Frontier in Relationship Marketing." *International Marketing Review,* Vol. 13, No. 3, 1996, pp. 24–42, special issue on Global Marketing Implementation.

Yip, George S., Pierre M. Loewe, and Michael Y. Yoshino. "How to Take Your Company to the Global Market." *Columbia Journal of World Business,* Winter 1988, pp. 37–48.

Yip, George S., Johan Roos, and Johny K. Johansson. "Effects of Nationality on Global Strategy." *Management International Review,* Vol. 37, No. 4, October–December 1997, pp. 365–84.

Yip, George S., Javier B. Gomez, and Joseph Monti. "Role of the Internationalization Process in the Performance of Newly Internationalizing Firms." *Journal of International Marketing,* Vol. 8, No. 3, 2000, pp. 10–35.

Yip, George S., G. Tomas M. Hult, and Audrey Bink, "Static Triangular Simulation as a Methodology for Strategic Management Research," In *Research Methodology In Strategy and Management,* Vol. 4, David J. Ketchen and Donald D. Bergh, Eds., Oxford, United Kingdom: Elsevier JAI, 2007, pp. 121–160.

Yoffie, David B., and Helen V. Milney. "An Alternative to Free Trade or Protectionism: Why Corporations Seek Strategic Trade Policy." *California Management Review,* Summer 1989, pp. 111–31.

Yunker, Penelope J. "A Survey Study of Subsidiary Autonomy, Performance Evaluation and Transfer Pricing in Multinational Corporations." *Columbia Journal of World Business,* Fall 1983, pp. 51–64.

COMPANY INDEX

Italicized page numbers refer to boxed text or illustrations.

SUBJECT INDEX

Italicized page numbers refer to boxed text or illustrations.

AUTHOR INDEX

Italicized page numbers refer to boxed text or illustrations.